A-Z SHEFFIELD Street Atlas

CONTENTS

REFERENCE

Motorway	**M1**	Car Park	**P**
'A' Road	**A61**	Church or Chapel	†
'B' Road	**B6150**	Fire Station	■
Dual Carriageway		Hospital	Ⓗ
One Way Street	→	House Numbers 'A' and 'B' Roads only	8 13
One Way traffic flow on 'A' Roads is indicated by a heavy line on the drivers left.			
Pedestrianized Road	[- - - - - - -]	Information Centre	🛈
Restricted Access		National Grid Reference	385
Railway	Level Crossing Station	Police Station	▲
Map Continuation	🔺 85	Post Office	●
County Boundary	+ + + + +	Toilet	▽
District Boundary	- · - · - · -	Toilet with Disabled Facilities	♿
Ambulance Station	✚	Viewpoint	☀

Map Pages 6-141
1:18103 (3½ inches to 1 mile)

Miles 0 — ¼ — ½
Metres 0 — 250 — 500 — 750

Central Area 4-5
1:9051 (7 inches to 1 mile)

Miles 0 — ⅛ — ¼
Metres 0 — 100 — 200 — 300

Geographers' A-Z Map Co. Ltd.

Head Office
Vestry Road, Sevenoaks, Kent, TN14 5EP
Telephone 0732-451152

Showrooms
44 Gray's Inn Road, London, WC1X 8LR
Telephone 01-242 9246

Edition 1

D0234730

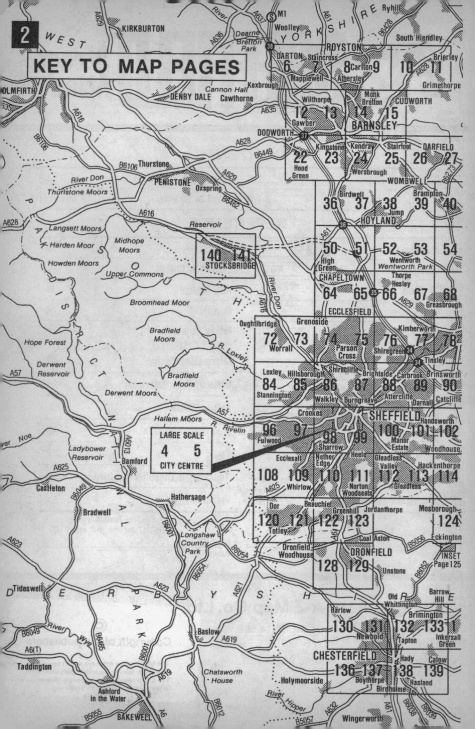

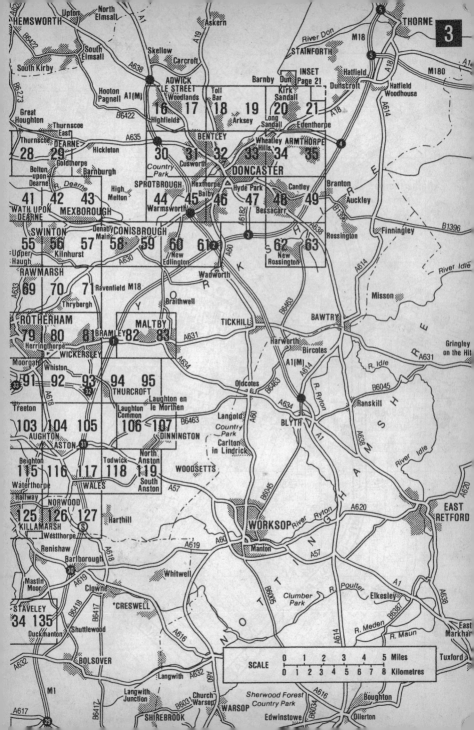

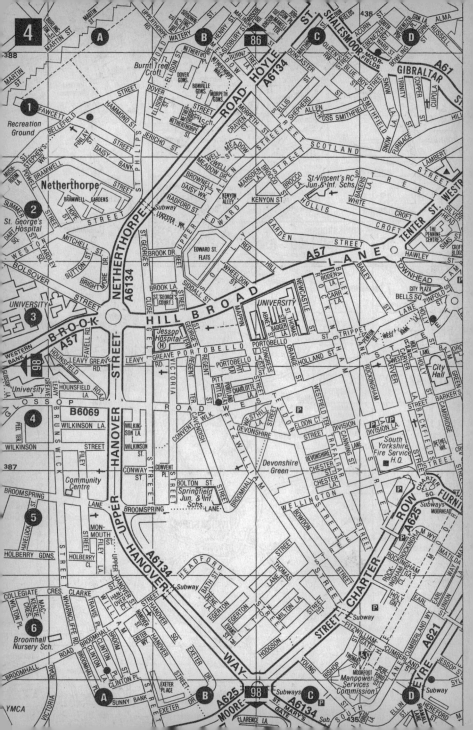

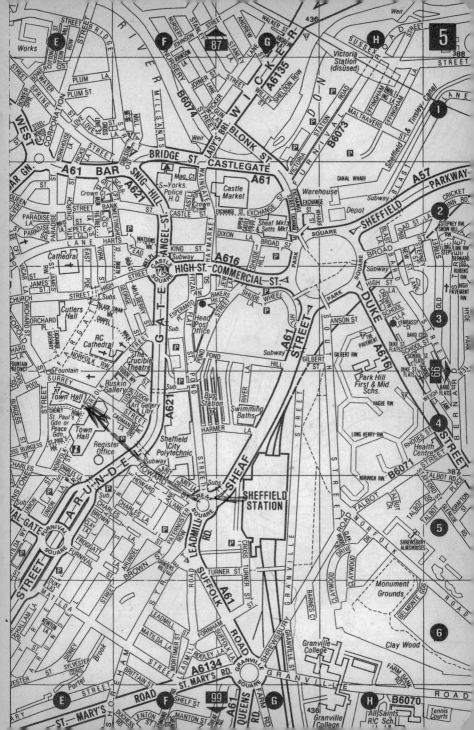

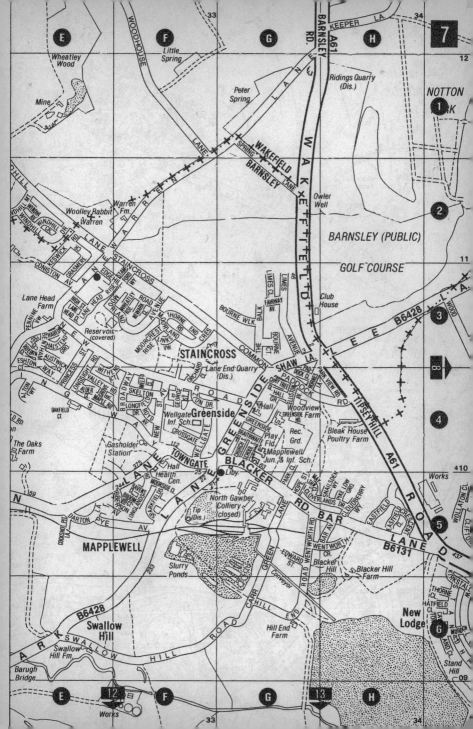

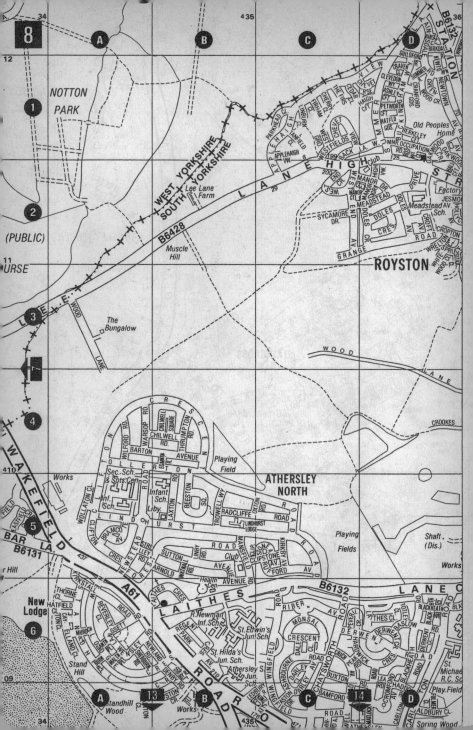

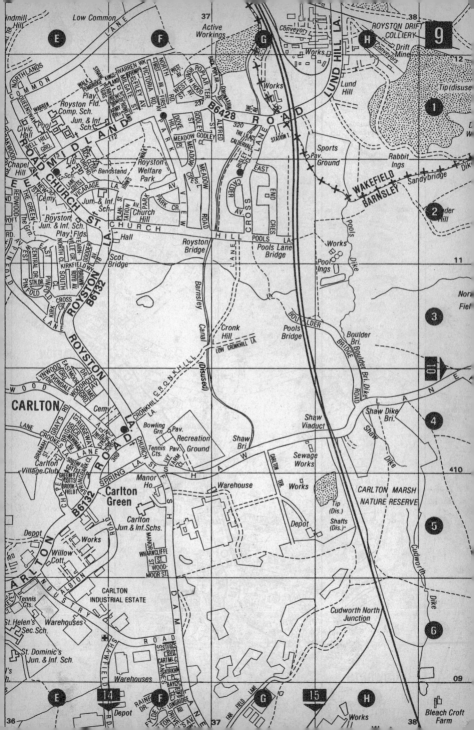

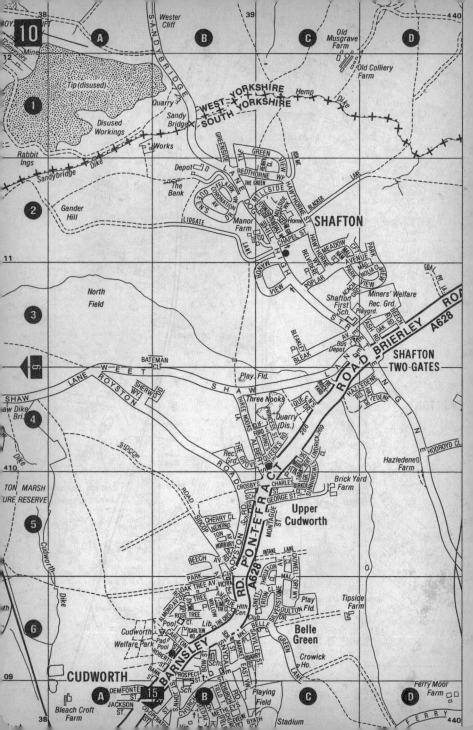

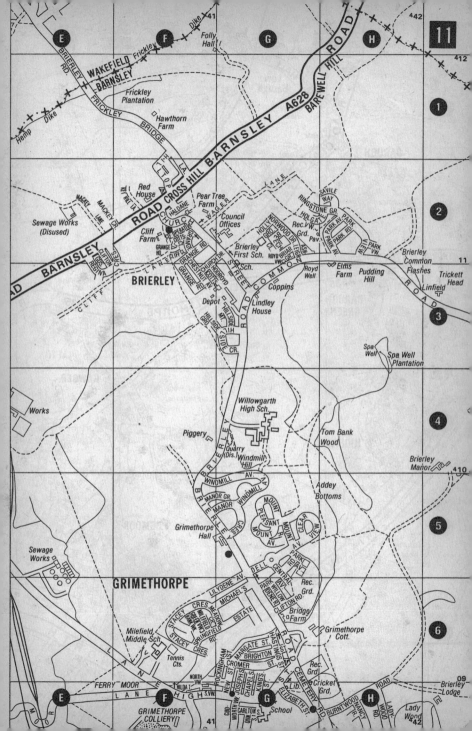

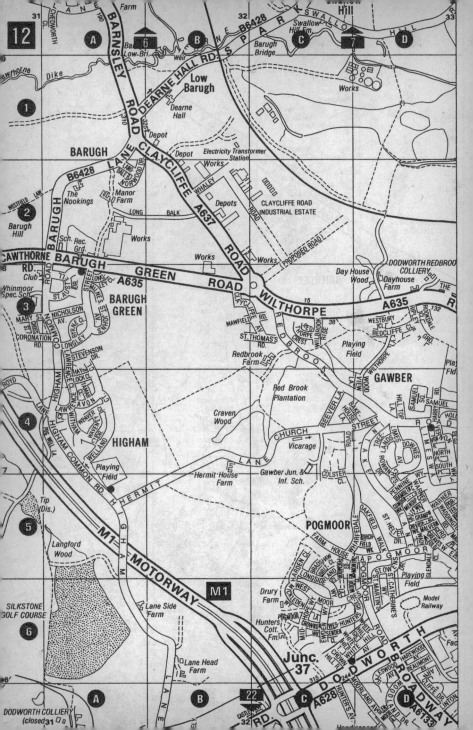

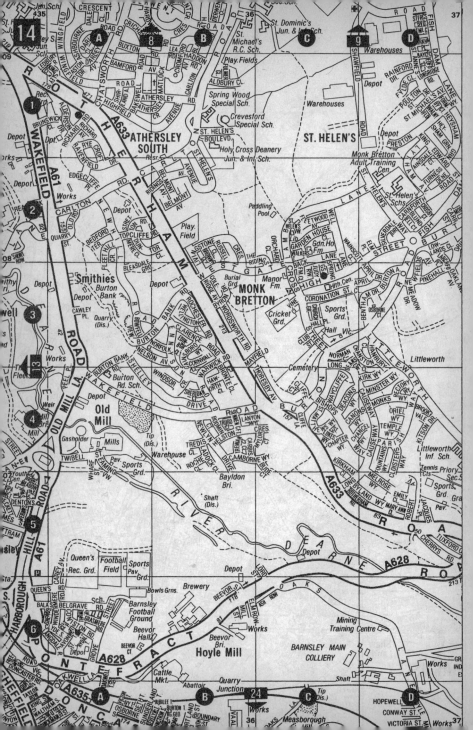

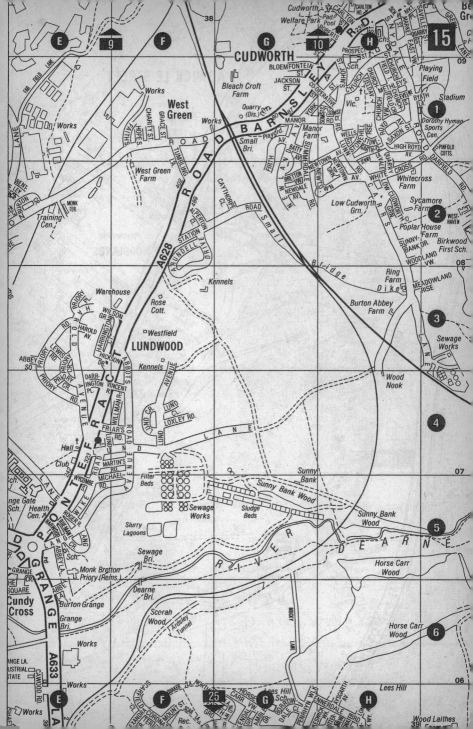

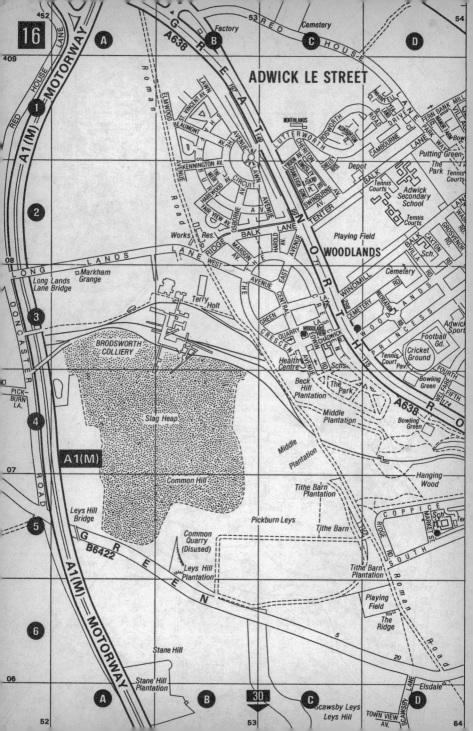

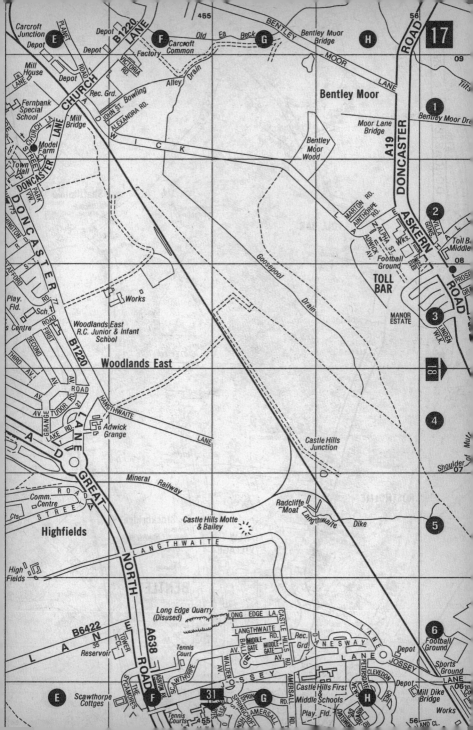

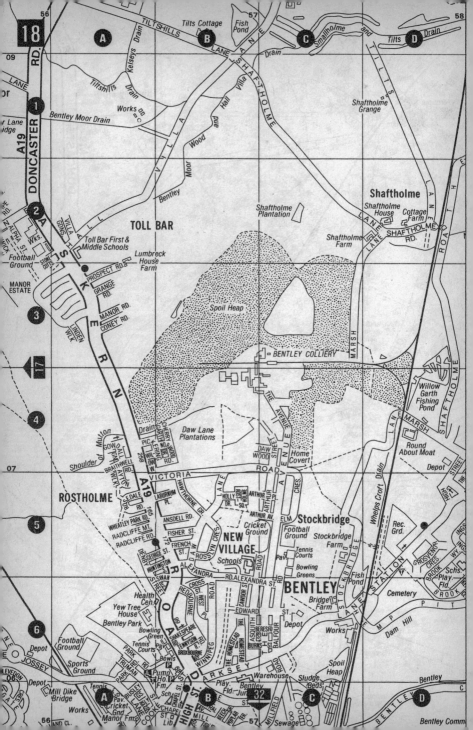

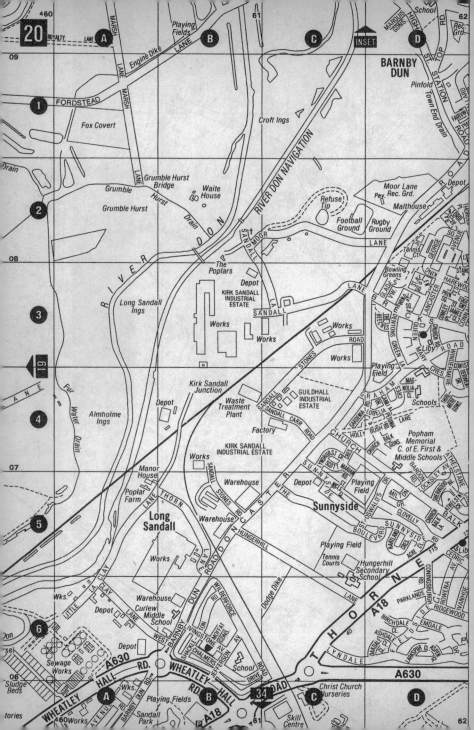

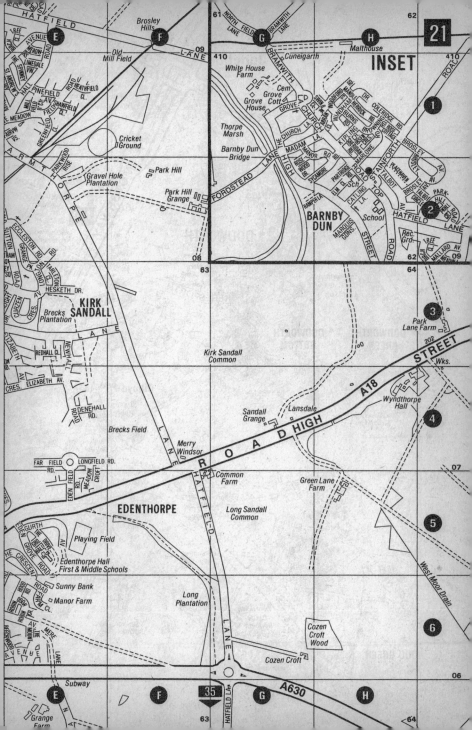

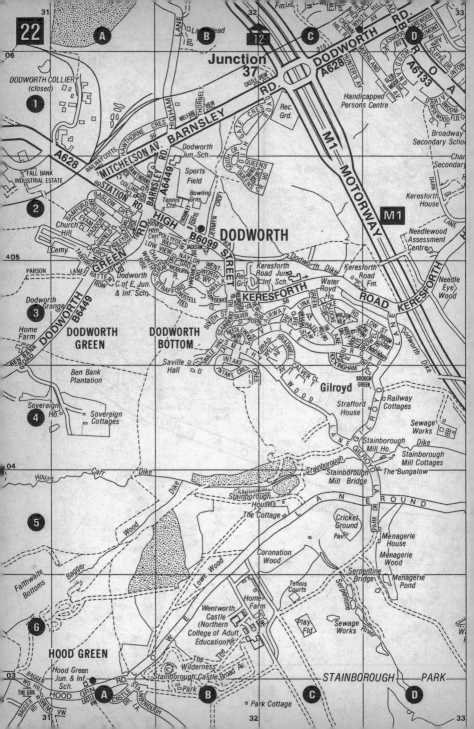

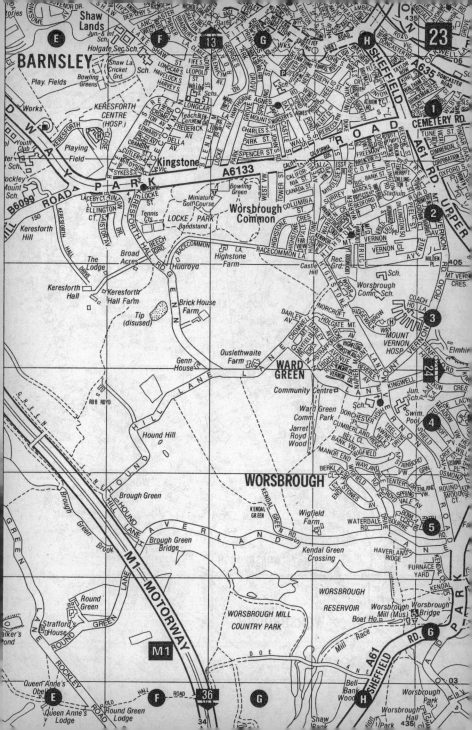

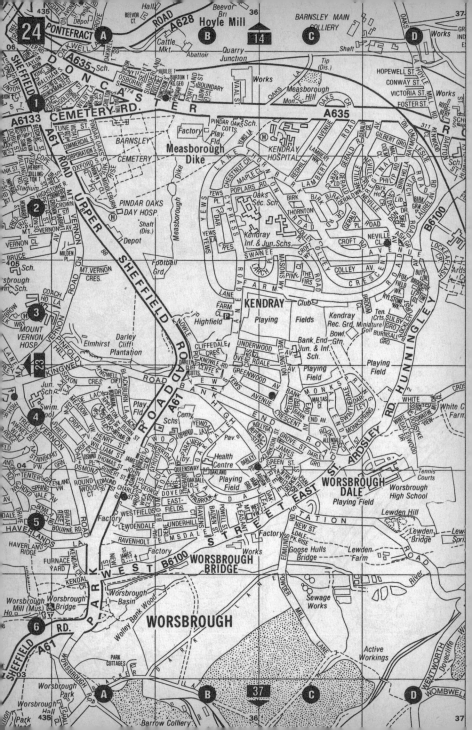

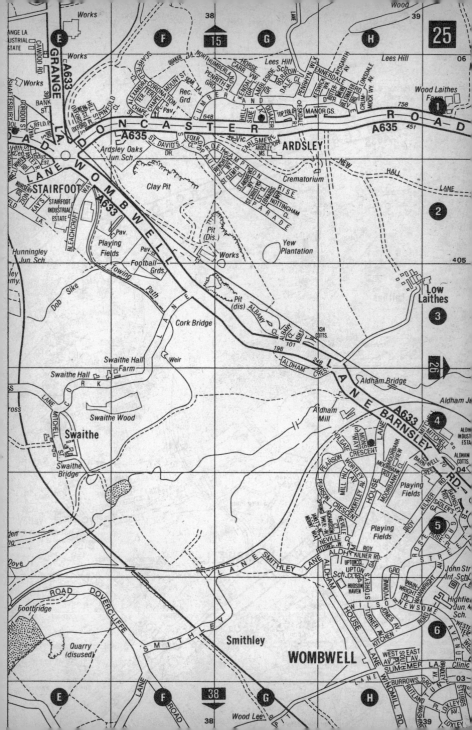

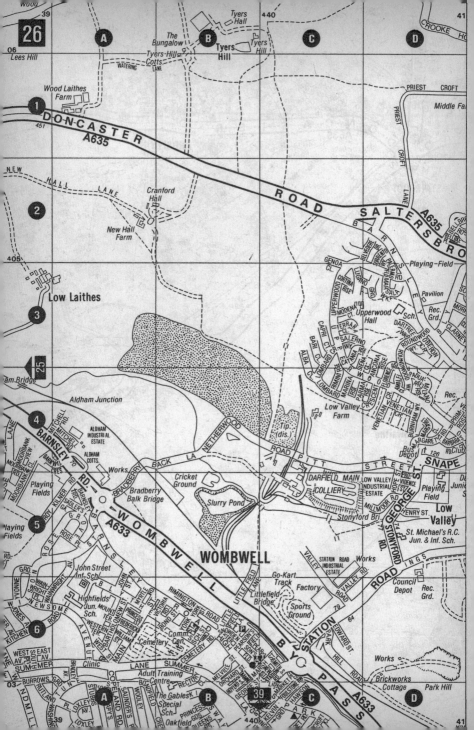

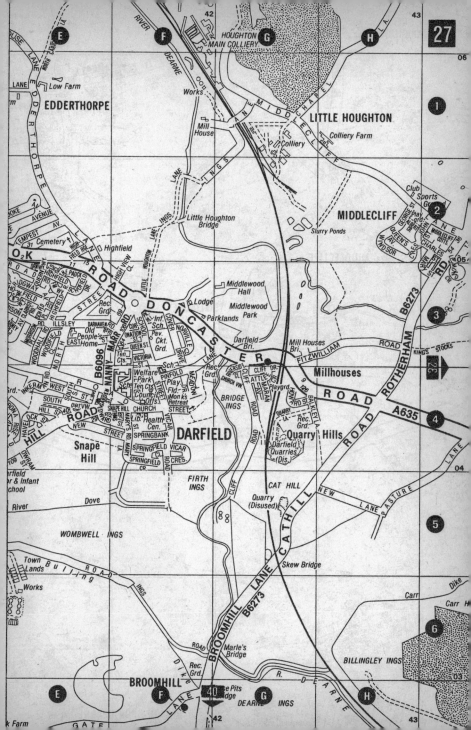

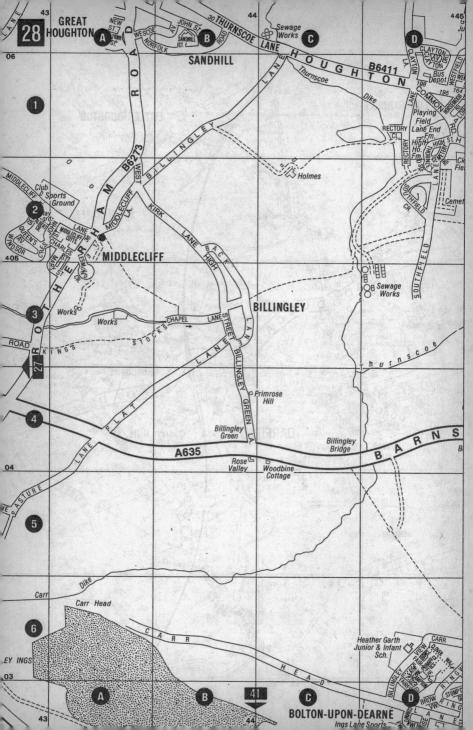

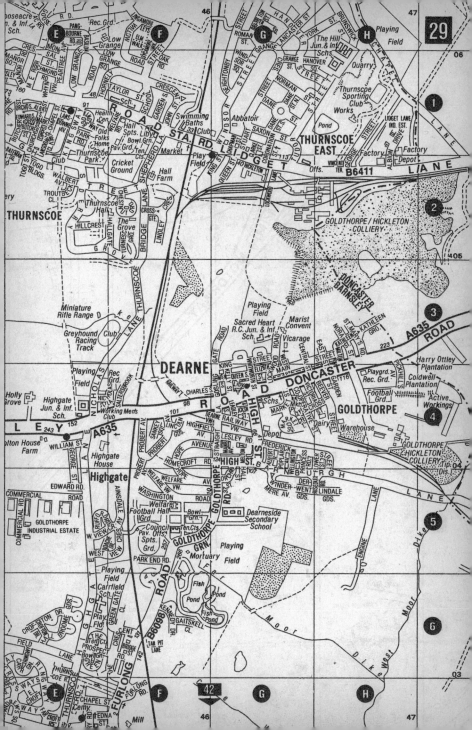

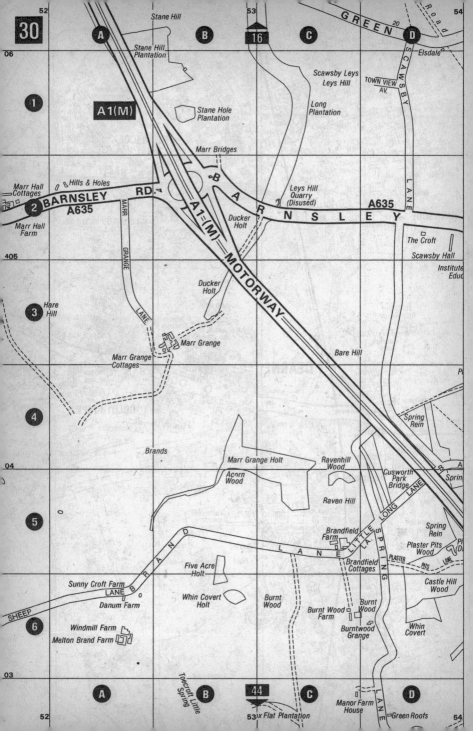

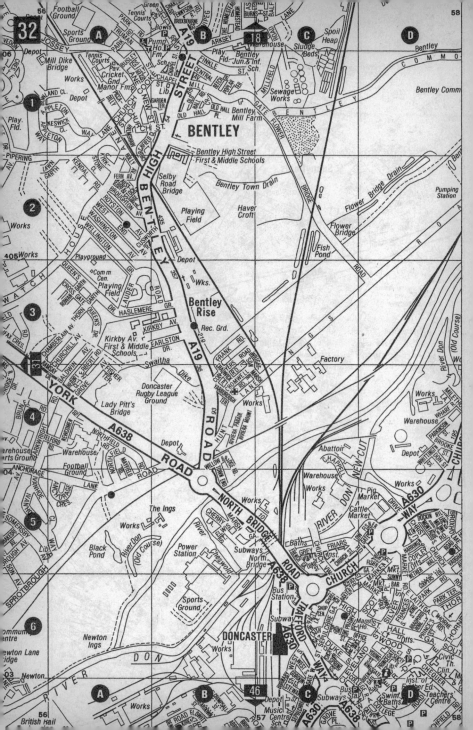

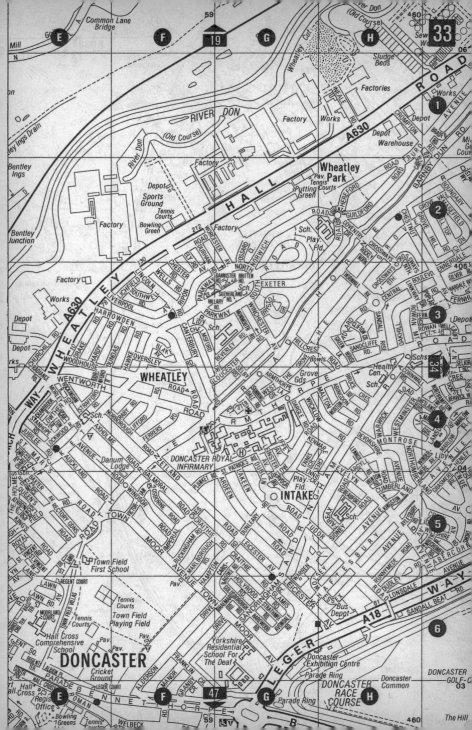

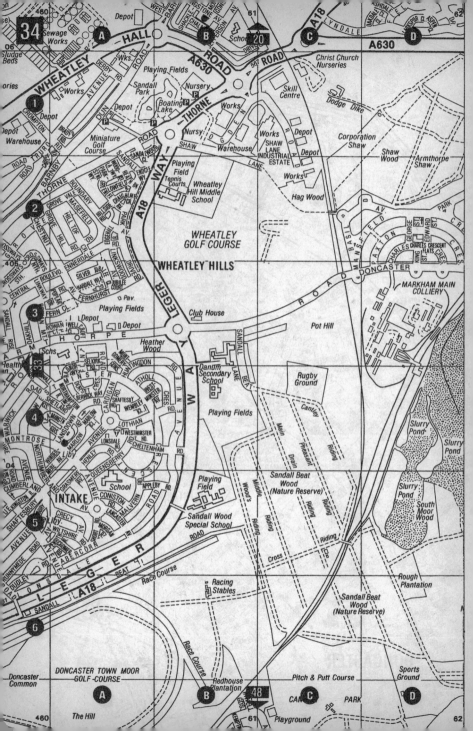

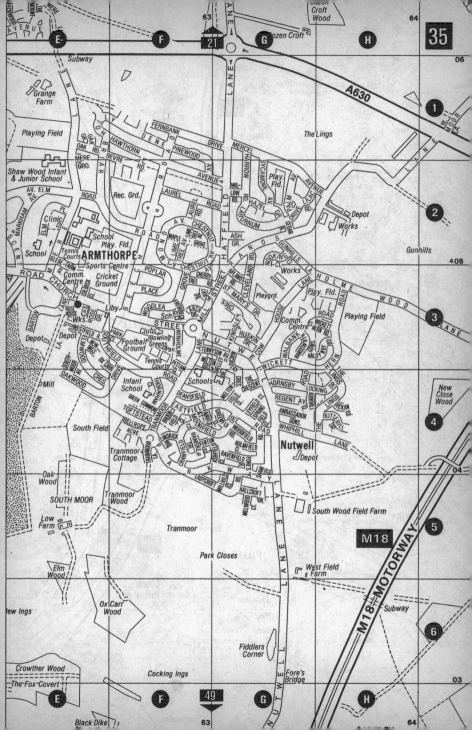

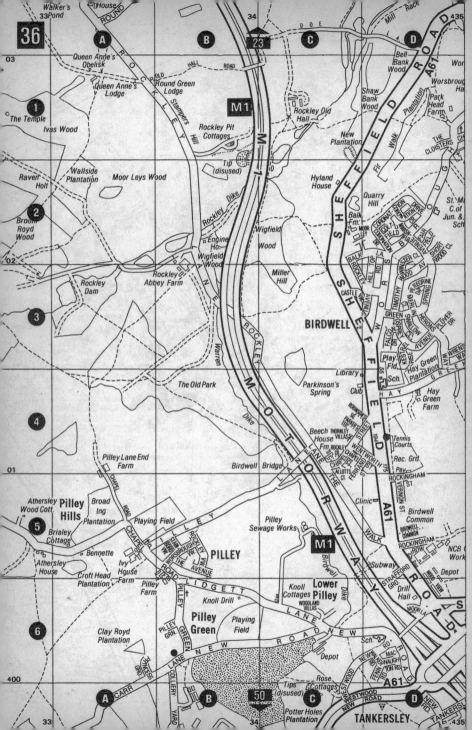

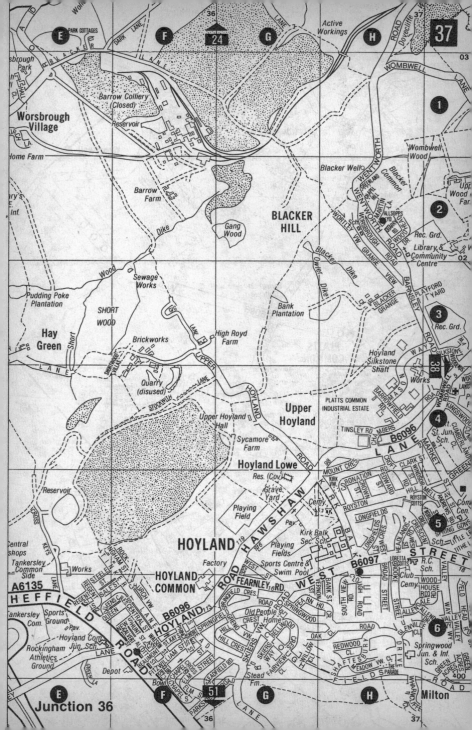

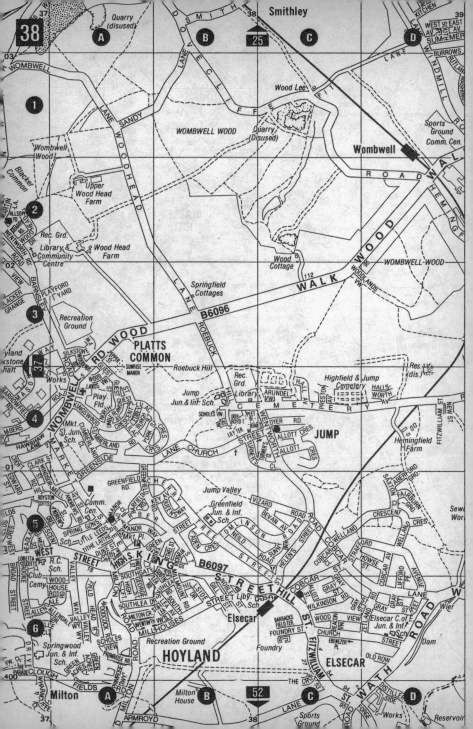

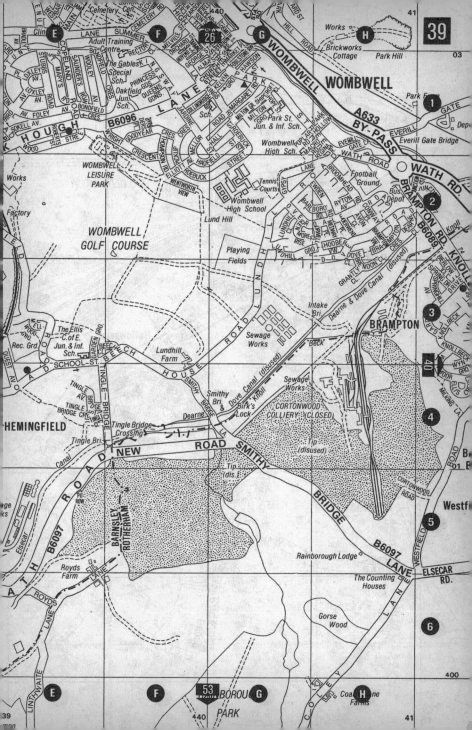

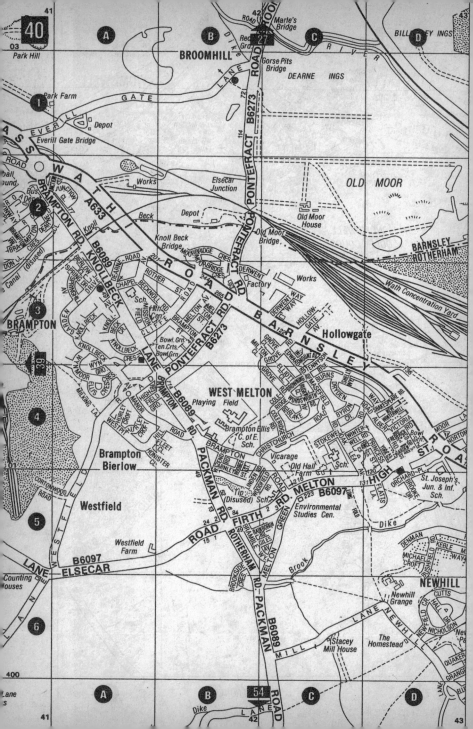

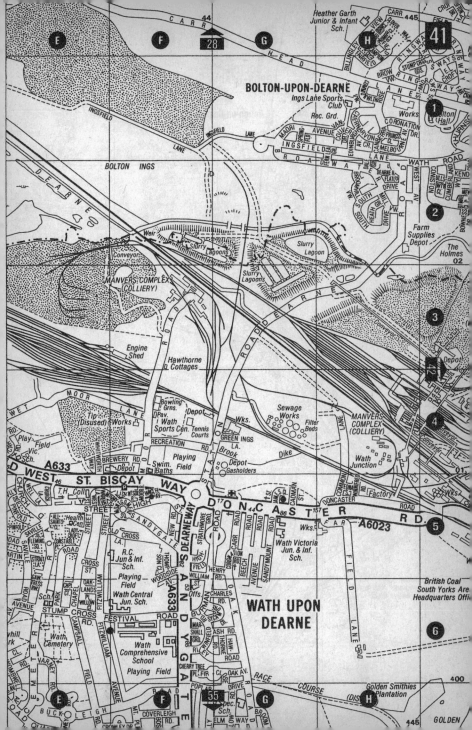

BOLTON-UPON-DEARNE

E F 44 G H

CARR 28 HEAD

Heather Garth
Junior & Infant
Sch.

CARR. 445

Ings Lane Sports
Club
Rec. Grd.

Works

Bolton
Hall

1

INGSFIELD

BOLTON INGS

INGSFIELD

2

DEARNE

Weir

Slurry
Lagoons

Slurry
Lagoon

Slurry
Lagoons

Farm
Supplies
Depot

The
Holmes
02

Conveyor

MANVERS COMPLEX
(COLLIERY)

3

Depot
42

Engine
Shed

Hawthorne
Cottages

DEARNE

4

MOOR

LANE

WET

Tip
(Disused)

Works

Bowling
Grns.
Pav.
Wath
Sports Cen.

Depot

Tennis
Courts

GREEN INGS
LA.
Brook

Sewage
Works

Filter
Beds

MANVERS
COMPLEX
(COLLIERY)

Play
Field
Vic.
Sch.

RECREATION

Dike

Wath
Junction

BREWERY RD.

Depot

Playing
Field

Swim.
Baths

Depot
Gasholders

Wks.

D WEST ST. BISCAY WAY

A633

DONCASTER RD.

Factory

5

DEARNE WAY

A6023

Wath Victoria
Jun. & Inf.
Sch.

Wks.

British Coal
South Yorks Are
Headquarters Offi

R.C.
Jun & Inf.
Sch.

Playing
Field

Wath Central
Jun. Sch.

A633

SANDYGATE

WATH UPON
DEARNE

6

Wath
Cemetery

Wath
Comprehensive
School
Playing Field

FESTIVAL

RACE

COURSE

Golden Smithies
Plantation
(DIS)

400

E F 55 G H

BUCK

COVERLEIGH

Rec. Sch.

GOLDEN

446

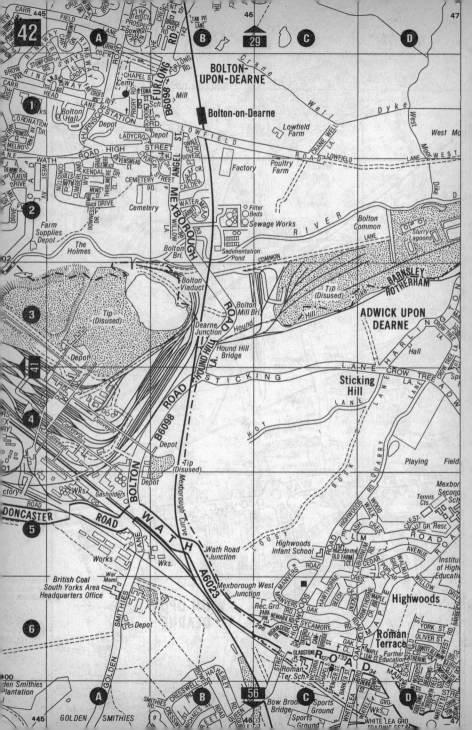

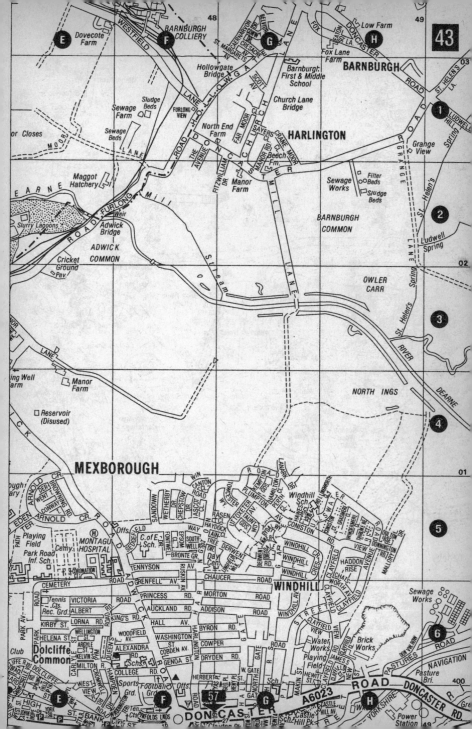

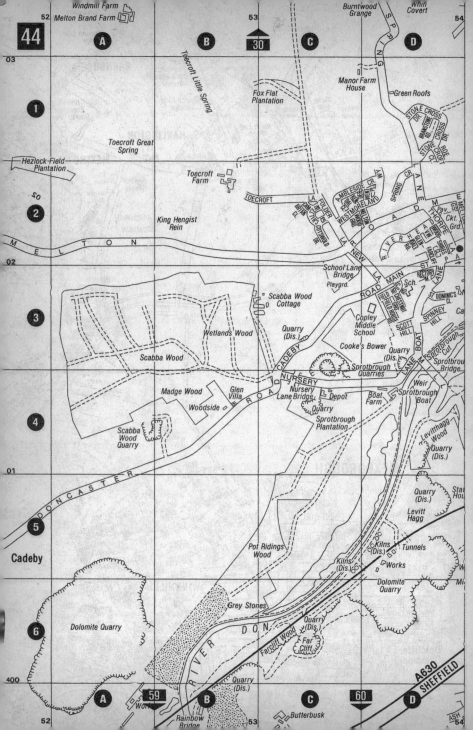

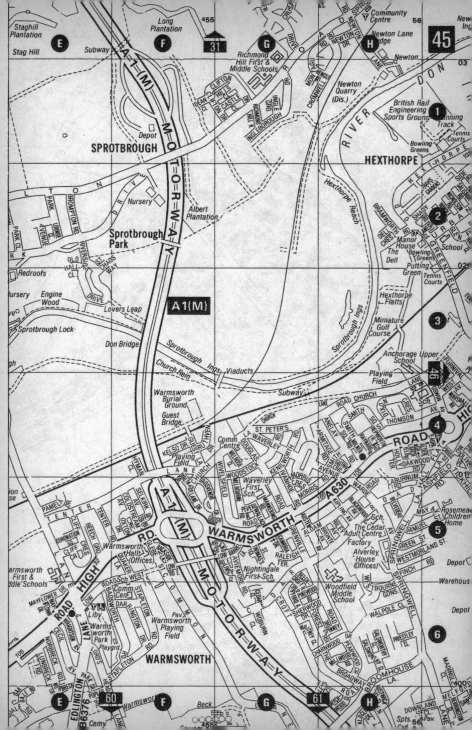

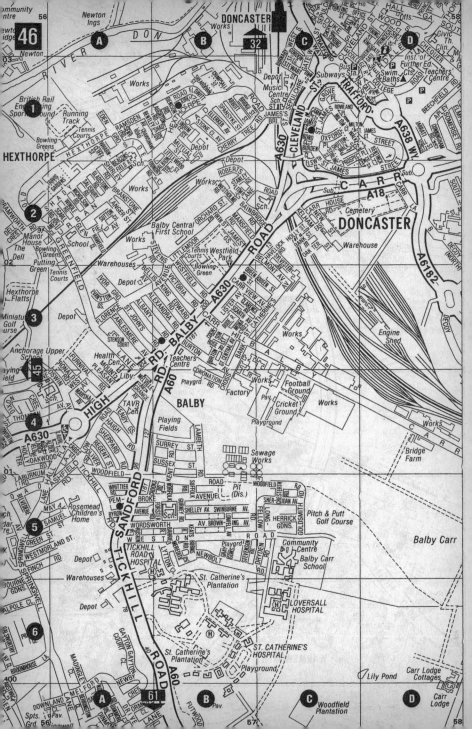

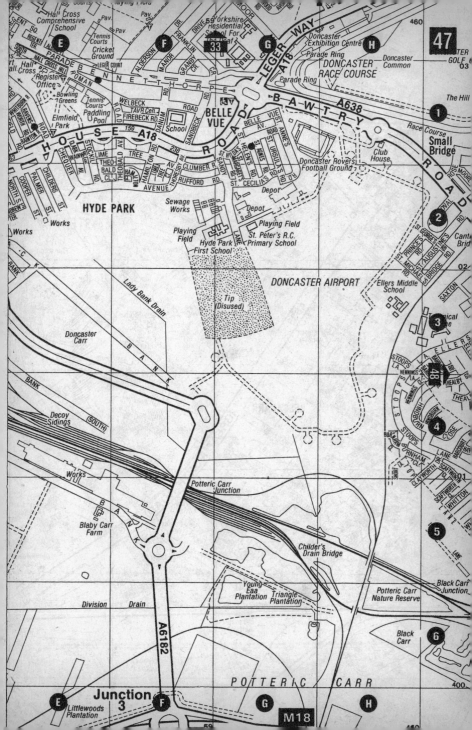

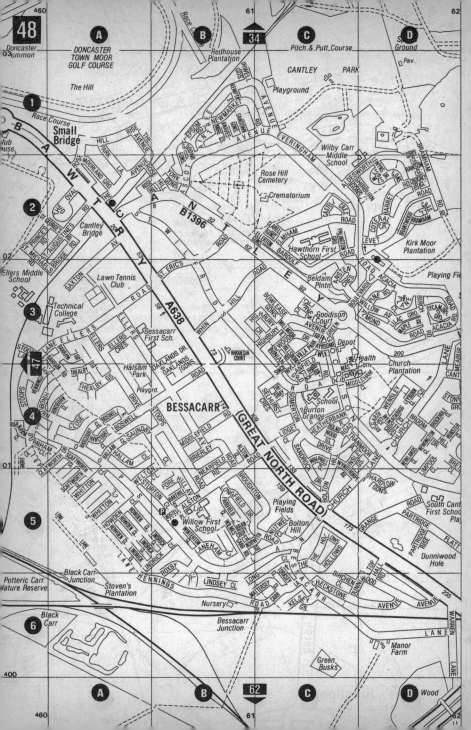

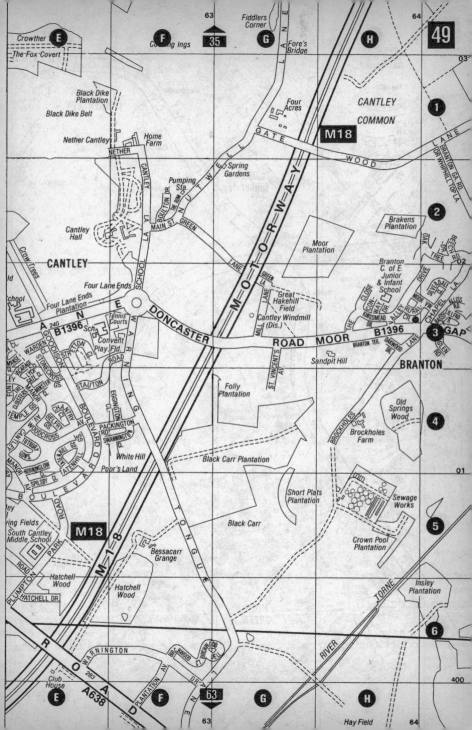

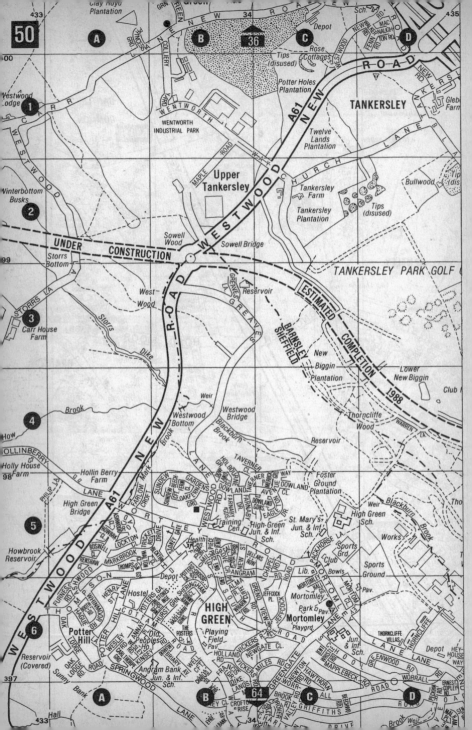

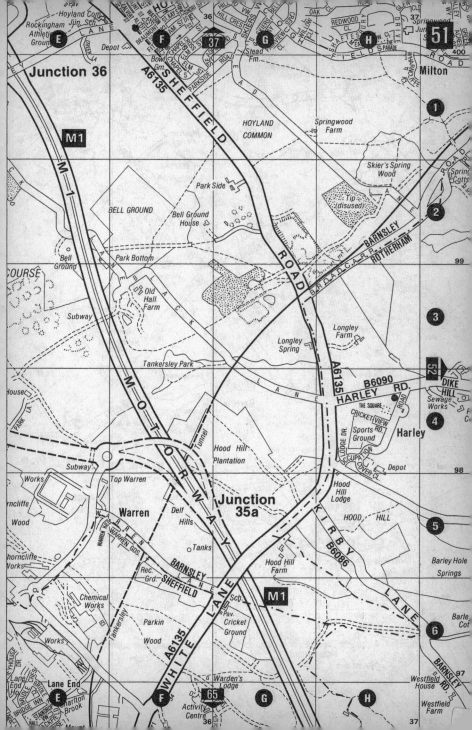

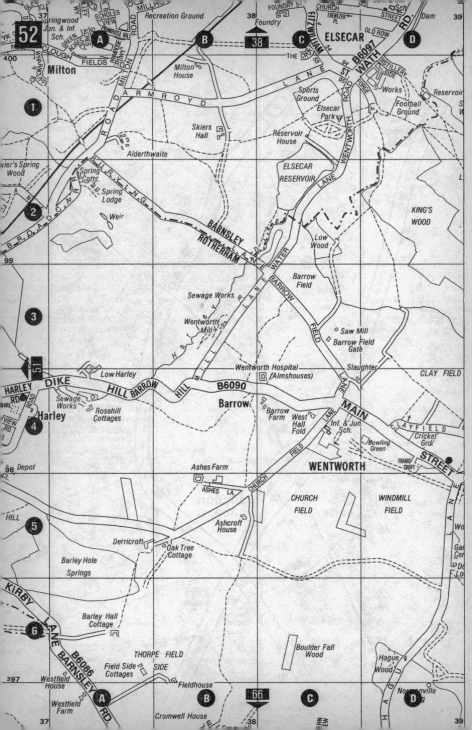

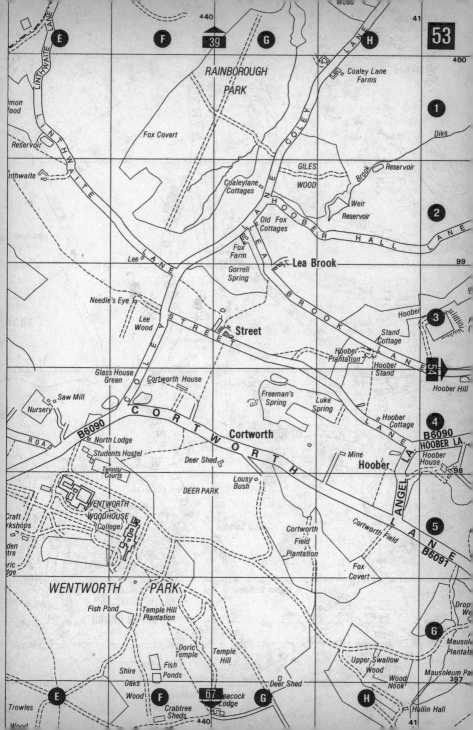

RAINBOROUGH PARK

Coaley Lane Farms

LINTHWAITE LANE

imon Wood

1

Reservoir

COLEY LANE

Fox Covert

Dike

nthwaite

GILES WOOD

Brook

Reservoir

Coaleylane Cottages

Weir
Reservoir

2

HOOBER HALL LANE

Old Fox Cottages

Fox Farm

99

LEA LANE

Lee LANE

Gorrell Spring

Lea Brook

LEA BROOK

Needle's Eye

Lee Wood

Hoober

LEY STREET

Street

Stand Cottage

3

Hoober Plantation

Hoober Stand

54

Glass House Green

Cortworth House

Freeman's Spring

Luke Spring

LANE

Hoober Hill

Saw Mill

Nursery

B6090

CORTWORTH

North Lodge

Cortworth

Hoober Cottage

Hoober

4

B6090 HOOBER LA.

ROAD

Students Hostel

Deer Shed

Mine

Hoober House

98

Tennis Courts

Lousy Bush

Hoober

ANGEL LANE

Craft rkshops

WENTWORTH WOODHOUSE (College)

DEER PARK

Cortworth Field Plantation

Cortworth Field

5

den tre

ric dge

B6091

Fox Covert

WENTWORTH PARK

Fish Pond

Temple Hill Plantation

Drop We

6

Doric Temple

Temple Hill

Mausole Plantati

Trowles

Shire Oaks Wood

Fish Ponds

Deer Shed

Upper Swallow Wood

Wood Nook

Mausoleum Pa

397

Crabtree Sheds

440

Wood

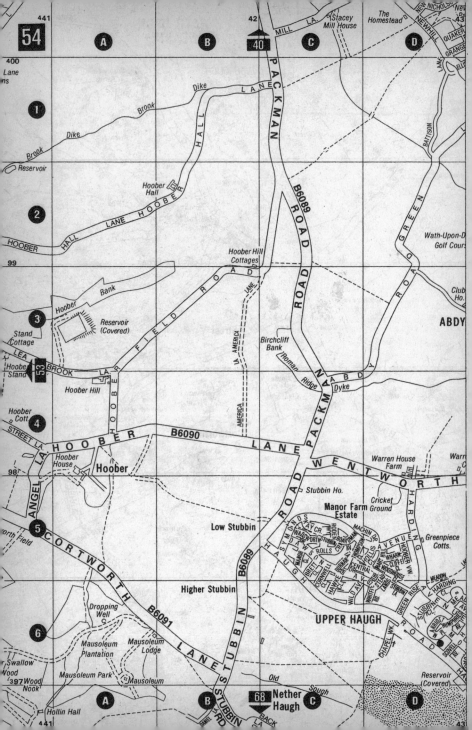

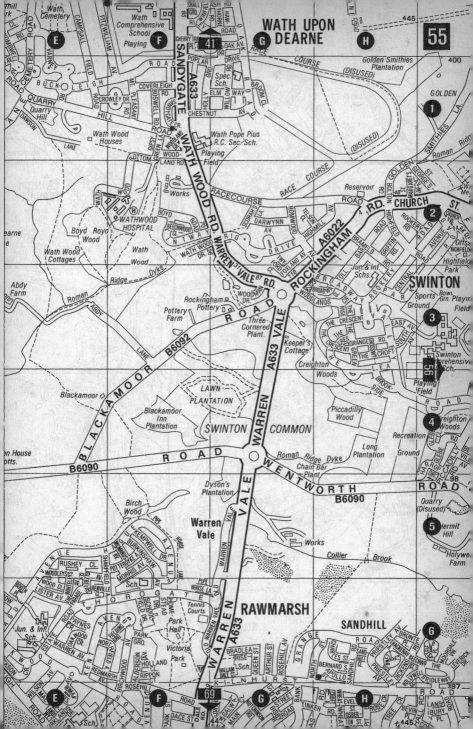

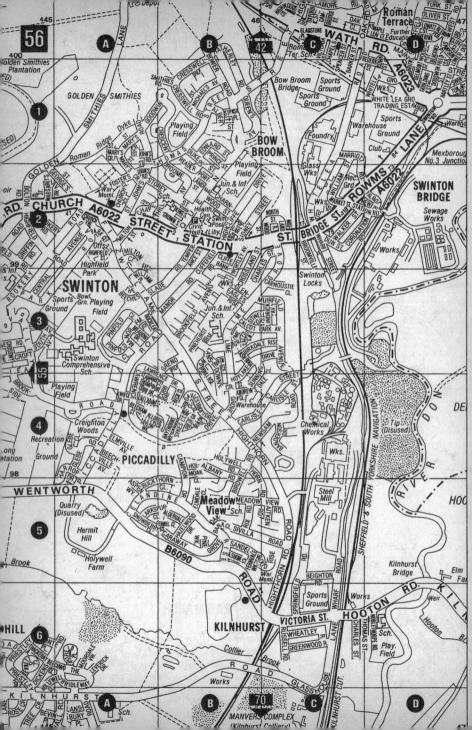

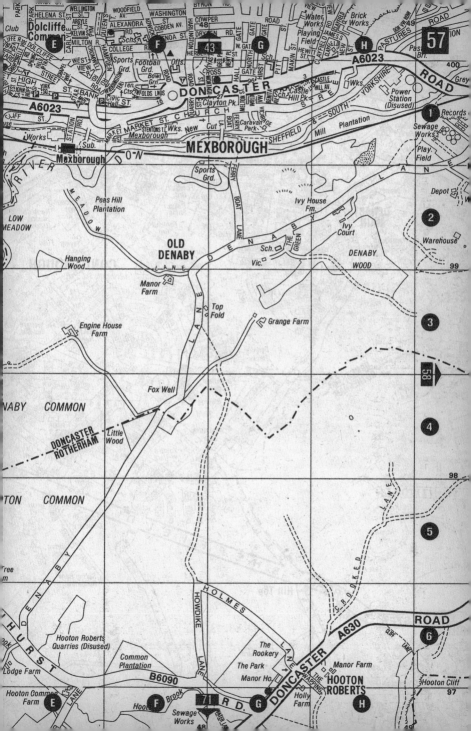

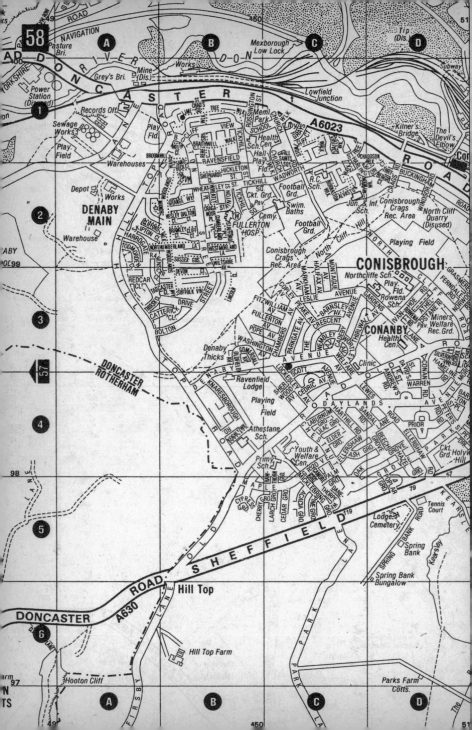

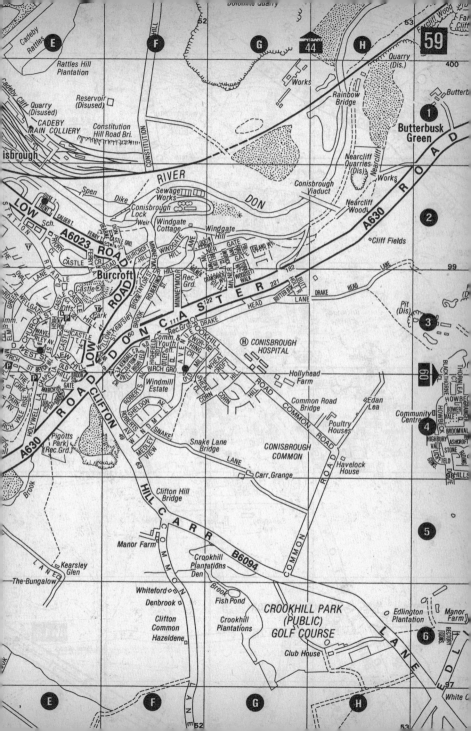

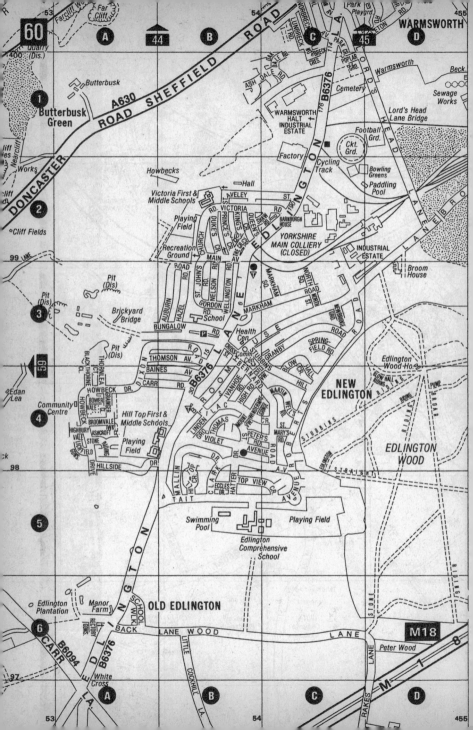

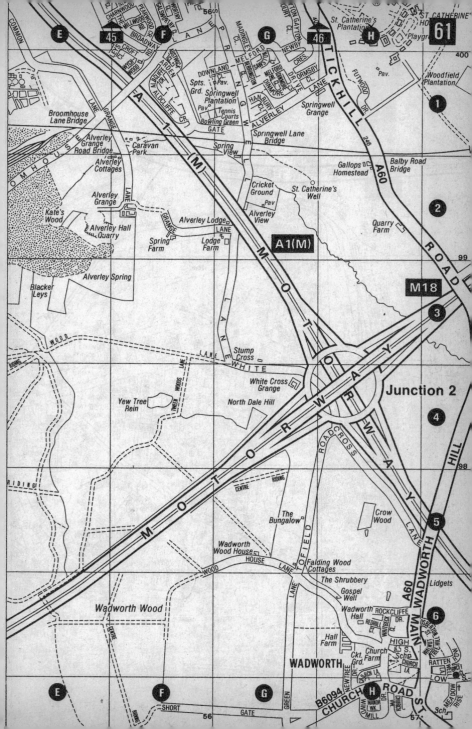

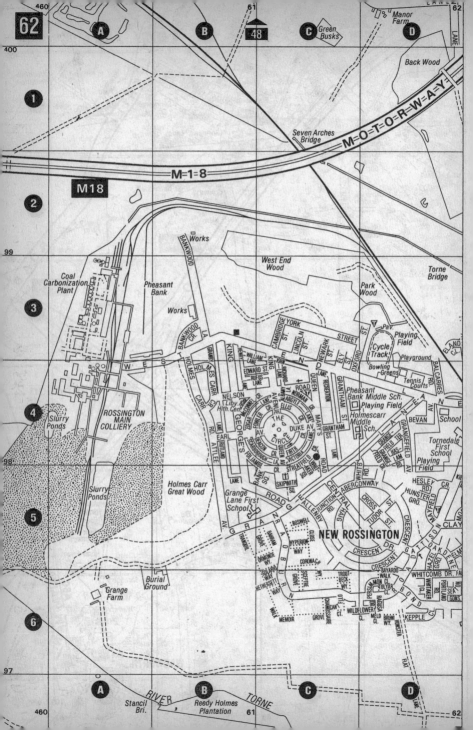

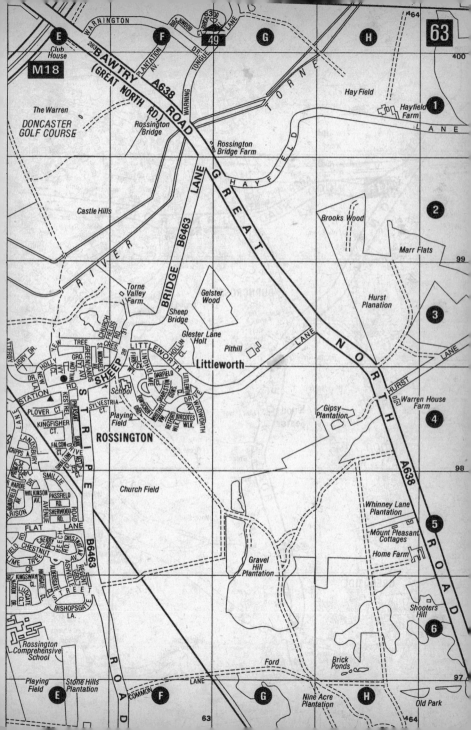

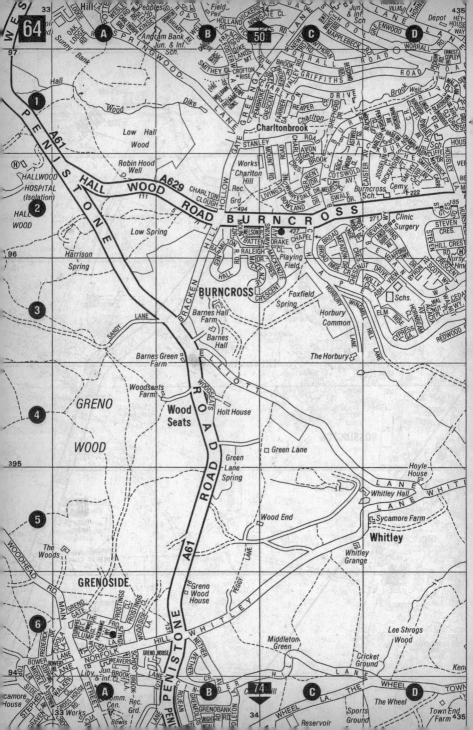

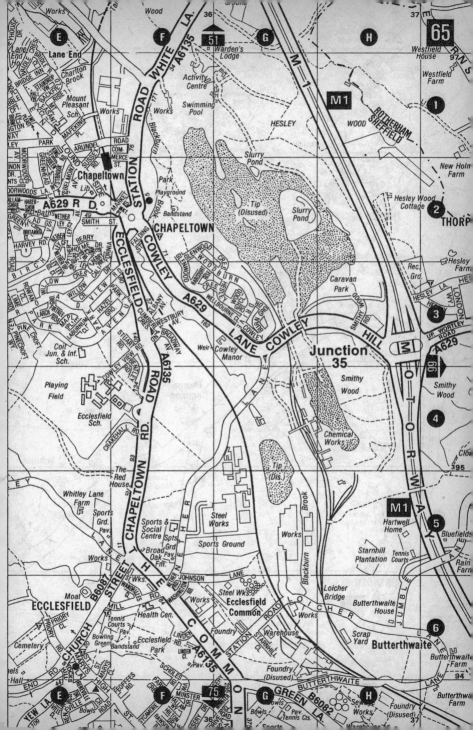

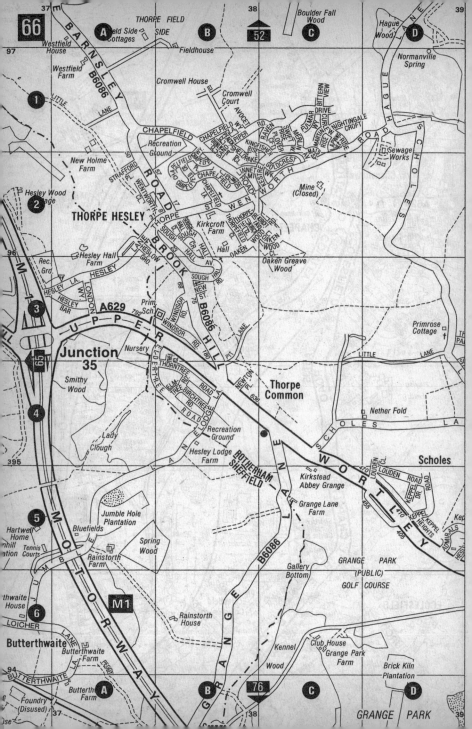

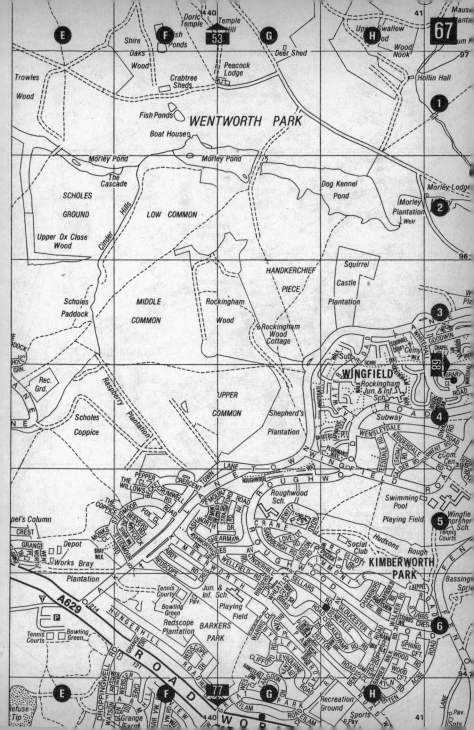

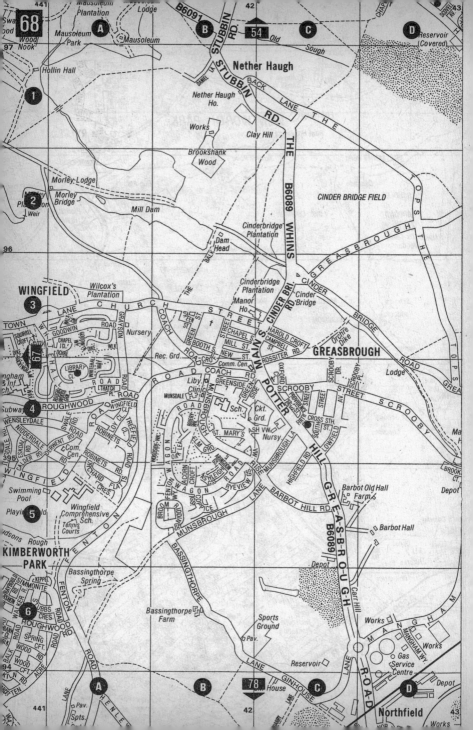

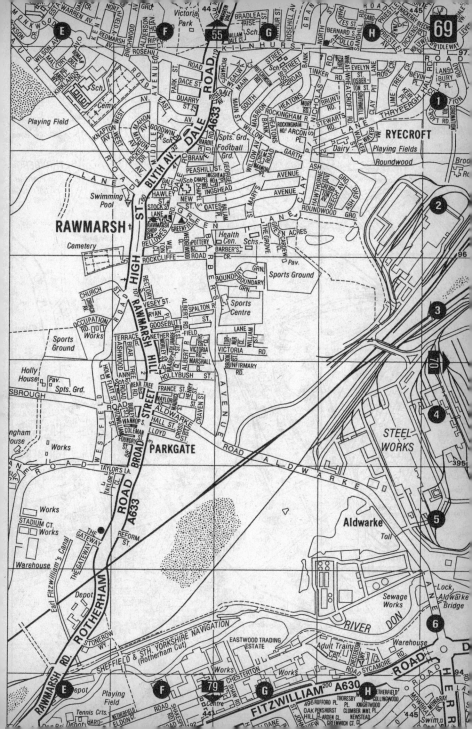

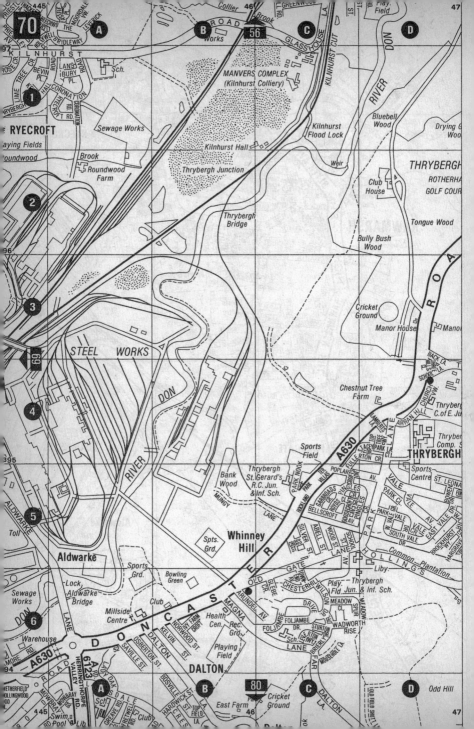

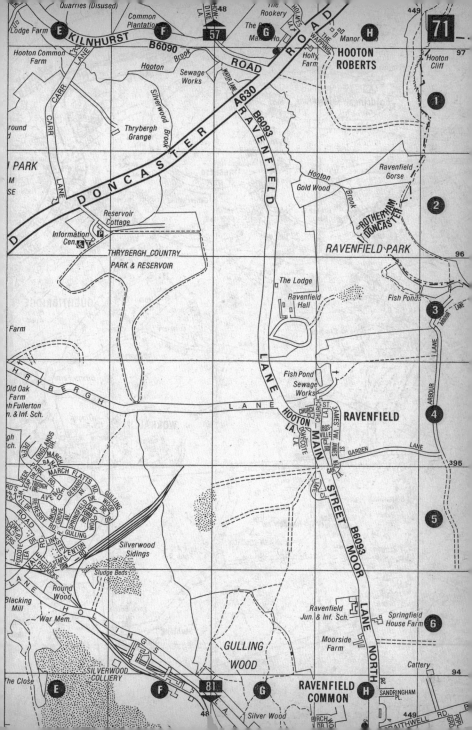

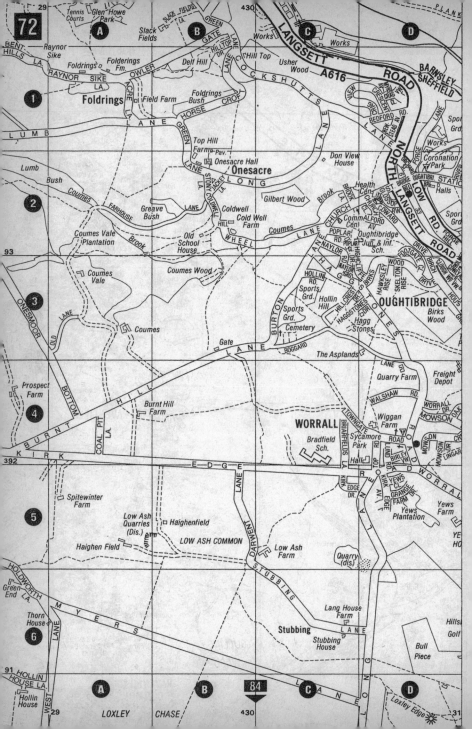

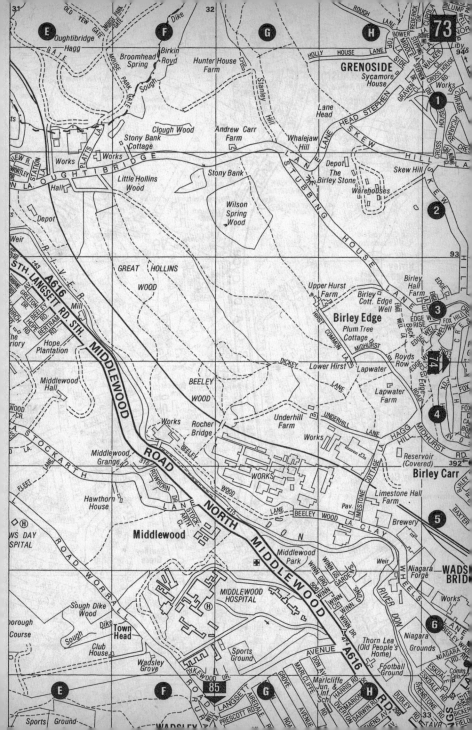

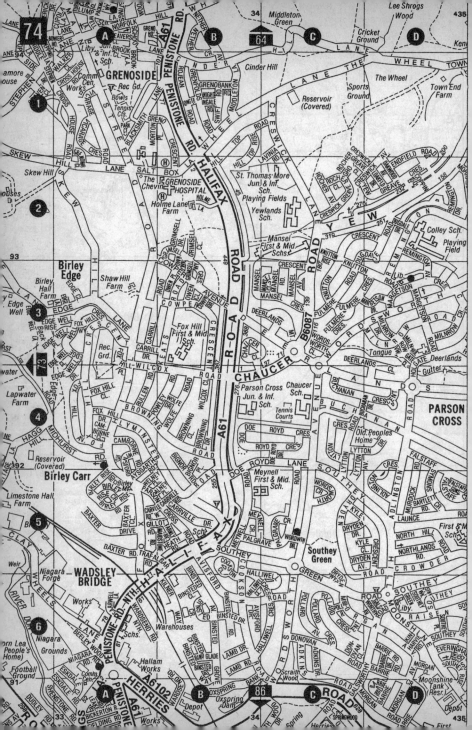

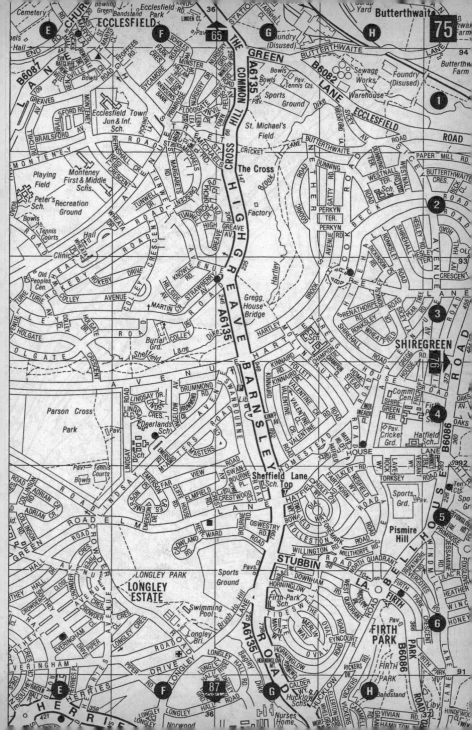

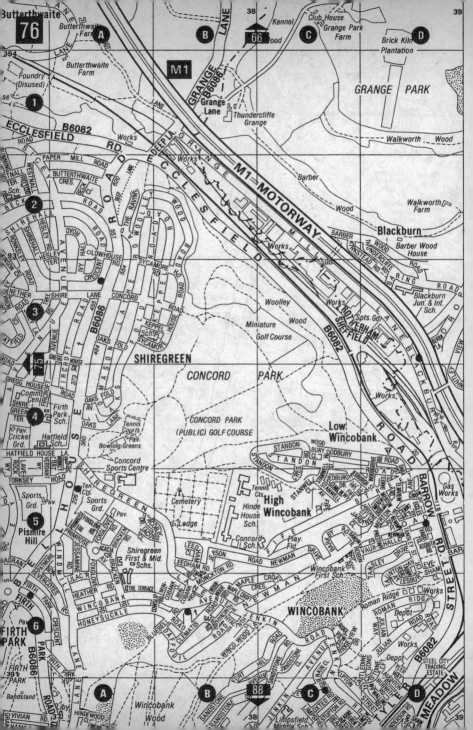

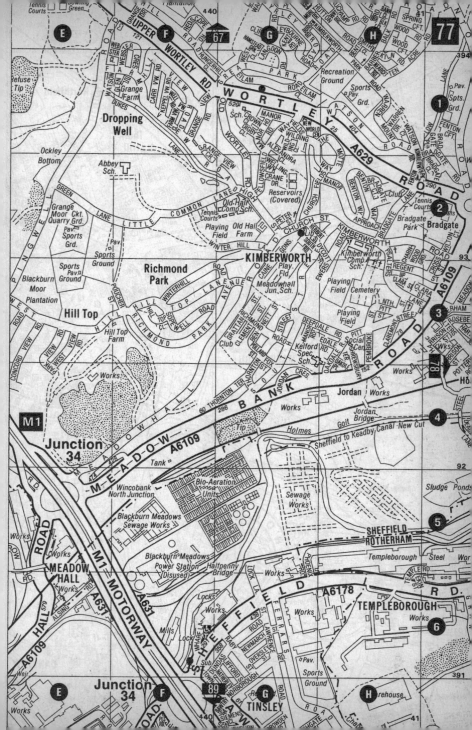

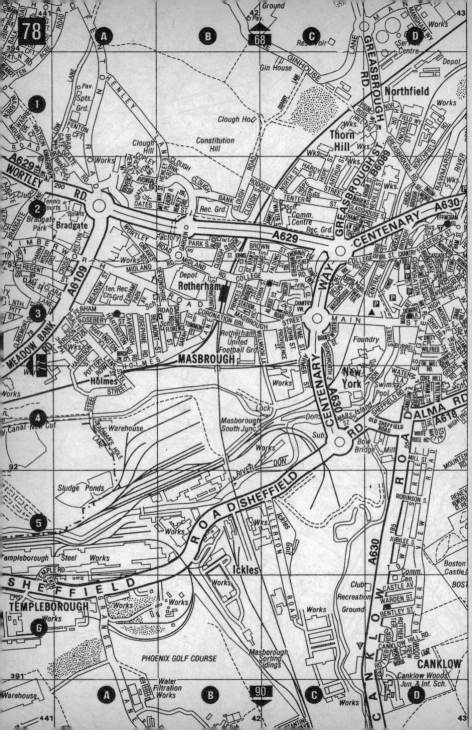

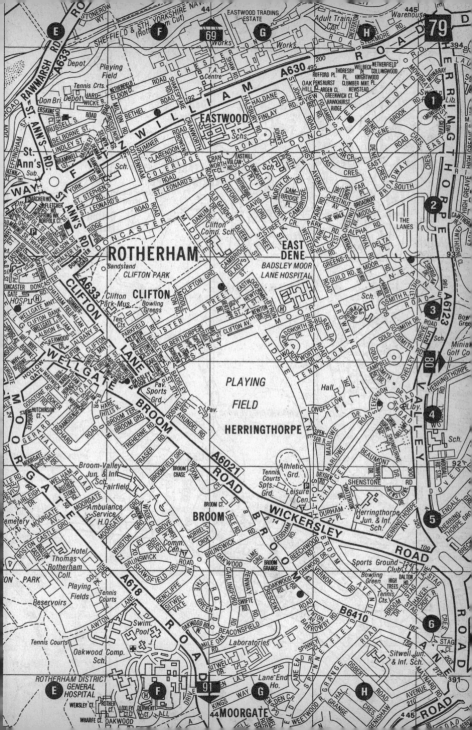

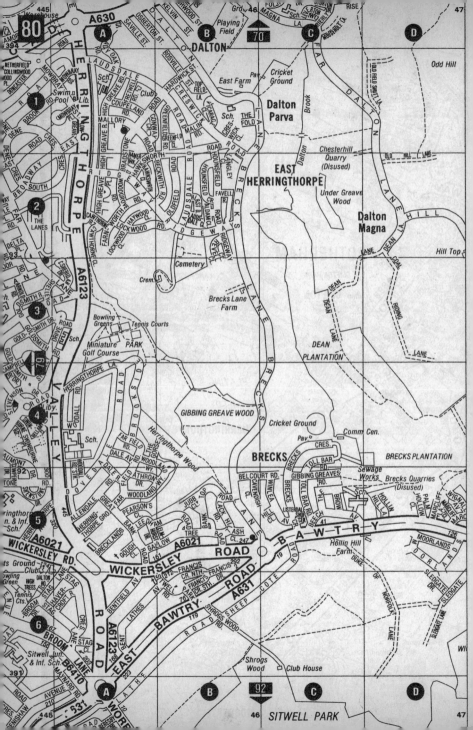

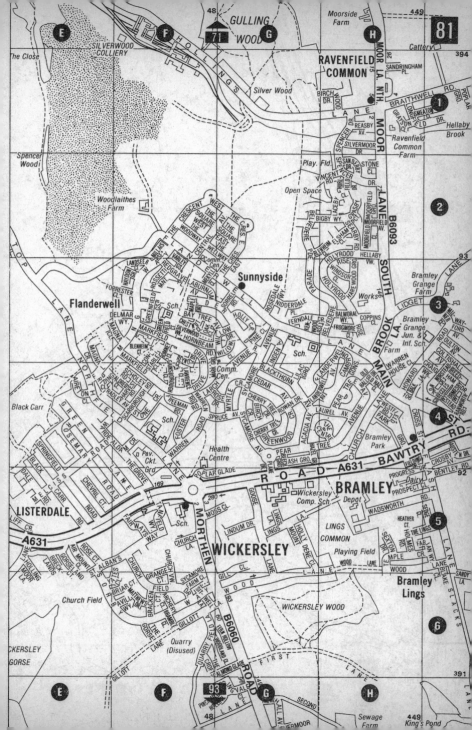

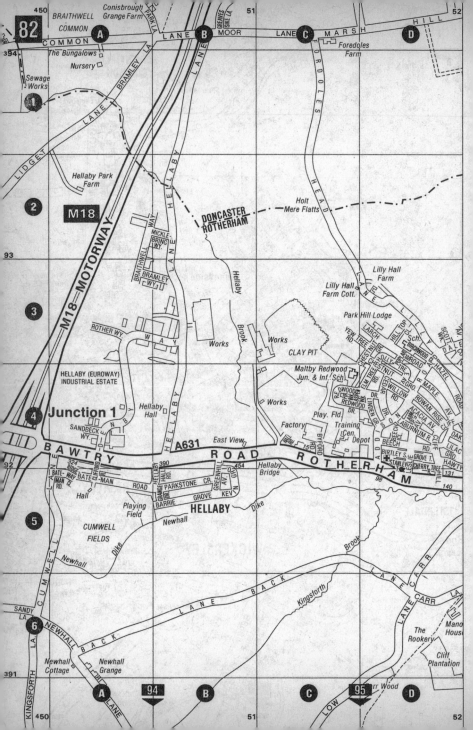

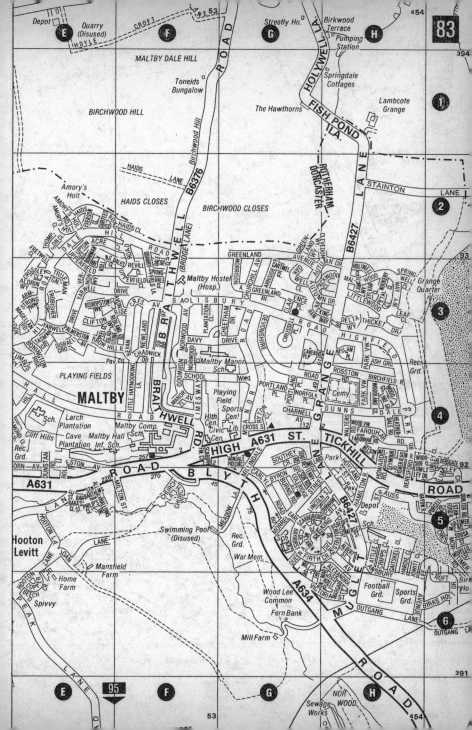

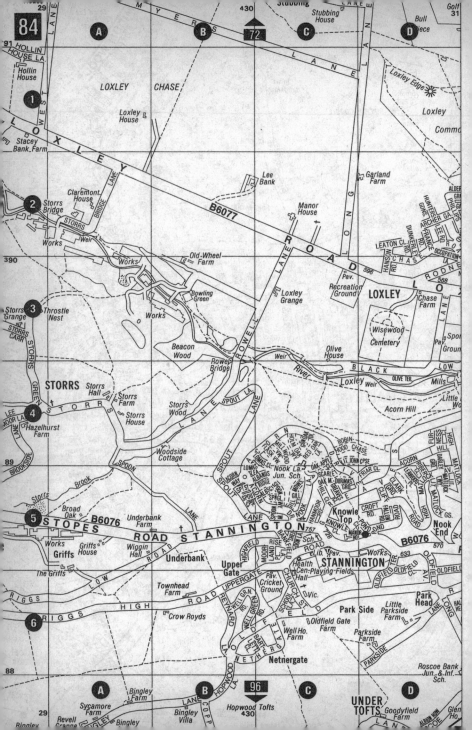

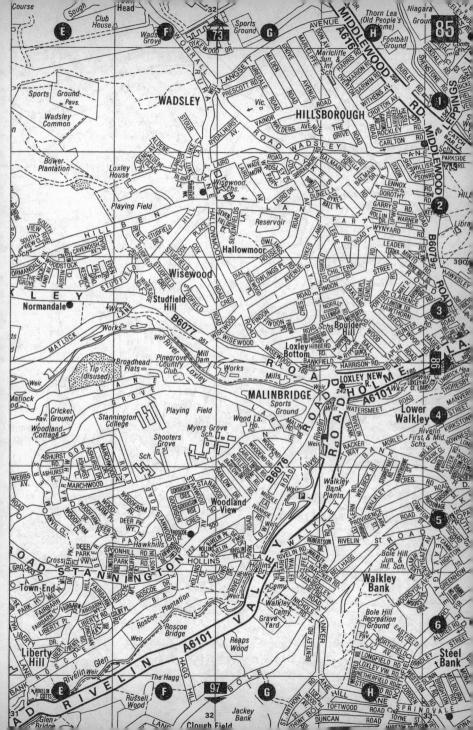

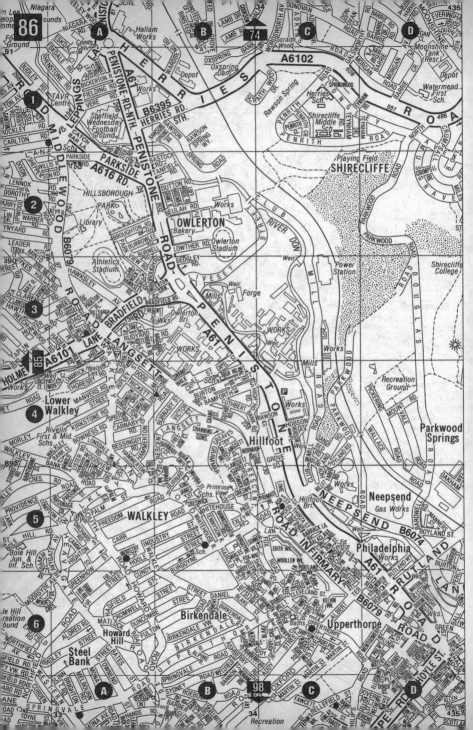

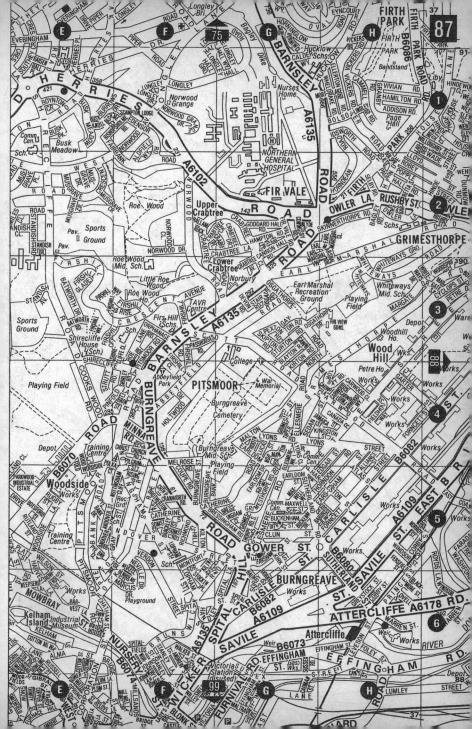

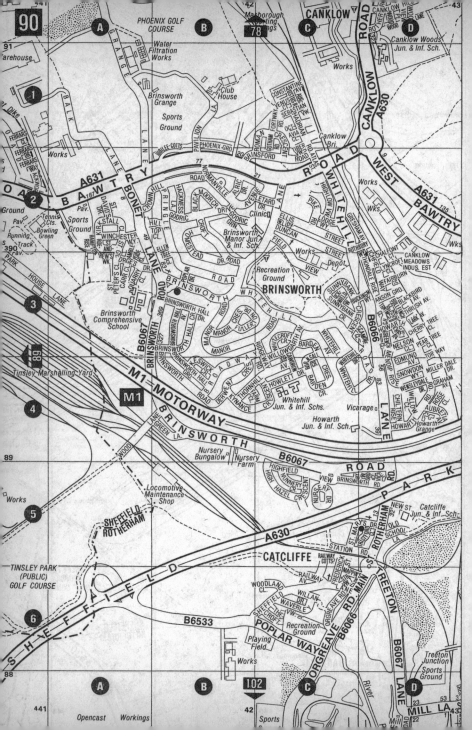

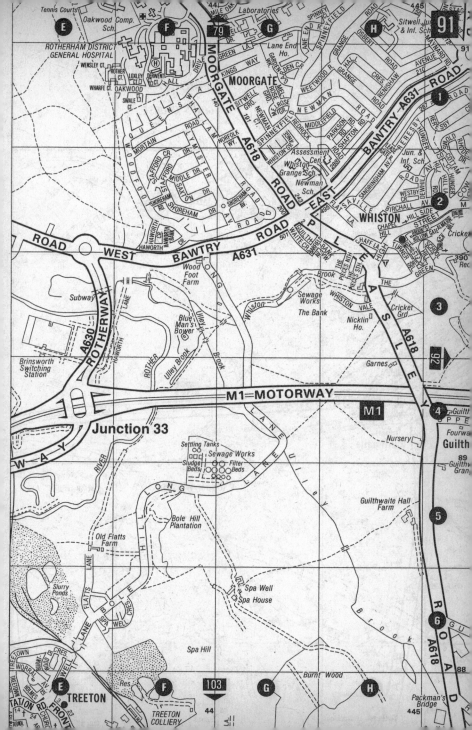

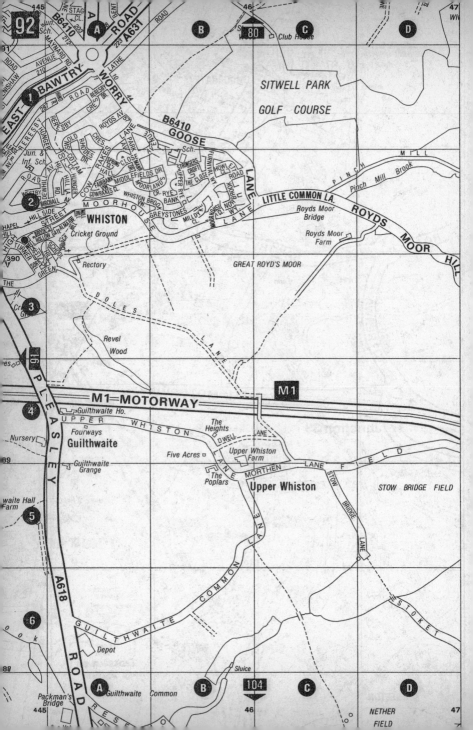

SITWELL PARK

GOLF COURSE

445
STAG CL.
Jun. Sch.
B6410
293
Jun. WE ROAD BENT CL.
A
ROAD
B
80 Club House
C
D
NSHAW
MAYNARD RD
272
2712
210
AVENUE
B6410
WORRY
LATHE
ROAD
223 A631
ROAD
47
WI

EAST
BAWTRY
1

THORESBY
WESTBY AV
RUNGER
OLD RHODES
RERESBY
COTTAM
ROYDS AV.
RAKES LANE
HEREStey CRE.
PARK LANE
B6410
GOOSE
Sch.
PINCH MILL
LANE

Jun. & Inf. Sch.
COW RD.
HALL
TARRAN
MIDDLEFIELDS DR.
DOORLANDS
STRINGERS CROFT
THE CLOSE
STUPPER RD.
FURNIVAL WY.
HOWL LANE
ROAD
LITTLE COMMON LA.
PINCH
Pinch Mill Brook
MILL

2
BIRCHALL
HILL
VIEWHILL
CRESWBY ROAD
COWRAKES CL.
WHISTON BROO
GREYSTONES
CR. RYE
BANK
MILLDYS CL.
MOORHOUSE
FULL NOOK
LANE WY.
LANE
Royds Moor Bridge
ROYDS
MOOR

HILL SIDE
CHAPEL
Street
WHISTON
MOORHOU
Royds Moor Farm

HILL
HIGH
TURNER
BROW SORBY
HOLLOW GATE HALM
Cricket Ground
GREEN
Rectory
GREAT ROYD'S MOOR
HILL

390
THE
3
Cr
DOLES
LANE

16
Revel
Wood
LANE

PLEASLEY

4
M1 MOTORWAY
M1
Guilthwaite Ho.
UPPER
WHISTON
The Heights
LANE
D WELL

Nursery
Fourways
Guilthwaite
Five Acres
Upper Whiston Farm
LANE
FIELD

89
Guilthwaite Grange
The Poplars
MORTHEN
LANE
STOW
STOW BRIDGE FIELD

waite Hall Farm
5
Upper Whiston
BRIDGE
LANE

A618
COMMON
LANE

6
GUILTHWAITE
STOKET

ROAD
Depot
A618
STOKET

88
ok
Sluice
104

Packman's Bridge
A
Guilthwaite Common
B
C
D

445
RESE
46
NETHER FIELD
47

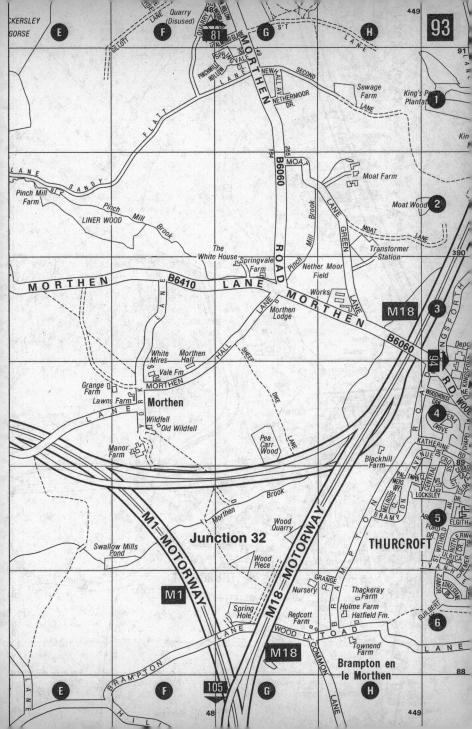

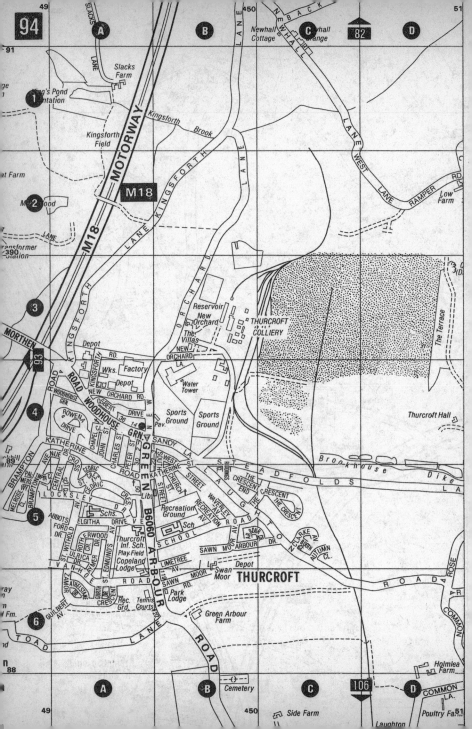

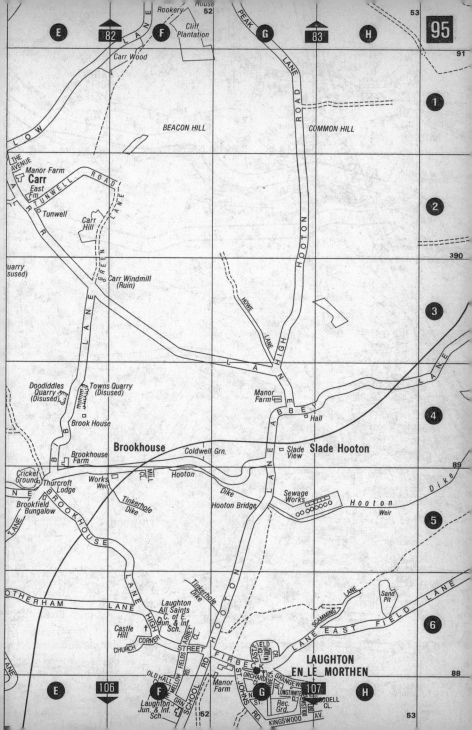

E 82 F Cliff Plantation PEAK G 83 H

Rookery House 52

53

91

Carr Wood

1

BEACON HILL COMMON HILL

LOW

THE AVENUE

Manor Farm

Carr East Fm

TUNWELL ROAD

2

390

Tunwell Carr Hill

GREEN LANE

LANE

HOOTON

Carr Windmill (Ruin)

HOWE LANE

HIGH

3

CARR

LANE

Doodiddles Quarry (Disused) Towns Quarry (Disused)

Manor Farm

ABBEY

4

Brook House Hall

Slade View Slade Hooton

Brookhouse

Brookhouse Farm Coldwell Grn.

Cricket Ground Thurcroft Lodge Works Weir Hooton MILL Dike

89

Brookfield Bungalow Tinkerhole Dike Hooton Bridge Sewage Works Hooton Dike Weir

BROOKHOUSE LANE

5

OTHERHAM LANE Tinkerhole Dike

HOOTON

LANE

SCAMMING LANE EAST FIELD LANE Sand Pit

6

Laughton All Saints C. of E. Jun. & Inf. Sch.

Castle Hill CORNER CHURCH

HIGH STREET

FIRBECK

88

LAUGHTON EN_LE_MORTHEN

E 106 F Laughton Jun. & Inf. Sch. OLD HALL MELLOW FIELDS GRN. RD. SCHOOL RD. ABBEY CL. Manor Farm ST. JOHNS RD. ORCHARD CL. G 107 H

52

KINGSWOOD

53

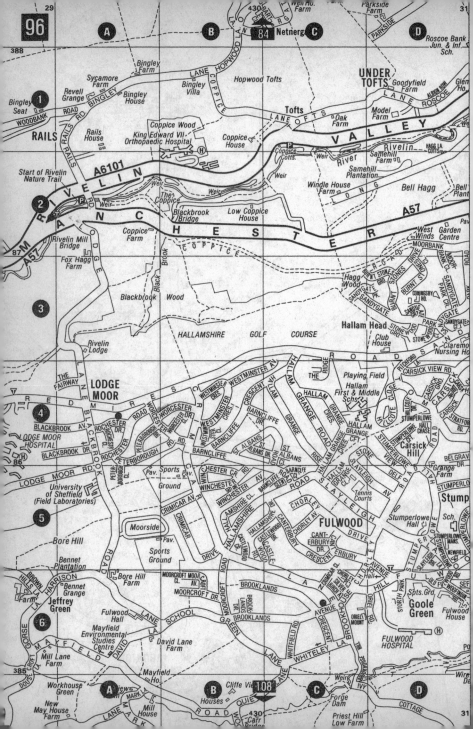

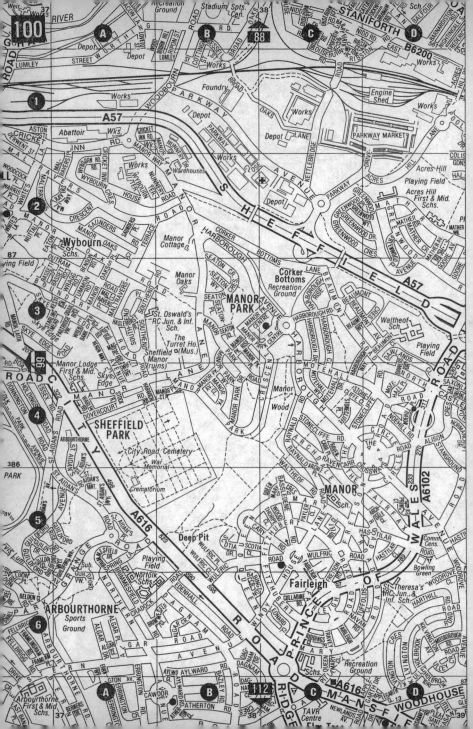

A   B   90   C   D

441

388

Opencast   Workings

1

2   ROTHERHAM
SHEFFIELD

Tip
(disused)

87

FINCH   MARSDEN
WELL   RD.

3

Sports
Ground
Pav.

Recreation
Ground
ST.

Sports
Ground
Pav.

102   Sch.
Lib.

4   HANDSWORTH   A57   ROAD

HANDSWORTH

Sports
Field

Cemy

MEDLOCK

Cemetery

CRESCENT
DRIVE

KIRKDALE   CRES.
KIRKDALE
DR.

BALLIFIELD

BALLIFIELD   AV.
BALLIFIELD
WY.
BALLIFIELD
PL.
BALLIFIELD
TCE.

BALLIFIELD
RISE

BALLIFIELD   ROAD

HANDSWORTH   GR.
CRES.

HANDW.
GRANGE   DR.
GRANGE   DR.

BALLIFIELD   CRES.

Ballifield
First & Mid.
Sch.

Beaver Hill
Sch.

SHUBERT

RETFORD

ORGREAVE   LANE

POPLAR   WAY   RD.
Recreation
Ground

Sports
Ground

Highfield
Farm

Works

ORGREAVE

Rotherwood

Sewage
Works

Garage

ORGREAVE

Warehouses

Works

ORGREAVE   RD.
ORGREAVE   PLACE
ORGREAVE   CRES.
ORGREAVE   CL.

Pav.

Orgreave
Common

Sports
Ground

Works

Works

Woodhouse
Mill

COALBROOK   AV.
COALBROOK   AV.
COALBROOK
GRO.

ROTHERHAM   ST.
ORGREAVE
ST.

Warehouse

TREETON   LA.
Treeton
Junction
Sports
Ground

MILL   LA.
B6067

River   Rother

Mill
Ho.

Coal Stocking
Ground

Orgreave   Works

Weir

Slurry
Ponds

Slur

42
(Playing
Field)

Slur

176

A57   ROAD

HORSE   WOOD   RD.

Woodhouse

Myrtle
Bank

SUNDOWN   RD.

5

BRAMLEY   PK.
REDTHORN   RD.
SUNDOWN
AVENUE

Sundown
Rise

HANDSWORTH
GRANGE
LANE

Playing
Field

Beaver
Avenue

BEAVER   DR.

BEAVER   HILL   ROAD

FLOCKTON

CRESCENT   AV.
FLOCKTON

FLOCKTON   AV.
FLOCKTON   RD.

Beaver
Hill

Richmond
College
Annexe

BADGER

GOATHLAND

Rec.
Ground
Richmond
Col.

GOATHLAND
RD.

B6064
RODGER

385

6

Shirtcliff

SEVERNSIDE   DR.
SEVERNSIDE   GDNS.
SEVERNSIDE

NEW   CROSS

NEW   CROSS

A   B   114   C   D

STRADBROKE   ROAD

441

Brook

Shirtcliff   Wood

WOODHOUSE

MAUNCER

MAUNCER
CR.

Cemetery

MAUNCER   LA.

TITHE   BARN

TITHE   BARN
CHAPEL   ST.

VICAR

Schubert
Bridge

Tithe   Barn

Grave
Yard

Recreation
Ground

STATION

Brunswick
First & Mid. Sch.
Playing Field

BEAVER   HILL   ROAD

B6066   BEAVER

B6066   HIGHFIELD   LA.

RETFORD   ROAD

ROTHERHAM   RD.

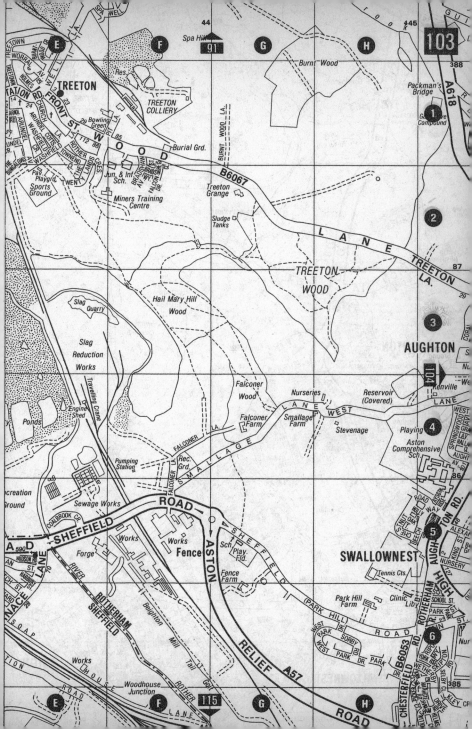

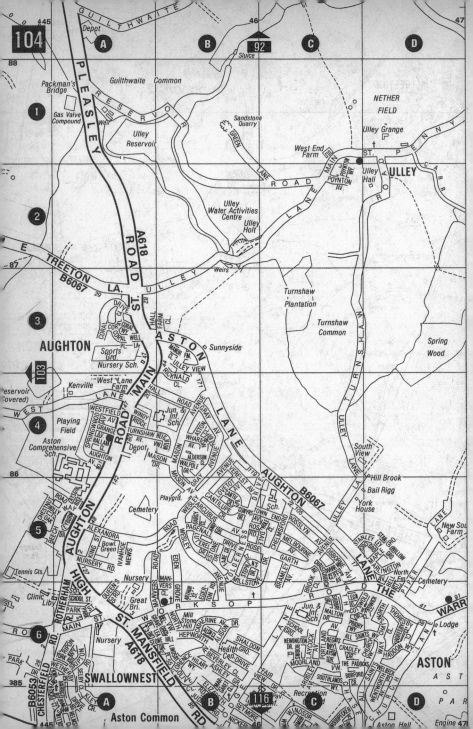

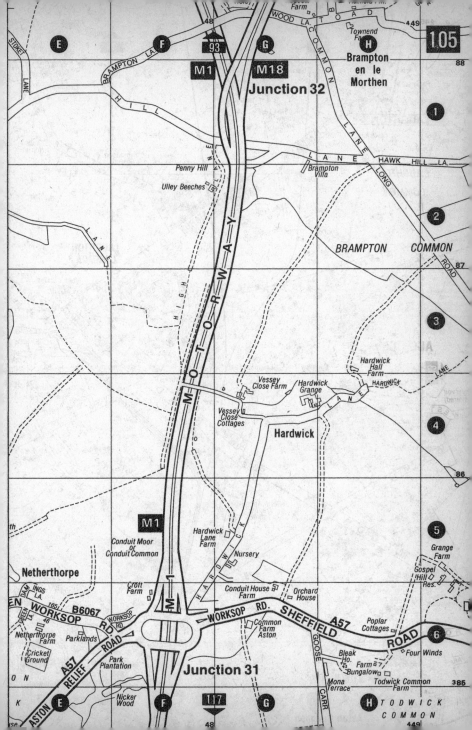

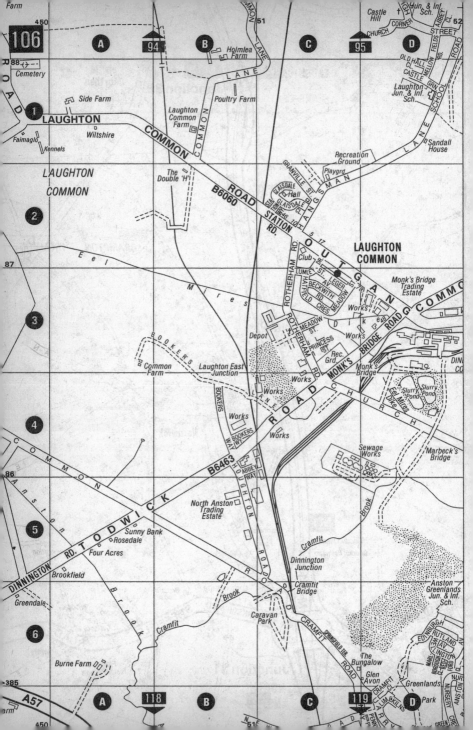

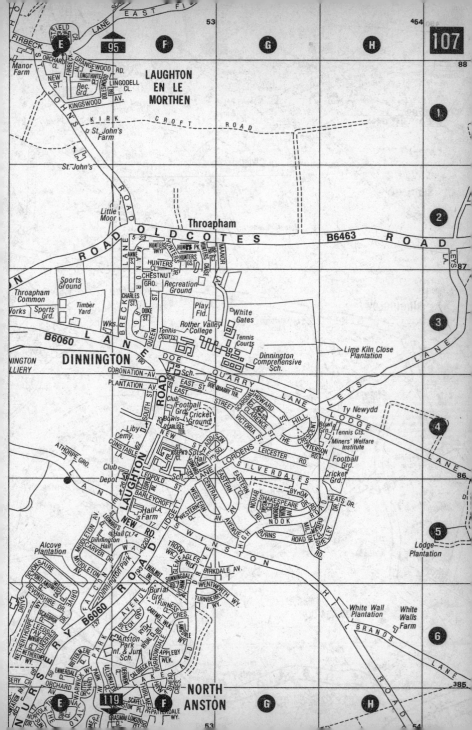

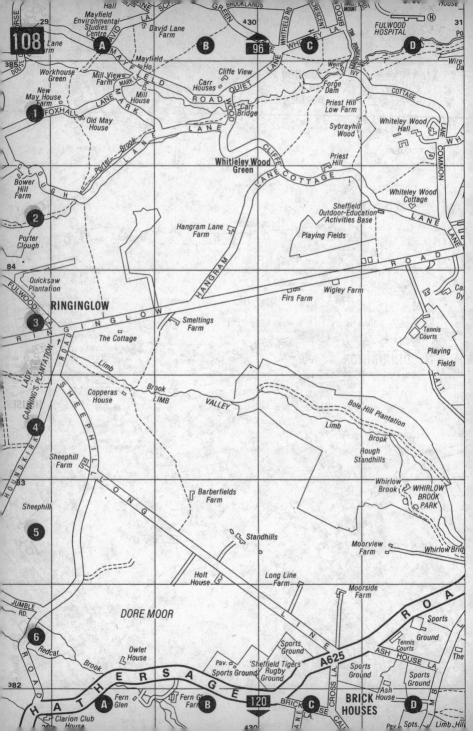

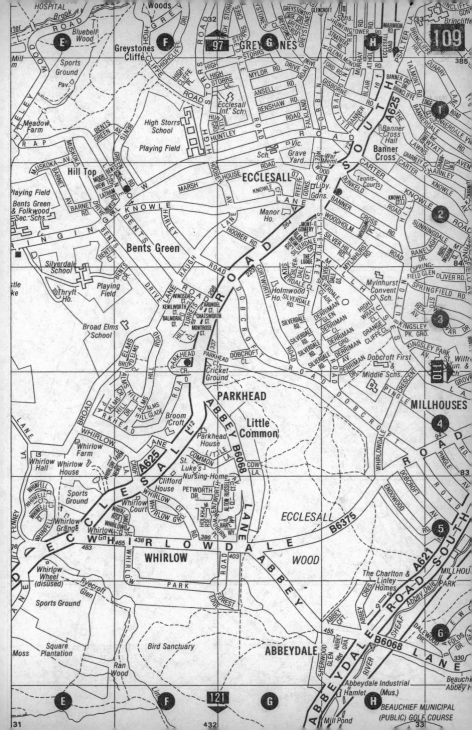

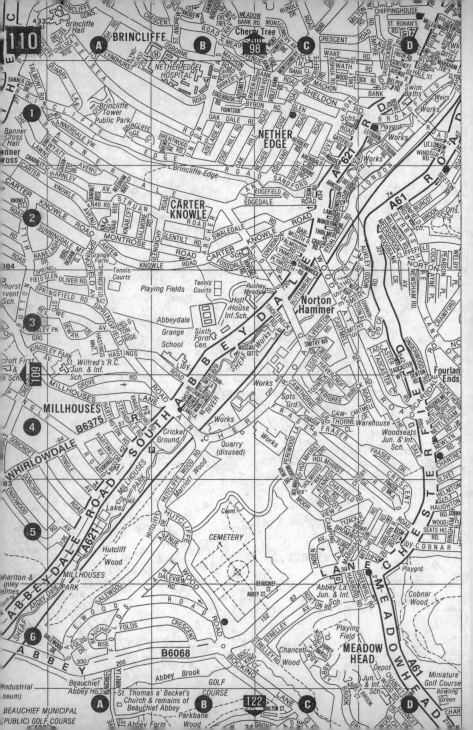

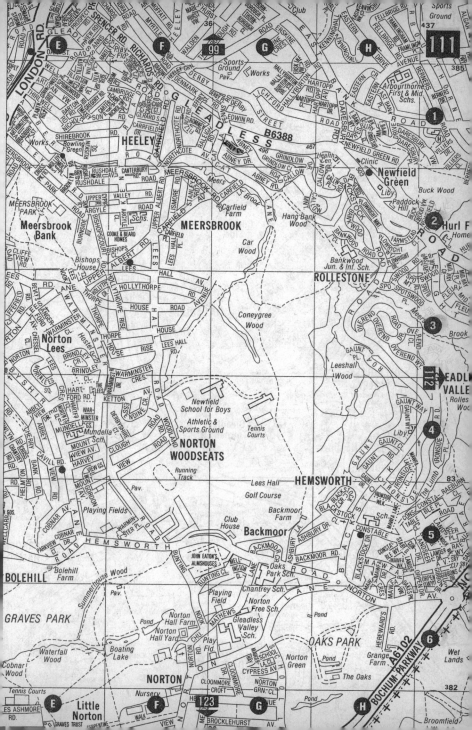

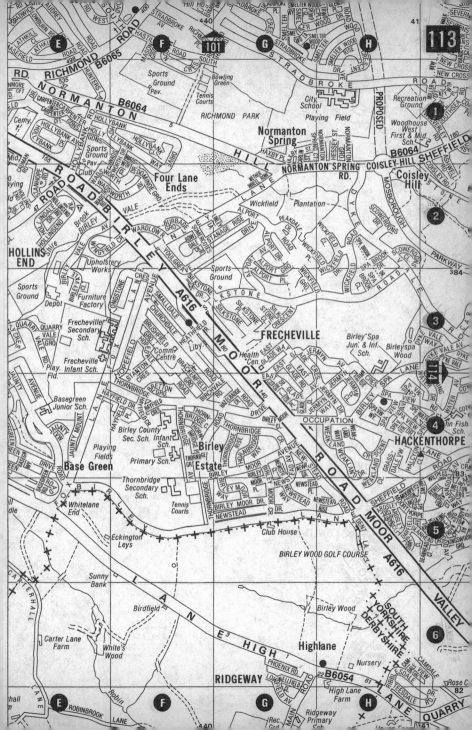

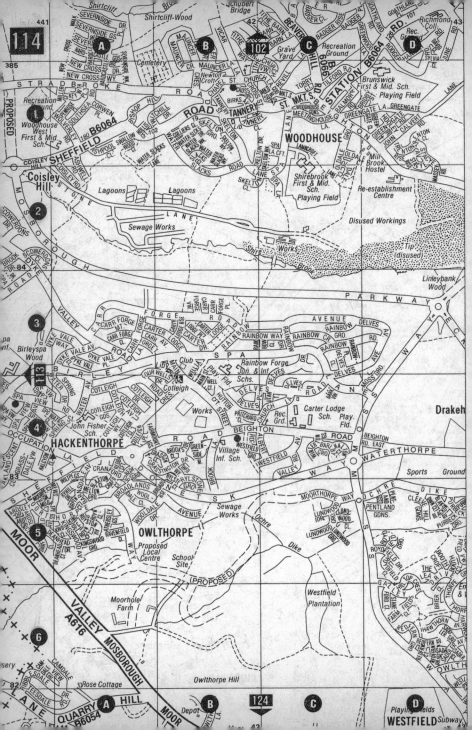

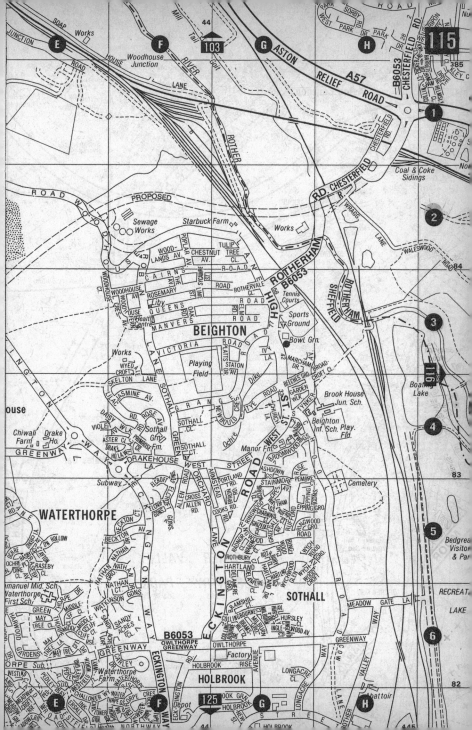

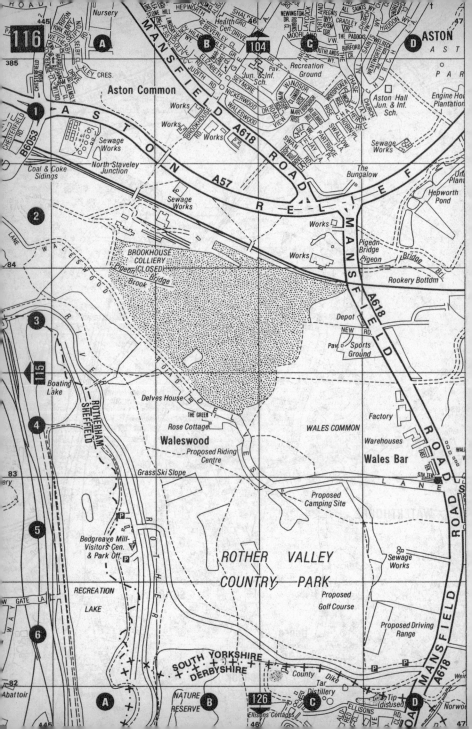

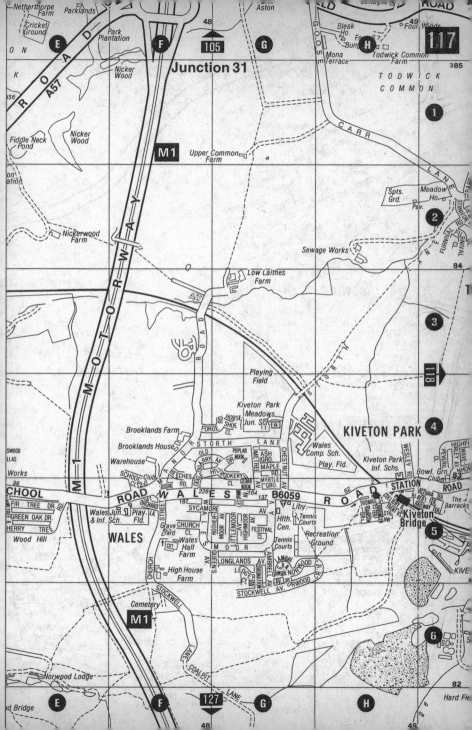

Netherthorpe Farm
Parklands
Aston
117
Cricket Ground
E
Park Plantation
F
48
105
G
Bleak Ho. Farm
49 Four Winds
H
Mona Terrace
Todwick Common Farm
385

Junction 31

T O D W I C K   C O M M O N

Nicker Wood
A57

M1

Upper Common Farm

1

Fiddle Neck Pond
Nicker Wood

Spts. Grd.
Meadow Ho.
Pav.
2

FURNIVAL RD
STANHOPE RD
CARNIVAL CL
FURNIVAL CL

Nickerwood Farm

Sewage Works

Low Laithes Farm

84

C A R R   L A N E

3

Playing Field

118

Kiveton Park Meadows Jun. Sch.

KIVETON PARK
4

Brooklands Farm
HORSE SHOE CL.
FORGE
RD.
POPLAR NOOK
LIME TREE AV.
ASH GRO.
MAPLE RD.
MYRTLE GRO.
CHESTNUT RD.
Wales Comp. Sch. Play. Fld.
Kiveton Park Inf. Schs.
HIGHFI
WAVE
RILEY CL
PEVERIL
WESLEY RD.
Bowl. Grn. Club
PL.

Brooklands House
Warehouse
SCHOOL CL
Club
BEECHES RD.
OLD QUARRY AV.
CEDAR NOOK
ROOKERY CL.

S T O R T H   L A N E

S T O R T H

R O A D

CHOOL
FIR TREE DR.
GREEN OAK DR.
HERRY TREE
Wood Hill
98
M1
R O A D
W A L E S
ORCHARD LA
SCHOOL ST
THE
228
187
SYCAMORE
Grave Yard
CHURCH CL.
WALES
Wales Jun. Play. & Inf. Sch. Fld.
Wales Hall Farm
High House Farm
CHURCH ST
Cemetery
STOCKWELL LANE
M1

MOOR
LITTLEMOOR AV
MOOR AV.
FESTIVAL CL.
164
137
B6059
MAPLE
AV.
Hlth. Cen.
Tennis Courts
Recreation Ground
Tennis Courts
Liby.
Wales
Works

R O A D
62
STATION
THOMAS ST
DAWSON TER.
COLLIERY R.
VICTORIA TER.
TRINITY ST.
TRINITY VW.
ALBERT TER.
WESLEY RD.
RAILWAY TER.
Kiveton Bridge
5
The Barracks
KIVE

Works

QUEEN'S AV.
LONGLANDS
LEDGER
STOCKWELL AV.
AMBRELL AV
CORONATION AV
GRISDE
NORWOOD
AMBRELL AV
NORWOOD CR.

6

82

Norwood Lodge
STOCKWELL LANE
COALPIT LANE

Bridge
E
F
48
127
G
H
Hard Fie

49

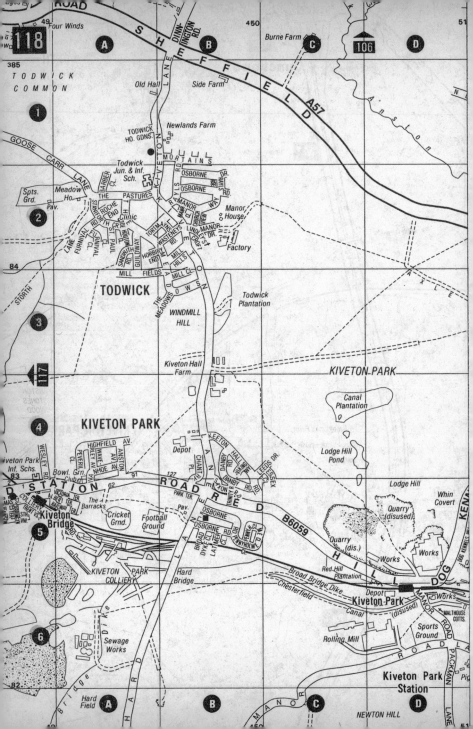

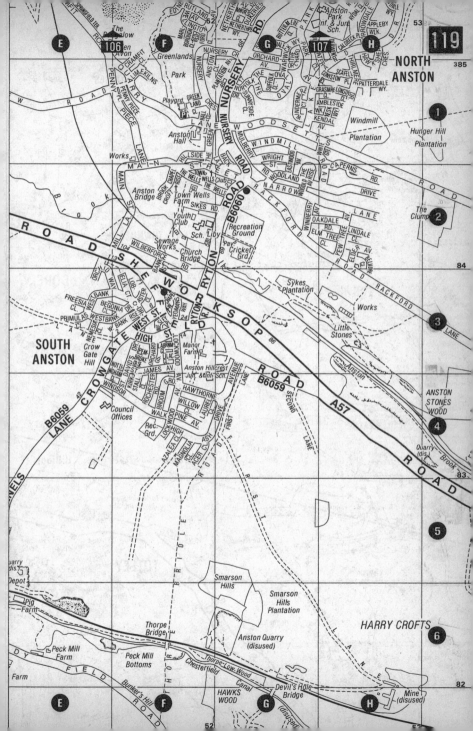

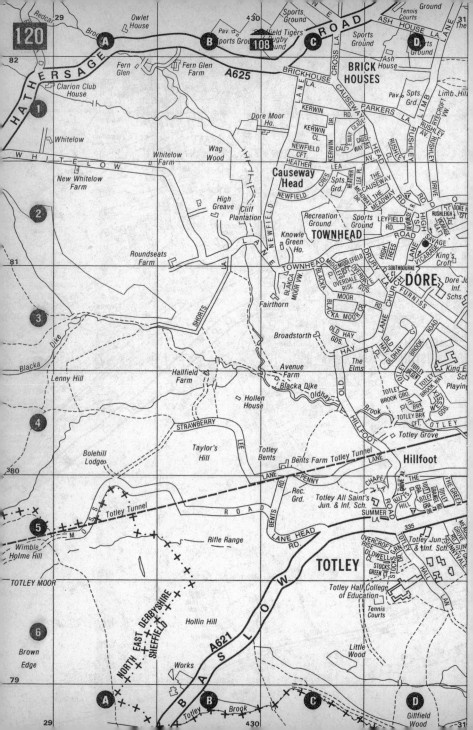

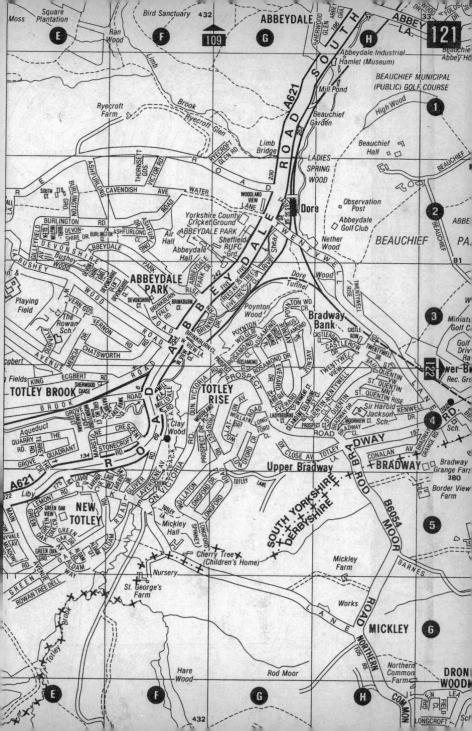

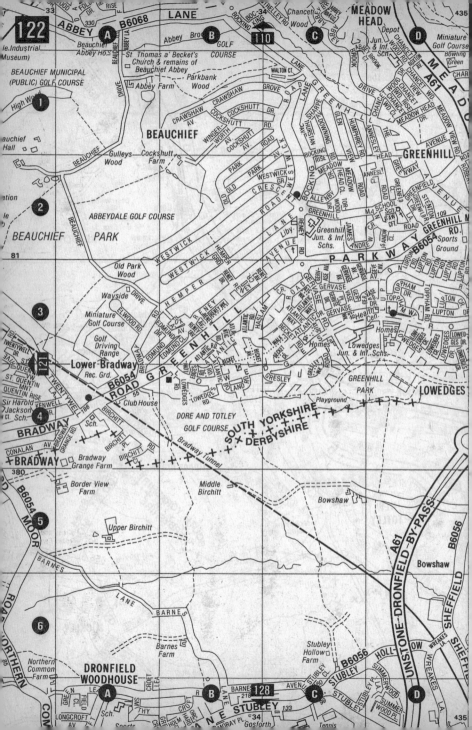

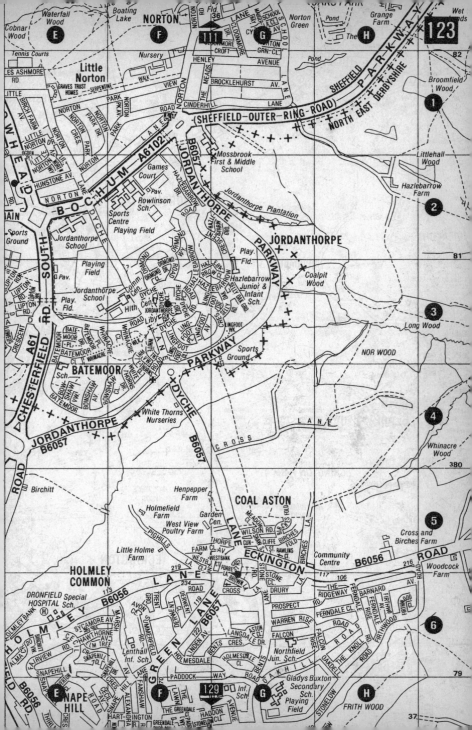

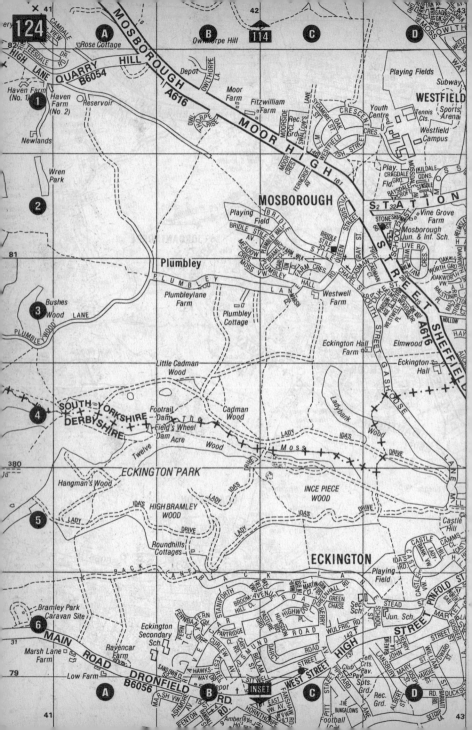

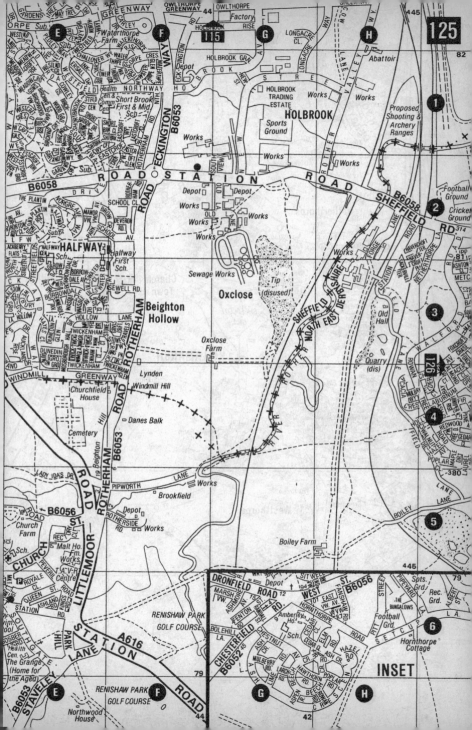

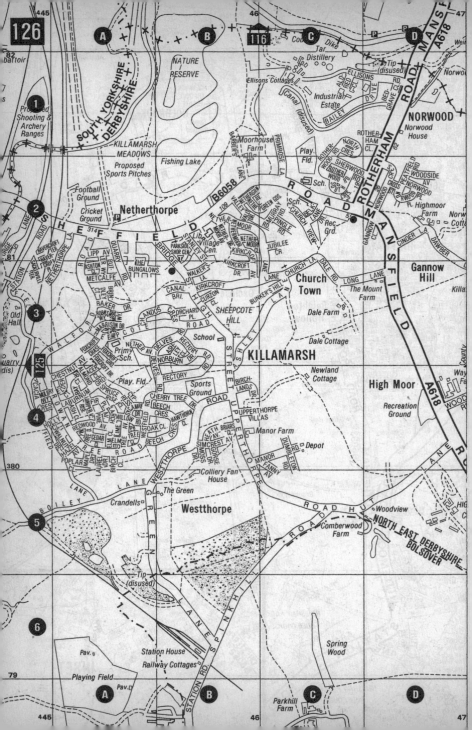

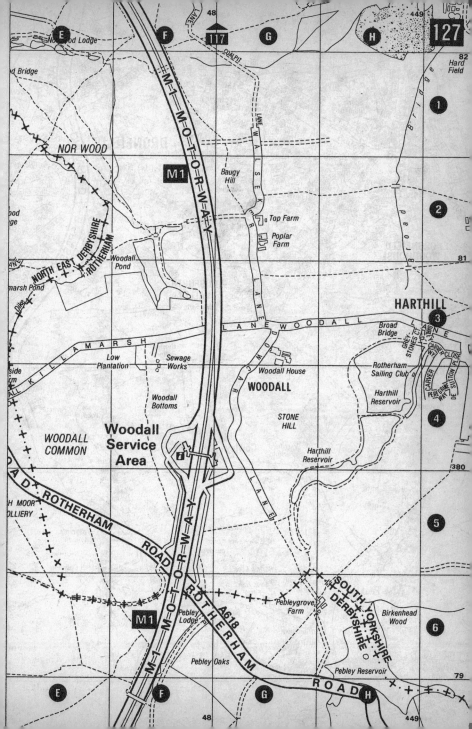

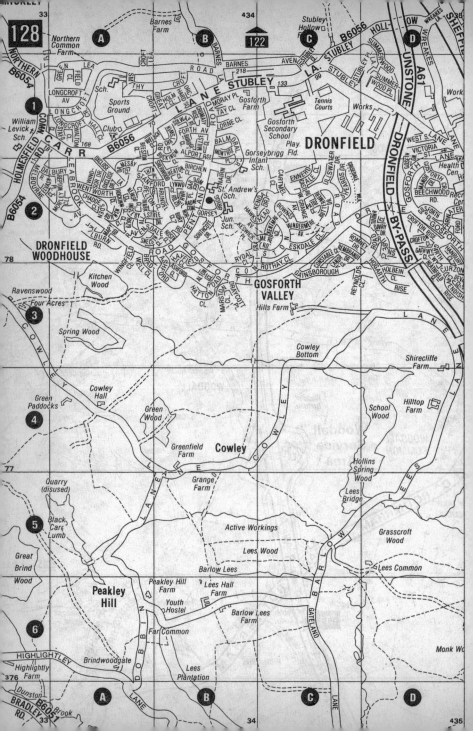

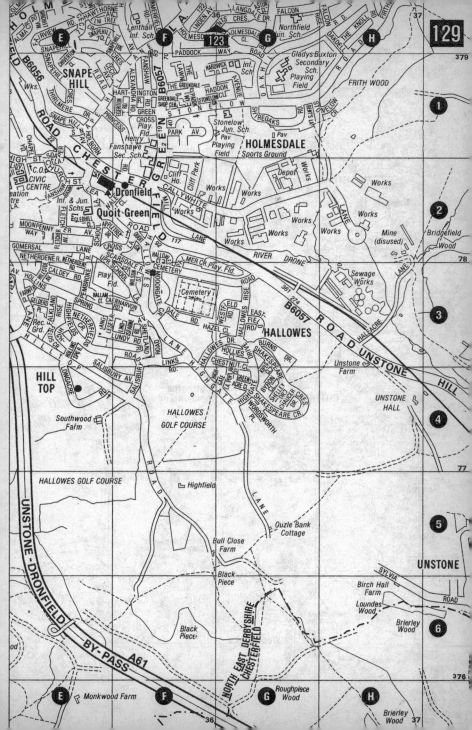

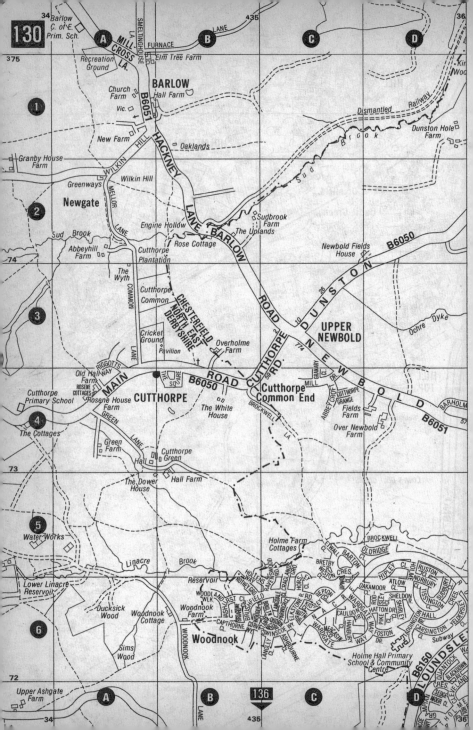

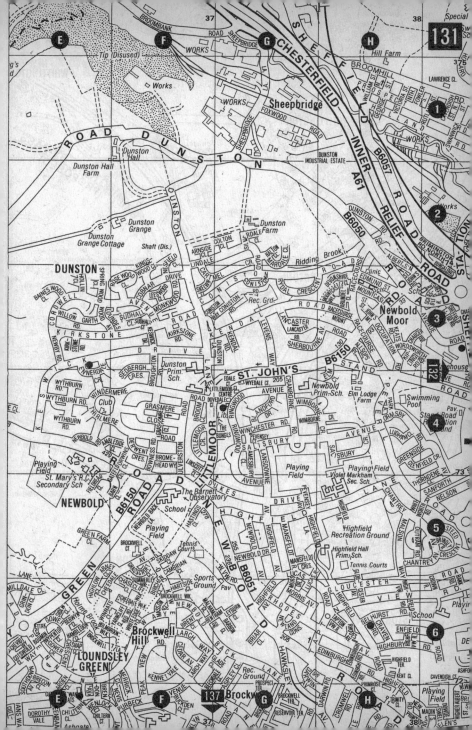

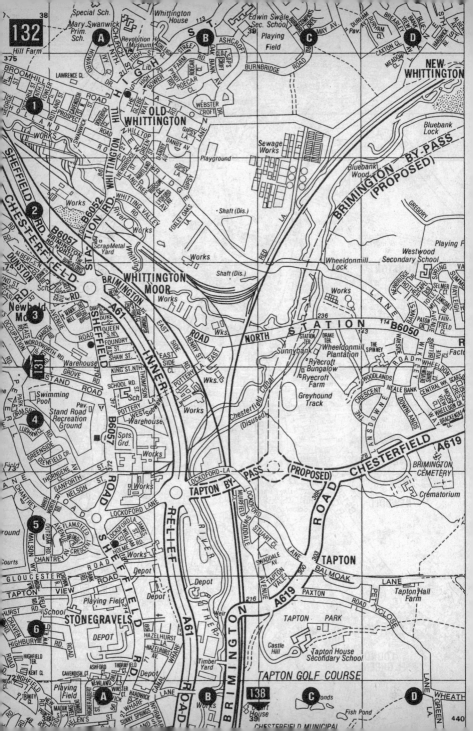

E Merrians Farm
F Staveley Up Sidings **G** **H**

Rec. Co.

376

ROTHER

1

RIVER

Tip (Disused)

Foundry

WORKS

R.

Dixon's Lock

Victoria Farm

Hounsfield Bridge

Sports Grd.

Club

Works

2

Open Cast Worki

HOLLINGWOOD
ROAD

Pondhouse Farm

Troughbrook Wood

74

New Brimington

KING ST.

QUEEN ST.

BOURNE
PRINCESS

DORSET CL.

CEDAR
SYCAMORE

LILAC ST.

LABURNUM ST.

FIR ST.

Brook

Playing Fld.

TROUGHBROOK

CRESCENT

Hollingwood Schs.

Swim. Pool

CHESTERFIELD
ROAD 277

Troughbrook Hill

3

PETERDALE

PETER

DALE
RD.

GEORGE S
JOHN
STREET
HEYWOOD
FOLJAMBE RD.
Sch.

CHAPEL ST.
BURNELL
ST.

DORSET AV.
Sch.

CAMBRGE
DRIVE

OXFORD
CL.

CORNWALL
CL.

117

CHESTERFIELD RD.
A619

60

8

RINGWOOD RD.

Hollingwood Estate

Ringwood Park

Ringwood Hall

Ringwood Lake

Ringwood Farm

Weir

INKERSALL

CROMFORD DR.
HOLESWELL
HUNTLEY
LUTON

134

TURNER DR.
ATTLEE
SUTTON
CRIC

4

Rec. Grd.

Lib.

CEMETERY
MONTPL.

Grove Farm

Ivy House Farm

BRIMINGTON

CHURCH ST.

HALL
ROAD

COTTERHILL LA.

BRADLEY GRANT
FRANCIS ST.

BRIARVIEW

MANOR AV.

BROOM GDS.

MANOR DR.

MANOR
ROAD

Manor Farm

Parker's Wood

INKERSALL GREEN

SHINWELL AV.

WILKINSON DR.

SMITH AV.

STANLEY

HILLMAN ROAD

BEVAN PLACE

DADE
PL.

DOBSON PL.

MADIN DR.

JERVIS

BRADSHAW RD.

McMAHON RD.

73

AVENUE
CURVE

LATHKILL
AV.

ASHOVER
ELLIOTT

5

BONDFIELD RD.

FURNACE

LANE

Furnace Farm

WEST WOOD

KINDER
DRIVE

DOVEDALE RD.

CURBAR

CASTLETON GRO.

BEELEY CL.
BEELEY WAY
MATLOCK
BAKEWELL

A M

6

Fish Pond

TAPTON GROVE

TAPTON GRANGE

GROVE
ROAD

Recreation Ground
RECREATION RD.

ANDERSON LA.

BROOKE

VICTORIA PARK

GROVE WAY

Manor Inf. Sch.

ELIOT CL.

CHESTERTON CL.

Lodge Farm

BRIMINGTON COMMON

WESTWOOD LA.

LODGE

E **F** SOUTH CL.
BARRY
WH

Oldfield Farm

139

G **H**

41 42

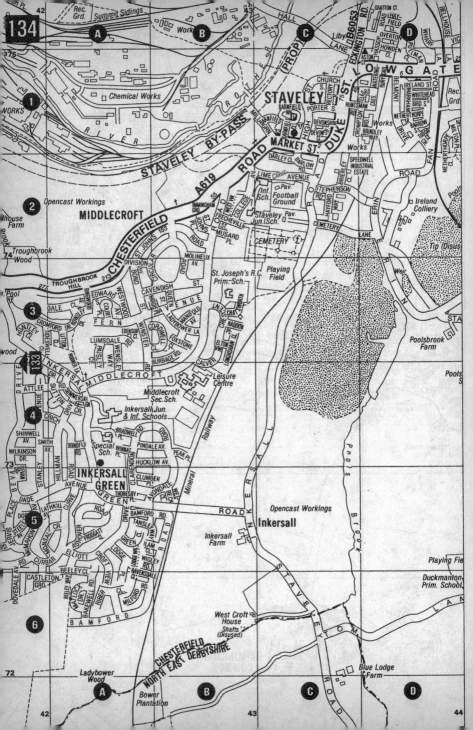

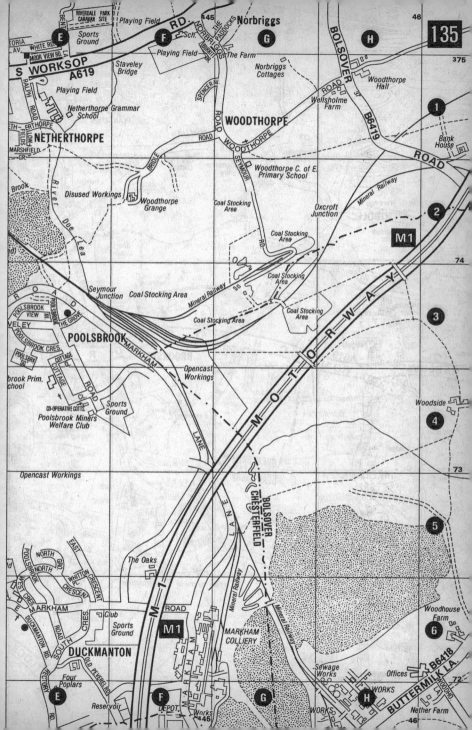

Norbriggs

WOODTHORPE

NETHERTHORPE

POOLSBROOK

CHESTERFIELD

DUCKMANTON

S WORKSOP

A619

Riverdale Park Caravan Site

Playing Field

Sports Ground

Staveley Bridge

Playing Field

Netherthorpe Grammar School

Playing Field

The Farm

Norbriggs Cottages

Wellsholme Farm

Woodthorpe Hall

Bank House

Woodthorpe C. of E. Primary School

Oxcroft Junction

Mineral Railway

M1

Disused Workings

Woodthorpe Grange

Coal Stocking Area

Coal Stocking Area

Coal Stocking Area

Coal Stocking Area

Coal Stocking Area

Coal Stocking Area

Seymour Junction

Coal Stocking Area

Mineral Railway

M O T O R W A Y

Poolsbrook View Av.

THE GROVE

Opencast Workings

Woodside

Poolsbrook Cres.

Co-operative Cotts.

Poolsbrook Miners Welfare Club

Sports Ground

Opencast Workings

brook Prim. chool

MARKHAM

LANE

The Oaks

Woodhouse Farm

North Cres.

Whitton Pl.

Crescent

MARKHAM

Club

Sports Ground

ROAD

M1

DUCKMANTON

Four Poplars

Reservoir

DEPOT.

MARKHAM COLLIERY

Mineral Railway

Mineral Railway

Sewage Works

Offices

WORKS

BOLSOVER CHESTERFIELD

BUTTERMILK LA.

B6418

Nether Farm

BOLSOVER ROAD

B6419

375

46

74

73

72

46

445

445

BENT

VICTORIA AV.

WHITE RD.

MOOR VIEW RD.

RALPH

ROAD

NETHERTHORPE FIELDS

MARSHFIELD

Brook

River Doe Lea

BRIDLE

ROAD

SPENCER AV.

NORBRIGGS

THE PADDOCKS

Sch.

BURNETT DRI.

SEYMOUR

RD.

ROAD

ROAD WOODTHORPE

ROAD

POOLSBROOK

CL.

COTTAGE CL.

COTTAGE CL.

EAST CRESCENT

NORTH

WEST CRES.

POOLSBROOK

SOUTH CRES.

DUCKMANTON ROAD

OLD RECTORY RD.

OLD PEVEREL RD.

Works

E

F

G

H

1

2

3

4

5

6

E

F

G

H

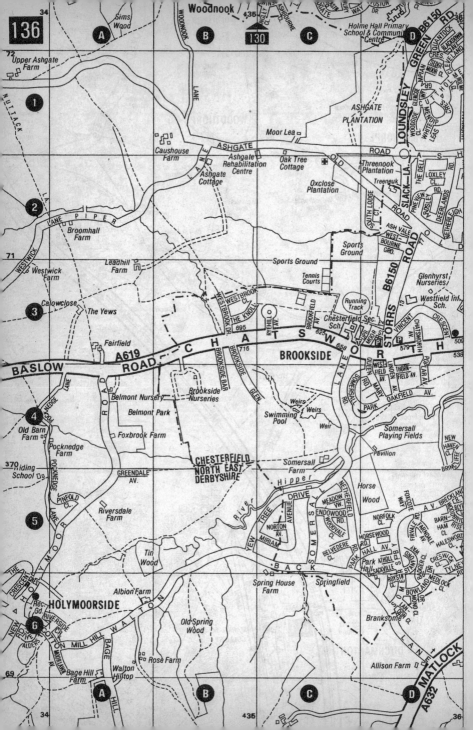

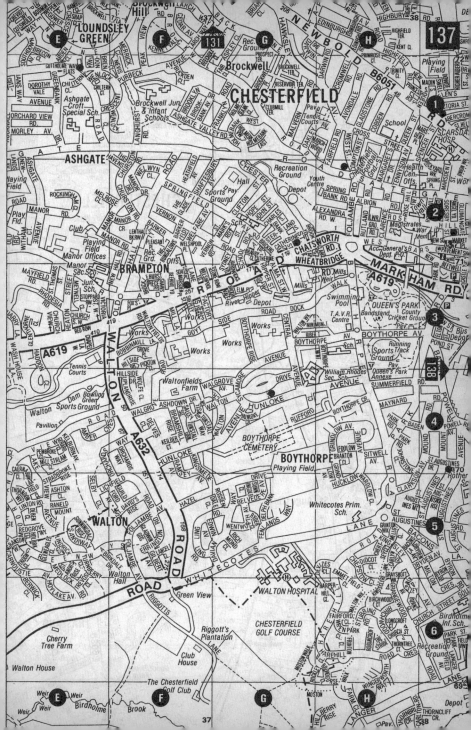

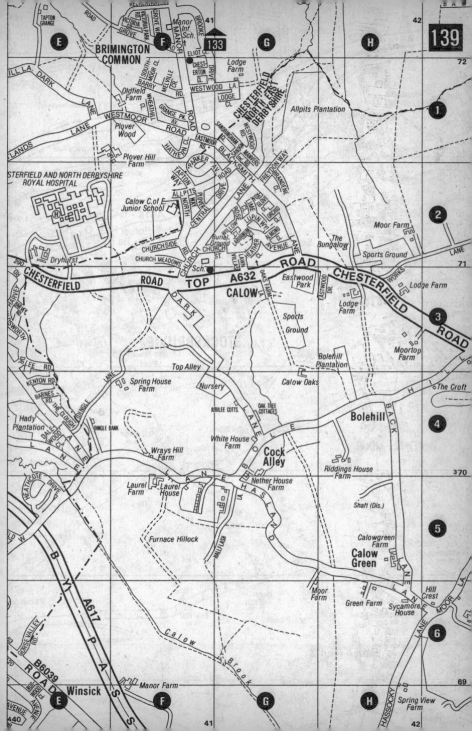

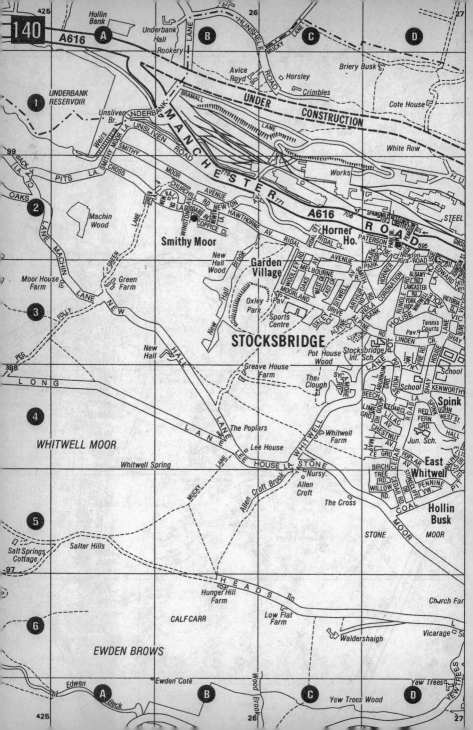

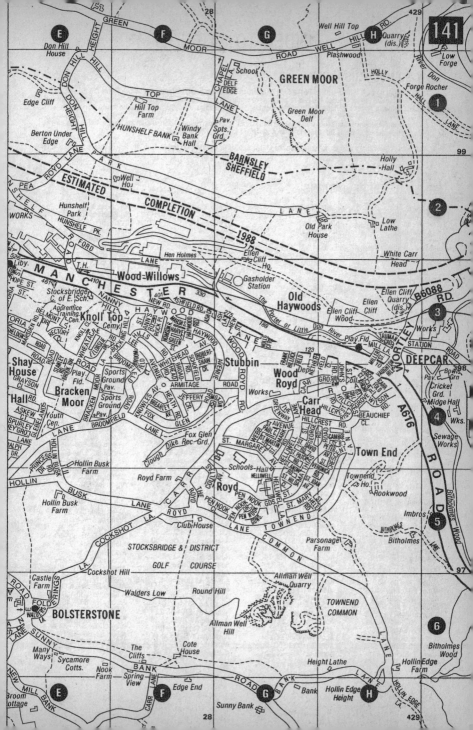

INDEX TO STREETS

HOW TO USE THIS INDEX

1. Each street name is followed by its Postal District and then by its map page reference; e.g. Abbey Brook Clo. S8—6C 110 is in the Sheffield 8 Postal District and it is to be found in square 6C on page 110. However, with the now general usage of Postal Coding, it is not recommended that this index should be used as a means of addressing mail.

2. A strict alphabetical order is followed in which Av., Rd., St. etc. (even though abbreviated) are read in full and as part of the street name; e.g. Abbots Rd. appears after Abbotsford Dri. but before Abbott St.

3. Streets & Subsidiary names not shown on the Maps, appear in the Index in Italics with the thoroughfare to which it is connected shown in brackets.

GENERAL ABBREVIATIONS

All : Alley	Cotts : Cottages	Junct : Junction	Rd : Road
App : Approach	Ct : Court	La : Lane	S : Sheffield
Arc : Arcade	Cres : Crescent	Lit : Little	S : South
Av : Avenue	DN : Doncaster	Lwr : Lower	Sq : Square
Bk : Back	Dri : Drive	Mnr : Manor	Sta : Station
Boulevd : Boulevard	E : East	Mans : Mansions	St : Street
Bri : Bridge	Embkmt : Embankment	Mkt : Market	Ter : Terrace
B'way : Broadway	Est : Estate	M : Mews	Up : Upper
Bldgs : Buildings	Gdns : Gardens	Mt : Mount	Vs : Villas
Chu : Church	Ga : Gate	N : North	WF : Wakefield
Chyd : Churchyard	Gt : Great	Pal : Palace	Wlk : Walk
Circ : Circle	Grn : Green	Pde : Parade	W : West
Cir : Circus	Gro : Grove	Pk : Park	Yd : Yard
Clo : Close	Ho : House	Pas : Passage	
Comn : Common	Ind : Industrial	Pl : Place	

142

Albert Rd. S63—4G 29
(Goldthorpe)
Albert Rd. S63—4D 40
(Wath upon Dearne)
Albert St. S64—6E 43
Albert St. S31—6D 124
Albert St. S60—3C 78
Albert St. S63—1E 29
Albert St. S64—1B 56
Albert St. S66—5H 83
Albert St. S70—6H 13
Albert St. S72—4C 10
Albert St. E. S70—6H 13
Albert St. N. S41—2H 131
Albert Ter. S31—5A 118
Albert Ter. Rd. S6—6C 86
Albion Dri. S63—1H 29
Albion Ho. S70—1H 23
Albion Pl. DN1—6E 33
Albion Rd. S40—2H 137
Albion Rd. S60—3E 79
Albion Rd. S71—6E 9
Albion Row. S6—1D 96
Albion St. S6—1C 98
Albion Ter. DN4—2B 46
Albion Ter. S70—1B 24
Alcester Rd. S7—6D 98
Aldam Clo. S17—5E 121
Aldam Clo. S65—2B 80
Aldam Croft. S17—5E 121
Aldam Rd. DN4—5G 45
Aldam Rd. S17—5F 121
Aldam Way. S17—5E 121
Aldbury Clo. S71—1B 14
Aldcliffe Cres. DN4—1F 61
Aldene Av. S6—2F 85
Aldene Glade. S6—2F 85
Aldene Rd. S6—1F 85
Alder Clo. S75—4E 7
Alder Gro. DN4—4A 46
Alder La. S9—2G 101
Alderney Rd. S2—6E 99
Aldersgate Clo. DN11—6E 63
Aldersgate Ct. S66—4H 83
Alders Grn. S6—2D 84
Alderson Av. S62—6F 55
Alderson Clo. S31—4B 104
Alderson Dri. DN2—6F 33
Alderson Dri. S71—1A 14
Alderson Pl. S2—5E 99
Alderson Rd. S2—5E 99
Alderson Rd. N. S2—5E 99
Alders, The. S42—6A 136
Aldervale Clo. S64—5B 56
Aldesworth Rd. DN4—2C 48
Aldfield Way. S5—2F 87
Aldham Cotts. S73—4A 26
Aldham Cres. S73—3G 25
Aldham Ho. La. S73—5H 25
Aldham Ind. Est. S73—4A 26
Aldine Ct. S1—3F 5
Aldred Clo. S31—1C 126
Aldred Clo. S66—4F 81
Aldred Rd. S10—6A 86
Aldred St. S65—4E 79
Aldrin Way. S66—3E 83
Aldwarke La. S65—5H 69
Aldwarke Rd. S62—4F 69
Alexandra Clo. S61—1G 77
Alexandra Rd. DN4—3B 46
Alexandra Rd. DN5—5B 18
Alexandra Rd. DN6—1F 17
Alexandra Rd. S2—6F 99
Alexandra Rd. S18—1F 129
Alexandra Rd. S31—5A 104
Alexandra Rd. S64—6F 43
Alexandra Rd. E. S41—3C 138
Alexandra Rd. W. S40—2H 137

Alexandra St. DN5—6B 18
Alexandra St. S66—6H 83
Alexandra Ter. S71—1F 25
Alford Av. S30—2D 72
Alfred Rd. S9—4B & 3C 88
(in three parts)
Alfred St. S71—1G 9
Algar Clo. S2—6A 100
Algar Cres. S2—6B 100
Algar Dri. S2—6A 100
Algar Pl. S2—6A 100
Algar Rd. S2—6A 100
Alice Rd. S61—2B 78
Alison Clo. S31—6B 104
Alison Cres. S2—4D 100
Alison Dri. S31—6B 104
Allan St. S65—3E 79
Allatt Clo. S70—1H 23
Alldred Cres. S64—4A 56
Allenby Cres. DN11—5C 62
Allenby Dri. S8—2C 122
Allendale. S70—4C 24
Allendale Clo. S70—4C 24
Allendale Dri. S74—6A 38
Allendale Rd. DN5—6H 31
Allendale Rd. S65—5A 80
Allendale Rd. S74—6H 37
Allendale Rd. S75—3G 13
(Barnsley)
Allendale Rd. S75—5B 6
(Darton)
Allende Way. S9—5D 88
Allen Rd. S19—5F 115
Allen St. S3—1C 4 & 1D 98
Allerton St. DN1—5D 32
Allestree Dri. S18—2A 128
All Hallows Dri. S66—5E 83
Alliance St. S4—4H 87
Alliss Rd. DN3—3H 49
Allott Cres. S74—4C 38
Allotts Ct. S70—4C 36
Allott St. S74—6C 38
(Elsecar)
Allott St. S74—6F 37
(Hoyland)
Allpits Rd. S44—2F 139
All Saints Clo. S63—5E 41
All Saints Sq. S60—3D 78
All Saints Sq. S64—2C 58
All Saints Way. S31—6D 104
Allsopps Yd. S74—2H 37
Allsops Pl. S41—3H 131
Allt St. S62—3F 69
Alma Cres. S18—6E 123
Alma Rd. S30—6B 50
Alma Rd. S60—4D 78
Alma Row. S60—2A 92
Alma St. S3—6E 87
Alma St. S70—6F 13
Alma St. S73—1F 39
Alma St. W. S40—3G 137
Almholme Rd. DN5—4E 19
Almond Av. DN3—2F 35
Almond Av. S72—6B 10
Almond Clo. S44—2G 139
Almond Clo. S66—4E 83
Almond Dri. S31—4A 126
Almond Glade. S66—6G 81
Almond Pl. S43—4E 133
Almond Rd. DN4—3D 48
Almond Tree Rd. S31—5E 117
Alms Hill Cres. S11—4F 109
Alms Hill Dri. S11—4F 109
Alms Hill Glade. S11—4F 109
Alms Hill Rd. S11—4F 109
Alney Pl. S6—5A 74
Alnwick Dri. S12—2E 113
Alnwick Rd S12—2C 112

Alperton Clo. S71—2F 15
Alpha Rd. S65—2H 79
Alpha St. DN5—2H 17
Alpine Clo. S30—3C 140
Alpine Rd. S6—6B 86
Alpine Rd. S30—3C 140
Alport Av. S12—3G 113
Alport Dri. S12—2G 113
Alport Gro. S12—2G 113
Alport Pl. S12—3G 113
Alport Rise. S18—1B 128
Alport Rd. S12—2G 113
Alric Dri. S60—2B 90
Alsing Rd. S9—6E 77
Alston Clo. DN4—4B 48
Alston Rd. DN4—5B 48
Alton Clo. S11—5G 109
Alton Clo. S18—3B 128
Alton Way. S75—4E 7
Alum Chine Clo. S41—5C 138
Alvaston Wlk. DN12—2C 58
Alverley La. DN4—1G 61
Alwyn Av. DN5—2G 31
Amalfi Clo. S73—4D 26
Ambassador Gdns. DN3—4G 35
Amber Cres. S40—4E 137
Amberley Rd. S9—4C 88
Amberley St. S9—3C 88
Ambleside Clo. S19—3E 125
Ambleside Clo. S41—4E 131
Ambleside Clo. S60—3A 90
Ambleside Cres. DN5—2C 44
Ambleside Gro. S71—1G 25
Ambleside Wlk. S31—1H 119
Amen Corner. S60—2C 78
America La. S62—4B 54
Amersall Cres. DN5—1G 31
Amersall Rd. DN5—1G 31
Amesbury Clo. S41—4G 131
Amory's Holt Clo. S66—2E 83
Amory's Holt Rd. S66—2E 83
Amos Rd. S9—1D 88
Anchorage Cres. DN5—5A 32
Anchorage La. DN5—5H 31
Ancona St. S73—4D 26
Anderson La. S43—6F 133
Andover Dri. S3—5E 87
Andover St. S3—5F 87
Andrew La. S3—1G 5
Andrew St. S3—6F 87
Anelay Rd. DN4—4H 45
Anfield Rd. DN4—4C 48
Angel La. S62—5H 53
Angel St. S3—2F 5 & 1F 99
Angel St. S63—2B 42
Angel Yd. S40—2A 138
Angerford Av. S8—3E 111
Anglesey Rd. S18—3E 129
Angram Rd. S30—5B 50
Annat Pl. S30—6A 50
Annesley Clo. S8—2D 122
Annesley Clo. S41—5C 138
Annesley Rd. S8—1D 122
Anne St. S31—2F 107
Anns Rd. S2—6E 99
Anns Rd. N. S2—6F 99
Ann St. S42—4F 69
Ansdell Rd. DN5—5B 18
Ansell Rd. S11—1G 109
Anson Gro. S60—3D 90
Anson St. S2—3H 5 & 2G 99
Ansten Cres. DN4—3C 48
Anston Av. S31—4A 118
Anston Clo. S31—1F 119
Antrim Av. S10—3B 98
Anvil Clo. S6—5E 85
Anvil Cres. S30—1F 75
Apley Rd. DN1—1D 46

Apollo St. S62—6H 55
Appleby Rd. DN2—5A 34
Appleby Wlk. S31—6F 107
Applegarth Clo. S12—1D 112
Applegarth Dri. S12—1D 112
Applehaigh View. S71—1C 8
Appleton Way. DN5—1H 31
Appleton Way. S70—4A 24
Appletree Dri. S18—2E 129
April Clo. S71—3D 14
April Dri. S71—3D 14
Aqueduct St. S71—4H 13
Arbour Clo. S41—6D 138
Arbour Cres. S66—5B 94
Arbour Dri. S66—5B 94
Arbour La. S65—4H 71
Arbourthorne. S2—4A 100
Arbourthorne Rd. S2
—6H 99 to 2B 112
Arcade, The. S70—6H 13
Archdale Clo. S2—5D 100
Archdale Pl. S2—5C 100
Archdale Rd. S2—4C 100
Archer Ga. S6—2D 84
Archer Ho. S65—2E 79
Archer La. S7—2B 110
Archer Rd. S8—4B 110
Archery Clo. S66—6F 81
Archibald Rd. S7—1C 110
Arcon Pl. S62—1G 69
Arcubus Av. S31—5B 104
Arden Clo. S40—1E 137
Arden Clo. S65—1H 79
Arden Ga. DN4—1F 61
Arden Rd. DN2—5G 33
Ardmore St. S9—6C 88
Ardsley Av. S31—6C 104
Ardsley Clo. S19—5H 113
Ardsley Dri. S19—5H 113
Ardsley Gro. S19—5H 113
Ardsley M. S71—1G 25
Ardsley Rd. S40—2D 136
Ardsley Rd. S70—4C 24
Argyle Clo. S8—2F 111
Argyle La. DN11—4C 62
Argyle Rd. S8—2E 111
Argyle St. S64—6E 43
Argyll Av. DN2—4H 33
Arklow Clo. S41—5B 138
Arklow Rd. DN2—5G 33
Arkwright Rd. DN5—4H 31
Arley St. S2—4E 99
Arlington Av. S31—5D 104
Armer St. S60—3C 78
Armitage Rd. DN4—4H 45
Armitage Rd. S30—4F 141
Armley Rd. S9—3C 88
Armroyd La. S74—1A 52
Arms Park Dri. S19—3F 125
Armstead Rd. S19—4G 115
Armstrong Wlk. S66—3E 83
Armthorpe La. DN2—4G 33
Armthorpe La. DN3
—1E to 4F 21
Armthorpe Rd. DN2
—4G 33 to 3C 34
Armthorpe Rd. S11—5F 97
Army Row. S71—1F 9
Arncliffe Dri. S30—1D 64
Arncliffe Dri. S70—1D 22
Arndale Precinct. S66—4G 83
Arnold Av. S12—5C 112
Arnold Av. S71—5B 8
Arnold Cres. S64—5E 43
Arnold Rd. S65—3H 79
Arnold St. S6—4A 86

143

Arnside Clo. S41—2F 131
Arnside Rd. S8—2C 110
Arnside Rd. S66—3G 83
Arnside Ter. S8—2C 110
Arran Clo. DN3—1H 21
Arran Hill. S65—4D 70
Arran Rd. S10—2H 97
Arras St. S9—6B 88
Arrowsmith Ho. S65—2E 79
(off Carlisle St.)
Arthington St. S8—1E 111
Arthur Av. DN5—5C 18
Arthur Pl. DN5—5C 18
Arthur Rd. S30—3C 140
Arthur St. DN5—5C 18
Arthur St. S31—6B 104
Arthur St. S60—2C 78
Arthur St. S62—6G 55
Arthur St. S70—4A 24
Artisan View. S8—1E 111
Arundel Av. S60—1E 103
Arundel Av. S65—6B 70
Arundel Clo. S18—2B 128
Arundel Clo. S41—3H 131
Arundel Cotts. S60—1E 103
Arundel Ct. S11—3F 109
Arundel Cres. S60—1E 103
Arundel Gdns. DN5—1H 31
Arundel Ga. S1—5E 5 & 3E 99
Arundel La. S1—5F 5 & 3F 99
(in two parts)
Arundel Dri. S71—2F 15
Arundel Rd. S30—1E 65
Arundel Rd. S60—1E 103
Arundel Rd. S65—4F 79
Arundel St. S1—6E 5 & 3E 99
Arundel St. S60—1E 103
Arundel View. S74—4C 38
Ascot Av. DN4—2B 48
Ascot Clo. S64—5F 43
Ascot Dri. DN5—3F 31
Ascot St. S2—4E 99
Ashberry Gdns. S6—6B 86
Ashberry Rd. S6—6B 86
Ashbourne Clo. S40—6C 130
Ashbourne Gro. S13—4H 101
Ashbourne Gro. S30—3E 73
Ashbourne Rd. S13—4H 101
Ashbourne Rd. S71—6C 8
Ashburnham Gdns. DN5—6G 31
Ashburton Clo. DN6—1C 16
Ashbury Dri. S8—5G 111
Ashbury La. S8—5G 111
Ash Clo. S31—4A 126
Ash Clo. S65—5B 80
Ash Cres. S30—3F 141
Ash Cres. S31—6G 125
Ash Cres. S64—5C 42
Ashcroft Clo. DN12—4A 60
Ashcroft Dri. S41—1B 132
Ashdale Clo. DN3—6D 20
Ash Dale Rd. DN4—1B 60
Ashdell. S10—3A 98
Ashdell La. S10—3A 98
Ashdell Rd. S10—3A 98
Ashdene Ct. S64—5B 56
Ashdown Dri. S40—4F 137
Ashdown Gdns. S19—4G 115
Ashdown Pl. DN5—1H 31
Ash Dyke Clo. S75—6F 9
Asher Rd. S7—5D 98
Ashes La. S62—5B 52
Ashfield Clo. DN3—4G 35
Ashfield Clo. S12—3B 112
Ashfield Clo. S75—4E 13
Ashfield Dri. S12—3B 112
Ashfield Rd. DN4—5A 46

Ashfield Rd. S30—3F 141
Ashfield Rd. S41—5D 138
Ashford Clo. S18—3B 128
Ashford Ct. S41—6A 132
Ashford Rd. S11—5B 98
Ashford Rd. S18—2B 128
Ashfurlong Clo: S17—2F 121
Ashfurlong Dri. S17—2F 121
Ashfurlong Rd. S17—2E 121
Ashgate Av. S40—2E 137
Ashgate Clo. S10—3A 98
Ashgate La. S10—3A 98
Ashgate Rd. S10—3A 98
Ashgate Rd. S42 & S40—1B 136
Ashgate Valley Rd. S40
—1F 137
Ash Gro. DN3—2G 35
Ash Gro. DN12—4C 58
Ash Gro. S10—3B 98
Ash Gro. S31—4G 117
Ash Gro. S62—2H 69
Ash Gro. S66—3H 83
(Maltby)
Ash Gro. S66—4G 81
(Wickersley)
Ash Gro. S70—2D 24
Ash Ho. La. S17—6D 108
Ashland Clo. S13—4G 101
Ashland Rd. S31—6E 125
Ash La. S30—3G 141
Ashleigh. S72—2G 11
Ashleigh Clo. S41—1B 132
Ashleigh Gdns. S61—5B 68
Ashley Clo. S31—3B 126
Ashley Croft. S71—1D 8
Ashley Gro. S31—6B 104
Ashley La. S31—3B 126
Ashmore Av. S31—4G 125
Ash Mt. S72—1C 10
Ashover Clo. S70—5A 24
Ashover Rd. S43—5A 134
Ashpool Clo. S13—1A 114
Ash Ridge. S64—3B 56
Ash Rd. S63—6G 41
Ash Rd. S72—3D 10
Ash Row. S71—6C 14
Ash St. S6—5C 86
Ash St. S19—1C 124
Ash St. S73—3G 25
Ashton Av. DN5—1F 31
Ashton Clo. S31—3A 126
Ashton Clo. S40—5E 137
Ashurst Clo. S6—5E 85
Ashurst Clo. S40—6B 130
Ashurst Dri. S6—4E 85
Ashurst Pl. S6—5E 85
Ashurst Rd. S6—4E 85
Ash Vale. W. S40—2D 136
Ash View. S30—3D 64
Ash View. S61—4B 68
Ashville. DN11—5E 63
Ashwell Rd. S13—1A 114
Ashwood Clo. S30—5A 50
Ashwood Rd. S30—6A 50
Ashwood Rd. S62—3F 69
Ashworth Dri. S61—5F 67
Askern Ho. DN1—1C 46
(off Oxford Pl.)
Askern Rd. DN5—2H 17 to 6B 18
Askern St. S9—2D 88
Askew Ct. S30—4E 141
Askrigg Clo. DN4—4D 48
A line Rd. S2—5E 99
Aspen Clo. DN3—6D 20
Aspen Rd. S31—6G 125
Aspen Way. S64—5A 56
Aspley Clo. S40—6G 131

Asquith Rd. DN5—6B 18
Asquith Rd. DN5—5D 76
Aster Clo. S19—4F 115
Aster Clo. S31—3F 119
Aston Clo. S18—6G 123
Aston Clo. S31—4B 104
Aston Ct. S43—1D 134
Aston Dri. S71—1A 14
Aston La. S31—3B 104
Aston Relief Rd. S 13 & S31
—5G 103
Aston St. S2—1H 99
Astwell Gdns. S30—1C 64
Athelstan Clo. S13—4G 101
Athelstane Dri. S66—6A 94
Athelstane Rd. DN12—3D 58
Athelstan Rd. S13—4G 101
Athelstone Cres. DN3—4D 20
Athersley Cres. S71—1A 14
Athersley Gdns. S19—5A 114
Athersley Rd. S71—1B 14
Atherton Clo. S2—1B 112
Atherton Rd. S2—1B 112
Atholl Clo. S42—5D 136
Atholl Cres. DN2—4A 34
Athol Rd. S8—3C 110
Athorpe Gro. S31—4E 107
Athron Dri. S65—5A 80
Athron St. DN1—5E 33
Atkin Pl. S2—5E 99
Atlantic Cres. S8—3C 122
Atlantic Dri. S8—3C 122
Atlantic Rd. S8—3B 122
Atlantic Wlk. S8—3C 122
Atlantic Way. S8—3C 122
Atlas St. S4—5H 87
Atlas St. S60—2C 90
Atlow Clo. S40—6D 130
Atterby Dri. DN11—3E 63
Attercliffe Comn. S9—4C 88
Attercliffe Rd. S4 & S9—6H 87
Attlee Av. DN11—4B 62
Attlee Clo. S66—5H 83
Attlee Cres. S73—4G 27
Attlee Rd. S43—4H 133
Aubretia Av. S60—4D 90
Auburn Rd. DN12—3B 60
Auckland Av. S6—3E 85
Auckland Dri. S19—3D 124
Auckland Rise. S19—3E 125
Auckland Rd. DN2—4E 33
Auckland Rd. S64—6F 43
Auckland's Pl. S40—3A 138
Auckland Way. S19—3E 125
Audrey Rd. S13—6E 101
Aughton Av. S31—4A 104
Aughton Clo. S13—6F 101
Aughton Cres. S13—5E 101
Aughton Dri. S13—5E 101
Aughton La. S31—5C 104
Aughton Rd. S31—5A 104
Augustus Rd. S60—1C 90
Aukley Rd. S8—2D 110
Aunby Dri. S31—5B 104
Austen Av. DN4—5G 45
Austen Dri. S66—4H 81
Austerfield Av. DN5—2A 32
Austin Clo. S6—3E 85
Austin Ct. S6—2E 85
Austwick Clo. DN4—1F 61
Austwick Clo. S75—3E 7
Austwick Wlk. S70—5G 13
Autumn Clo. S66—5C 94
Autumn Dri. S66—3G 83
Avenue 1. S41—5B 138
Avenue 2. S41—5B 138
Avenue 3. S41—5B 138
Avenue 4. S41—5B 138

Avenue 5. S41—5B 138
Avenue 6. S41—5B 138
Avenue 7. S41—5B 138
Avenue 8. S41—5B 138
Avenue Ct. S10—5G 97
Avenue Rd. DN2—4E 33
Avenue Rd. S7—1D 110
Avenue Rd. S41—3A 132
Avenue Rd. S63—5G 41
Avenue, The. DN4—2A 48
Avenue, The. DN5—6C 18
(Bentley)
Avenue, The. DN5—1F 43
(Harlington)
Avenue, The. S9—1E 101
Avenue, The. S18—1F 129
Avenue, The. S19—3F 115
Avenue, The. S66—2E 95
Avenue, The. S71—1G 9
Avenue, The. S75—5B 36
Aviemore Rd. DN4—5G 45
Avill Way. S66—6F 81
Avisford Dri. S5—6B 74
Avisford Rd. S5—5B 74
Avoca Av. DN2—5G 33
Avocet Way. S61—1B 66
Avon Clo. S18—6F 123
Avon Clo. S66—3F 83
Avon Clo. S73—2H 99
Avon Clo. S75—4A 12
Avondale Dri. S71—4E 9
Avondale Rd. DN1—6G 33
Avondale Rd. S6—3H 85
Avondale Rd. S40—1H 137
Avondale Rd. S43—5B 134
Avondale Rd. S61—2A 78
Avon Gro. S30—1C 64
Avon Mt. S61—2A 78
Avon St. S71—6A 14
Axholme Rd. DN2—4E 33
Axle La. S31—3D 118
Aylesbury Cres. S9—6D 76
Aylesbury Rd. DN2—5H 33
Aylesford Clo. S71—4H 13
Aylsham Dri. S31—6C 104
Aylward Clo. S2—6B 100
Aylward Rd. S2—6B 100
Aymer Dri. S66—5A 94
Ayrsome Wlk. DN4—3C 48
Aysgarth Av. S71—1H 25
Aysgarth Clo. DN4—4D 48
Aysgarth Rise. S31—5A 104
Aysgarth Rd. S6—4A 74
Ayton Wlk. DN5—5A 18
Azalea Clo. S31—4F 119

Babington Cres. S2—6B 100
Babur Rd. S4—5H 87
Backfield Rise. S30—1E 65
Backfields. S1—6D 4 & 2E 99
Back La. DN5—4D 30
Back La. DN12—6A 60
Back La. S10—1F 97
Back La. S17—4F 121
Back La. S30—2A 140
Back La. S31—1G 119
(Anston)
Back La. S31—5A 124
(Eckington)
Back La. S44—4H 139
Back La. S62—1C 68
Back La. S65—3D 70
Back La. S66—6A 82
Back La. S71—2C 14
Back La. S72—2B 28
Back La. W. S71—1C 8
Backmoor Cres. S8—5G 111

Backmoor Rd. S8—5G 111
Back Poplar Ter. S71—1G 9
Backside La. DN4—5F 45
Bacon La. S9—6A 88
Bacons La. S40—5H 137
Baden Powell Av. S40—4H 137
Baden Powell Rd. S40—3A 138
Baden St. S60—2C 78
Baden St. S70—5B 24
Badger Clo. S13—6C 102
Badger Clo. S42—5D 136
Badger Dri. S13—6C 102
Badger La. S1—3C 4
Badger Pl. S13—6C 102
Badger Rise. S13—6C 102
Badger Rd. S13—6C 102
Badsley Ct. S65—3G 79
Badsley Moor La. S65—4F 79
Badsley St. S65—3F 79
Badsley St. S. S65—4F 79
Badsworth Rd. DN4—6F 45
Bage Hill. S42—6A 136
Bagger Wood Hill. S75—6A 22
Bagger Wood Rd. S75—6A 22
Bagley Rd. S4—2H 87
Bagshaw's Rd. S12—1D 112
Bagshot St. S11—5B 98
Bahram Gro. DN11—5C 62
Bahram Rd. DN4—3A 48
Baildon St. S9—4C 88
Bailey Dri. S31—1C 126
Bailey La. S1—3C 4 & 2D 98
Bailey St. S1—3D 4 & 2E 99
Bailey St. S70—6H 13
Bainbridge Rd. DN4—2B 46
Baines Av. DN12—4A 60
Baines Wood Clo. S41—3E 131
Bainton Dri. S7—2F 23
Bakehouse La. S31—6D 124
Bakehouse La. S75—4D 12
Baker Dri. S31—3A 126
Bakers Hill. S1—3G 5
Bakers La. S1—2D 4 & 1E 99
Baker St. S9—5B 88
Baker St. S70—6H 13
(in two parts)
Bakewell Rd. S43—6A 134
Bakewell Rd. S71—1A 14
Balaclava La. S6—5C 86
Balaclava Rd. S6—5C 86
Bala St. S71—6H 13
Balby Carr Bank. DN4—3C 46
Balby Rd. DN4—3B 46
Balcarres Rd. DN11—4D 62
Baldwin Av. DN5—4A 32
Baldwin St. S9—6B 88
Balfour Rd. DN5—6C 18
Balfour Rd. S9—6D 88
Balk La. S60—1A 90
Balk La. S66—4H 81
Balk La. S70—2C 36
Balkley La. S73—4G 27
Balk, The. DN5—2D 18
Balk, The. S61—3B 68
Balk, The. S75—3G 7
Ballam Av. DN5—6G 17
Ballfield Av. S75—5A 6
Ballfield La. S75—5A 6
Ballifield Av. S13—4A 102
Ballifield Clo. S13—4B 102
Ballifield Cres. S13—4B 102
Ballifield Dri. S13—4B 102
Ballifield Pl. S13—4A 102
Ballifield Rise. S13—4B 102
Ballifield Rd. S13—4A 102
Ballifield Way. S13—4A 102
Ball Rd. S6—3H 85
Ball St. S3—6D 86

Balmain Dri. S6—2H 85
Balmain Rd. S6—2H 85
Balm Grn. S1—3D 4 & 2E 99
Balmoak La. S41—5C 132
Balmoral Ct. S11—3F 109
Balmoral Cres. S18—1B 128
Balmoral Dri. DN2—5F 33
Balmoral Rd. S13—1C 114
Balmoral Way. S66—3H 81
Baltic Rd. S9—5B 88
Baltic Way. S9—5B 88
Bamford Av. S71—1A 14
Bamford Clo. S75—2A 22
Bamford Rd. S43—6A 134
Bamforth St. S6—4B 86
Banderson Dri. S62—4C 56
Bank Clo. S7—1C 110
Bank Clo. S61—6H 67
Bank End Av. S70—4C 24
Bank End Rd. S70—4B 24
Bankfield La. S6—5C 84
Bankfield Rd. S6—3G 85
Bank Ho. Rd. S6—6A 86
Bank La. S30—6G 141
Bank Rd. S41—5A 132
Bank Sq. DN11—5C 62
Bank St. DN1—2C 46
Bank St. S1—2E 5 & 1F 99
Bank St. S31—2F 119
Bank St. S40—2G 137
Bank St. S43—3D 132
Bank St. S64—1E 57
Bank St. S70—2H 23
Bank St. S71—1E 25
Bank St. S72—6B 10
Bank St. S74—2H 111
Bank Ter. S10—2A 98
(off Parker's La.)
Bank Top Rd. S65—5B 80
Bank View. S12—4C 114
Bank View. S60—2H 91
Bankwood Clo. S14—2H 111
Bankwood Cres. DN11—3B 62
Bankwood La. DN11—2B 62
Bankwood Rd. S14—2H 111
Banner Ct. S11—1H 109
Banner Cross Dri. S11—1H 109
Banner Cross Rd. S11—2H 109
Bannerdale Clo S11—1A 110
Bannerdale Rd. S11 & S7
—1A 110
Bannerdale View. S11—1A 110
Bannham Rd. S9—1F 101
Bannister Ho. DN2—3G 33
Bannon St. S6—6B 86
Bar Av. S75—5H 7
Barber Balk Clo. S61—6H 67
Barber Balk Rd. S61—1H 77
Barber Clo. S31—2A 118
Barber Cres. S10—1B 98
Barber Pl. S10—1B 98
Barber Rd. S10—1B 98
Barber's Av. S62—2F 69
Barber's Cres. S62—2G 69
Barber's La. S31—1B 126
Barber's Path. S64—6D 42
Barber St. S74—5A 38
Barber Wood Rd. S61—2C 76
Barbon Clo. S40—6G 131
Barbot Hill Rd. S61—5C 68
Bard Ct. S2—3H 5
Barden Cres. S60—3C 90
Bardolf Rd. DN4—2C 48
Bardon Rd. DN3—4D 20
Bard St. S2—2H 5 & 2G 99
Bard St. Flats. S2—2H 5
Bardwell Rd. S3—5D 86
Barewell Hill S72—1H 11

Barfield Av. S60—2G 91
Barfield Rd. S74—5A 38
Barholme Clo. S41—4D 130
Barholm Rd. S10—3F 97
Bari Clo. S73—3C 26
Baring Rd. S61—3D 76
Barkby Rd. S9—5C 76
Barker Field. S40—2F 137
Barker La. S40—2F 137
Barkers Croft. S61—4H 67
Barker's Pl. S6—2A 86
Barker's Pool. S1—4D 4 & 2E 99
Barker's Rd. S7—1B 110
Barker St. S64—1C 56
Bar La. S75—5H 7
Barlborough Rd. S73—2G 39
Barlby Gro. S12—4C 114
Barleycroft La. S31—5F 107
Barleywood Rd. S9—5E 89
Barlow Dri. S6—5G 85
Barlow Lees La. S18—6C 128
Barlow Rd. S6—5G 85
Barlow Rd. S41—2B 130
Barlow Rd. S43—2C 134
Barmouth Rd. S7—2C 110
Barnabas Wlk. S71—4H 13
Barnard Av. S18—6H 123
Barnardiston Rd. S9—6D 88
Barnburgh Ho. DN12—2C 60
Barnburgh La. S63—5G 29
Barnby Dun Rd. DN2
—2A 34 to 5B 20
Barncliffe Clo. S10—5C 96
Barncliffe Cres. S10—4B 96
Barncliffe Dri. S10—4B 96
Barncliffe Glen. S10—5C 96
Barncliffe Rd. S10—4B 96
Barn Clo. S41—5F 131
Barnes Av. S18—1B 128
Barnes Ct. S2—6G 5 & 3F 99
Barnes Ct. S64—4A 56
(off Lawrence Dri.)
Barnes Hall Rd. S30—3B 64
Barneslai Clo. S70—5G 13
Barnes La. S18—5H 121
Barnes Rd. S41—4E 139
Barnet Av. S11—2E 109
Barnet Rd. S11—2E 109
Barnfield Av. S10—2E 97
Barnfield Clo. S10—2E 97
Barnfield Dri. S10—3E 97
Barnfield Rd. S10—2E 97
Barnfield Ter. S43—1C 134
Barnfield Wlk. S43—1C 134
Barnham Clo. S40—5D 136
Barnsdale Av. S19—5A 114
Barnsley Av. DN12—3C 58
Barnsley Rd. DN5
—2A 30 to 3G 31
Barnsley Rd. S4 & S5—3F 87
Barnsley Rd. S61
—6A 52 to 2B 66
Barnsley Rd. S63—4D 28 to
(Highgate, Goldthorpe) 4G 29
Barnsley Rd. S63—3C 40
(Wath upon Dearne)
Barnsley Rd. S72—3E to 1H 11
(Brierley)
Barnsley Rd. S72—1G 15
(Cudworth)
Barnsley Rd. S73—2D 26
(Darfield)
Barnsley Rd. S73
—4H 25 & 5A 26
(in three parts, Wombwell)
Barnsley Rd. S74—3H 37

Barnsley Rd. S75—5C 6 to
(Darton)   1A 12
Barnsley Rd. S75—1B 22
(Dodworth)
Barnsley Rd. WF4—1H 7
(Grange Moor)
Barnsley Western Rf. Rd. S70
—6G 13
Barnwell Cres. S73—4H 25
Baron St. S1—4E 99
Barrack La. S6—5C 86
Barracks Field Ter. S74—6C 38
Barracks Sq. S40—2A 138
Barratt Rd. S31—6D 124
Barrel La. DN4—5G 45
Barret Rd. DN4—2D 48
Barretta St. S4—2H 87
Barrie Cres. S5—1D 86
Barrie Dri. S5—6D 74
Barrie Gro. S66—5B 82
Barrie Rd. DN4—5B 46
Barrie Rd. S5—6D 74
Barrowby Rd. S60—6H 79
Barrow Field La. S62—3C 52
Barrowfield Rd. S74—4H 37
Barrow Hill. S62—4A 52
Barrow Rd. S9—5D 76
Barrow St. S43—1D 134
Barry Rd. S43—1F 139
Bartholomew St. S73—6A 26
Bartle Av. S12—3B 112
Bartle Dri. S12—3B 112
Bartle Rd. S12—3B 112
Bartlett Clo. S6—6C 84
Bartlett Rd. S5—5D 74
Bartle Way. S12—3B 112
Barton Av. S71—4A 8
Barton Cres. S40—5C 130
Barton La. DN3—3E 35
Barton Pl. DN12—4D 58
Barton Rd. S8—1E 111
Barugh Grn. Rd. S75—2A 12
Barugh La. S75—2A 12
Basegreen Av. S12—4D 112
Basegreen Clo. S12—4D 112
Basegreen Cres. S12—4D 112
Basegreen Dri. S12—4D 112
Basegreen Pl. S12—4D 112
Basegreen Rd. S12—4D 112
Basegreen Way. S12—4E 113
Basford Clo. S9—4E 89
Basford Dri. S9—4E 89
Basford Pl. S9—6E 89
Basford St. S9—6D 88
Basil Av. DN3—2C 34
Basildon Rd. S63—1E 29
Baslow Cres. S75—2A 22
Baslow Rd. S17
—6B 120 to 4F 121
Baslow Rd. S42—4A 136
Baslow Rd. S71—6D 8
Bassett Pl. S2—3H 99
Bassett Rd. S2—3A 100
Bassey Rd. DN3—3H 49
Bassingthorpe La. S61—6B 68
Bassledene Rd. S2—5C 100
Bass Ter. DN1—6E 33
Bastock Rd. S6—2B 86
Bateman Clo. S72—3F 9
Bateman Rd. S66—5A 82
(in two parts)
Bateman Sq. S63—1E 29
Batemoor Clo. S8—3E 123
Batemoor Dri. S8—3E 123
Batemoor Pl. S8—3E 123
Batemoor Rd. S8—3E 123
Batemoor Wlk. S8—3E 123
(off Batemoor Clo.)

Bates St. S10—6A 86
Bath St. S1—6B 4 & 3D 98
Battison La. S63—1D 54
Batt St. S8—5E 99
Batty Av. S72—1G 15
Batworth Dri. S5—3E 87
Batworth Rd. S5—3E 87
Bawtry Ga. S9—1G 89
Bawtry Rd. DN4—1G 47 to 1F 63
Bawtry Rd. S9—1G 89
Bawtry Rd. S60—2A 90
Bawtry Rd. S66—5C 80 to 4B 82
Baxter Av. DN1—5E 33
Baxter Clo. S6—5A 74
Baxter Dri. S6—5A 74
Baxter Ga. DN1—6C 32
Baxter Rd. S6—5A 74
Bayardo Wlk. DN11—6D 62
Baycliff Clo. S71—1D 14
Bay Ct. S31—4A 126
Baysdale Croft. S19—2D 124
Bay Tree Av. S66—3F 81
Bazley Rd. S2—1B 112
Beacon Clo. S9—1B 88
Beacon Croft. S9—1B 88
Beacon Rd. S9—1B 88
Beaconsfield Rd. DN4—2A 46
Beaconsfield Rd. S60—6G 79
Beaconsfield St. S64—6D 42
Beaconsfield St. S70—1G 23
Beacon View. S74—6C 38
Beacon Way. S9—1B 88
Beancroft Clo. DN11—6H 61
Bear Tree Rd. S62—3F 69
Bear Tree St. S62—4F 69
Beauchamp Rd. S61—6H 67
Beauchief Abbey La. S8
—1A 122
Beauchief Clo. S30—4H 141
Beauchief Ct. S8—6C 110
Beauchief Dri. S8 & S17
—2A 122
Beauchief Rise. S8—6A 110
Beaufort Rd. DN2—5H 33
Beaufort Rd. S10—2B 98
Beaumont Av. DN6—1B 16
Beaumont Av. S2—3C 100
Beaumont Av. S70—6D 12
Beaumont Clo. S2—3D 100
Beaumont Cres. S2—3C 100
Beaumont Dri. S65—4H 79
Beaumont Rd. S75—6A 6
Beaumont Rd. N. S2—3C 100
Beaumont St. S74—6F 37
Beaumont Way. S2—3C 100
Beaver Av. S13—5B 102
Beaver Clo. S13—5B 102
Beaver Dri. S13—5B 102
Beaver Hill Rd. S13—5B 102
Beaver Pl. S40—3F 137
Beccles Way. S66—4H 81
Beck Clo. S5—2A 76
Beck Clo. S64—4B 56
Becket Av. S8—3B 122
Becket Cres. S8—3C 122
Becket Cres. S61—5F 67
Becket Rd. S8—3C 122
Beckett Hospital Ter. S70
—1H 23
Beckett Rd. DN2—4E to 2G 33
Beckett St. S71—5H 13
Beckford La. S5—1H 75
Becknoll Rd. S73—3A 40
Beck Rd. S5—2H 75
Beckton Av. S19—5F 115
Beckton Ct. S19—5F 115
Beckwith Rd. S31—3C 106

Beckwith Rd. S65—2B 80
Bedale Rd. DN5—2F 31
Bedale Rd. S8—1D 110
Bedale Wlk. S72—2C 10
Bedford Clo. S31—6D 106
Bedford Rd. S30—1D 72
Bedford St. S6—6D 86
Bedford St. S66—5H 83
Bedford St. S70—2H 23
Bedford Ter. S71—2A 14
Bedgrave Clo. S31—1D 126
Beecham Ct. S64—4A 56
Beech Av. S62—2H 99
Beech Av. S65—5C 80
Beech Av. S72—5B 10
Beech Clo. S66—4D 82
Beech Clo. S72—2G 11
Beech Clo. S73—3F 39
Beech Cres. S31—6G 125
(Eckington)
Beech Cres. S31—4A 126
(Killamarsh)
Beech Cres. S64—6C 42
Beechcroft Rd. DN4—5G 45
Beechdale Clo. S40—1F 137
Beech Dri. DN3—2H 49
Beeches Av. S2—5G 99
Beeches Dri. S2—5G 99
Beeches Gro. S19—4G 115
Beeches Rd. S31—4F 117
Beeches, The. DN3—3D 20
Beeches, The. S64—3A 56
Beechfern Clo. S30—5B 50
Beechfield Rd. DN1—1D 46
Beech Gro. DN4—5E 45
Beech Gro. DN5—1B 32
Beech Gro. DN12—4D 58
Beech Gro. S31—6F 107
Beech Gro. S66—4G 81
Beech Gro. S70—2F 23
Beech Hill. DN12—3E 59
Beech Hill Rd. S10—3A 98
Beech Ho. Rd. S73—3F 39
Beech Rd. DN11—5E 63
Beech Rd. S63—5G 41
Beech Rd. S66—4D 82
Beech Rd. S72—3D 10
Beech St. S43—2G 133
Beech St. S70—1H 23
Beechville Av. S64—4A 56
Beech Way. S18—6E 123
Beech Way. S31—5A 104
Beechwood Clo. DN3—6E 21
Beechwood Clo. S62—6H 55
Beechwood Clo. S63—2F 55
Beechwood Rd. S6—3H 85
Beechwood Rd. S18—2D 128
Beechwood Rd. S30—1C 64
(High Green)
Beechwood Rd. S30—4D 140
(Stocksbridge)
Beechwood Rd. S60—5G 79
Beechwood Wlk. DN12—4A 60
(off Broomvale Wlk)
Beehive Rd. S10—1B 98
Beehive Yd. S40—3F 137
Beeley Clo. S43—5A 134
Beeley Rd. S30—3E 73
Beeley St. S2—4D 98
Beeley Way. S43—6A 134
Beeley Wood La. S6—5G 73
Beeley Wood Rd. S6—6A 74
Beeston Clo. S18—1A 128
Beeston Sq. S71—5B 8
Bee St. S9—3D 88
Beeton Rd. S8—2D 110
Beet St. S3—3B 4 & 2D 98

Beetwell St. S40—3A 138
Beever La. S75—4C 12
Beeversleigh. S65—3E 79
(off Clifton La.)
Beevers Rd. S61—5F 67
Beever St. S63—4H 29
Beevor Ct. S71—6A 14
Beevor St. S71—6B 14
Begonia Clo. S31—3F 119
Beighton Rd. S12—4B 114
Beighton Rd. S13—1C 114
Beighton Rd. S62—5C 56
Beighton Rd. E. S19—4D 114
Beighton St. S9—1E 101
Belcourt Rd. S65—5B 80
Beldon Clo. S2—6H 99
Beldon Pl. S2—6H 99
Beldon Rd. S2—6H 99
Belfry Gdns. DN4—4E 49
Belgrave Dri. S10—4D 96
Belgrave Pl. S31—6B 104
Belgrave Rd. S10—4E 97
Belgrave Rd. S71—6A 14
Belgrave Sq. S2—5E 99
Belklane Dri. S31—2C 126
Bellamy Clo. S65—4H 79
Bell Bank View. S70—4H 23
Bellbrooke Av. S73—2D 26
Bellbrooke Pl. S73—2D 26
Bellefield St. S3—1A 4 & 1C 98
Belle Grn. La. S72—6C 10
Belle Vue Av. DN4—1G 47
Belle Vue Clo. S43—3D 132
Belle Vue Rd. S64—6E 43
Bellhagg Rd. S6—5H 85
Bellhouse La. S43—1D 134
Bellhouse Rd. S5
—6H 75 to 2A 76
Bellis Av. DN4—3A 46
Bellowes Rd. S62—2F 69
Bellrope Acre. DN3—4F 35
Bellscroft Av. S65—5C 70
Bells Sq. S1—3D 4 & 2E 99
Bell St. S31—6D 104
Bellwood Cres. S74—6G 37
Belmont Av. DN4—2C 46
Belmont Av. S30—2E 65
Belmont Av. S71—2B 14
Belmont Dri. S30—3E 141
Belmont Dri. S43—1D 134
Belmonte Gdns. S2
—6H 5 & 3G 99
Belmont St. S41—3A 132
Belmont St. S61—3A 78
Belmont St. S64—1D 56
Belmoor Rd. S9—4C 88
Belper Rd. S7—1D 110
Belsize Rd. S10—5E 97
Beltoft Way. DN12—2G 59
Belton Clo. S18—2A 128
Belvedere. DN4—5H 45
Belvedere Av. S40—5G 137
Belvedere Clo. S31—2H 119
Belvedere Clo. S40—5C 136
Belvedere Clo. S72—3C 10
Belvedere Dri. S73—2D 26
Belvedere Pde. S66—2G 81
Belvis Row. S2—2G 99
Belvoir Av. DN5—1G 43
Ben Bank Rd. S75—3A 22
Bence Clo. S75—6C 6
Bence La. S75—5A 6
Ben Clo. S6—2F 85
Benita Av. S64—1G 57
Ben La. S6—2F 85
Bennett Clo. S62—6H 55
Bennetthorpe. DN2—1E 47
Bennett St. S2—5D 98

Bennett St. S61—3G 77
Benson Rd. S2—3A 100
Bentfield Av. S60—6A 80
Bentham Dri. S71—3D 14
Bentham Rd. S40—6G 131
Bentham Way. S75—3E 7
Bent Hills La. S30—1A 72
Bentinck Clo. DN1—1D 46
Bentink St. DN12—3F 59
Bent La. S43—1E 135
Bent Lathes Av. S60—6A 80
Bentley Av. DN4—1A 46
Bentley Clo. S71—2E 15
Bentley Comn. La. DN5—1C 32
Bentley Moor La. DN5—1G 17
Bentley Rd. DN5—2A 32
Bentley Rd. S6—6G 85
Bentley Rd. S30—4F 65
Bentley St. S66—5H 81
Bentley St. S60—6D 78
Benton Ter. S64—4B 56
Benton Way. S61—2H 77
Bents Clo. S11—2E 109
Bents Clo. S30—2E 65
Bents Cres. S11—3F 109
Bents Cres. S18—6G 123
Bents Dri. S11—2E 109
Bents Grn. Av. S11—1E 109
Bents Grn. Pl. S11—2F 109
Bents Grn. Rd. S11—1F 109
Bents La. S18—6G 123
Bents Rd. S11—2F 109
Bents Rd. S17—5C 120
Bents Rd. S61—6H 67
Bents View. S11—2E 109
Benty La. S10—2F 97
Beresford Rd. S66—5H 83
Beresford St. DN5—6E 18
Berkeley Croft. S71—1D 8
Berkeley Precinct. S11—5B 98
Berkley Clo. S70—4H 23
Berkley Rd. S9—4C 88
Berkley St. S9—4C 88
Bernard Clo. S43—3F 133
Bernard Gdns. S2—2H 5
Bernard Rd. DN12—4B 60
Bernard Rd. S2 & S4—1H 99
Bernard St. S2—2G 99
Bernard St. S60—4E 79
Bernard St. S62—6H 55
Berners Clo. S2—1A 112
Berners Dri. S2—1A 112
Berners Pl. S2—1A 112
Berners Rd. S2—1A 112
Bernshall Cres. S5—1F 75
Berresford Rd. S11—5B 98
Berrington Clo. DN4—1G 61
Berry Av. S31—6C 124
Berrydale. S70—4B 24
Berry Holme Clo. S30—2E 65
Berry Holme Ct. S30—2E 65
Berry Holme Dri. S30—2E 65
Bertram Rd. S30—3E 73
Berwick Clo. S40—6E 137
Berwick Way. DN2—4A 34
Berwyn Clo. S40—6E 131
Bessacarr La. DN4—5C 48
Bessemer Pl. S9—6A 88
Bessemer Rd. S9—5A 88
Bessemer Ter. S30—2D 140
Bessingby Rd. S6—4A 86
Bethel Rd. S65—1F 79
Bethel Sq. S74—5B 38
(off Bethel St.)
Bethel St. S74—5B 38
Bethel Wlk. S1—4D 4
Beulah Rd. S6—2B 86
Bevan Av. DN11—4D 62

146

Bevan Av. S74—5C 38
Bevan Cres. S66—3F 83
Bevan Dri. S43—5H 133
Bevan Way. S30—2D 64
Bevercotes Rd. S5—6H 75
Beverley Av. S70—3H 23
Beverley Clo. S31—6B 104
Beverley Clo. S71—6A 8
Beverley Gdns. DN5—4F 31
Beverley Rd. DN2—3G 33
Beverleys Rd. S8—3E 111
Beverley St. S9—5C 88
Bevin Pl. S62—1H 69
Bevre Rd. DN3—1F 35
Bewdley Ct. S71—1F 9
Bewicke Av. DN5—3F 31
Bhatia Clo. S64—6E 43
Bib La. S31—4E 95
Bickerton Rd. S6—1A 86
Bierlow Clo. S73—3A 40
Bigby Way. S66—2H 81
Bignor Pl. S6—4B 74
Bignor Rd. S6—4B 74
Bilam Pl. S61—6G 67
Bilby La. S43—2E 133
Billam St. S31—6B 124
Billingley Grn. La. S72—3B 28
Billingley La. S72—2B 28
Billingley View. S63—1H 41
Bilston Rd. S6—4B 86
Bilton Rd. S9—6D 88
Binders Rd. S61—6G 67
Binfield Rd. S8—2D 110
Bingham Ct. S10—5G 97
Bingham Pk. Cres. S11—5G 97
Bingham Pk. Rd. S11—6G 97
Bingham Rd. S8—5D 110
Bingley La. S6—1A 96
Bingley St. S75—5F 13
Binsted Av. S5—6B 74
Binsted Clo. S5—6B 74
Binsted Cres. S5—6B 74
Binsted Croft. S5—6B 74
Binsted Dri. S5—6B 74
Binsted Gdns. S5—6B 74
Binsted Glade. S5—6B 74
Binsted Gro. S5—6B 74
Binsted Rd. S5—6B 74
Binsted Way. S5—6B 74
Birchall Av. S30—2H 91
Birch Av. S30—3E 65
Birch Clo. S31—4A 126
Birch Cres. S66—4G 81
Birchdale Clo. DN3—6D 20
Birchen Clo. DN4—6C 48
Birchen Clo. S18—2B 128
Birchen Clo. S40—6F 131
Birches Fold. S18—5G 123
Birches La. S18—5G 123
Birch Farm Av. S8—1E 123
Birchfield Rd. S66—4H 83
Birchfield Wlk. S75—5D 12
Birch Gro. DN12—3F 59
Birch Gro. S30—3E 73
Birch Ho. Av. S30—3D 72
Birchitt Clo. S17—4A 122
Birchitt Pl. S17—4A 122
Birchitt Rd. S17—4A 122
Birchitt View. S18—6E 123
Birchlands Dri. S31—4B 126
Birch La. S43—2G 133
Birch Pk. Ct. S61—3A 78
Birch Rd. DN4—3D 48
Birch Rd. S9—5A 88
Birch Rd. S70—2D 24
Birch Tree Clo. DN3—1E 21
Birch Tree Rd. S30—4D 140
Birchtree Rd. S61—4B 66

Birchvale Rd. S12—4F 113
Birchwood Av. S62—6F 55
Birchwood Clo. S19—1E 125
Birchwood Clo. S66—3D 82
Birchwood Ct. DN4—6F 49
Birchwood Ct. S40—6H 137
Birchwood Cres. S40—6H 137
Birchwood Croft. S19—1E 125
Birchwood Dell. DN4—6F 49
Birchwood Dri. S65—1H 81
Birchwood Gdns. S19—1E 125
Birchwood Gro. S19—1E 125
Birchwood Rise. S19—1E 125
Birchwood View. S19—1E 125
Birchwood Way. S19—1E 125
Bircotes Wlk. DN11—4F 63
Bird Av. S73—1E 39
Birdholme Cres. S40—5A 138
Bird St. S43—1D 134
Birdwell Comn. S70—5D 36
Birdwell Rd. S4—2B 88
Birdwell Rd. S62—5B 56
Birdwell Rd. S75—3D 22
Birk Av. S70—2C 24
Birkbeck Ct. S30—5B 50
Birk Cres. S70—2C 24
Birkdale Av. S31—5G 107
Birkdale Clo. S72—5C 10
Birkdale Dri. S40—5E 137
Birkdale Rise. S64—3B 56
Birkdale Rd. S71—1D 8
Birkendale. S6—6B 86
Birkendale Rd. S6—6B 86
Birkendale View. S6—6B 86
Birk Grn. S70—2D 24
Birk Ho. La. S70—2D 24
Birklands Av. S13—4G 101
Birklands Clo. S13—4G 101
Birklands Dri. S13—4G 101
Birk Rd. S70—2C 24
Birks Av. S13—1B 114
Birks Holt Dri. S66—6H 83
Birks Rd. S61—6G 67
Birks Wood Dri. S30—3D 72
Birk Ter. S70—2C 24
Birley La. S12—5E 113
Birley Moor Av. S12—4G 113
Birley Moor Clo. S12—4G 113
Birley Moor Cres. S12—4G 113
Birley Moor Dri. S12—5G 113
Birley Moor Pl. S12—5G 113
Birley Moor Rd. S12—2E 113
Birley Moor Way. S12—5G 113
Birley Rise Cres. S6—5A 74
Birley Rise Rd. S6—5A 74
Birley Spa La. S12
                  —4H 113 to 4C 114
Birley Spa Wlk. S12—3B 114
(off Carter Lodge Dri.)
Birley Vale Av. S12—3E 113
Birley Vale Clo. S12—3E 113
Birley View. S30—4D 72
Birthwaite Rd. S75—1D 6
Birtley St. S66—4D 82
Bisby Rd. S62—1G 69
Biscay Way. S63—5F 41
Bishop Hill. S13—1A 114
Bishops Clo. S8—2F 111
Bishopscourt Rd. S8—2E 111
Bishopsgate La. DN11—6E 63
Bishopsholme Clo. S5—1E 87
Bishopsholme Rd. S5—1E 87
Bishopston Wlk. S66—3E 83
Bishop St. S3—6C 4 & 3D 98
Bishops Way. S71—4C 14
Bisley Clo. S71—2G 9
Bismarck St. S70—2H 23
Bitholmes La. S30—5H 141

Bittern View. S61—1C 66
Blacka Moor Cres. S17—3C 120
Blacka Moor Rd. S17—3C 120
Blackamoor Rd. S64—4E 55
Blacka Moor View. S17
                         —3C 120
Black Bank. DN4—2D 46
Blackberry Flats. S19—2E 125
Blackbird Av. S60—3D 90
Blackbrook Rd. S10—4A 96
Blackbrook Dri. S10—4A 96
Blackbrook Rd. S10—4A 96
Blackburn Cres. S30—1C 64
Blackburn Croft. S30—1D 64
Blackburn La. S61—3D 76
Blackburn La. S70—4A 24
Blackburn La. S75—5F 13
Blackburn Rd. S61
                  —4D 76 to 5E 77
Blackburn St. S70—4A 24
Black Carr Rd. S66—5E 81
Blackdown Av. S19—5D 114
Blackdown Av. S42—6D 130
Blackdown Clo. S19—5D 114
Blacker Grange. S74—3H 37
Blacker La. S70—1E 37
Blacker La. S72—2C 10
Blacker Rd. S75—4G 7
Blackheath Clo. S71—6D 8
Blackheath Rd. S71—6D 8
Blackheath Wlk. S71—6D 8
Black La. S6—4D 84
Black La. S74—1D 50
Blackmoor Cres. S60—2B 90
Blackmore St. S4—6H 87
Blacksmith La. S30—1A 74
Blacksmith La. S44—1G 139
Blackstock Clo. S14—5H 111
Blackstock Cres. S14—5H 111
Blackstock Dri. S14—5H 111
Blackstock Rd. S14
                  —5H to 2H 111
Black Swan Wlk. S1—3E 5
Blackthorn Av. S66—4G 81
Blackthorn Clo. S30—5B 50
Blackthorne Clo. DN12—4A 60
Blackwood Av. DN4—5H 45
Blaco Rd. S9—4D 88
Blagden St. S2—2G 99
Blair Athol Rd. S11—1H 109
Blake Av. DN2—3F 33
Blake Av. S63—4C 40
Blake Clo. S66—5H 81
Blake Gro. Rd. S6—6C 86
Blakeley Clo. S71—6E 9
Blakeney Rd. S10—2A 98
Blake St. S6—6B 86
Blandford Dri. S41—4G 131
Bland La. S6—2F & 2F 85
(in two parts)
Bland St. S4—3A 88
Blast La. S2—2H 5
Blast La. S4—2H 5 & 1G 99
Blaxton Clo. S19—5A 114
Blayton Rd. S4—3G 87
Bleachcroft Way. S70—2E 25
Bleak Av. S72—3C 10
Bleakley Clo. S72—3C 10
Bleasdale Gro. S71—3B 14
Blenheim Av. S70—1G 23
Blenheim Clo. S66—2G 81
Blenheim Ct. S66—3F 81
Blenheim Cres. S64—6D 42
Blenheim Gdns. S11—2G 109
Blenheim Gro. S70—1G 23

Blenheim Rd. S70—2F 23
Bloemfontein St. S72—1G 15
Blonk St. S1—1G 5 & 1F 99
Bloomfield Rd. S75—4D 6
Blossom Cres. S12—4D 112
Blow Hall Cres. DN12—3C 60
Blow Hall Riding. DN12—4D 60
Blucher St. S70—6G 13
Bluebank View. S43—1D 132
Bluebell Rd. S5—6B 76
Bluebell Rd. S75—2C 6
Bluebird Hill. S31—1C 116
Blue Boy St. S3—1C 4 & 1D 98
Blundell Clo. DN4—4C 48
Blundell Ct. S71—2D 14
Blyde Rd. S5—2G 87
Bly Rd. S73—3D 26
Blyth Av. S62—2F 69
Blyth Clo. S40—5D 136
Blythe St. S73—6A 26
Blyth Rd. S66—1A 82
Boardman Av. S62—5C 54
Boat La. DN5—3D 44
Bobbinmill La. S40—3F 137
Bochum Parkway. S8
                  —2E 123 to 6A 112
Bocking Clo. S8—6B 110
Bocking Hill. S30—3F 141
Bocking La. S8—6B 110
Bocking Rise. S8—1C 122
Boden La. S1—3C 4
Boden Pl. S9—6E 89
Bodmin Ct. S71—4B 14
Bodmin St. S9—5B 88
Bodmin Way. S42—6E 131
Boggard La. S30—3C 72
Boiley La. S31—5A 126
Boland Rd. S8—4B 122
Bole Hill. S44—4G 139
Bole Hill. S60—6F 91
Bole Hill La. S10—1H 97
Bolehill La. S31—6G 125
Bole Hill Rd. S6—1F 97 to 5H 85
Bolsover Rd. S5—1H 87
Bolsover Rd. S43—1H 135
Bolsover Rd. E. S5—2H 87
Bolsover St. S3—3A 4 & 2C 98
Bolton Hill Rd. DN4—5C 48
Bolton Rd. S63—5A 42
Bolton Rd. S64—2H 55
Bolton St. DN12—1B 58
Bolton St. S3—5B 4 & 3D 98
Bond Clo. DN1—1C 46
Bondfield Rd. DN11—5E 63
Bondfield Cres. S73—1E 39
Bondfield Rd. S43—4A 134
Bond Rd. S75—4F 13
Bond St. DN11—6D 62
Bond St. S43—3A 134
Bond St. S73—6B 26
Bonet La. S60—2A 90
Bonington Rise. S66—3E 83
Bonville Gdns. S3—1B 4
Booker Rd. S8—5C 110
Booker's La. S31—3B 106
Bookers Way. S31—4B 106
Booth Clo. S19—5D 114
Booth Clo. S66—5C 94
Booth Croft. S70—5D 114
Booth Pl. S62—6E 55
Booth Rd. S30—6A 50
Booth St. S61—3B 68
Booth St. S74—5B 38
Borough Rd. S6—3A 86
Borrowdale Av. S19—3E 125
Borrowdale Clo. S19—3E 125

Borrowdale Clo. S71—1G 25
Borrowdale Cres. S31—6F 107
Borrowdale Dri. S19—3E 125
Borrowdale Rd. S19—3E 125
Boston Castle Gro. S60—5E 79
Boston Castle Ter. S60—5E 79
Boston St. S2—4D 98
Bosville Clo. S65—4H 71
Bosville Rd. S10—2H 97
Bosville St. S65—1B 80
Boswell Clo. DN11—5C 62
Boswell Clo. S30—5A 50
Boswell Clo. S71—1D 8
Boswell Rd. DN4—4A 48
Boswell Rd. S63—1F 55
Boswell St. S65—4F 79
Bosworth Rd. DN6—1C 16
Bosworth St. S10—1H 97
Botanical Rd. S11—4A 98
Botham St. S4—3A 88
Botsford St. S3—5E 87
Boulder Bri. Rd. S71—3G 9
Boulevard, The. DN3—5C 20
Boulton Clo. S40—6C 130
Boulton Dri. DN3—2F 49
Boundary Av. DN2—2A 34
Boundary Grn. S62—3G 69
Boundary Rd. S2—3H 99
Boundary St. S70—1B 24
Bourne Clo. S43—2E 133
Bourne Ct. S75—3G 7
Bourne Rd. S5—5G 75
Bourne Rd. S70—5H 23
Bourne Wlk. S75—3G 7
Bowden Wood Av. S9—3E 101
Bowden Wood Clo. S9—3E 101
Bowden Wood Cres. S9
—3E 101
Bowden Wood Dri. S9—3E 101
Bowden Wood Pl. S9—3E 101
Bowden Wood Rd. S9—3E 101
Bowdon St. S1—5C 4 & 3D 98
Bowen Dri. S65—5D 70
Bowen Rd. S65—1F 79
Bower Farm Rd. S41—1B 132
Bower Fold. DN1—6D 32
Bower Ho. S30—6A 64
Bower La. S30—6A 64
Bower Rd. S10—1B 98
Bower Rd. S64—6B 42
Bower Spring. S3—1E 5 & 1E 99
Bower St. S3—1E 5 & 1E 99
Bower Vale. DN12—4A 60
Bowfell View. S71—3A 14
Bowfield Rd. S5—5G 75
Bowland Clo. DN5—1H 31
Bowland Cres. S70—5H 23
Bowland Dri. S30—2C 64
Bowland Rd. S42—6D 136
Bowlease Gdns. DN4—3C 48
Bowling Grn. St. S3
—1D 4 & 6E 87
Bowman Clo. S12—5B 112
Bowman Dri. S12—5B 112
Bowman Dri. S66—3E 83
Bowness Clo. S18—2C 128
Bowness Dri. S63—2A 42
Bowness Rd. S6—4A 86
Bowness Rd. S41—4F 131
Bowood Rd. S11—5B 98
Bowshaw. S18—5D 122
Bowshaw Av. S8—4E 123
Bowshaw Clo. S8—4E 123
Bowshaw View. S8—4E 123
Bow St. S72—6B 10
Boyce St. S6—6B 86
Boyd Rd. S63—2F 55
Boyland St. S3—5D 86

Boynton Cres. S5—1E 87
Boynton Rd. S5—1E 87
Boythorpe Av. S40—3G 137
Boythorpe Cres. S40—4H 137
Boythorpe Mt. S40—3H 137
Boythorpe Rise. S40—3G 137
Boythorpe Rd. S40—3H 137
Bracken Ct. S66—6F 81
Brackendale Clo. S43—4D 132
Brackenfield Gro. S12—3F 113
Bracken Hill. S30—3B 64
Bracken Moor La. S30—4E 141
Bracken Rd. S5—5A 76
Brackley St. S3—5F 87
Bradberry Back La. S73—5A 26
Bradbury Clo. S40—2G 137
Bradbury's Clo. S62—4F 69
Bradbury St. S8—1E 111
Bradbury St. S70—6F 13
Bradfield Rd. S6—3A 86
Bradford Rd. DN2—1A 34
Bradford Row. DN1—6D 32
Bradford St. S9—4C 88
Bradgate Clo. S61—2A 78
Bradgate Ct. S61—2H 77
Bradgate La. S61—2H 77
Bradgate Pl. S61—1A 78
Bradgate Rd. S61—1A 78
Bradlea Rise. S62—6G 55
Bradley Av. S73—6A 26
Bradley Clo. S43—4E 133
Bradley Rd. S18—6A 128
Bradley St. S10—6A 86
Bradley Way. S43—4E 133
Bradshaw Av. S60—2F 103
Bradshaw Clo. S75—5C 12
Bradshaw Rd. S43—5H 133
Bradshaw Way. S60—2F 103
Bradstone Rd. S65—2A 80
Bradway Clo. S17—4H 121
Bradway Dri. S17—4H 121
Bradway Grange Rd. S17
—4A 122
Bradway Rd. S17—4H to 3G 121
Bradwell Av. S75—3C 22
Bradwell Clo. S18—2A 128
Bradwell Pl. S43—4A 134
Bradwell St. S2—1F 111
Braemar Rd. DN2—6G 33
Braemore Rd. S6—2G 85
Brailsford Av. S5—1E 75
Brailsford Rd. S5—1E 75
Brairfield Rd. S12—4C 112
Brairfields La. S30—4C 72
Braithwaite St. S75—4G 7
Braithwell Rd. DN5—4A 18
Braithwell Rd. S65—1H 81
Braithwell Rd. S66—4F 83
Braithwell Wlk. DN12—1B 58
Braithwell Way. S66—3A 82
Bramah St. S71—4E 9
Bramall La. S2—4E 99
Bramall La. S30—1B 140
Bramble Clo. S66—6F 81
Bramble Way. S63—5B 40
Brambling Ct. S41—2C 138
Bramcote Av. S71—5A 8
Brameld Rd. S62—2F 69
Brameld Rd. S64—2H 55
Bramham Rd. DN4—2D 48
Bramham Rd. S9—6D 88
Bramley Av. S13—5H 101
Bramley Av. S31—5C 104
Bramley Clo. S19—2C 124
Bramley Ct. DN12—2B 58
Bramley Ct. S10—2H 97
Bramley Dri. S13—4H 101
Bramley Hall Rd. S13—5H 101

Bramley La. S13—4H 101
Bramley La. S65—1A 82
Bramley Pk. Caravan Site. S31
—6A 124
Bramley Pk. Rd. S13—4H 101
Bramley Way. S66—3A 82
Brampton Av. S66—5H 93
Brampton Ct. S19—5A 114
Brampton Cres. S73—2H 39
Brampton La. S31—1F 105
Brampton Rd. S63—4B 40
Brampton Rd. S66—6H 93
Brampton Rd. S73—2H 39
Brampton St. S73—3B 40
Brampton View. S73—2H 39
Bramshill Clo. S19—6G 115
Bramshill Ct. S19—6G 115
Bramshill Rise. S40—4F 137
Bramwell Gdns. S3
—2A 4 & 1C 98
Bramwell St. S3—2A 4 & 1C 98
Bramwell St. S65—2E 79
Bramwith La. DN3—1G 21
Bramwith Rd. S11—5F 97
Bramworth Rd. DN4—2H 45
Brancroft Clo. DN4—5B 48
Brandene Clo. S44—2G 139
Brand La. DN5—5B 30
Brandon St. S3—4F 87
Brandreth Clo. S6—6C 86
Brandreth Rd. S6—6C 86
Brands La. S31—6H 107
Branksome Av. S70—6E 13
Branksome Chine Av. S70
—6C 138
Bransby St. S6—6B 86
Branstone Rd. DN5—1D 44
Branstone St. DN4—2A 46
Branton Clo. S40—4H 137
Branton Ga. Rd. DN3—1H 49
Branton Ter. DN3—3H 49
Brantwood Cres. DN4—2D 48
Brathay Clo. S4—2B 88
Brathay Rd. S4—2B 88
Bray St. S9—6C 88
Bray Wlk. S61—5E 67
Brearley Av. S30—4F 141
Brearley Av. S43—1D 132
Breckland Rd. S40—5D 136
Brecklands. S60—5A 80
Brecklands. S66—5E 81
Breck La. S31—3F 107
Brecks Cres. S65—5C 80
Brecks La. DN3—3D 20
Brecks La. S65—2B 80
Brecon Clo. S19—5G 115
Brecon Clo. S40—6E 131
Brendon Av. S40—1E 137
Brendon Clo. S73—3H 39
Brent Clo. S40—6F 131
Brent La. S43—1E 135
Brentwood Av. S11—1B 110
Brentwood Rd. S11—1B 110
Bressingham Clo. S4—5C 87
Bressingham Rd. S4—5G 87
Bretby Clo. DN4—4D 48
Bretby Rd. S40—5C 130
Brett Clo. S62—5C 54
Bretton Clo. S75—5A 6
Bretton Gro. S12—4F 113
Bretton Ho. DN1—1C 46
(off St James St.)
Bretton Rd. S75—5A 6
Bretton View. S72—2G 15
Brewery Rd. S63—4F 41
Brewery St. S41—2B 138
Breydon Av. DN5—4G 31
Briar Clo. S41—6G 131

Briar Ct. S66—6F 81
Briardene Clo. S40—6B 130
Briarfield Av. S12—4C 112
Briarfield Cres. S12—4C 112
Briarfield Rd. S12—4C 112
Briarfields La. S30—4C 72
Briar Gro. S72—2G 11
Briar Rise. S70—5A 24
Briar Rd. DN3—1E 35
Briar Rd. S7—1C 110
Briars Clo. S31—4B 126
Briar View. S43—4E 133
Briary Av. S30—6B 50
Brickhouse La. S17—1C 120
Brickhouse Yd. S40—2G 137
Brick St. S10—1H 97
Brickyard, The. S72—4C 10
Brickyard Wlk. S40—2A 138
Bridby St. S13—1D 114
Bridge Gdns. S71—4H 9
Bridgegate. S60—2D 78
Bridge Gro. DN5—4H 31
Bridge Hill. S30—2D 72
Bridgehouses. S3—1F 5 & 6E 87
Bridge Inn Rd. S30—1E 65
Bridge Stile Clo. S19—2C 124
Bridge St. DN4—1B 46
Bridge St. S3—1F 5 & 6E 87
Bridge St. S31—2B 126
Bridge St. S40—5A 138
Bridge St. S60—2D 78
Bridge St. S63—6F 29
Bridge St. S64—2C 56
Bridge St. S70—1E 25
Bridge St. S71—5H 13
Bridge St. S75—4C 6
Bridle Clo. S30—1E 65
Bridle Cres. S30—1E 65
Bridle Rd. S43—2F 135
Bridle Stile. S19—2C 124
Bridle Stile Av. S19—2B 124
Bridle Stile Clo. S19—2C 124
Bridleway, The. S62—6A 56
Bridport Rd. S9—6D 88
Brier Clo. S19—6D 114
Brierfield Clo. S75—5E 13
Brierley Clo. S43—2C 134
Brierley Rd. DN4—4B 48
Brierley Rd. S72—5F 11
(Grimethorpe)
Brierley Rd. S72—3D 10
(Shafton)
Brierley Rd. S72—1E 11
(S. Hiendley)
Brierly Dri. S65—6C 70
Brier St. S6—3A 86
Briery Wlk. S61—4B 68
Briggs St. S71—4E 9
Brightmore Dri. S3
—3A 4 & 2C 98
Brighton St. S9—3D & 2D 88
Brighton St. S72—6G 11
Brighton Ter. Rd. S10—1A 98
Brightside La. S9—4A 88
Bright St. S9—2D 88
Brimington Rd. S41—1B 138
Brimington Rd. N. S41—2A to
(in two parts)   3A 132
Brimmesfield Clo. S2—6A 100
Brimmesfield Dri. S2—5A 100
Brimmesfield Rd. S2—6A 100
Brinckman St. S70—1A 24
Brincliffe Clo. S40—4D 136
Brincliffe Cres. S11—6A 98
Brincliffe Edge Clo. S11
—1A 110

148

Brincliffe Edge Rd. S11
—1H 109 to 2C 110
Brincliffe Gdns. S11—6A 98
Brincliffe Hill. S11—6H 97
Brindley Clo. S8—3E 111
Brindley Ct. S31—3A 126
Brindley Cres. S8—3E 111
Brindley Rd. S41—5A 132
Brindley Way. S43—1D 134
Brinkburn Clo. S17—3F 121
Brinkburn Ct. S17—3F 121
Brinkburn Dri. S17—3F 121
Brinkburn Vale Rd. S17
—3F 121
Brinsford Rd. S60—2C 90
Brinsworth Hall Av. S60—3B 90
Brinsworth Hall Cres. S60
—3B 90
Brinsworth Hall Dri. S60
—3B 90
Brinsworth Hall Gro. S60
—4B 90
Brinsworth La. S60—3B 90
Brinsworth Rd. S60—3B to
(in three parts)   5C 90
Brinsworth St. S9—5B 88
Brinsworth St. S60—3C 78
Bristol Gro. DN2—3G 33
Bristol Rd. S11—4A 98
Britain St. S64—1D 56
Britannia Clo. S70—1H 23
Britannia Ct. S30—2E 65
Britannia Ho. S70—1H 23
Britannia Rd. S9—1E 101
(in two parts)
Britannia Rd. S40—6B 138
Britland Clo. S75—5C 12
Britnall St. S9—5C 88
Briton Sq. S63—1G 29
Briton St. S63—1G 29
Brittain St. S1—6F 5 & 3F 99
Britten Ho. DN2—3G 33
Broachgate. DN5—1G 31
Broadcarr Rd. S74—3B 52
Broadcroft Clo. S19—4G 115
Broad Dyke Clo. S31—5B 118
Broad Elms Clo. S11—3F 109
Broad Elms La. S11—4F 109
Broadfield Rd. S8—1D 110
Broadgorse Clo. S40—6H 137
Broadhead Rd. S30—4F 141
Broad Inge Cres. S30—2C 64
Broadlands Av. S19—5A 114
Broadlands Rise. S19—5B 114
Broad La. S1—3B 4 & 2D 98
Broadley Rd. S13—6E 101
Broad Oaks. S9—6B 88
Broad Pavement. S40—2A 138
Broad Riding. DN12—4D 60
Broad St. S2—2G 5 & 1F & 1G 99
(in two parts)
Broad St. S62—4F 69
Broad St. S74—5H 37
Broad St. La. S2—2H 5 & 1G 99
Broadwater. S63—1G 41
Broadway. S60—4B 90
Broadway. S64—3H 55
Broadway. S65—2H 79
Broadway. S70—6D 12
Broadway. S75—4F 7
Broadway Av. S30—3F 65
Broadway Clo. S64—3H 55
Broadway E. S65—2H 79
Broadway, The. DN4—6H 45
Brocco Bank. S11—5A 98
Brocco La. S3—2C 4 & 1D 98
Brocco St. S3—2C 4 & 1D 98
Brockfield Clo. S70—4A 24

Brockhill Ct. S43—3F 133
Brockhole Clo. DN4—4D 48
Brockholes Clo. DN3—4H 49
Brockhurst Way. S65—5D 70
Brocklehurst Av. S8—1G 123
Brocklehurst Av. S70—3D 24
Brocklehurst Piece. S40
—3F 137
Brockwell Ct. S40—5F 131
Brockwell La. S40—5D 130 to
(in two parts)   6E 131
Brockwell La. S42—4B 130
Brockwell Pl. S40—1G 137
Brockwell Ter. S40—1G 137
Brockwell Wlk. S40—6F 131
Brodsworth Ho. DN1—1C 46
(off St James St.)
Bromehead Way. S41—4F 131
Brompton Rd. DN5—2E 45
Brompton Rd. S9—4C 88
Bromwich Rd. S8—5C 110
Bronte Av. DN4—5H 45
Bronte Clo. S71—4B 14
Bronte Gro. S64—5F 43
Bronte Pl. S62—6H 55
Brookbank Av. S40—1F 137
Brook Clo. S30—6A 64
Brook Clo. S31—6C 104
Brook Croft. S31—2F 119
Brook Dri. S3—2B 4 & 1D 98
Brooke Dri. S43—6F 133
Brooke Dri. S63—5D 40
Brooke St. DN1—4D 32
Brooke St. S74—5H 37
Brookfield Av. S40—3C 136
Brookfield Av. S64—3B 56
Brookfield Clo. DN3—4F 35
Brookfield Rd. S7—6D 98
Brookfield Ter. S71—5E 9
Brook Hill. S3—3A 4 & 2C 98
Brook Hill. S61—3B 66
Brookhill Rd. S75—5A 6
Brookhouse Hill. S10—6C 96
Brookhouse La. S31—5E 95
Brookhouse Rd. S31—1B 116
Brooklands Av. S10—6B 96
Brooklands Cres. S10—6B 96
Brooklands Dri. S10—6B 96
Brook La. S3—3B 4 & 2D 98
Brook La. S30—1A 74
(Grenoside)
Brook La. S30—2C 72
(Oughtibridge)
Brook La. S66—3H 81
Brooklyn Dri. S40—1F 137
Brooklyn Pl. S8—2E 111
Brooklyn Rd. S8—2E 111
Brook Rd. DN12—3F 59
Brook Rd. S8—2D 110
Brook Rd. S30—1C 64
Brook Rd. S65—1H 79
Brook Row. S40—4E 141
Brookside. DN12—4E 59
Brookside. S64—4H 55
Brookside. S65—4A 80
Brookside Bar. S40—3B 136
Brookside Clo. S12—4B 114
Brookside Ct. S62—5D 68
Brookside Cres. S63—6B 40
Brookside Dri. S70—3D 24
Brookside Glen. S40—3B 136
Brookside La. S6—4A 84
Brook Sq. DN12—4E 59
Brook St. S60—2H 91
Brook St. S62—4G 69
Brook Vale. S40—3G 137
Brookvale. S71—4D 14

Brook Way. DN5—6D 18
Brook Yd. S40—2G 137
Broom Av. S60—5H 79
Broombank Rd. S41—1F 131
Broom Chase. S60—5F 79
Broom Clo. S2—4D 98
Broom Clo. S41—4F 131
Broom Clo. S63—6D 28
(Bolton-upon-Dearne)
Broom Clo. S63—1G 55
(Wath upon Dearne)
Broom Clo. S70—3D 24
Broom Ct. S60—5G 79
(Broom Rd.)
Broom Ct. S60—5F 79
(Wade Clo.)
Broom Cres. S60—5F 79
Broomcroft. S75—3D 22
Broom Dri. S60—6H 79
Broome Av. S64—2B 56
Broomfield Av. S41—6D 138
Broomfield Clo. S70—1D 22
Broomfield Ct. S30—3F 141
Broomfield Ct. S71—1F 9
Broomfield Gro. S60—5F 79
Broomfield La. S30—4E 141
Broomfield Rd. S10—3B 98
Broomfield Rd. S30—3F 141
Broom Gdns. S43—4F 133
Broom Grange. S60—5G 79
Broom Gro. S31—4F 119
Broom Gro. S60—4F 79
Broomgrove Cres. S10—3B 98
Broomgrove Hall. S10—3B 98
Broomgrove La. S10—3B 98
Broomgrove Rd. S10—3B 98
Broomhall Pl. S10
—6A 4 & 3C 98
Broomhall Rd. S10
—6A 4 & 4C 98
Broomhall St. S3—6A 4 &
(in three parts)   3C to 3D 98
Broomhead Ct. S75—5F 7
Broomhead Rd. S73—2H 39
Broomhill. DN12—1B 58
Broomhill Clo. S31—6B 124
Broom Hill Dri. DN4—4D 48
Broomhill La. S63—6G 27
Broomhill Rd. S41—1H 131
Broomhill View. S63—2H 41
Broomhouse La. DN12 & DN4
—4B 60
Broom La. S60—5G 79
Broom Ridings. S61—5B 68
Broom Rd. S60—4F 79
Broomroyd. S70—5B 24
Broomspring La. S10
—5A 4 & 3C 98
Broom St. S10—6A 4 & 3C 98
Broom Ter. S60—4F 79
Broomvale Wlk. DN12—4A 60
Broom Valley Rd. S60—4F 79
Broomville St. S64—2C 56
Broomwood Clo. S19—4G 115
Broomwood Gdns. S19—4G 115
Brosley Av. DN3—1H 21
Brotherton St. S3—5F 87
Brough Grn. S75—4D 22
Broughton Av. DN5—2A 32
Broughton La. S9—3D 88
Broughton Rd. DN4—5B 48
Broughton Rd. S6—2A 86
Broughton Rd. S41—4F 131
Brow Clo. S70—3H 23
Brow Cres. S19—2E 125
Brow Hill Rd. S66—3E 83
Brownell St. S3—2B 4 & 1D 98
Brown Hills La. S10—6A 96

Browning Av. DN4—5B 46
Browning Clo. S6—4B 74
Browning Clo. S71—2B 14
Browning Dri. S6—4B 74
Browning Dri. S65—3H 79
Browning Rd. DN3—1H 21
Browning Rd. S6—4A 74
Browning Rd. S63—4C 40
Browning Rd. S64—5E 43
Browning Rd. S65—3H 79
Brown La. S1—5E 5 & 3E 99
Brown La. S18—6G 123
Brownroyd Av. S71—3E 9
Brown St. S1—5F 5 & 3F 99
Brown St. S60—2B 78
Brow, The. S65—5A 80
Brow View. S63—1H 41
Broxbourne Gdns. DN5—6B 18
Broxholme La. DN1—5D 32
Broxholme Rd. S8—4D 110
Bruce Av. S70—2H 23
Bruce Cres. DN2—4H 33
Bruce Rd. S11—5B 98
Brunel Dri. DN5—4H 31
Bruni Way. DN11—6D 62
Brunswick Clo. S71—1H 13
Brunswick Rd. S3—6F 87
Brunswick Rd. S60—5F 79
Brunswick St. S10
—4A 4 & 2C 98
Brunswick St. S41—1A 138
Brunswick St. S63—1H 29
Brunt Rd. S62—1H 69
Brushfield Gro. S12—3F 113
Brushfield Rd. S40—6B 130
Bubwith Rd. S9—1D 88
Buchanan Cres. S5—4C 74
Buchanan Dri. S5—4D 74
Buchanan Dri. S5—4D 74
Buckden Clo. S40—1F 137
Buckden Rd. S70—5F 13
Buckenham Dri. S4—5G 87
Buckenham St. S4—5G 87
Buckingham Clo. S18—1B 128
Buckingham Rd. DN2—5F 33
Buckingham Rd. DN12—2D 58
Buckingham Way. S60—3D 90
Buckingham Way. S66—3G 83
Buckingham Way. S71—1D 8
Buckleigh Rd. S63—1E 55
Buckley Ct. S70—1H 23
Buckthorne Clo. S64—5A 56
Buckwood View. S14—2H 111
Bude Ct. S71—4C 14
Bude Rd. DN4—3B 46
Bullen Rd. S6—4A 74
Bullfinch Clo. S60—3D 90
Bungalow Rd. DN12—3B 60
Bungalows, The. S31—6H 125
(Eckington)
Bungalows, The. S31—3A 126
(Killamarsh)
Bungalows, The. S40—2F 137
(Newbold)
Bungalows, The. S41—4G 131
(Piccadilly)
Bungalows, The. S41—2B 138
(Whittington Moor)
Bungalows, The. S60—1E 103
Bungay Row. S2—1H 99
Bunker's Hill. S31—3C 126
Bunting Clo. S8—5F 111
Bunting Nook. S8—5F 111
Burbage Clo. S18—1B 128
Burbage Gro. S12—2F 113

149

Burbage Rd. S43—3B 134
Burcot Rd. S8—2D 110
Burcroft Hill. DN12—2F 59
Burden Clo. DN1—1C 46
Burford Av. DN4—6G 45
Burford Cres. S31—6C 104
Burgen Rd. S61—6G 67
Burgess Clo. S41—6D 138
Burgess Rd. S9—5B 88
Burgess St. S1—4E 5 & 2E 99
Burgoyne Clo. S6—5B 86
Burgoyne Rd. S6—5B 86
Burkinshaw Av. S62—5F 55
Burkitt Dri. S43—1F 135
Burleigh St. S70—1H 23
Burley Clo. S40—6A 138
Burlington Arc. S70—6H 13
(off Eldon St.)
Burlington Clo. S17—2E 121
Burlington Ct. S6—6C 86
Burlington Glen. S17—2E 121
Burlington Gro. S17—2E 121
Burlington Rd. S17—2E 121
Burlington St. S6—6C 86
Burlington St. S40—2A 138
Burman Rd. S63—6F 41
Burnaby Ct. S6—4B 86
Burnaby Cres. S6—5B 86
Burnaby Grn. S6—5B 86
Burnaby St. DN1—1C 46
Burnaby St. S6—4B 86
Burnaby Wlk. S6—5B 86
Burnaston Clo. S18—2A 128
Burnaston Wlk. DN12—2C 58
Burnbridge Rd. S41—1B 132
Burncross Rd. S30—2C 64
Burnell Rd. S6—2A 86
Burnell St. S43—3F 133
Burngreave Bank. S4—5F 87
Burngreave Rd. S3—4F 87
Burngreave St. S3—5F 87
Burn Gro. S30—3G 65
Burngrove Pl. S3—4F 87
Burnham Clo. DN4—4H 47
Burnham Gro. DN5—1H 31
Burnham Way. S73—4D 26
Burn Pl. S71—6A 8
Burnsall Cres. S60—4C 90
Burnsall Gro. S70—3D 24
Burns Clo. S40—6H 137
Burns Dri. S18—3G 129
Burns Dri. S30—2D 64
Burns Dri. S65—3H 79
Burnside Av. S8—2E 111
Burns Rd. DN3—1H 21
Burns Rd. DN4—5B 46
Burns Rd. S6—1B 98
Burns Rd. S31—5G 107
Burns Rd. S65—3G 79
Burns Rd. S66—5G 83
Burns St. DN5—6B 18
Burns Way. S63—4C 40
Burnt Hill La. S30—4A 72
Burnt Ho. La. S31—1G 103
Burnt Stones Clo. S10—3D 96
Burnt Stones Dri. S10—3D 96
Burnt Stones Gro. S10—3D 96
Burnt Tree La. S3—1B 4 & 1D 98
Burntwood Cres. S60—6E 91
Burnt Wood La. S60—1G 103
Burntwood Rd. S72—6H 11
Burrell St. S60—3D 78
Burrowlee Rd. S6—2A 86
Burrows Dri. S5—1E 87
Burrows Gro. S73—6H 25
Bursden Clo. S41—2A 132
Burton Av. DN4—3B 46
Burton Av. S71—3D 14

Burton Bank Rd. S71—4A to
(in two parts)   3B 14
Burton Cres. S71—2E 15
Burton La. S30—3C 72
Burton Rd. S3—5D 86
Burton Rd. S71—4C 14 to 1F 15
Burton St. S6—4B 86
Burton St. S71—4G 13
Burton Ter. DN4—3B 46
Burton Ter. S70—1B 24
Burying La. S62—2A 52
Bushey Wood Rd. S17—3E 121
Bushfield Rd. S63—5D 40
Busk Knoll. S5—1E 87
Busk Meadow. S5—1E 87
Busk Pk. S5—1E 87
Busley Gdns. DN5—1A 32
(in two parts)
Butcher St. S63—1E 29
Butchill Av. S5—1E 75
Bute St. S10—2H 97
Butler Rd. S6—4G 85
Butler Way. S31—2A 126
Butterbusk. DN12—3G 59
Butterill Dri. DN3—4H 35
Butterley Dri. S70—3D 24
Buttermere Clo. S31—6E 107
Buttermere Clo. S63—2A 42
Buttermere Clo. S64—5G 43
Buttermere Dri. S18—2C 128
Buttermere Rd. S7—3C 110
Buttermere Way. S71—1H 25
Buttermilk La. S44—6H 135
Butterthwaite Cres. S5—2A 76
Butterthwaite La. S30—6H 65
Butterthwaite Rd. S5—1H 75
Butterton Dri. S40—6C 130
Butt Hole Rd. DN12—3G 59
Button Hill. S11—3H 109
Button Row. S30—3D 140
Butts Hill. S17—5D 120
Buxton Rd. S71—6C 8
Byath La. S72—1H 15
Byford Rd. S66—4C 82
Byland Way. S71—5D 14
Byrley Rd. S61—6G 67
Byrne Clo. S75—3A 12
Byron Av. DN4—5A 46
Byron Av. DN5—5H 31
Byron Av. S30—3D 64
Byron Clo. S18—4G 129
Byron Cres. S63—4C 40
Byron Dri. S65—3G 79
Byron Dri. S71—3B 14
Byron Rd. S7—1C 110
Byron Rd. S19—5G 115
Byron Rd. S31—5G 107
(in two parts)
Byron Rd. S40—5A 138
Byron Rd. S64—6F 43
Byron Rd. S66—5G 83
Byron St. S40—4B 138

Cadeby Av. DN12—3C 58
Cadeby Ho. DN1—1C 46
(off St James St.)
Cadeby Rd. DN5—3C 44
Cadman Ct. S19—3D 124
Cadman La. S1—4F 5 & 2E 99
Cadman Rd. S12—1E 113
Cadman St. S4—1G 99
Cadman St. S19—3C 124
Cadman St. S63—5G 41
Cadwell Clo. S72—5C 10
Caernarvon Clo. S40—4E 137
Caernarvon Cres. S63—1H 41
Caernarvon Dri. DN5—1G 43

Caernarvon Rd. S18—3E 129
Caine Gdns. S61—3G 77
Cairns Rd. S10—3G 97
Cairns Rd. S19—3F 115
Caister Av. S30—2D 64
Caistor Av. S70—2E 23
Cait La. S11—4D 108
Calcot Grn. S64—3B 56
Calcot Pk. Av. S64—3B 56
Caldbeck Gro. S30—5B 50
Caldbeck Rd. S31—6F 107
Calder Av. S71—2G 9
Calder Cres. S70—2D 24
Calder Rd. S61—5H 67
Calder Rd. S63—2B 42
Calder Ter. DN12—2E 59
Caldervale. S71—1G 9
Calder Way. S5—1G 87
Caldey Rd. S18—3E 129
Califonia Cres. S70—2H 23
California Dri. S30—3E 65
California Gdns. S70—1H 23
California St. S70—2G 23
California Ter. S70—2G 23
Calladine Way. S64—4A 56
Callow Dri. S14—2H 111
Callow Mt. S14—2G 111
Callow Pl. S14—2H 111
Callow Rd. S14—2G 111
Callywhite La. S18—2F 129
Calow Grn. S44—5G 139
Calow La. S41 & S44—6D 138
Calver Clo. S75—4C 22
Calver Cres. S43—3B 134
Calvert Rd. S9—5E 89
Calvert St. S74—6F 37
Camborne Clo. S6—4A 74
Camborne Rd. S6—4A 74
Camborne Way. S71—4B 14
Cambourne Clo. DN6—1D 16
Cambria Dri. DN4—5G 45
Cambrian Clo. DN5—2C 44
Cambrian Clo. S40—5F 131
Cambridge Cres. S65—2G 79
Cambridge Pl. S65—2G 79
Cambridge Rd. S8—1F 111
Cambridge Rd. S30—4H 141
Cambridge Rd. S43—3F 133
Cambridge St. DN11—3C 62
Cambridge St. S1—4D 4 & 2E 99
Cambridge St. S64—6C 42
Cambridge St. S65—2G 79
Cambron Gdns. S66—4H 41
Camdale Rise. S12—6H 113
Camdale View. S12—6A 114
Camden Pl. DN1—1C 46
Camellia Dri. DN3—4D 20
Cammell Rd. S5—1H 87
Camms Clo. S31—5D 124
Camm St. S6—5A 86
Campbell Dri. S65—4H 79
Campbell Rd. S9—3D 88
Campbell St. S61—3C 68
Camping La. S8—5C 110
Campion Clo. S63—6D 28
Campion Dri. S64—4B 56
Campo La. S1—3D 4 & 1E 99
Campsall Dri. S10—2G 97
Campsall Field Rd. S63—6E 41
Canada Dri. S4—4H 87
Canada St. S70—2G 23
Canal Bri. S31—3B 126
Canal St. S4—6H 87
Canal St. S71—4H 13
Canal Wharf S2—2H 5 & 1G 99
Canal Wharf. S41—1B 138
Canberra Rise. S63—1H 41
Canklow Hill Rd. S60—6D 78

Canklow Meadows Ind. Est.
                      S60—3D 90
Canklow Rd. S60—1D 90
Canning St. S1—4C 4 & 2D 98
Cannock St. S6—3A 86
Cannon Hall Rd. S5—2G 87
Canons Way. S71—4C 14
Cantello Ct. DN11—6C 62
Canterbury Av. S10—5C 96
Canterbury Clo. DN5—3G 31
Canterbury Cres. S10—5C 96
Canterbury Dri. S10—5C 96
Canterbury Rd. DN2—3F 33
Canterbury Rd. S8—2F 111
Cantilupe Cres. S31—5B 104
Cantley La. DN4 & DN3—2A 48
Cantley Mnr. Av. DN4—4E 49
Capel Rise. S43—3D 132
Capel St. S6—4B 86
(in two parts)
Caperns Rd. S31—2H 119
Capri Ct. S73—3C 26
Capthorne Clo. S40—6B 130
Caraway Gro. S64—5B 56
Carbis Clo. S71—4B 14
Carbrook Hall Ind. Est. S9
                      —2D 88
Carbrook St. S9—3D 88
Cardew Clo. S62—2G 69
Cardiff St. S9—3C 88
Cardigan Rd. DN2—4A 34
Cardoness Dri. S10—3E 97
Cardoness Rd. S10—3F 97
Carey Av. S71—6A 14
Carfield Av. S8—2F 111
Carfield La. S8—2G 111
Carfield Pl. S8—2F 111
Carisbrooke Rd. DN2—5G 33
Carlby Rd. S6—4G 85
Carley Dri. S19—6F 115
Carlingford Rd. S60—6G 79
Carlin St. S13—1G 113
Carlise St. S65—2E 79
Carlisle Pl. S65—2E 79
(off Nottingham St.)
Carlisle Rd. DN2—2H 33
Carlisle Rd. S4—3A 88
Carlisle St. S4—6G 87
Carlisle St. S62—4B 56
Carlisle St. E. S4
                      —5H 87 to 3B 88
Carlisle Ter. S31—4F 107
Carlthorpe Gro. S30—6A 50
Carlton Av. S65—3F 79
Carlton Clo. S19—3C 124
Carlton Ho. DN1—1C 46
(off Bond Clo.)
Carlton Ho. S72—6B 10
Carlton Ind. Est. S71—6E 9
Carlton Rd. DN1—4E 33
Carlton Rd. S6—1H 85
Carlton Rd. S40—6A 138
Carlton Rd. S71—2A 14 to 4F 9
Carlton St. S71—3G 13
Carlton St. S72—6B 10
(Cudworth)
Carlton St. S72—6G 11
(Grimethorpe)
Carlton Ter. S71—4G 9
Carltonville Rd. S9—3D 88
Carlyle Rd. S66—5G 83
Carlyle St. S64—6E 43
Carlyon Gdns. S40—5H 137
Carnaby Rd. S6—4A 86
Carnarvon St. S6—6C 86
Carnforth Rd. S71—2D 14
Carnley St. S71—3D 14
Carnoustie Av. S40—5E 137

Carnoustie Clo. S64—3C 56
Carpenter Croft. S12—1E 113
Carpenter Gdns. S12—1E 113
Carpenter M. S12—1E 113
Carr Bank Clo. S11—5F 97
Carr Bank Dri. S11—5E 97
Carr Bank La. S11—5E 97
Carr Clo. S60—3A 90
Carrcroft Ct. S30—4H 141
Carrfield Clo. S75—5B 6
Carrfield Ct. S8—1F 111
Carrfield Dri. S8—1F 111
Carr Field La. S63—6D 28
Carrfield Rd. S8—1F 111
Carrfield St. S8—1F 111
Carr Fold. S30—4H 141
Carr Forge Clo. S12—3A 114
Carr Forge La. S12—3A 114
Carr Forge Mt. S12—3A 114
Carr Forge Pl. S12—3B 114
Carr Forge Rd. S12—3A 114
Carr Forge Ter. S12—3A 114
Carr Forge View. S12—3B 114
Carr Forge Wlk. S12—3B 114
  (off Carter Lodge Dri.)
Carr Grn. S63—6E 29
Carr Grn. La. S75—6G 7
Carr Gro. S30—4G 141
Carr Head La. S63
            —6B 28 to 1A 42
Carr Hill. DN4—3B 46
Carr Ho. Rd. DN1 & DN4—2C 46
Carrill Dri. S6—3A 74
Carrill Rd. S6—3A 74
Carrington Av. S75—3G 13
Carrington Rd. S11—5H 97
Carrington St. S65—4F 79
Carrington St. S75—4F 13
Carrington Ter. S31—5H 117
Carr La. DN4—6C 48
  (Bessacarr)
Carr La. DN4—2D 46
  (Hyde Park)
Carr La. DN12—2F 59
Carr La. S1—3C 4 & 2D 98
Carr La. S18—1A 128
Carr La. S30—6F 141
Carr La. S31—3F 95
  (Slade Hooton)
Carr La. S31—2D 104
  (Ulley)
Carr La. S65—1E 71
Carr La. S66—2E 95
  (Carr, Maltby)
Carr La. S66—6D 82
  (Hooton Levitt)
Carr La. S75—1A 50
Carr Rd. DN12—4A 60
Carr Rd. S6—5A 86
Carr Rd. S30—5F 141
Carr Rd. S63—5G 41
Carrs La. S72—2H 15
Carr St. S71—2D 14
Carr View Av. DN4—3B 46
Carr View Rd. S61—1F 77
Carrville Dri. S6—5B 74
Carrville Rd. S6—5B 74
Carrville Rd. W. S6—5A 74
Carrwell La. S6—6A 74
Carsick Gro. S10—4D 96
Carsick Hill Cres. S10—4D 96
Carsick Hill Dri. S10—4E 97
Carsick Hill Rd. S10—4D 96
Carsick Hill Way. S10—4D 96
Carsick View Rd. S10—4D 96
Carsington Clo. S40—6D 130
Carson Mt. S12—4D 112
Carson Rd. S10—2H 97

Carterhall La. S12—5E 113
Carterhall Rd. S12—5D 112
Carter Knowle Av. S11—2A 110
Carter Knowle Av. S11—2A 110
Carter Knowle Rd. S11 & S7
            —2H 109
Carter Lodge Av. S12—3B 114
Carter Lodge Dri. S12—3B 114
Carter Lodge Pl. S12—3B 114
Carter Lodge Rise. S12—3B 114
Carter Lodge Wlk. S12—3B 114
  (off Carter Lodge Dri.)
Carter Pl. S8—1F 111
Carter Rd. S8—1E 111
Carter St. S4—4H 87
Cartmel Clo. S18—2C 128
Cartmel Clo. S66—3G 83
Cartmel Ct. S71—6F 9
Cartmel Cres. S41—3F 131
Cartmell Cres. S8—4D 110
Cartmell Rd. S8—3C 110
Cartmel Wlk. S31—6F 107
Car Vale Dri. S13—5E 101
Car Vale View. S13—5E 101
Carver Clo. S31—4H 127
Carver Dri. S31—5E 107
Carver La. S1—3D 4 & 2E 99
Carver St. S1—3D 4 & 2E 99
Carver Way. S31—3H 127
Carwood Clo. S4—4H 87
Carwood Grn. S4—4H 87
Carwood Gro. S4—4H 87
Carwood La. S4—4H 87
Carwood Rd. S4—4H 87
Carwood Way. S4—4H 87
Cary Rd. S2—5B 100
Cary Rd. S31—6B 124
Cascades Shopping Centre.
            S60—2D 78
Castell Cres. DN4—2C 48
Castle Av. DN12—3E 59
Castle Av. S60—6D 78
Castlebeck Av. S2—4D 100
Castlebeck Ct. S2—4E 101
Castlebeck Croft. S2—4E 101
Castle Clo. DN5—1G 45
Castle Clo. S75—3C 22
Castle Cres. DN12—2E 59
Castledine Croft. S9—6D 76
Castledine Gdns. S9—6D 76
Castle Dri. S75—6A 22
Castlegate. S3—2G 5 & 1F 99
Castle Grn. S3—2F 5 & 1F 99
Castle Grn. S31—1D 106
Castle Gro. DN12—2F 59
Castle Hill. DN12—3E 59
Castle Hill. S31—5D 124
Castle Hill Av. S64—1H 57
Castle Hill Clo. S31—5D 124
Castle Hills Rd. DN5—6G 17
Castle Mkt. S1—2G 5 & 1F 99
Castlereagh St. S70—6G 13
Castlerigg Way. S18—2C 128
Castle Row. S17—3H 121
Castlerow Clo. S17—3H 121
Castlerow Dri. S17—3H 121
Castle Sq. S1—2F 5 & 1F 99
Castle St. DN12—3E 59
Castle St. S3—2F 5 & 1F 99
Castle St. S70—1G 23
Castle Ter. DN12—3E 59
Castleton Gro. S43—6H 133
Castle View. DN12—4B 60
Castle View. S31—6D 124
Castle View. S70—3C 36
Castle View. S75—1C 22
  (Dodworth)

Castle View. S75—6A 22
  (Hood Green)
Castlewood Cres. S10—5B 96
Castlewood Dri. S10—5C 96
Castlewood Rd. S10—5B 96
Castle Yd. S40—3A 138
Castor Rd. S9—4B 88
Catania Rise. S73—3C 26
Catch Bar La. S6—1A 86
Catcliffe Rd. S9—1E 101
Catherine Av. S31—6B 104
Catherine Ct. S40—2G 137
Catherine Rd. S4—5G 87
Catherine St. DN1—1D 46
Catherine St. S3—5F 87
Catherine St. S40—2G 137
Catherine St. S64—6D 42
Catherine St. S65—3E 79
Cathill Rd. S63—5G 27
Cat La. S2 & S8—1G 111
Catley Rd. S9—6E 89
Catling La. DN3—2H 21
Cattal St. S9—6D 88
Catterick Clo. DN12—3A 58
Cauldon Dri. S40—6C 130
Causeway Gdns. S17—1C 120
Causeway Glade. S17—1C 120
Causeway Head Rd. S17
            —1C 120
Causeway, The. S17—2D 120
Cavendish Av. S6—2E 85
Cavendish Av. S17—2F 121
Cavendish Clo. S65—5B 80
Cavendish Ct. S41—6A 132
Cavendish Pl. S66—3G 83
Cavendish Rise. S18—3D 128
Cavendish Rd. S11—6A 98
Cavendish Rd. S61—3A 78
Cavendish Rd. S75—4G 13
Cavendish St. S3—4B 4 & 2D 98
Cavendish St. S40—2A 138
Cavendish St. S43—3B 134
Cavendish St. N. S41—1A 132
Cave St. S9—6B 88
Cavill Rd. S8—4E 111
Cawdor Rd. S2—1A 112
Cawdor Rd. S60—4C 90
Cawdor St. DN5—6B 18
Cawley Pl. S71—3A 14
Cawood Rd. S71—1E 25
Cawston Rd. S4—3G 87
Cawthorne. S75—3C 22
Cawthorne Clo. S8—4C 110
Cawthorne Clo. S65—2A 80
Cawthorne Gro. S8—4C 110
Cawthorne La. S75—6A 6
Cawthorne Rd. S65—2A 80
Cawthorne Rd. S75—2A 12
Caxton Clo. S43—1D 132
Caxton La. S10—3H 97
Caxton Rd. DN6—2D 16
Caxton Rd. S10—3A 98
Caxton St. S70—4G 13
Caythorpe Clo. S71—2G 15
Cayton Clo. S71—6A 8
Cecil Av. DN4—6E 45
Cecil Av. S18—1E 129
Cecil Rd. S18—6E 123
Cecil Sq. S2—5D 98
Cedar Av. S40—6F 131
Cedar Av. S64—5D 42
Cedar Av. S66—4G 81
Cedar Clo. DN4—6G 45
Cedar Clo. S30—4D 140
Cedar Clo. S31—6G 125
  (Eckington)
Cedar Clo. S31—4A 126
  (Killamarsh)

Cedar C[...]
Cedar Dr[...]
Cedar Gro[...]
Cedar Noo[...]
Cedar Rd. D[...]
Cedar Rd. DN[...]
Cedar Rd. S30—[...]
Cedar Way. S30[...]
Cedric Av. DN12[...]
Cedric Cres. S66[...]
Cedric Rd. DN3—5D [...]
Celandine Ct. S17—4C[...]
Celandine Gdns. S17—[...]
Celandine Rise. S64—5A[...]
Cemetery Av. S11—4B 98
Cemetery La. S43—2C 134
Cemetery Rd. DN6—3C 16
Cemetery Rd. S11—5G 99
Cemetery Rd. S18—3F 129
Cemetery Rd. S41—3C 138
Cemetery Rd. S63—2A 42
  (Bolton-upon-Dearne)
Cemetery Rd. S63—1D 28
  (Thurnscoe)
Cemetery Rd. S63—1E 55 to
  (Wath upon Dearne)   5E 41
Cemetery Rd. S64—6E 43
Cemetery Rd. S70—1A 24
Cemetery Rd. S72—6G 11
Cemetery Rd. S73—4D 38
  (Hemingfield)
Cemetery Rd. S73—6B 26
  (Wombwell)
Cemetery Rd. S74—4C 38
Cemetery Ter. S43—4E 133
Centenary Way. S60 & S65
            —4C 55
Central Av. DN5—1B 32
Central Av. DN6—3C 16
Central Av. S31—5F 107
Central Av. S40—3G 137
Central Av. S64—3H 55
Central Av. S65—2H 79
Central Av. S66—2F 81
Central Av. S72—5G 11
Central Boulevd. DN2—3H 33
Central Dri. DN11—5C 62
Central Dri. S44—2F 139
Central Dri. S62—5C 54
Central Dri. S66—5A 94
Central Dri. S71—2E 9
Central Pavement. S40
  (off Market Pl.)   —2A 138
Central Rd. S60—3D 78
Central St. S41—4C 138
Central St. S63—3G 29
Central St. S74—6F 37
Central Ter. S40—3B 138
Central Wlk. S43—4D 132
Centre Riding. DN11
            —6F & 5G 61
Centre, The. S66—4H 81
Century St. S9—5D 88
Chaddesden Clo. S18—2A 128
Chaddson Wlk. DN12—1D 58
Chadwick Dri. S66—3F 83
Chadwick Rd. DN5—4B 32
Chadwick Rd. DN6—3C 16
Chadwick Rd. S13—6E 101
Chaffinch Av. S60—3D 90
Chaff La. S60—2H 91
Chalfont Ct. S60—3D 90
Challenger Dri. DN5—6G 31
Challoner Grn. S19—1E 125
Challoner Way. S19—1E 125
Chalmers Dri DN2—6B 20

Chestnut Gro. S63—2F 29
Chestnut Gro. S64—5D 42
Chestnut Gro. S66—3D 82
Chestnut Rd. S31—5H 103
Chevet Ho. DN1—1C 46
(off Grove Pl.)
Chevet Rise. S71—1D 8
Chevet View. S71—1C 8
Cheviot Dri. DN5—2H 31
Cheviot Wlk. S75—5D 12
Cheviot Way. S40—6E 131
Chevril Ct. S66—5E 81
Chichester Rd. S10—1H 97
Childers St. DN4—2E 47
Chiltern Clo. S40—1E 137
Chiltern Ct. S40—1E 137
Chiltern Cres. DN5—2C 44
Chiltern Rise. S60—4D 90
Chiltern Rd. DN5—2H 31
Chiltern Rd. S6—3H 85
Chiltern Wlk. S75—5D 12
Chilton St. S70—1A 24
Chilwell Rd. S71—4B 8
Chilwell Sq. S71—4B 8
Chinley St. S9—6C 88
Chippingham Pl. S9—5B 88
Chippingham St. S9—5C 88
Chippinghouse Rd. S7 & S8
—6D 98
Chiverton Clo. S18—1E 129
Chorley Av. S10—5C 96
Chorley Dri. S10—5C 96
Chorley Pl. S10—6C 96
Chorley Rd. S10—6C 96
Christchurch Av. S31—5C 104
Christ Chu. Rd. DN1—5D 32
Christ Chu. Rd. S3—4F 87
Christchurch Rd. S63—4C 40
Christ Chu. Ter. DN1—6E 33
Church Av. S62—3E 69
Church Balk. DN3—4C 20
Church Balk Gdns. DN3—4D 20
Church Clo. S30—2D 72
Church Clo. S31—5F 117
(Kiveton Park)
Church Clo. S64—2A 56
Church Clo. S65—4G 71
Church Clo. S66—5F 83
Church Corner. S31—6F 95
Churchdale Rd. S12—3F 113
Church Dri. S72—3F 11
Churchfield. S70—5G 13
Churchfield Av. S72—1H 15
Churchfield Av. S75—5A 6
Churchfield Clo. DN5—1A 32
Churchfield Clo. S75—5A 6
Churchfield Ct. S70—5G 13
Churchfield Cres. S72—1H 15
Church Field Dri. S66—5F 81
Church Field La. S62—5C 52
Churchfield La. S75—5A 6
Church Fields. S61—2G 77
Church Fields Rd. DN11—3E 63
Churchfield Ter. S72—1H 15
Church Gro. S71—3C 14
Church Hill. S60—2A 92
Church Hill. S71—2F 9
Churchill Av. DN5—3A 32
Churchill Av. S66—3G 83
Churchill Rd. DN1—3E 33
Churchill Rd. S10—2A 98
Churchill Rd. S30—2B 140
Church La. DN3—1G 21
Church La. DN4—5C 48
(Bessacarr)
Church La. DN4—4F 45
(Warmsworth)
Church La. DN5—1G 43

Church La. DN6—1E 17
Church La. DN11—6H 61
(in two parts)
Church La. S9—5B 88
Church La. S12—4C 114
(Hackenthorpe)
Church La. S13—1B 114
Church La. S17—3D 120
Church La. S19—4G 115
Church La. S31—1D 116
(Aston)
Church La. S31—4D 106
(Dinnington)
Church La. S31—3C 126
(Killamarsh)
Church La. S40—2A 138
Church La. S44—2F 139
Church La. S60—1E 103
Church La. S63—5E 41
Church La. S65—4H 71
Church La. S66—4H 81
(Bramley)
Church La. S66—5F 83
(Maltby)
Church La. S66—5F 81
(Wickersley)
Church La. S70—5G 13
(Barnsley)
Church La. S70—1E 37
(Worsbrough)
Church La. S75—2C 50
Church Meadows. S44—2F 139
Church Rd. DN3—1G 21
(Barnby Dun)
Church Rd. DN3—3D 20
(Kirk Sandall)
Church Rd. DN11—6H 61
Church Rd. DN12—1C 58
(Denaby Main)
Church Rd. DN12—2B 60
(Edlington)
Churchside. S41—6D 138
Churchside. S44—2F 139
Churchside La. S41—6D 138
Church St. DN1—5C 32
Church St. DN3—3E 35
Church St. DN5—1A 32
Church St. DN12—3E 59
Church St. S1—3E 5 & 2E 99
Church St. S6—6C 84
Church St. S18—2E 129
(Dronfield)
Church St. S30—6E 65
(Ecclesfield)
Church St. S30—2C 72
(Oughtibridge)
Church St. S31—5E 125
(Eckington)
Church St. S31—5F 117
(Wales)
Church St. S43—3E 133
(Brimington)
Church St. S43—1C 134
(Staveley)
Church St. S44—2F 139
Church St. S60—3D 78
Church St. S61—3A 68
(Greasbrough)
Church St. S61—2G 77
(Kimberworth)
Church St. S62—3E 69
Church St. S63—1A 42
(Bolton-upon-Dearne)
Church St. S63—1E 29
(Thurnscoe)
Church St. S63—5E 41
(Wath upon Dearne)

Church St. S64—1F 57
(Mexborough)
Church St. S64—2H 55
(Swinton)
Church St. S66—5B 94
Church St. S70—5G 13
Church St. S71—4F 9
(Carlton)
Church St. S71—2E 9
(Royston)
Church St. S72—2F 11
(Brierley)
Church St. S72—1H 15
(Cudworth)
Church St. S73—4F 27
(Darfield)
Church St. S73—1F 39
(Wombwell)
Church St. S74—6C 38
(Elsecar)
Church St. S74—4B 38
(Jump)
Church St. S75—5C 6
(Darton)
Church St. S75—4C 12
(Gawber)
Church St. S75—4G 7
(Mapplewell)
Church St. Clo. S63—1E 29
Church St. N. S41—1A 132
Church St. S. S40—6A 138
(in two parts)
Church St. W. S40—3E 137
Church Ter. S75—2A 22
Church View. DN1—5C 32
Church View. DN11—6H 61
Church View. S13—1C 114
Church View. S31—6D 104
(Aston)
Church View. S31—2C 126
(Killamarsh)
Church View. S31—2B 118
(Todwick)
Church View. S40—3E 137
Church View. S64—2A 56
Church View. S65—4D 70
Church View. S66—5F 81
Church View. S72—1H 15
Church View. S73—4G 27
Church View. S74—6F 37
Church View. S75—4E 13
Church Wlk. DN12—1C 58
Church Wlk. S40—2A 138
(off Stephenson Pl.)
Church Wlk. S63—1E 29
(off Church St.)
Church Way. DN1—5C 32
Church Way. S40—2A 138
Churston Rd. S40—2F 137
Cinder Bri. Rd. S61—3C 68
Cinderhill La. S8—1F 123
Cinder Hill La. S30—1B 74
Cinderhill Rd. S61—5G 67
Cinder La. S31—2D 126
Circle, The. DN11—4C 62
Circle, The. S2—4D 100
Circle, The. S30—6C 50
Circuit, The. DN6—1B 16
Circular Rd. S41—5B 138
Circular Rd. S43—3B 134
City Plaza. S1—3D 4
City Rd. S2 & S12—3H 99
Clanricarde St. S71—3G 13
Clara St. S61—3H 77
Clarefield Rd. S9—3D 88
Clarehurst Rd. S73—3E 27
Clarell Gdns. DN4—2C 48
Claremont Cres. S10—2B 98

Claremont Pl. S10—2B 98
Claremont St. S61—3H 77
Clarence Av. DN4—3B 46
Clarence La. S3—4D 98
Clarence Pl. S66—3G 83
Clarence Rd. S6—3H 85
Clarence Rd. S40—2H 137
Clarence Rd. S71—3B 14
Clarence Sq. S31—4G 107
Clarence St. S31—4G 107
Clarence St. S40—2H 137
Clarence St. S63—4D 40
Clarence Ter. S63—1G 29
(off Clarke St.)
Clarendon Ct. S11—5E 97
Clarendon Dri. S10—5E 97
Clarendon Rd. S10—6E 97
Clarendon Rd. S43—5A 134
Clarendon Rd. S65—2F 79
Clarendon St. S70—6F 13
Clark Av. DN4—1E 47
Clark Av. DN12—5B 60
Clarke Av. S66—5C 94
Clarke Dell. S10—4B 98
Clarke Dri. S10—4B 98
Clarkegrove Rd. S10—4B 98
Clarkehouse Rd. S10—4A 98
Clarke Sq. S2—5D 98
Clarke St. S10—6A 4 & 3C 98
Clarke St. S63—1G 29
Clarke St. S75—4F 13
Clark Gro. S6—5D 84
Clarkson Av. S40—5H 137
Clarkson St. S10—2C 98
Clarkson St. S70—4C 24
Clark St. S74—4H 37
Clarney Av. S73—3D 26
Clarney Pl. S73—3E 27
Claycliffe Av. S75—3B 12
Claycliffe Rd. S75—1B 12
Claycliffe Rd. Ind. Est. S75
—2C 12
Claycliffe Ter. S63—4G 29
Claycliffe Ter. S70—1F 23
Clayfield Av. S64—6H 43
Clayfield Clo. S64—6H 43
Clayfield Ct. S64—6H 43
Clayfield Rd. S62—4D 52
Clayfield Rd. S64—6H 43
Clayfield View. S64—5H 43
Clay Flat La. DN11—5D 62
Clay La. DN2—5A 20
Clay La. S1—5E 5
Clay La. W. DN2—6A 20
Clay Pit La. S62—2G 69
Clay Pits La. S30—2A 140.
Clayroyd. S70—5B 24
Clay St. S9—4B & 4C 88
(in two parts)
Clayton Av. S63—1D 28
Clayton Cres. S19—5E 115
Clayton Dri. S63—1D 28
Clayton Hollow. S19—5E 115
Clayton La. S63—1D 28
Clayton St. S41—3B 138
Clay Wheels La. S6—5H 73
Claywood Dri. S2—5H 5 & 3G 99
Claywood Rd. S2—5H 5 &
(in two parts)   3G & 4G 99
Clayworth Dri. DN4—4A 48
Clear View. S72—5G 11
Cleeve Hill Gdns. S19—5D 114
Clematis Rd. S5—6B 76
Clementson Rd. S10—1A 98
Clement St. S9—5D 88
Clement St. S61—3G 77
Clevedon Cres. DN5—6H 17
Clevedon Way. S66—2H 83

Cookson St. DN4—3B 46
Cooks Rd. S19— 5G 115
Cooks Wood Rd. S3- 4E 87
Coombe Pl. S10—2A 98
Coombe Rd. S10— 2A 98
Co-operative Cotts S43
　　　　　　　　—4E 135
Co-operative Cotts S72
　　　　　　　　—2F 11
Co-operative St. S63– 4G 29
　(Goldthorpe)
Co-operative St. S63– 4D 40
　(Wath upon Dearne)
Co-operative St. S72—1G 15
Cooper Rd. S75—5A 6
Cooper Row. S75—3B 22
　(off Stainborough Row.)
Coopers Ter. DN1—6D 32
Cooper St. DN4—2E 47
Copeland Rd. S73—6A 26
Cope St. S70—2H 23
Copley Av. DN12—3C 58
Copley Cres. DN5—3E 31
Copley Pl. S61—2A 78
Copley Rd. DN1—5D 32
Copley St. S8—1E 111
Copper Beech Cres. S66– 6E 83
Copper Clo. S70—1H 23
Copper St. S3—1D 4 & 1E 99
Coppice Clo. S30—2B 140
Coppice Clo. S41—6D 138
Coppice Gdns. S61—5B 68
Coppice La. S6—1B 96
Coppice Rd. DN6—5D 16
Coppice Rd. S10—2B 96
Coppice, The. S61—5E 67
Coppice View. S10—2F 97
Coppins Clo. S66—3H 81
Coppin Sq. S5—2D 74
Coral Clo. S31—3A 104
Coral Dri. S31—3A 104
Coral Pl. S31—3A 104
Coral Way. S31—3A 104
Corby Rd. S4—2B 88
Corby St. S4—6H & 5H 87
　(in two parts)
Cordwell Av. S41—3E 131
Cordwell Clo. S43—3B 134
Corker Bottoms La. S2
　　　　　　　　—2B 100
Corker Rd. S12—1C 112
Cork La. S70—4E 25
Corn Hill. DN12—4G 59
Cornish St. S6—6D 86
Cornwall Av. S43—3F 133
Cornwall Clo. S43—3F 133
Cornwall Clo. S71—3B 14
Cornwall Dri. S43—3F 133
Cornwall Rd. DN2—4H 33
Cornwell Clo. S62—5C 54
Coronach Way. DN11—5C 62
Coronation Av. S31—3F 107
　(Dinnington)
Coronation Av. S31—5G 117
　(Kiveton Park)
Coronation Av. S71—1G 9
Coronation Av. S72—2B 10
Coronation Bri. S61 & S60
　　　　　　　　—3B 78
Coronation Ct. S64—5E 43
Coronation Cres. S70—2D 36
Coronation Dri. S63—1H 41
Coronation Dri. S70—2D 36
Coronation Gdns. DN4—5E 45
Coronation Rd. DN4—4B 46
Coronation Rd. S30—3D 140
Coronation Rd. S43—3E 133
Coronation Rd. S62—1A 70

Coronation Rd S63　5G 41
Coronation Rd S64　2C 56
Coronation Rd S74　5H 37
Coronation Rd S75– 3A 12
Coronation St S63—2G 29
Coronation St S71—3C 14
Coronation St S73—3F 27
Coronation Ter S71—1F 25
Corporation St S3
　　　　　　　　—1E 5 & 1E 99
Corporation St S41—2B 138
Corporation St S60—3D 78
Corporation St S70—1A 24
Cortina Rise S73—3C 26
Cortonwood Ho. DN1—1C 46
　(off Bond Clo.)
Cortworth La. S62—4F 53
Cortworth Rd. S11—3G 109
Corve Way S40—6B 130
Corwen Pl S13—1A 114
Cossey Rd S4—5H 87
Coteral Cres DN4—2D 48
Cotleigh Av. S12—4A 114
Cotleigh Clo. S12—4A 114
Cotleigh Cres. S12—4A 114
Cotleigh Dri. S12—4A 114
Cotleigh Gdns. S12—4A 114
Cotleigh Pl. S12—4A 114
Cotleigh Rd. S12—4A 114
Cotleigh Way. S12—4A 114
Cotswold Av. S30—2C 64
Cotswold Clo. S40—6E 131
Cotswold Cres. S60—2A 92
Cotswold Dri. DN5—2C 44
Cotswold Dri. S31—6C 104
Cotswold Gdns. DN5—2H 31
Cotswold Rd. S6—3H 85
Cottage Clo. S43—4E 133
Cottage La. S11—2C 108
Cottam Clo. S60—2A 92
Cottam Rd. S30—6A 50
Cottenham Rd. S65—2F 79
Cotterhill La. S43—4E 133
Cottesmore Clo. S75—4E 13
Cottingham St. S9—1B 100
Cotton Mill Hill. S42—6A 136
Cotton Mill Rw. S3
　　　　　　　　—1E 5 & 6E 87
Cotton Mill Wlk. S3—6E 87
Cotton St. S3—1E 5 & 6E 87
Coulston St. S3—1F 5 & 1F 99
Coultas Av. S30—5F 141
Countess Rd. S1—4E 99
County Way. S70—5H 13
Coupeland Rd. S65—1A 80
Coupe Rd. S3—5F 87
Court Clo. DN5—3F 31
Court Pl. S43—3A 134
Coventry Gro. DN2—2H 33
Coventry Rd. S9—6E 89
Cover Clo. S62—4H 51
Coverdale Rd. S7—2C 110
Cover Dri. S73—3F 27
Coverleigh Rd. S63—1F 55
Coward Dri. S30—2D 72
Cow Ho. La. DN3—3G 35
Cow La. S11—6G 97
　(Greystones)
Cow La. S11—4G 109
　(Parkhead)
Cow La. S19—6H 115
Cow La. S43—2E 133
Cowley Dri. S30—3G 65
Cowley Gdns. S19—1E 125
Cowley Hill. S30—3G 65
Cowley La. S18—4A to 3D 128
Cowley La. S30—2F 65
Cowley Pl. DN3—3D 20

Cowley Rd S30—3D 72
Cowley View Rd. S30—3F 65
Cowlishaw Rd. S11—5A 98
Cowood St. S64—1D 56
Cowper Av. S6—3B 74
Cowper Cres. S6—3B 74
Cowper Dri. S6—3B 74
Cowper Dri. S65—5H 79
Cowper Rd. S64—6F 43
Cowpingle La. S43—2E 133
Cowrakes Clo S60—2A 92
Cow Rakes La. S60—2A 92
Cowslip Rd. S5—6B 76
Cox Pl. S6—2F 85
Cox Rd. S6—2F 85
Crabtree Av. S5—3G 87
Crabtree Clo. S5—2E 87
Crabtree Cres. S5—2F 87
Crabtree Dri. S5—2G 87
Crabtree La. S5—2G 87
Crabtree Pl. S5—2G 87
Crabtree Rd. S5—2F 87
Cradley Dri. S31—6C 104
Cradock Rd. S2—6A 100
Craganour Pl. DN12—2B 58
Cragdale Gro. S19—2D 124
Craglands Gro. S40—6C 130
Crags Rd. DN12—2D 58
Crag View Clo. S30—1D 72
Crag View Cres. S30—1D 72
Cragholme Cres. DN2—2A 34
Craig Wlk. S66—4H 81
Craithie Rd. DN2—5F 33
Crakehall Rd. S30—4F 65
Cramfit Clo. S31—1F 119
Cramfit Rd. S31—6C 106
Cranborne Rd. S41—4G 131
Cranbrook Rd. DN1—4E 33
Cranbrook St. S70—2F 23
Crane Dri. S61—2G 77
Crane Moor Clo. DN5—1G 43
Crane Rd. S61—5G 67
Crane Well La. S63—1C 42
Cranfield Clo. DN3—4F 35
Cranford Ct. S19—5A 114
Cranford Dri. S19—4A 114
Cranford Gdns. S71—1D 8
Cranleigh Gdns. DN6—2C 16
Cranston Clo. S71—3D 14
Cranswick Way. DN12—3G 59
Cranworth Clo. S65—2G 79
Cranworth Pl. S3—5F 87
Cranworth Rd. S3—5F 87
Cranworth Rd. S65—1F 79
Craven Clo. DN4—3C 48
Craven Clo. S9—6E 89
Craven Clo. S71—1D 8
Craven Rd. S41—6H 131
Craven St. S3—1B 4 & 1D 98
Craven St. S62—4F 69
Crawford Rd. S8—3D 110
Crawshaw Av. S8—1B 122
Crawshaw Gro. S8—1B 122
Crawshaw Rd. DN4—1A 46
Cream St. S2—4F 99
Crecy Av. DN2—5A 34
Creighton Av. S62—2H 69
Cresacre Av. DN5—1G 43
Crescent E., The. S66—2G 81
Crescent End, The. S66—5B 94
Crescent Rd. S7—6C 98
Crescent, The. DN3—4G 35
　(Armthorpe)
Crescent, The. DN3—5E 21
　(Edenthorpe)
Crescent, The. DN6—3B 16
Crescent, The. DN12—3C 58
　(Conisbrough)

Crescent, The. DN12—2B 60
　(Edlington)
Crescent, The. S17—4E 121
Crescent, The. S31—4G 107
　(Dinnington)
Crescent, The. S42—6D 138
Crescent, The. S43—4C 132
Crescent, The. S63—6F 29
Crescent, The. S64—3H 55
Crescent, The. S65—2E 79
Crescent, The. S66—5C 94
Crescent, The. S72—6B 10
Crescent, The. S75—3D 12
Crescent W., The. S66—2F 81
Cresswell Rd. S9—1E 101
Cresswell Rd. S64—1B 56
Cresswell St. S75—5E 13
Crest Rd. S5—5F 75
Crestwood Ct. S5—5G 75
Crestwood Gdns. S5—5G 75
Creswell St. S64—1D 56
Creswick Av. S5—2D 74
Creswick Clo. S40—5D 136
Creswick Clo. S65—1B 80
Creswick Greave. S30—2C 74
Creswick Greave Clo. S5
　　　　　　　　—2C 74
Creswick La. S30—1C 74
Creswick Rd. S65—1B 80
Creswick St. S6—5B & 5B 86
　(in two parts)
Creswick Way. S6—5B 86
Crewe Hall. S10—4A 98
Crich Av. S71—6C 8
Crich Rd. S43—4A 134
Cricket Inn Cres. S2—2A 100
Cricket Inn Gdns. S2—1G 99
Cricket Inn Rd. S2—1G 99
　(in two parts)　& 1A 100
Cricket La. S30—1G 75
Cricket View Rd. S62—4H 51
Crimicar Av. S10—5B 96
Crimicar Clo. S10—6C 96
Crimicar Dri. S10—5B 96
Crimicar La. S10—4B 96
Crimpsall St. DN4—1B 46
Cripps Av. DN11—4E 63
Cripps Clo. S66—5H 83
Crispin Clo. S12—3C 112
Crispin Dri. S12—3C 112
Crispin Gdns. S12—3C 112
Crispin Rd. S12—3C 112
Crochley Clo. DN4—2D 48
Croft Av. S71—2D 8
Croft Bldgs. S1—2D 4
Croft La. S11—4F 109
Croft Lea. S18—1A 128
Crofton Av. S6—1H 85
Crofton Clo. S18—2D 128
Crofton Dri. S63—6E 29
Crofton Rise. S18—2D 128
Crofton Rise. S30—1B 64
Croft Rd. DN4—6G 45
Croft Rd. S6—5D 84
Croft Rd. S12—2D 112
Croft Rd. S60—2B 90
Croft Rd. S70—2C 24
Croft Rd. S74—4H 37
Crofts Dri. S65—5C 70
Crofts, The. S60—3D 78
Crofts, The. S66—6F 81
Croft St. S61—3B 68
Croft St. S70—4A 24
Croft, The. DN5—4E 19
Croft, The. DN12—4E 59
Croft, The. S60—6C 90
Croft, The. S64—3H 55
Croft, The. S74—1C 52

155

Darrington Pl. S71—4E 15
Darton Hall Clo. S75—4D 6
Darton Hall Dri. S75—4D 6
Darton La. S75—5D 6
Darton St. S70—1D 24
Dartree Wlk. S73—3D 26
Dart Sq. S3—1C 98
Darwall Clo. S30—5B 50
Darwent La. S30—5B 72
Darwin Av. S40—6G 131
Darwin Clo. S10—3F 97
Darwin La. S10—3F 97
Darwin Rd. S6—1H 85
Darwin Rd. S40—1H 137
Darwynn Av. S64—2G 55
Davian Way. S40—5G 137
David Clo. S13—6D 102
David La. S10—6A 96
Davies Dri. S64—4B 56
Davis St. S65—2G 79
Davy Dri. S66—3F 83
Dawber La. S31—2D 126
Daw Croft Av. S70—4A 24
Dawlands Clo. S2—3D 100
Dawlands Dri. S2—4D 100
Daw La. DN5—5B 18
Dawson Av. S62—5C 54
Dawson La. S63—1E 55
Dawson Ter. S31—5H 117
Daw Wood. DN5—4C 18
Daykin Clo. S75—5B 6
Daylands Av. DN12—4C 58
Day St. S70—1G 23
Deacon Cres. DN11—4C 62
Deacon Cres. S66—5G 83
Deacons Way. S71—4C 14
Deadman's Hole La. S61
—4A 78
Deakins Wlk. S10—4F 97
Dean Clo. DN5—1F 45
Deane Field View. S19—5D 114
Deanhead Ct. S19—5A 114
Deanhead Dri. S19—5H 113
Dean La. S65—3C 80
Deansfield Clo. DN3—4F 35
Dean St. S70—6F 13
Deans Way. S71—3C 14
Dearden St. S30—1F 75
Dearne Clo. S73—2H 39
Dearne Ct. S9—1C 88
Dearne Hall Rd. S75—1B 12
Dearne Rd. S63—3G & 2H 41
Dearne Rd. S73—3A 40
Dearne Rd. Flatlets. S63—2H 41
Dearne St. DN12—2F 59
Dearne St. S9—1C 88
Dearne St. S75—4C 6
Dearne View. S63—4G 29
Dearneway. S63—5F 41
Dearnley View. S75—3F 13
Deben Clo. S40—5E 137
Decoy Bank N. DN4—2D 46
Decoy Bank S. DN4—3D 46
Deepdale Rd. S61—3G 77
Deep La. S5—2A 76
Deerlands Av. S5—3C 74
Deerlands Clo. S5—3C 74
Deerlands Mt. S5—3C 74
Deerlands Rd. S40—2D 136
Deer Leap Dri. S65—5E 71
Deer Pk. Clo. S6—5E 85
Deer Pk. Pl. S6—5E 85
Deer Pk. Rd. S6—5E 85
Deer Pk. Rd. S65—4E 71
Deer Pk. View. S6—5F 85
Deer Pk. Way. S6—5F 85
De Houton Clo. S31—2A 118
Deightonby St. S63—1G 29

De Lacy Dri. S70—4A 24
Delamere Clo. S19—5G 115
Delamere Gro. S19—5G 115
Delf Edge. S30—1G 141
Delf St. S2—6F 99
Della Av. S70—1F 23
Dell Av. S72—5G 11
Dell Cres. DN4—2H 45
Dell, The. S40—2D 136
Delmar Way. S66—3F 81
Delph Bank. S40—5G 137
Delph Ho. Rd. S10—2F 97
Delta Pl. S65—2H 79
Delta Way. S66—3H 83
Delves Av. S12—3C 114
Delves Clo. S12—3C 114
Delves Clo. S40—4F 137
Delves Dri. S12—4C 114
Delves La. S31—4B 116
Delves Pl. S12—4B 114
Delves Rd. S12—4B 114
Delves Rd. S31—3B 126
Delves Ter. S12—4C 114
Denaby Av. DN12—4B 58
Denaby La. DN12 & S65
—5E 57 to 1A 58
Den Bank Av. S10—2E 97
Den Bank Clo. S10—2F 97
Den Bank Cres. S10—2E 97
Den Bank Dri. S10—2E 97
Denby Rd. S71—6B 8
Denby Dri. DN5—5A 18
Denby St. S2—4D 98
Denby Way. S66—4A 82
Dene Clo. S66—5G 81
Dene Cres. S65—1H 79
Denehall Rd. DN3—4E 21
Dene La. S1—6B 4 & 3D 98
Dene Rd. S65—1H 79
Denham Rd. S11—4C 98
Denholme Clo. S3—6F 87
Denison Rd. DN4—1B 46
Denman Rd. S63—5D 40
Denman St. S65—1E 79
Denmark Rd. S2—1F 111
Denson Clo. S2—1F 111
Dent La. S12—5H 113
Dentons Grn. La. DN3—3D 20
Denton St. S71—5H 13
Derby Pl. S2—1G 111
Derby Rd. DN2—1A 34
Derby Rd. S40—6A 138
Derbyshire Ct. S8—4F 111
Derbyshire La. S8—2D 110
Derby St. S2—1F 111
Derby St. S70—6F 13
Derby Ter. S2—1G 111
Derriman Av. S11—3H 109
Derriman Clo. S11—3H 109
Derriman Dri. S11—3H 109
Derriman Glen. S11—3G 109
Derriman Gro. S11—3H 109
Derry Gro. S63—2E 29
Derwent Clo. S18—6F 123
Derwent Clo. S31—6F 107
Derwent Clo. S71—6D 8
Derwent Ct. S17—4G 121
Derwent Ct. S60—1F 91
Derwent Cres. S41—4F 131
Derwent Cres. S60—4B 90
Derwent Cres. S71—6D 8
Derwent Dri. DN3—4D 20
Derwent Dri. S30—2C 64
Derwent Dri. S64—5G 43
Derwent Gdns. S63—5G 29
Derwent Pl. DN5—2D 44
Derwent Pl. S73—2H 39
Derwent Rd. S18—6F 123

Derwent Rd. S61—4A 68
Derwent Rd. S64—5G 43
Derwent Rd. S71—6C 8
Derwent Row. S2—1H 99
Derwent St. S2—1H 99
Derwent Ter. S64—5E 43
Derwent Way. S63—3B 40
De Sutton Pl. S31—4H 127
Deveron Rd. S19—2F 125
Devizes Clo. S40—5H 137
Devon Ct. DN12—3B 58
Devon Dri. S43—3F 133
Devon Rd. S4—3G 87
Devonshire Av. E. S41—5C 138
Devonshire Clo. S17—3F 121
Devonshire Clo. S18—3D 128
Devonshire Clo. S41—3H 131
Devonshire Clo. S43—1C 134
Devonshire Ct. S17—3F 121
Devonshire Ct. S43—4D 132
Devonshire Dri. S17—2E 121
Devonshire Dri. S31—5E 107
Devonshire Dri. S75—3F 13
Devonshire Glen. S17—3E 121
Devonshire Gro. S17—3E 121
Devonshire La. S1
—4C 4 & 2D 98
Devonshire Rd. DN2—4H 33
Devonshire Rd. S17—2E 121
Devonshire Rd. S66—3G 83
Devonshire Rd. E. S41—5C 138
Devonshire St. S3
—4B 4 & 2D 98
Devonshire St. S41—2A 138
Devonshire St. S43—3E 133
(Brimington)
Devonshire St. S43—1C 134
(Staveley)
Devonshire St. S61—3B 78
Devonshire Ter. Rd. S17
—2D 120
Dewar Dri. S7—3A 110
Dewhill Av. S60—2H 91
Dial Ho. Rd. S6—3G 85
Dial Way. S5—5G 75
Diamond St. S73—6B 26
Dickan Gdns. DN3—4H 35
Dickenson Ct. S30—2D 64
Dickenson Rd. S41—4B 138
Dickens Rd. S62—6H 55
Dickey La. S6—4G 73
Dickinson Pl. S70—2H 23
Dickinson Rd. S5—2H 75
Dickinson Rd. S70—2H 23
Didcot Clo. S40—5H 137
Digby Clo. S61—1G 77
Dike Hill. S62—4A 52
Dikelands Mt. S30—1B 64
Dillington Rd. S70—2H 23
Dillington Sq. S70—2H 23
Dillington Ter. S70—2H 23
Dingle Bank. S44—4E 139
Dingle La. S44—4E 139
Dinmore Clo. DN4—1G 61
Dinnington Rd. S8—3D 110
Dinnington Rd. S31
—1B 118 & 5A 106
Dirleton Dri. DN4—5F 45
Disraeli Gro. S66—3E 83
Distillery Side. S74—1D 52
Ditchingham St. S4—5G 87
Division La. S1—4D 4 & 2E 99
Division St. S1—4C 4 & 2D 98
Division St. S43—3A 134
Dixon Cres. DN4—4H 45
Dixon La. S1—2G 5 & 1F 99
Dixon Rd. DN12—4A 60
Dixon Rd. S6—2H 85

Dixon Rd. S41—3B 138
Dixon St. S6—6D 86
Dixon St. S65—2E 79
Dobbin Hill. S11—1G 109
Dobbin La. S18—6A 128
Dobcroft Av. S7—4H 109
Dobcroft Clo. S11—3G 109
Dobcroft Rd. S11 & S7—3G 109
Dobie St. S70—1H 23
Dobroyd Ter. S74—4B 38
Dobson Pl. S43—5H 133
Dobsyke Clo. S70—4D 24
Dockin Mill Rd. DN1—5D 32
Dock Wlk. S40—3G 137
Doctor La. S9—5D 88
Dodd St. S6—4A 86
Dodson Dri. S13—3H 101
Dodsworth St. S64—1D 56
Dodworth Rd. S70—6C 12
Doe La. S70—6G 23
Doe Quarry La. S31—3F 107
Doe Quarry Ter. S31—4G 107
Doe Royd Cres. S5—4C 74
Doe Royd Dri. S5—4C 74
Doe Royd La. S5—4C 74
Dog Croft La. DN5—5G 19
Dog Hill. S72—2B 10
Dog Hill Dri. S72—2C 10
Dog Kennels Hill. S31—5D 118
Dog Kennels La. S31—5D 118
Dog La. S70—6G 13
(off Shambles St.)
Dolcliffe Clo. S64—6D 42
Dolcliffe Rd. S64—6E 43
Doles Av. S71—2D 8
Doles Cres. S71—2D 8
Doles La. S60—3A 92
Doleswood Dri. S31—1E 107
Domine La. S60—3D 78
Dominoe Gro. S12—2F 113
Don Av. S6—6G 73
Donavon Rd. S5—6C 74
Doncaster Ga. S65—3E 79
Doncaster La. DN6—2E 17
Doncaster Pl. S65—2G 79
Doncaster Rd. DN3—3D 34
(Armthorpe)
Doncaster Rd. DN3—3F 49
(Branton)
Doncaster Rd. DN3—5B to
(Kirk Sandall)   2D 20
Doncaster Rd. DN5—3A 16
(Adwick-le-Street)
Doncaster Rd. DN5—1H 43
(Barnburgh)
Doncaster Rd. DN5—1F 43
(Harlington)
Doncaster Rd. DN5—5A 44
(Sprotbrough)
Doncaster Rd. DN5—2H 17
(Toll Bar)
Doncaster Rd. DN12—3F 59
(Conisbrough)
Doncaster Rd. DN12—1A to
(Denaby Main)   2D 58
Doncaster Rd. S63—4G 29
(Goldthorpe)
Doncaster Rd. S63—5G 41
(Wath upon Dearne)
Doncaster Rd. S64—1F 57
Doncaster Rd. S65—6A 70
(Dalton, Thrybergh &
Hooton Roberts)
Doncaster Rd. S65—3E 79
(Rotherham)
Doncaster Rd. S70—1A 24
Doncaster Rd. S71
—1E 25 to 2C 26

157

Ebenezer Pl. S74—6C 38
Ebenezer St. S3—6E 87
Eben St. S9—1C 88
Ecclesall Rd. S11
—6H 97 to 4D 98
Ecclesall Rd. S. S11
—3E to 1H 109
Eccles Dri. DN12—5B 60
Ecclesfield Rd. S5
—1H 75 to 4D 76
Ecclesfield Rd. S30—2F 65
Eccles St. S9—5D 76
Eccleston Rd. DN3—2E 21
Eckington Rd. S18—5G 123
Eckington Rd. S19—1F 125
(in two parts)   to 6F 115
Eckington Rd. S43—1D 134
Eckington Way. S19
—3D 114 to 2F 125
Edale Ct. S41—4G 131
Edale Rise. S75—2A 22
Edale Rd. S11—1G 109
Edale Rd. S61—3H 77
Edderthorpe La. S73—1E 27
Eden Dri. S6—3E 85
Edenfield Clo. S71—1D 14
Eden Field Rd. DN3—5E 21
Eden Gro. DN4—1A 46
Eden Gro. S31—5B 104
Eden Gro. Rd. DN3—5E 21
Edenhall Rd. S2—6B 100
Edensor Ct. S43—3A 134
Edensor Rd. S5—1F 87
Eden Ter. S64—5E 43
Edgar La. DN11—4B 62
Edgar St. S4—4H 87
Edge Bank. S7—1C 110
Edgebrook Rd. S7—1B 110
Edgecliffe Pl. S71—2A 14
Edge Clo. S6—3A 74
Edgedale Rd. S7—2C 110
Edgefield Rd. S7—2C 110
Edge Grn. DN3—3D 20
Edgehill Rd. DN2—2A 34
Edge Hill Rd. S7—1B 110
Edgehill Rd. S75—3F 7
Edge La. S6—3A 74
Edgemount Rd. S7—2C 110
Edge Well Clo. S6—3A 74
Edge Well Cres. S6—3A 74
Edge Well Dri. S6—4A 74
Edge Well La. S6—3H 73
Edge Well Pl. S6—3A 74
Edge Well Rise. S6—3A 74
Edge Well Way. S6—3A 74
(off Edge Well Cres.)
Edinburgh Av. S63—1H 41
Edinburgh Clo. S71—3B 14
Edinburgh Dri. S31—6D 106
Edinburgh Rd. S41—6H 131
Edinburgh Rd. S74—4A 38
Edith Ter. DN5—2G 31
Edith Wlk. S6—5C 86
Edlington La. DN12 & DN4
—6E 45
Edlington Riding. DN12—4C 60
Edmonton Clo. S75—5C 12
Edmund Av. S17—3A 122
Edmund Av. S60—4D 90
Edmund Clo. S17—3B 122
Edmund Dri. S17—3B 122
Edmund Rd. S2—5F 99
Edmunds Rd. S70—5C 24
Edmund St. S41—3H 131
Edmund St. S70—5A 24
Edna St. S63—1A 42
(Bolton-upon-Dearne)
Edna St. S63—5H 41
(Wath upon Dearne)
Edstone Dri. S31—5B 104
Edward Rd. S9—4C 88
Edward Rd. S63—5E 29
(Goldthorpe)
Edward Rd. S63—3C 40
(Wath upon Dearne)
Edward St. DN3—2D 34
Edward St. DN5—6B 18
Edward St. DN11—4B 62
Edward St. S3—2B 4 & 1D 98
Edward St. S30—3D 140
Edward St. S31—4F 107
(Dinnington)
Edward St. S31—6D 124
(Eckington)
Edward St. S43—3A 134
Edward St. S63—1E 29
Edward St. S64—1B 56
Edward St. S73—4E 27
(Darfield)
Edward St. S73—6C 26
(Wombwell)
Edward St. S74—5H 37
Edward St. S75—5G 7
Edward St. Flats. S3
—2B 4 & 1D 98
Edwin Av. S40—5F 137
Edwin Rd. DN6—3C 16
Edwin Rd. S2—1G 111
Effingham La. S4—1H 5 & 1G 99
Effingham Rd. S4 & S9—6H 87
Effingham Sq. S65—2D 78
Effingham St. S4
—1H 5 & 1G 99 to 6H 87
Effingham St. S65—2E 79
(In two parts)
Egerton La. S1—5B 4 & 3D 98
Egerton Rd. S18—1F 129
Egerton Rd. S31—6B 104
Egerton St. S1—6B 4 & 3D 98
Eggington Clo. DN4—4F 49
Egmanton Rd. S71—4B 8
Eilam Clo. S61—1G 77
Eilam Rd. S61—1G 77
Ekin St. S60—6H 77
Eland Clo. DN11—3D 62
Elcroft Gdns. S19—5F 115
Elder Av. S31—2H 119
Elder Ct. S31—4A 126
Elder Dri. S66—3F 81
Elder Gro. DN12—4C 58
Eldertree Rd. S61—4B 66
Elder Way. S40—2A 138
Eldon Arc. S70—6H 13
(off Eldon St.)
Eldon Ct. S1—4C 4 & 2D 98
Eldon St. S65—1F 79
Eldon St. S1—4C 4 & 2D 98
Eldon St. S70—6H 13
Eldon St. N. S71—5H 13
Eleanor St. S9—5D 88
Elgin St. S10—2H 97
Elgitha Dri. S66—5A 94
Eliot Clo. S43—6F 133
Elizabeth Av. DN3—3E 21
Elizabeth Rd. S31—1B 116
Elizabeth St. S63—4G 29
Elizabeth St. S72—6G 11
Elizabeth Way. S60—3C 78
(off Vine Clo.)
Elkstone Rd. S40—6C 130
Elland Clo. S71—6A 8
Ella Rd. S4—4G 87
Ellenborough Rd. S6—3H 85
Ellen Tree Clo. S60—3B 90
Ellerker Av. DN4—1B 46
Ellers Av. DN4—3A 48
Ellers Cres. DN4—3A 48
Ellers Dri. DN4—3A 48
Ellershaw La. DN12—4C 58
Ellershaw Rd. DN12—4D 58
Ellers Rd. DN4—3A 48
Ellerton Gdns. DN4—2C 48
Ellerton Rd. S5—1H 87
Ellesmere Rd. S4—5G 87
Ellesmere Rd. N. S4—4G 87
Ellesmere Ter. S65—3F 79
Ellesmere Wlk. S4—4G 87
Ellington Ct. S70—2E 23
Ellin St. S1—6D 4 & 4E 99
Elliott Av. S73—2F 39
Elliott Clo. S63—4C 40
Elliott Dri. S43—5A 134
Elliott Dri. S61—5H 67
Elliott La. S30—4B 64
Elliott Rd. S6—1B 98
Elliottville St. S6—5A 86
Ellis Av. S63—1D 54
Ellis Cres. DN11—4C 62
Ellis Cres. S73—4A 40
Ellisons Rd. S31—1C 126
Ellison St. S3—1B 4 & 1D 98
(in two parts)
Ellis St. S3—1C 4 & 1D 98
Ellis St. S60—2C 90
Elliston Av. S75—4G 7
Ellorslie Dri. S30—3E 141
Elm Clo. DN3—2H 21
Elm Clo. S31—4A 126
Elm Clo. S41—4H 131
Elm Ct. S70—5B 24
Elm Cres. DN5—5C 18
Elm Cres. S19—1C 124
Elmdale Clo. S64—5B 56
Elm Dri. S31—4A 126
Elmfield Av. S5—5F 75
Elmfield Rd. DN1—1E 47
Elmfield Rd. DN11—5D 62
Elm Grn. La. DN12—3E 59
Elm Gro. S61—4B 68
Elmham Rd. DN4—2C 48
Elmham Rd. S9—1F 101
Elmhurst Dri. S65—5A 80
Elm La. S5—5F 75
Elmore Rd. S10—2A 98
Elm Pl. DN3—2E 35
Elm Pl. S40—3G 137
Elm Pl. S62—2G 69
Elm Pl. S71—2D 14
Elm Rise. S30—3D 64
Elm Rd. DN3—2E 35
Elm Rd. S19—3G 115
Elm Rd. S31—6H 125
Elm Rd. S64—5C 42
Elm Row. S71—6B 14
Elmsdale. S70—5B 24
Elm St. S43—2G 133
Elm St. S74—1F 51
Elm Tree Clo. S31—2H 119
Elm Tree Cres. S18—6E 123
Elmtree Rd. S61—4B 66
Elm Tree Rd. S66—4D 82
Elmview Rd. S9—5D 76
Elmville Av. S64—4A 56
Elm Wlk. S63—1F 29
Elm Way. S63—1G 55
Elmwood Av. DN6—1B 16
Elmwood Cres. DN3—3E 35
Elmwood Dri. S19—3D 124
Elsecar Ho. DN1—1C 46
Off Bond Clo.)
Elsecar Rd. S63—5A 40
Elsham Clo. S66—2H 81
Elstree Dri. S12—3D 112
Elstree Rd. S12—3D 112
Elsworth Clo. DN1—2C 46
Elton St. S40—3A 138
Elton View. S43—3B 134
Elvaston Clo. S18—2A 128
Elwis St. DN5—5B 32
Elwood Rd. S17—3A 122
Ely Rd. DN2—2F 33
Ely St. DN11—3C 62
Embankment. S10—2A 98
Embassy Ct. S2—3H 5
Emdale Dri. DN3—6D 20
Emerson Clo. S5—4F 75
Emerson Cres. S5—5F 75
Emerson Dri. S5—5F 75
Emily Clo. S71—5D 14
Emily Rd. S7—1C 110
Emley Dri. DN5—2E 31
Emley Ho. DN1—1C 46
(off St James St.)
Emmettfield Clo. S40—5H 137
Empire Rd. S7—6D 98
Empire Ter. S71—1F 9
Endcliffe Av. S10—4A 98
Endcliffe Cres. S10—4H 97
Endcliffe Edge. S10—4H 97
Endcliffe Glen Rd. S11—4A 98
Endcliffe Gro. Av. S10—4G 97
Endcliffe Hall Av. S10—4G 97
Endcliffe Rise Rd. S11—4A 98
Endcliffe Ter. Rd. S11—4A 98
Endcliffe Vale Av. S11—5A 98
Endcliffe Vale Rd. S10—4H 97
Endcliffe Way. DN2—2A 34
Endfield Rd. S5—1D 74
Endowood Rd. S7—5H 109
Endowood Rd. S40—5C 136
Enfield Pl. S13—3H 101
Enfield Rd. S41—6H 131
Engine La. S63—5H 29
Engine La. S72—4D 10 to 6F 11
Ennerdale Av. S19—3E 125
Ennerdale Clo. S18—2C 128
Ennerdale Clo. S31—6E 107
Ennerdale Clo. S64—5G 43
Ennerdale Cres. S41—4E 131
Ennerdale Dri. S19—3E 125
Ennerdale Rd. DN2—3A 34
Ennerdale Rd. S71—1H 25
Ennis Cres. DN2—4G 33
Entwhistle Rd. S30—6C 50
Epping Gdns. S19—5G 115
Epping Gro. S19—5G 115
Epsom Clo. S64—5F 43
Epsom Rd. DN4—1B 48
Erin Rd. S43—2D 134
Ernest Copley Ho. S30—1D 64
Errington Av. S2—1A 112
Errington Clo. S2—1A 112
Errington Cres. S2—1A 112
Errington Rd. S2—1A 112
Errington Rd. S40—5F 137
Errington Way. S2—6A 100
Erskine Cres. S2—6G 99
Erskine Rd. S2—6G 99
Erskine Rd. S65—1E 79
Erskine View. S2—1G 111
Eshton Ct. S75—3E 7
Eshton Wlk. S70—6F 13
(off Prospect St.)
Eskdale Clo. S6—1A 68
Eskdale Clo. S18—2C 128
Eskdale Dri. DN5—1H 31
Eskdale Rd. S6—1A 86
Eskdale Rd. S61—4H 67
Eskdale Rd. S71—1G 25
Eskdale Wlk. DN5—2E 31
Esperanto Pl. S1—3F 5

Essendine Cres. S8—4F 111
Essex Av. DN2—6H 33
Essex Clo. S31—4C 118
Essex Rd. S2—4H 99
Essex St. S70—2H 23
Estate Rd. S62—6E 55
Ettrick Clo. S40—6E 131
Etwall Clo. S40—5C 130
Etwall Way. S5—5G 75
Evans St. S3—6B 4
Evanston Gdns. DN4—3A 46
Eva Ratcliffe Ho. S5—1E 75
Eveline St. S72—1H 15
Evelyn Av. DN2—4H 33
Evelyn Rd. S10—2H 97
Evelyn St. S62—1H 69
Evelyn Ter. S70—1B 24
Everard Av. S17—4G 121
Everard Dri. S17—4G 121
Everard Glade. S17—4G 121
Everill Ga. La. S73—1H & 1H 39
(in two parts)
Everingham Clo. S5—6E 75
Everingham Cres. S5—6D 74
Everingham Rd. DN4—1C 48
Everingham Rd. S5—6E 75
Everson Clo. S66—2E 83
Everton Rd. S11—5A 98
Evesham Clo. S9—5D 76
Ewden Rd. S73—2H 39
Ewden Way. S75—6C 12
Ewers Rd. S61—3H 77
Ewood Dri. DN4—3C 48
Exchange Gateway. S1—3E 5
Exchange Pl. S2—2G 5
Exchange St. DN1—2D 46
Exchange St. S2—2G 5 & 1F 99
Exeter Dri. S3—6B 4 & 4D 98
Exeter Pl. S3—4D 98
Exeter Rd. DN2—3G 33
Exeter Way. S3—6A 4 & 3C 98
Exley Av. S6—5B 86
Eyam Clo. S75—2A 22
Eyam Rd. S10—2H 97
Eyncourt Rd. S5—6G 75
Eyre Gdns. S30—1B 64
Eyre La. S1—6E 5 & 3E 99
Eyre St. S1—6D 4 & 3E 99
Eyre St. E. S41—6C 138

Fabian Way. S66—5H 81
Factory La. DN1—6C 32
Factory St. S40—3F 137
Fairbank Rd. S5—2F 87
Fairbank View. S60—2A 92
Fairbarn Clo. S6—6E 85
Fairbarn Dri. S6—6E 85
Fairbarn Pl. S6—6E 85
Fairbarn Rd. S6—6E 85
Fairbarn Way. S6—6E 85
Fairburn Gdns. S30—3D 90
Fairburn Gro. S74—5D 38
Faircliff. DN5—2D 44
Fair Clo. S40—1G 137
Fairfax Rd. DN2—5H 33
Fairfax Rd. S2—5D 100
Fairfield. S63—6D 28
Fairfield. S70—2D 36
Fairfield Clo. DN4—5B 48
Fairfield Clo. S43—3D 132
Fairfield Ct. DN3—4F 35
Fairfield Rd. DN5—3H 31
Fairfield Rd. S40—1H 137
Fairford Clo. S40—6H 137
Fairleigh. S2—6C 100
Fairleigh Dri. S60—5E 79
Fairmount Gdns. S12—4A 114

Fairthorn Rd. S5—5H 75
Fairview. DN3—1D 20
Fair View Av. DN6—2B 16
Fairview Clo. S74—6G 37
Fair View Dri. S31—6C 104
Fairview Rd. S18—6E 123
Fairview Vs. DN3—1E 21
Fairway. S75—3C 22
Fairway Av. S75—3G 7
Fairways. S66—5F 81
Fairway, The. S10—4A 96
Fairways. S66—5F 81
Faith St. S71—1F 15
Falcon Ct. DN11—4E 63
Falcon Dri. S60—2F 103
Falcon Dri. S70—3D 36
Falconer La. S13—5F 103
Falcon Rd. S18—6G 123
Falcon St. S70—5G 13
Falcon Way. S31—6E 107
Falcon Yd. S40—2A 138
(off Low Pavement)
Falding St. S30—2F 65
Falding St. S60—3C 78
Falkland Rise. S18—3E 129
Falkland St. S11—1G 109
Fall Bank Ind. Est. S75—1B 22
Fallon Rd. S6—5D 84
Falmouth Rd. S7—2C 110
Falstaff Cres. S5—5D 74
Falstaff Gdns. S5—5D 74
Falstaff Rd S5—4D 74
Fane Cres. S31—5B 104
Fanny Av. S31—4C 126
Fan Rd. S43—2D 134
Fanshaw Bank. S18—2E 129
Fanshaw Rd. S18—1F 129
Fanshaw Rd. S31—6H 125
Faraday Rd. S9—5A 88
Faranden Rd. S9—6C 88
Far Cres. S65—2H 79
Far Croft. S63—1A 42
Farcroft Gro. S4—2B 88
Far Dalton La. S65—1C 80
Far Field La. S63—5H 41
Far Field La. S71—1E 15
Far Field Rd. DN3—4E 21
Farfield Rd. S3—5C 86
Far Field Rd. S65—4A 80
Fargate. S1—3E 5 & 2E 99
Farhouse La. S30—2A 72
Farish Pl. S2—1F 111
Far La. S6—2H 85
Far La. S65—1H 79
Farlow Croft. S30—5A 50
Farm Bank Rd. S2
—6H 5 & 3G 99
Farm Clo. DN3—6E 21
Farm Clo. S12—5D 112
Farm Clo. S18—5F 123
Farm Clo. S40—6H 137
Farm Clo. S60—4C 90
Farm Clo. S70—3B 24
Farm Clo. S71—3C 14
Farm Cres. S19—3C 124
Farm Fields Clo. S19—6D 114
Farm Ho. La. S75—5C 12
Far Moor Clo. DN5—1G 43
Farm Rd. S2—4F 99
Farm Rd. S70—3B 24
Farmstead Clo. S14—2H 111
Farmsworth Ct. S41—5D 138
Farm View Clo. S61—1F 77
Farm View Rd. S61—1F 77
Farm Wlk. S19—2C 124
Farm Way. S73—3E 27
Farnaby Dri. S30—5B 50
Farnaby Gdns. S30—5B 50

Farndale Av. S42—5D 136
Farndale Rd. DN5—2F 31
Farndale Rd. S6—1A 86
Farnley Av. S6—5B 74
Farnsworth Ct. S41—5D 138
Farnsworth St. S41—5C 138
Farnworth Rd. S65—2A 80
Far Pl. S65—2H 79
Farquhar Rd. S66—4H 83
Farrah St. S70—6F 13
Farrar Rd. S7—6D 98
Farrier Ga. S30—1C 64
Farringdon Dri. DN11—6E 63
Far View Rd. S5—5F 75
Farwater Clo. S18—3E 129
Farwater La. S18—2D 128
Favell Rd. S3—3A 4
Favell Rd. S65—2B 80
Fawcett St. S3—1A 4 & 1C 98
Fearnehough St. S9—6C 88
Fearn Ho. Cres. S74—6G 37
Fearnley Rd. S74—6G 37
Fearnville Gro. S71—2E 9
Felkin St. S41—2B 138
Fellbrigg Rd. S2—6H 99
Fellowesfield Way. S61—2G 77
Fellows Wlk. S73—5H 25
Fell Pl. S9—3B 88
Fell Rd. S9—4C 88
Fell St. S9—3B 88
Fenlands Way. S40—5G 137
Fennel Gdns. S64—5B 56
Fenney La. S11—5E 109
Fenn Rd. S75—6D 36
Fensome Way. S73—3E 27
Fenton Clo. DN3—4F 35
Fenton Croft. S61—1A 78
Fenton Rd. S61—6A 68
Fenton St. S31—6G 125
Fenton St. S61—2H 77
Fentonville St. S11—5C 98
Fenton Way. S61—5B 68
Feoffees Rd. S30—6F 65
Ferguson St. S9—5B 88
Ferham Pk. Av. S61—3A 78
Ferham Rd. S61—3A 78
Fern Av. DN5—2A 32
Fern Av. S19—3F 115
Fern Av. S43—3A 134
Fern Bank. DN6—1D 16
Fernbank Dri. DN3—1F 35
Fernbank Dri. S61—8B 124
Fern Clo. DN2—3A 34
Fern Clo. S31—6B 124
Ferncroft Av. S19—2C 124
Ferndale Clo. S18—6H 123
Ferndale Dri. S66—3G 81
Ferndale Rise. S18—6H 123
Ferndale Rd. DN12—3D 58
Ferndale Rd. S18—6H 123
Fern Hollow. S66—6G 81
Fernhurst Rd. DN2—3A 34
Fern Lea Gro. S30—1F 75
Fern Lea Gro. S63—1H 41
Fern Rd. S6—5H 85
Fernvale Wlk. S64—5B 56
Fern Way. S31—6B 124
Ferrand St. S70—4C 36
Ferrara Clo. S73—3C 26
Ferrars Clo. S9—1H 89
Ferrars Dri. S9—2H 89
Ferrars Rd. S9—6G 77
Ferrars Way. S9—2H 89
Ferrers Rd. DN2—4F 33
Ferriby Rd. S6—1H 85

Ferry Boat La. DN12 & S64
(in two parts)   —2G 57
Ferry La. DN12—2E 59
Ferry Moor.La. S72—6D 10
Ferrymore Ho. DN1—1C 46
(off St James St.)
Ferry Ter. DN12—2E 59
Fersfield St. S4—5H 87
Festival Clo. S3—5G 117
Festival Rd. S63—6F 41
Field Clo. S18—1A 128
Field Clo. S73—3E 27
Fieldhead Clo. S41—5E 131
Fieldhead Rd. S8—6E 99
Field Ho. Rd. DN5—3D 44
Fieldhouse Way. S4—4H 87
Fielding Dri. S66—4H 81
Fielding Gro. S62—6F 55
Fielding Rd. S6—1A 86
Field La. S31—3H 125
Field La. S60 & S66—4D 92
Field La. S70—2E 25
Fields End Gdns. S30—1F 75
(off Minster Rd)
Fieldside. DN3—6D 20
Field View. S60—2C 90
Field Vw. S40—6A 138
Field Way. S60—1D 78
Fife Clo. S9—5C 76
Fife Gdns. S9—5C 76
Fife St. S9—5C 76
Fife St. S70—1F 23
Fife Way. S9—5C 76
Fifth Av. DN6—4D 16
Fig Tree La. S1—2E 5
Filby Rd. DN5—4G 31
Filey Av. S71—1F 9
Filey La. S3—6A 4 & 3C 98
Filey St. S10—4A 4 & 2C 98
Finch Clo. S65—5E 71
Finch Rise. S31—1C 116
Finch Rd. DN4—5H 45
Finchwell Clo. S13—3H 101
Finchwell Cres. S13—3H 101
Finchwell Rd. S13—3H 101
Findon Cres. S6—3G 85
Findon Pl. S6—3G 85
Findon Rd. S6—3G 85
Findon St. S6—3H 85
Finkle St. DN5—1B 32
Finlay Rd. S65—1G 79
Finlay St. S3—6A 4 & 1C 98
Firbeck Av. S31—1E 107
Firbeck Ho. DN1—1C 46
(off Camden Pl.)
Firbeck La. S31—6G 95
Firbeck Rd. S8—4C 110
Firbeck Way. DN11—3F 63
Fir Clo. S63—6F 41
Fircroft Av. S5—4H 75
Fircroft Rd. S5—4H 75
Firebeck Rd. DN4—1F 47
Firham Clo. S71—1C 8
Firsby La. DN12—6A 58
Firshill Av. S4—3F 87
Firshill Clo. S4—3F 87
Firshill Cres. S4—3E 87
Firshill Croft. S4—3E 87
Firshill Gdns. S4—3E 87
Firshill Glade. S4—3F 87
Firshill Rise. S4—3F 87
Firshill Rd. S4—3F 87
Firshill Wlk. S4—3E 87
Firshill Way. S4—3E 87

First Av. DN6—3E 17
First Av. S65—2G 79
First Av. S71—1F 9
Firs, The. S70—3C 24
Firs, The. S71—1C 8
First La. S31—4G 119
First La. S66—6G 81
Fir St. S6—6A 86
Fir St. S43—2H 133
Firth Av. S72—1G 15
Firth Cres. DN11—4C 62
Firth Cres. S66—5G 83
Firth Pk. Av. S5—6A 76
Firth Pk. Cres. S5—6H 75
Firth Pk. Rd. S5—2H 87
Firth Rd. S63—5B 40
Firth's Homes. S11—5F 97
Firth St. DN4—2B 46
Firth St. S61—4C 68
Firth St. S71—5H 13
Firthwood Av. S18—6H 123
Firthwood Clo. S18—6H 123
Firthwood Rd. S18—6H 123
Fir Tree Dri. S31—5E 117
Firtree Rise. S30—3E 65
Fir Vale Pl. S5—2G 87
Fir Vale Rd. S5—2G 87
Firvale Rd. S42—5D 136
Fir View Gdns. S4—3H 87
Fir Wlk. S66—4C 82
Fish Dam La. S71—2D 14 to 5F 9
Fisher Clo. S60—3C 78
Fisher La. S9—6E 89
Fisher Rd. S66—4H 83
Fisher St. DN5—5B 18
Fisher Ter. DN5—4A 32
Fish Pond La. S66—1H 83
Fishponds Rd. S13—5E 101
Fishponds Rd. W. S13—6E 101
Fitzalan Rd. S13—4H 101
Fitzalan Sq. S1—3F 5 & 2F 99
Fitzgerald Rd. S10—1H 97
Fitzhubert Rd. S2—5C 100
Fitzmaurice Rd. S9—5D 88
Fitzroy Rd. S2—1F 111
Fitzwalter Rd. S2—3H 99
Fitzwilliam Av. DN12—3C 58
Fitzwilliam Dri. DN5—2G 43
Fitzwilliam Ga. S1
　　　　—6C 4 & 3E 99
Fitzwilliam Rd. S65—2E 79
Fitzwilliam Rd. S73 & S72
　　　　—3G 27
Fitzwilliam Sq. S61—3B 68
(off Croft St.)
Fitzwilliam St. S1
　　　　—4B 4 & 2D 98
Fitzwilliam St. S62—4F 69
Fitzwilliam St. S63—6E 41
Fitzwilliam St. S64—2A 56
Fitzwilliam St. S70—6G 13
Fitzwilliam St. S73—4D 38
Fitzwilliam St. S74—6C 38
(Elsecar)
Fitzwilliam St. S74—6F 37
(Hoyland)
Five Trees Av. S17—3G 121
Five Trees Clo. S17—3G 121
Five Trees Dri. S17—3G 121
Fixby Ho. DN1—1C 46
(off Grove Pl.)
Flamstead Cres. S41—5A 142
Flanderwell Av. S66—4G 81
Flanderwell La. S66—2F 81
Flash La. S66—5H 81
Flask View. S6—4C 84
Flat La. S60—2H 91

Flat La. S72—4A 28
Flat St. S1—3F 5 & 2F 99
Flatts La. S60—6E 91
Flatts La. S63—5D 40
Flaxby Rd. S9—6D 88
Flax Lea. S70—4A 24
Fleet Clo. S63—4B 40
Fleethill Cres. S71—2A 14
Fleet La. S30—5E 73
Fleet St. S9—4B 88
Fleet St. S70—1H 23
Fleetwood Av. S71—2C 14
Fleming Pl. S70—1G 23
Fleming Sq. S63—5E 41
Fleming Way. S66—4E 81
Fletcher Av. S18—2E 129
Fletcher Ho. S65—2E 79
Fleury Clo. S14—3A 112
Fleury Cres. S14—3A 112
Fleury Pl. S14—3A 112
Fleury Rise. S14—3A 112
Fleury Rd. S14—3A 112
Flint Rd. DN2—3A 34
Flintway. S63—2F 55
Flockton Av. S13—5C 102
Flockton Cres. S13—5B 102
Flockton Dri. S13—5C 102
Flockton Rd. S13—5B 102
Flodden St. S10—1H 97
Floodgate Dri. S30—1F 75
Flora St. S6—5C 86
Florence Av. DN4—3A 46
Florence Av. S31—6B 104
Florence Rise. S73—3D 26
Florence Rd. S8—5C 110
Florence Rd. S61—3B 78
Flower Bri. Rd. DN5—1C 32
Flower St. S63—4H 29
Flowitt St. DN4—1B 46
Flowitt St. S64—6D 42
Folderings La. S30—6E 141
Folder La. DN5—2C 44
Folds Cres. S8—6A 110
Folds Dri. S8—6A 110
Folds La. S8—6A 110
Fold, The. S65—1B 80
Foley Av. S73—1E 99
Foley St. S4—6H 87
Foljambe Av. S40—5F 137
Foljambe Cres. DN11—4B 62
Foljambe Dri. S65—6C 70
Foljambe Rd. S40—2H 137
Foljambe Rd. S43—3E 133
Foljambe Rd. S65—1H 79
Foljambe St. S62—3F 69
Follett Rd. S5—4G 75
Fontwell Dri. S64—5F 43
Foolow Av. S40—4H 137
Footgate Clo. S30—2D 72
Forbes Rd. S6—4A 86
Ford Clo. S18—2D 128
Ford La. S30—2E 141
Ford Rd. S11—1H 109
Fordstead La. DN5 & DN3
　　　　—2F 19
Fore Hill Av. DN4—5B 48
Foremark Rd. S5—5H 75
Fore's Rd. DN3—4G 35
Forest Edge. S11—6G 109
Forest Rise. DN4—6G 45
Forest Rd. S71—5A 8
Forge Hill. S30—2D 72
Forge La. S1—6D 4 & 4E 99
Forge La. S30—2D 72
Forge La. S31—2H 125
Forge La. S60—3D 78
Forge La. S74—1D 52

Forge Rd. S31—4F 117
Formby Ct. S71—1D 14
Forncett St. S4—5H & 4H 87
(in two parts)
Fornham St. S2—6F 5 & 3F 99
Forres Av. S10—2G 97
Forres Rd. S10—2G 97
Forrester Clo. S66—3F 81
Forrester's La. S18—5G 123
Forster Rd. DN4—5B 46
Forth Av. S18—1B 128
Fort Hill Rd. S9—6B 76
Fortway Rd. S60—1C 90
Fossard Clo. DN2—2G 33
Fossdale Rd. S7—2B 110
Foster Rd. S66—4F 81
Foster's Clo. S64—2A 56
Fosters, The. S30—6B 50
Foster St. S70—1D 24
Foster Way. S30—5B 50
Foston Dri. S40—6D 130
Foulstone Row. S73—1G 39
Foundry Ct. S3—4F 87
Foundry Rd. DN4—2B 46
Foundry St. S41—3A 132
Foundry St. S62—4F 69
Foundry St. S70—1G 23 to
(in two parts)　　　　6G 13
Foundry St. S74—6C 38
Fountain Clo. S75—4C 6
Fountain Precinct. S1—3E 5
Fountain Sq. S75—4C 6
Fountains Way. S71—4D 14
Fountside. S7—1B 110
Fourth Av. DN6—3D 16
Fourwells Dri. S12—3A 114
Fowler Cres. DN11—4C 62
Fowler St. S41—1H 131
Fox Clo. S61—5F 67
Foxcote Lea. S65—5E 71
Foxcote Way. S42—5D 136
Fox Ct. S64—4B 56
Foxcroft Chase. S31—3A 126
Foxcroft Dri. S31—3A 126
Foxcroft Gro. S31—3A 126
Foxdale Av. S12—2D 112
Foxfield Wlk. S70—3D 24
Fox Glen Rd. S30—4F 141
Foxglove Clo. S44—2G 139
Foxglove Rd. S5—5A 76
Foxhall La. S10—1A 108
Fox Hill. S3—5F 87
Fox Hill Clo. S6—4A 74
Fox Hill Cres. S6—4A 74
Fox Hill Dri. S6—4A 74
Fox Hill Pl. S6—3A 74
Fox Hill Rd. S6—5A to 2A 74
Fox Hill Way. S6—3A 74
Foxland Av. S64—3G 55
Fox La. DN5—1G 43
Fox La. S12—5E 113
Fox La. S17—3B 122
Foxley Oaks La. S41—2B 132
Fox Rd. S6—5C 86
Foxroyd Clo. S71—1F 25
Fox's Pl. S40—3F 137
Foxstone Clo. S43—3B 134
Fox St. S3—5F 87
Fox St. S61—3G 77
Fox Wlk. S6—5B 86
Foxwood Av. S12—1D 112
Foxwood Clo. S41—6D 138
Foxwood Dri. S12—1D 112
Foxwood Gro. S12—2D 112
Foxwood Rd. S12—1D 112
Foxwood Rd. S41—1G 131
Framlingham Pl. S2—6H 99

Framlingham Rd. S2—6H 99
France Rd. S6—2D 84
Frances St. DN1—6D 32
France St. S62—4F 69
Francis Clo. S43—4E 133
Francis Cres. N. S60—5B 80
Francis Cres. S. S60—5B 80
Francis Dri. S60—5B 80
Francis Gro. S30—6B 50
Francis St. S60—4E 79
Frank Hillock Field. S30
　　　　—3G 141
Franklin Cres. DN2—6F 33
Franklyn Rd. S40—1G 137
Frank Pl. S9—4C 88
Frank Rd. DN5—3B 32
Fraser Clo. S8—4C 110
Fraser Cres. S8—4C 110
Fraser Dri. S8—4D 110
Fraser Rd. S8—4C 110
Fraser Rd. S60—4F 79
Fraser Wlk. S8—5D 110
Frecheville St. S43—2B 134
Frederick Av. S70—1F 23
Frederick Dri. S30—6A 64
Frederick Pl. S70—2H 23
Frederick Rd. S7—6D 98
Frederick St. S9—6D 88
Frederick St. S60—6C 90
(Catcliffe)
Frederick St. S60—2D 78
(Rotherham)
Frederick St. S63—4G 29
(Goldthorpe)
Frederick St. S63—4D 40
(Wath upon Dearne)
Frederick St. S64—6D 42
Frederick St. S73—6A 26
Freedom Ct. S6—4B 86
Freedom Rd. S6—5A 86
Freeman Gdns. S30—1B 64
Freeman Rd. S66—4F 81
Freeman St. S70—1H 23
Freemans Yd. S70—6H 13
Freesia Clo. S31—3E 119
Freeston Pl. S9—4C 88
French Ga. DN1—5C 32
(in two parts)
Frenchgate Shopping Cen. DN1
(off French Ga.)　　　—6C 32
French St. DN5—5B 18
Fretson Rd. S2—5C 100
Fretwell Clo. S66—2E 83
Fretwell Rd. S65—1A 80
Freydon Way. S44—2G 139
Friar Clo. S6—5D 84
Friar's Rd. S71—4E 15
Frickley Bri. La. S72—1E 11
Frickley Rd. S11—5F 97
Frinton Clo. S40—6H 137
Frithbeck Clo. DN3—3F 35
Frith Clo. S12—2D 112
Frith Rd. S12—2D 112
Frobisher Gro. S66—3E 83
Froggatt Clo. S43—5A 134
Froggatt La. S1—5E 5 & 3E 99
Frogmore Clo. S66—3H 81
Frog Wlk. S11—5C 98
Front St. S60—1E 103
Frostings Clo. S30—6A 64
(in two parts)
Frostings, The. S30—6A 64
Fulford Clo. S9—6E 89
Fulford Pl. S9—6E 89
Fulford Way. DN12—2G 59
Fuller Gro. S64—4B 56
Fullerton Av. DN12—3C 58
Fullerton Cres. S65—4D 70

Gomersal La S18—2E 129
Gomersall Av DN12 3B 58
Gooder Av S71—2E 9
Goodison Boulevd DN4—3E 49
Goodison Cres. S6—5F 85
Goodison Rise. S6—5F 85
Goodwin Av S62—1F 69
Goodwin Cres. S64—1A 56
Goodwin Rd. S8—1E 111
Goodwin Rd S61—3A 68
Goodwin Way S61—3A 68
Goodwood Gdns DN4—1B 48
Goodyear Cres. S73—1F 39
Goore Av S9—3D 100
Goore Dri. S9—2D 100
Goore Rd S9—3D 100
Goosebutt St S62—3F 69
Goose Carr La. S31—6H 105
Goosecroft Av. S65—5C 70
Goose La S66—5G 81
Gordon Av S8—5E 111
Gordon Rd. DN12—3B 60
Gordon Rd. S11—5B 98
Gordon St. DN1—6C 32
Gordon St S70—1E 25
Gordon Ter S65—3F 79
Gorseacre La. S63—1E 29
Gorse Dri. S31—4B 126
Gorseland Ct. S66—5E 81
Gorse La S10—6A 96
Gorse, The. S65—4A 80
Gorse, The. S66—6F 81
Gorse Valley Rd. S41—6E 139
Gorsey Brigg. S18—2B 128
Gosber Rd. S31—6E 125
Gosber St S31—6D 124
Gosforth Clo. S18—2D 128
Gosforth Cres. S18—2D 128
Gosforth Dri. S18—2B 128
Gosforth Grn. S18—2D 128
Gosforth La. S18—2D 128
Gosling Gate Rd. S63—4G 29
Gotham Rd. S60—1C 90
Gough Clo S65—5A 80
Gough St. S60—2D 78
Goulder Pl S9—3D 88
Goulding St. S64—1D 56
Gowdall Grn. DN5—4A 18
Gower Cres. S40—6E 131
Gower St. S4—5G 87
Goyt Side Rd. S40—3F 137
Grace St S71—1F 15
Grafton St. S2—3G 99
Grafton St. S70—6F 13
Graham Av. S60—4D 90
Graham Ct. S10—5F 97
Graham Knoll. S10—5F 97
Graham Rise. S10—5F 97
Graham Rd. DN3—4D 20
Graham Rd S10—5F 97
Graham's Orchard. S70—6G 13
Grainger Clo. DN12—4A 60
Grainger Ct. S10—4E 97
Grammar St. S6—4B 86
Grampian Clo S75—5D 12
Grampian Cres S40—1D 136
Granary Clo. S41—4C 130
Granby Cres. DN2—1F 47
Granby La. DN11—3B 62
Granby Rd. DN12—3C 60
Granby Rd. S5—1H 87
Grange Av. DN4—4A 46
Grange Av. S18—2C 128
Grange Av. S31—4A 104
Grange Cliffe Clo. S11—3H 109
Grange Clo. S66—6H 93
Grange Clo. S72—2F 11
Grange Ct. S66—6F 81

Grange Cres. S11—5C 98
Grange Cres. S63—1G 29
Grange Cres. S71—5E 15
Grange Cres. Rd. S11—5C 98
Grange Dri. S61—6F 67
Grange Dri. S66—5B 82
Grange Farm Dri. S30—5D 72
Grangefield Av DN11—4D 62
Grangefield Cres. DN11—4D 62
Grangefield Ter. DN11—4D 62
Grange Ho. S72—2F 11
Grange La. DN5—1H 43
Grange La DN11—5B 62
(New Rossington)
Grange La DN11—1E 61
(Wadworth, in two parts)
Grange La. S5 & S61—1B 76
Grange La. S13—5A 102
Grange La. S60—6A 78
Grange La. S66—4G 83
Grange La Ind. Est. S71—6E 15
Grange Mill La S5 & S9—1B 76
Grange Pk. DN3—2E 21
Grange Pk Av S43—1F 139
Grange Rd DN4—5D 48
Grange Rd DN5—3A 18
Grange Rd. DN6—4E 17
Grange Rd S11—5C 98
Grange Rd S19—4F 115
Grange Rd. S60—1H 91
Grange Rd S62—6G 55
Grange Rd S63—6D 40
Grange Rd S64—3H 55
Grange Rd S71—2C 8
Grange Rd S72—2F 11
Grange St. S63—1G 29
Grange Ter S63—1G 29
(off Chapman St.)
Grange, The. S61—5E 67
Grange View. S74—2H 37
Grange View Cres S61—1F 77
Grange View Rd. S61—1F 77
Grange Way. DN12—2B 58
Grangewood Rd. S31—1E 107
Grangewood Rd. S40—6H 137
Gransden Way. S40—5E 137
Grantham St. DN11—4C 62
Grantly Clo. S73—3H 39
Granton Pl. S71—6A 8
Grant Rd. S6—2B 86
Granville Clo. S41—5D 138
Granville Rd. S2—6G 5 & 3F 99
Granville Sq. S2—6G 5 & 3F 99
Granville St. S2—6G 5 & 3F 99
Granville St. S31—2C 106
Granville St. S75—4F 13
Granville Ter. S65—3F 79
Grasby Ct. S66—2H 81
Grasmere Av. DN2—5A 34
Grasmere Clo. S41—4F 131
Grasmere Clo. S63—2A 42
Grasmere Clo. S64—5H 43
Grasmere Cres. S75—3E 7
Grasmere Rd. DN12—3D 58
Grasmere Rd. S8—2C 110
Grasmere Rd. S18—2B 128
Grasmere Rd. S71—6A 14
Grasscroft Clo. S40—5F 131
Grassdale View. S12—4H 113
Grassington Clo. S12—4B 114
Grassington Dri. S12—4B 114
Grassington Way. S30—1D 64
Grassmoor Clo. S12—2B 112
Grassthorpe Rd. S12—3D 112
Gratton Ct. S43—1D 134
Gratton St. S61—3G 77
Graven Clo. S30—1H 73

Graves Trust Homes. S8
—1E 123
Graves Trust Homes. S12
—2C 112
Gray Av. S31—4B 104
Gray Gdns. DN4—5B 46
Grays Ct. DN12—1C 58
Grayshott Wlk. S40—5H 137
Grayson Clo. S30—4E 141
Grayson Clo. S65—1H 81
Grayson Rd. S61—3A 68
Gray's Rd. S71—4E 9
Gray St. S3—5F 87
Gray St. S19—2C 124
Gray St. S74—6C 38
Greasbro Rd. S9—1F 89
Greasbrough La S62—2D 68
Greasbrough Rd S61 & S60
(in two parts) —5C 68
Greasbrough Rd S62—4D 68
Greasbrough St S60—2C 78
Great Bank Rd S65—5A 80
Gt. Central Av DN4—3B 46
Gt. Croft. S18—1B 128
Gt. North Rd DN6 & DN5—1B 16
Gt. North Rd. DN11—2G 63
Gt. Park Rd. S61—1G 77
Greaves Clo. S6—5C 84
Greaves Fold. S75—5D 12
Greaves La. S6—5C 84
Greaves La. S30—3B 50
Greaves Rd. S5—1E 75
Greaves Rd. S61—2A 78
Greaves Sike La. S66—1B 83
Greaves St. S6—4B 86
Greenacre Clo. S18—4G 129
Green Acres. S62—2G 69
Greenacres. S74—6A 38
Green Arbour Rd. S66—5A 94
Greenbank Dri. S40—1E 137
Greenbank Wlk S72—6F 11
Green Boulevarde DN4—3C 48
Green Chase. S31—6C 124
Green Clo. S43—5A 134
Green Common. DN3—4F 35
Green Cross. S18—1F 129
Greendale Av. S42—5A 136
Greendale Ct. S18—1F 129
Greendale Shopping Centre
S18—1F 129
Green Farm Clo. S40—5E 131
Greenfield. S62—2F 69
Greenfield Clo. DN3—4G 35
(Armthorpe)
Greenfield Clo. DN3—1E 21
(Barnby Dun)
Greenfield Clo. S8—2D 122
Greenfield Clo. S65—1B 80
Greenfield Cotts. S71—5E 9
Greenfield Ct. S66—3F 81
Greenfield Dri. S8—2D 122
Greenfield Gdns. S66—3F 81
Greenfield La. DN4—2A 46
Greenfield Rd. S8—2D 122
Greenfield Rd. S65—1B 80
Greenfield Rd. S74—5A 38
Greenfields. S31—6C 124
Greenfinch Clo. S60—3D 90
Greenfoot Clo. S75—4F 13
Greenfoot La. S75—3F to 4E 13
(in two parts)
Greengate Clo. S13—1D 114
Green Gate Clo. S63—6F 29
Greengate La. S13—1C 114
Greengate La. S30—1B 64
Greengate Rd. S13—1D 114
Greenhall Rd. S31—6C 124
Greenhead Gdns. S30—2E 65

Greenhead La. S30—2E 65
Greenhill Av. S8—1C 122
Greenhill Av. S66—5B 82
Greenhill Av. S71—4H 13
Greenhill Main Rd. S8—2C 122
Greenhill Parkway. S8—4A 122
Greenhill Rd. S8—5D 110
Green Ho. La. DN2—3H 33
Greenhow St. S6—6A 86
Green Ings La. S63—4G 41
Greenland. S74—2H 37
Greenland Av. S66—3G & 2G 83
(in two parts)
Greenland Clo. S9—5E 89
Greenland Clo. S31—1F 119
Greenland Ct. S9—5E 89
Greenland Dri. S9—5E 89
Greenland Rd. S9—4E 89
Greenlands Av. DN11—3E 63
Greenland View S9—6E 89
Greenland View. S70—5H 23
Greenland Wlk. S9—5E 89
Greenland Way S9—4E & 5E 89
(in two parts)
Greenland Way. S66—2G 83
Green La. DN3—2F 49
Green La. DN5—5A 16 to 6F 17
Green La. DN6—3C 16
Green La. DN11—6G 61
Green La. S3—6D 86
Green La. S18—2F 129
Green La. S30—1E 75
(Ecclesfield)
Green La. S30—1B 72
(Onesacre)
Green La. S30—2A 140
(Stocksbridge)
Green La. S30—1B 72
(Wharncliffe Side)
Green La. S31—6E 105
(Aston)
Green La. S31—5A 126
(Killamarsh)
Green La. S31—1B 104
(Ulley)
Green La. S41—1D 138
Green La. S42—4A 130
Green La. S60—4B 90
(Brinsworth)
Green La. S60—1G 91
(Rotherham)
Green La. S61—2E 77
Green La. S62—2H 69
Green La. S63—2D 54
Green La. S66—3E 95
(Carr, Maltby)
Green La. S66—2H 93
(Thurcroft)
Green La. S66—4E 81
(Wickersley)
Green La. S70—4E 23
Green La. S74—6E 37
Green La. S75—3C 22
Green Lea. S18—1A 128
Greenleafe Av. DN2—2A 34
Green Moor Rd. S30—1F 141
Green Oak Av. S17—5E 121
Green Oak Cres. S17—5E 121
Green Oak Dri. S17—5E 121
Green Oak Dri. S31—5E 117
Green Oak Gro. S17—5E 121
Green Oak Rd. S17—6E 121
Green Oak View. S17—5E 121
Greenock St. S6—3H 85
Green Rise. S62—6D 54
Green Rd S75—3A 22
Greenside. S61—4B 68
Greenside. S72—1B 10

163

Greenside. S75—4G 7
Greenside Av. S31—5G 117
Greenside Av. S41—4H 131
Greenside Av. S75—4G 7
Greenside Ho. S75—4G 7
Greenside La. S74—5A 38
Greenside M. S12—4B 114
Green Spring Av. S70—3D 36
Greens Rd. S65—3H 79
Green St. DN4—5H 45
Green St. S30—3F 141
Green St. S41—1A 132
Green St. S31—3B 68
Green St. S70—4C 24
Green St. S74—5A 38
Green, The. DN12—2G 57
Green, The. S9—1E 101
Green, The. S17—5D 120
Green, The. S31—1F 119
(Anston)
Green, The. S31—4B 116
(Waleswood, Kiveton Park)
Green, The. S41—6D 138
Green, The. S60—6F 79
(Rotherham)
Green, The. S60—3H 91
(Whiston)
Green, The. S63—6E 29
Green, The. S64—3H 55
Green, The. S71—2E 9
Green, The. S72—2C 10
Green, The. S75—6A 22
Green View, The. S72—1B 10
Greenways. S40—5E 137
Greenway, The. S8—1D 122
Greenway, The. S30—4G 141
Greenwich Ct. S65—1H 79
Greenwood Av. S9—2D 100
Greenwood Clo. S9—2D 100
Greenwood Cres. S9—2C 100
Greenwood Cres. S66—4G 81
Greenwood Cres. S71—1D 8
Greenwood Dri. S9—2C 100
Greenwood La. S13—6D 102
Greenwood Rd. S9—2D 100
Greenwood Rd. S30—6D 56
Greenwood Rd. S62—6C 56
Greenwood Ter. S70—5G 13
Greenwood Way. S9—2D 100
Greeton Dri. S30—3E 73
Gregg Ho. Cres. S5—4H 75
Gregg Rd. S5—3H 75
Gregory La. S43—2D 132
Gregory Rd. S8—1E 111
Grenfell Av. S64—6F 43
Grenfolds Rd. S30—1B 74
Greno Cres. S30—1B 74
Greno Ga. S30—6A 64
Greno Ho. S30—6A 64
Grenomoor Clo. S30—2A 74
Greno Rd. S64—3B 56
Greno View. S74—6G 37
Greno View. S75—6A 22
Greno View Rd. S30—6C 50
Grenville Pl. S75—4E 13
Grenville Rd. DN4—5G 45
Gresham Av. S60—2C 90
Gresham Rd. S6—5A 86
Gresley Rd. S8—4C 122
Gresley Wlk. S8—4C 122
Greyfriars. S11—6G 97
Grey Friars Rd. DN1—5C 32
Greystock St. S4—6H 87 &
(in two parts)   5A 88
Greystones Av S11—5H 97
Greystones Av. S70—5H 23

Greystones Clo. S11—6G 97
Greystones Ct. S11—6G 97
Greystones Ct. S31—3H 127
Greystones Cres. S11—6G 97
Greystones Dri. S11—6G 97
Greystones Grange. S11
                    —6G 97
Greystones Grange Cres. S11
                    —6G 97
Greystones Grange Rd. S11
                    —6G 97
Greystones Hall Rd. S11—5G 97
Greystones Rise. S11—6G 97
Greystones Rd. S11—6F 97
Greystones Rd. S60—2B 92
Grice Clo. DN4—1D 48
Griffin Rd. S64—2H 55
Griffiths Clo. S62—3F 69
Griffiths Rd. S30—1C 64
Grimesthorpe Rd. S4—5G 87
(in three parts)   to 3A 88
Grimesthorpe Rd. S. S4—5G 87
Grimsell Clo. S6—2B 74
Grimsell Cres. S6—2B 74
Grimsell Dri. S6—2B 74
Grimsell Way. S6—3B 74
Grinders Hill. S1—5F 5
Grinders Wlk. S6—2F 85
Grindlow Av. S40—4H 137
Grindlow Clo. S14—1G 111
Grindlow Dri. S14—1G 111
Grindon Clo. S40—6E 131
Grinton Wlk. S40—5H 137
Grisedale Wlk. S18—2C 128
Grizedale Av. S19—5G 115
Grizedale Clo. S19—5G 115
Grosvenor Cres. DN4—5F 45
Grosvenor Cres. DN5—5D 18
Grosvenor Dri. S70—6E 13
Grosvenor Rd. DN6—2D 16
Grosvenor Rd. S65—1F 79
Grosvenor Sq. S2—5D 98
Grosvenor Ter. DN4—5G 45
Grouse Croft. S6—5B 86
Grouse St. S6—4A 86
Grove Av. DN5—4A 32
Grove Av. S6—1G 85
Grove Av. S17—5D 120
Grove Clo. S63—3C 40
Grove Hall Clo. DN3—5E 21
Grove Hill Rd. DN2—2A 34
Grove Ho. Ct. S17—4E 121
Grove Pl. DN1—1C 46
Grove Pl. S40—3F 137
Grove Rd. S7—4A 110
Grove Rd. S17—4E 121
Grove Rd. S30—4H 141
Grove Rd. S41—4A 132
Grove Rd. S43—6F 133
Grove Rd. S60—4D 78
Grove Rd. S63—3C 40
Grove Rd. S75—4E 7
Grove Sq. S6—4C 86
Grove St. S41—5C 138
Grove St. S70—4C 24
Grove St. S71—6A 14
Grove Ter. S66—4D 82
Grove, The. DN2—4G & 3H 33
(in two parts)
Grove, The. DN3—1G 21
Grove, The. S6—3E 85
Grove, The. S17—4D 120
Grove, The. S43—3E 135
Grove, The. S62—2G 69
Grove, The. S65—2H 79
Grove, The. S66—5F 81
Grove, The. S72—4B 10
Grove Vale. DN2—2A 34

Grove Wlk. S17—4E 121
(off Grove Rd.)
Grove Way. S43—6F 133
Guernsey Rd. S2—6E 99
Guest La. DN4—4F 45
Guest Pl. S60—5F 79
Guest Pl. S74—4A 38
Guest Rd. S11—5A 98
Guest Rd. S60—5F 79
Guest St. S75—4F 13
Guest St. S74—4A 38
Guilbert Av. S66—6A 94
Guildford Av. S2—5H 99
Guildford Av. S40—5F 137
Guildford Clo. S2—5H 99
Guildford Dri. S2—5H 99
Guildford Rise. S2—6A 100
Guildford Rd. DN2—2H 33
Guildford Rd. S71—1D 8
Guildford View. S2—6A 100
Guildford Wlk. S2—5G 99
Guildford Way. S2—5H 99
Guildhall Ind. Est. DN3—4C 20
Guild Rd. S65—3H 79
Guildway. S31—2A 118
Guilthwaite Comn. La. S60
                    —6A 92
Guilthwaite Cres. S60—2G 91
Gullane Dri. DN4—5F 45
Gulling Wood Dri. S65—5E 71
Gunhills La. DN3—2G 35
Gun La. S3—1G 5 & 1F 99
Gurney Rd. DN4—5B 46
Gurth Av. DN3—5E 21
Gurth Dri. S66—6A 94
Gypsy La. S73—2G 39

Habershon Ct. S30—2E 65
Habershon Dri. S30—1D 64
Habershon Rd. S61—6H 67
Hackness La. S60—2B 90
Hackney La. S18—1B 130
Hackthorn Rd. S8—4D 110
Haddon Clo. S18—1F 129
Haddon Clo. S40—3E 137
Haddon Clo. S75—2A 22
Haddon Pl. S43—3B 134
Haddon Rise. S64—5H 43
Haddon Rd. S71—1B 14
Haddon St. S3—5D 86
Haddon Way. S31—6D 104
Haden St. S3—3A 86
Hadfield St. S6—6A 86
Hadfield St. S73—2F 39
Hadrian Rd. S60—1C 90
Hady Cres. S41—3C 138
Hady Hill. S41—3B 138
Hady La. S41—3D 138
Haggard Rd. S6—3B 86
Hagg Hill. S6—6F 85
(Clough Field)
Hagg Hill. S6—4H 73
(Wadsley Bridge)
Hagg La. S10—2E 97
Hagg La. Cotts. S10—2D 96
Haggstones Dri. S30—3C 72
Haggstones Rd. S30—3C 72
Hague Av. S62—6E 55
Hague La. S30—6A 50
Hague La. S62—1D 66
Hague Row. S2—4H 5 & 2G 99
Haids Clo. S66—2F 83
Haids La. S66—2F 83
Haids Rd. S66—2E 83
Haig Cres. DN11—5C 62
Haigh Croft. S71—1D 8
Haigh La. S75—1A 6

Haigh Moor Clo. S13—5G 101
Haigh Moor Rd. S13—5H 101
Haigh Moor Wlk. S13—5G 101
Haigh Rd. DN4—4A 46
Hail Mary Dri. S13—5D 102
Hakehill Clo. DN4—5B 48
Halcyon Clo. S12—4H 113
Haldane Clo. S72—2F 11
Haldane Rd. S65—1G 79
Haldene. S70—5A 24
Haldynby Gdns. DN3—3H 35
Hale St. S8—1D 110
Halesworth Clo. S40—5D 136
Halesworth Rd. S13—3G 101
Halfacre La. S18—3H 129
Halfway Centre. S19—2E 125
Halfway Dri. S19—2E 125
Halfway Gdns. S19—2E 125
Halifax Av. DN12—3C 58
Halifax Cres. DN5—3H 31
Halifax Hall. S10—4A 98
Halifax Rd. S6 & S30—5B 74
Halifax St. S71—3G 13
Hallam Chase. S10—4H 97
Hallam Clo. DN4—4A 48
Hallam Clo. S31—4A 104
Hallam Ct. S18—3E 129
Hallam Dale Ct. S62—6G 55
Hallamgate Rd. S10—2F 97
Hallam Grange Clo. S10—5C 96
Hallam Grange Cres. S10
                    —4C 96
Hallam Grange Croft. S10
                    —4C 96
Hallam Grange Rise. S10
                    —4C 96
Hallam Grange Rd. S10—4C 96
Hallam La. S1—6E 5 & 3E 99
Hallam Pl. S62—2G 69
Hallam Rd. S60—1F 91
Hallam Rock. S5—2F 87
Hallamshire Clo. S10—5B 96
Hallamshire Ct. S30—2E 65
Hallamshire Dri. S10—5B 96
Hallamshire Rd. S10—5B 96
Hallam Way. S30—1F 75
Hall Av. S64—6F 43
Hall Av. S74—4C 38
Hall Balk La. S75—4F 13
Hall Broome Gdns. S63—6E 29
Hallcar St. S4—6G 87
Hall Clo. S18—1A 128
Hall Clo. S31—1F 119
Hall Clo. S70—1E 37
Hall Clo. Av. S60—2A 92
Hall Cres. S60—1H 91
Hallcroft Dri. DN3—5G 35
Hall Croft Rise. S71—2D 8
Hall Cross Hill. DN1—1E 47
Hall Dri. S63—6D 40
Hall Farm Clo. S13—3B 104
Hall Flat Rd. DN4—4A 46
Hall Ga. DN1—6D 32
Hallgate. S63—2F 29
Hall Ga. S64—1G 57
Hallgate Rd. S10—2G 97
Hall Gro. S60—4E 79
Hall Gro. S75—4G 7
Halliwell Clo. S5—6B 74
Halliwell Cres. S5—6C 74
Hallowes Ct. S18—2F 129
Hallowes Dri. S18—3F 129
Hallowes La. S18—2F 129
Hallowes Rise. S18—3G 129
Hallowmoor Rd. S6—2F 85
Hall Pk. Head. S6—6E 85
Hall Pk. Hill. S6—6E 85
Hall Pk. Mt. S6—6E 85

Hall Pl. S71—3C 14
Hall Rd. S9—2G 101
Hall Rd. S13—3H 101
Hall Rd. S31—4B 104
Hall Rd. S43—4E 133
Hall Rd. S60—4E 79
Hall Rd. S66—4C 82
Hall St. S60—3C 78
Hall St. S62—4F 69
Hall St. S63—5G 29
Hall St. S73—1G 99
Hall St. S74—5A 38
Hallsworth Av. S73—4D 38
Hall View. S30—1E 65
Hall Villa La. DN5—2A 18
Hall Wood Rd. S30—2A 64
Hallyburton Clo. S2—1G 111
Hallyburton Dri. S2—1G 111
Hallyburton Rd. S2—1G 111
Halmshaw Ter. DN5—1A 32
Halsall Av. S9—2E 101
Halsall Dri. S9—2E 101
Halsall Rd. S9—2E 101
Halsbury Rd. S65—1G 79
Halstead Gro. S75—3E 7
Halsteads. S13—4G 101
Halton Clo. S41—2G 131
Halton Ct. S12—4C 114
Hambledon Clo. S40—6E 131
Hambleton Clo. S75—5D 12
Hameline Rd. DN12—3D 58
Hamer Wlk. S65—2A 80
Hamilton Clo. DN4—2F 47
Hamilton Clo. S64—5G 43
Hamilton Pk. Rd. DN5—3F 31
Hamilton Rd. DN4—2F 47
Hamilton Rd. S5—1H 87
Hamilton Rd. S66—5H 83
Hammerton Clo. S6—4A 86
Hammerton Rd. S6—4A 86
Hammond St. S3—1A 4 & 1C 98
Hampden Rd. S64—6F 43
Hampton Rd. DN2—5F 33
Hampton Rd. S5—2C 87
Hampton St. S41—6D 138
Hamstead Grn. S61—6G 67
Hanbury Clo. DN4—1G 61
Hanbury Clo. S18—2D 128
Hanbury Clo. S40—6C 130
Hanbury Clo. S71—3D 14
Handby St. S41—5D 138
Handley St. S3—6F 87
Hands Rd. S10—1A 98
Handsworth Av. S9—2F 101
Handsworth Cres. S9—2F 101
Handsworth Gdns. DN3—3G 35
Handsworth Grange Clo. S13
—4A 102
Handsworth Grange Cres. S13
—4B 102
Handsworth Grange Dri. S13
—4B 102
Handsworth Grange Rd. S13
—4A 102
Handsworth Grange Way. S13
—4B 102
Handsworth Rd. S9 & S13
—2G 101
Hangingwater Clo. S11—5F 97
Hangingwater Rd. S11—6F 97
Hangram La. S11—3B 108
Hangsman La. S31—2C 106
Hangthwaite La. DN6—4F 17
Hanmoor Rd. S6—5C 84
Hannah Rd. S13—6D 102
Hanover Ct. S3—6A 4 & 3C 98
Hanover Sq. S3—6B 4 & 3D 98
Hanover Sq. S63—1G 29

Hanover St. S3—6B 4 & 3D 98
(in two parts)
Hanover St. S63—1G 29
Hanover Way. S3—5A 4 & 3D 98
Hanson Rd. S6—3D 84
Hanson St. S70—5H 13
Harbord Rd. S8—5C 110
Harborough Av. S2
—2B to 5D 100
Harborough Clo. S2—3C 100
Harborough Dri. S2—3C 100
Harborough Hill Rd. S71
—6H 13
Harborough Rise. S2—3C 100
Harborough Rd. S2—3C 100
Harborough Way. S2—4C 100
Harbury St. S13—5E 103
Harcourt Clo. DN4—4A 48
Harcourt Cres. S10—1B 98
Harcourt Rise. S30—3F 65
Harcourt Rd. S10—2B 98
Harcourt Ter. S65—3F 79
Hardale Wlk. DN2—3A 34
Hardcastle Dri. S13—6A 102
Hardcastle Gdns. S13—6A 102
Hardcastle Rd. S13—1A 114
Harden Clo S75—5C 12
Hardie Clo. S66—5H 83
Hardie Pl. S43—3B 134
Hardie Pl. S62—1F 69
Hardie St. S31—6D 124
Harding Av. S62—5D 54
Harding Clo. S62—6D 54
Harding St. S9—5D 88
Hardwick Clo. S18—1F 129
Hardwick Clo. S31—6D 104
Hardwick Clo. S70—5A 24
Hardwick Cres. S11—5A 98
Hardwick Cres. S71—6D 8
Hardwicke Rd. S65—1E 79
Hardwick Gro. S75—3B 22
Hardwick La. S31—5G 105
Hardwick St. S41—1A 138
Hardwick St. S65—1B 80
Hardwicks Yd. S40—3G 137
Haredon Clo. S75—3E 7
Harefield Rd. S11—5B 98
Harehill Rd. S40—6H 137
Harehills Rd. S60—4E 79
Harewood Av. DN3—3D 20
Harewood Av. DN6—2B 16
Harewood Av. S70—6D 12
Harewood Gro. S66—3H 81
Harewood Rd. DN2—6G 33
Harewood Rd. S6—2B 86
Harewood Way. S11—5G 109
Hargrave Pl. S65—5D 70
Harland Rd. S11—4C 98
Harlech Clo. S30—1D 64
Harleston St. S4—5H 87
Harley Rd. S11—2F 109
Harley Rd. S62—4H 51
Harlington Ct. DN12—1C 58
Harlington Rd. S64—3D 42
(Adwick upon Dearne)
Harlington Rd. S64—6F 43
(Mexborough)
Harmer La. S1—4F 5 & 2F 99
Harmony Way. S60—5C 90
Harney Clo. S9—6E 89
Harold Av. DN6—2C 16
Harold Av. S71—3E 15
Harold Croft. S61—3C 68

Harold St. S6—5B 86
Harperhill Clo. S40—6H 137
Harriet Clo S70—2A 24
Harrington Ct. S71—3E 15
Harrington Rd. S2—6E 99
Harrington St DN1—5D 32
Harrison La. S10—6A 96
Harrison Rd. S6—3H 85
Harrison St. S61—3A 78
Harris Rd. S6—1H 85
Harrogate Dri. DN12—2A 58
Harrogate Rd. S31—1A 116
Harrop Dri. S64—4A 56
Harrowden Ct. S9—1G 89
Harrowden Rd. DN2—3E 33
Harrowden Rd. S9—1G 89
Harrow Rd. DN2—2G 35
Harrow St. S11—4D 98
Harry Firth Clo. S9—6C 88
Harry Rd. S75—4D 12
Hartfield Clo. S41—6D 138
Hartford Clo. S8—4E 111
Hartford Rd. S8—4E 111
Hart Hill. S62—5D 54
Harthill Rd. DN12—4C 58
Harthill Rd. S13—6D 100
Hartington Av. S7—4A 110
Hartington Clo. S61—3A 78
Hartington Ct. S18—1F 129
(off Hartington Rd.)
Hartington Dri. S71—3H 13
Hartington Rd. S7—4A 110
Hartington Rd. S18—1F 129
Hartington Rd. S41—3C 138
Hartinton Rd. S61—3A 78
Hartland Av. S19—5G 115
Hartland Ct S19—5G 115
Hartland Cres. DN3—5D 20
Hartland Dri. S19—5G 115
Hartland Way. S41—2A 132
Hartley Brook Av. S5—3G 75
Hartley Brook Rd. S5—3G 75
Hartley St. S2—6E 99
Hartley St. S64—1D 56
Hartopp Av. S2—1H 111
Hartopp Clo. S2—1G 111
Hartopp Dri. S2—1H 111
Hartopp Rd. S2—1H 111
Harts Head. S1—2F 5 & 1F 99
Hartside Clo. S40—6F 131
Harvest La. S3—6E 87
Harvest Rd. S66—4F 81
Harvey Clough Rd. S8—4E 111
Harvey Rd. S30—2E 65
Harvey Rd. S41—3E 139
Harvey St. S30—3F 141
Harvey St. S70—1F 23
Harwell Rd. S8—6D 98
Harwich Rd. S2—4A 100
Harwood Clo. S2—5E 99
Harwood Dri. S19—6D 114
Harwood Gdns. S19—6E 115
Harwood St. S2—5E 99
Harwood Ter. S71—5E 15
Haslam Cres. S8—3B 122
Haslam Pl. S66—3H 83
Haslam Rd. DN11—4D 62
Hasland By Pass. S41
—4B 138 to 6F 139
Hasland La. S44—5G 139
Hasland Rd. S41—4B to 4B 138
(in two parts)
Haslehurst Rd. S2—3A 100
Haslemere Gro. DN5—3A 32
Hassocky La. S44—6H 139
Hassop Rd. S43—1D 134
Hastilar Clo. S2—5D 100

Hastilar Rd. S2—5D 100
(in two parts)
Hastilar Rd. S. S13—5E 101
Hastings Clo. S41—5F 131
Hastings Mt. S2—3A 110
Hastings Rd. S7—3A 110
Hastings St. S72—6G 11
Hatchell Dri. DN4—6E 49
Hatfield Clo. S71—6A 8
Hatfield Cres. S31—3C 106
Hatfield Gdns. S71—1D 8
Hatfield Ho. DN1—1C 46
(off Grove Pl.)
Hatfield Ho. Ct. S5—4H 75
Hatfield Ho. Croft. S5—4H 75
Hatfield Ho. La. S5—5G 75
Hatfield La. DN3—2G 35 to
(Armthorpe)   5F 21
Hatfield La. DN3—2H 21
(Barnby Dun)
Hatherley Rd. S9—1G 89
Hatherley Rd. S64—6B 42
Hatherley Rd. S65—1E 79
Hathern Clo S43—1F 139
Hathersage Rd. S17
—1A 120 to 5E 109
Hatter Dri. DN12—5B 60
Hatton Clo. S18—3B 128
Hatton Rd. S40—6D 130
Hatton Rd. S6—4B 86
Haugh La. S11—2F 109
Haugh Rd S62—5C 54
Haughton Rd. S8—5D 110
Havelock Rd. DN4—2C 46
Havelock St. S10—3C 98
Havelock St. S70—1F 23
Havelock St. S73—4E 27
Havens, The. S40—2F 137
Havercroft Pl. S31—2H 125
Havercroft Rd. S8—3C 110
Havercroft Rd S60—6A 80
Havercroft Ter. S31—2H 125
Haverlands La. S70—5F 23
Haverlands Ridge S70—5H 23
Hawes Clo. S64—5G 43
Hawfield Clo. DN4—2A 46
Hawke Clo. S62—6C 54
Hawke Rd. DN2—3F 33
Hawke St. S9—3C 88
Hawk Hill La. S66—1H 105
Hawkhurst Ridge. S65—1H 79
Hawkins Av. S30—2C 64
Hawkshead Av. S18—2B 128
Hawkshead Cres. S31—6F 107
Hawkshead Rd. S4—2B 88
Hawksley Av. S6—3A 86
Hawksley Av. S40—6G 131
Hawksley Rise. S30—3D 72
Hawksley Rd. S6—3A 86
Hawksway. S31—6B 124
Hawksworth Clo. S65—2A 80
Hawksworth Rd. S6—5B 86
Hawksworth Rd. S65—2A 80
Hawley St. S1—2D 4 & 1E 99
Hawley St. S62—2F 69
Haworth Bank. S60—2F 91
Haworth Clo. S71—4B 14
Haworth Cres. S60—2F 91
Hawshaw La. S74—5G 37
Hawson St. S73—1G 39
Hawthorn Av. DN3—1F 35
Hawthorn Av. S19—6D 114
Hawthorn Av. S66—4D 82
Hawthorne Av. S18—6E 123
Hawthorne Av. S30—2B 140
Hawthorne Av. S31—4F 119
Hawthorne Av. S62—2G 69

Hawthorne Cres. S64—6C 42
Hawthorne Cres. S75—1A 22
Hawthorne Flats. S63—1F 29
 (off Lingamore Leys.)
Hawthorne Gro. DN5—5B 18
Hawthorne Rd. S63—6G 41
Hawthorne St. S6—5H 85
Hawthorne St. S40—4A 138
Hawthorne St. S70—1G 23
Hawthorne St. S72—2C 10
Hawthorne Way. S72—2C 10
Hawthorn Gro. DN12—5C 58
Hawthorn Rd. S6—3H 85
Hawthorn Rd. S30—6C 50
Hawthorn Rd. S31—6G 125
Hawthorn Ter. S10—2A 98
 (off Parker's La.)
Haxby Pl. S13—1G 113
Haxby St. S13—1G 113
Haybrook Ct. S17—4E 121
Haydn Rd. S66—5H 83
Haydock Clo. S64—5F 43
Haydon Gro. S66—3F 81
Hayes Ct. S19—3E 125
Hayes Croft. S70—6H 13
Hayes Dri. S19—3E 125
Hayfield Clo. S18—2B 128
Hayfield Clo. S43—1D 134
Hayfield Clo. S75—2A 22
Hayfield Cres. S12—4F 113
Hayfield Dri. S12—4F 113
Hayfield La. DN9—2G 63
Hayfield Pl. S12—4F 113
Hayfield View. S31—6B 124
Hayfield Wlk. S61—6G 67
 (off Byrley Rd.)
Hayford Way. S43—2C 134
Hay Grn. La. S70—4D 36
Hayhurst Cres. S66—5G 83
Hayland St. S9—1D 88
Haylock Clo. S75—4A 12
Haymarket. S1—2F 5 & 1F 99
Haythorne Way. S64—4B 56
Haywood Av. S30—3F 141
Haywood Clo. S65—2A 80
Haywood La. S30—3F 141
Hazel Av. S31—4A 126
Hazelbadge Cres. S12—4G 113
Hazel Clo. S18—3F 129
Hazel Dri. S40—5F 137
Hazel Gro. DN3—2G 35
Hazel Gro. DN11—5D 62
Hazel Gro. DN12—4D 58
Hazel Gro. S30—3E 65
Hazel Gro. S66—4G 81
Hazelhurst S8—3F 123
 (off Jordanthorpe Centre)
Hazelhurst Av. S41—6B 132
Hazelhurst La. S8—6B 112
Hazelhurst La. S41—6A 132
Hazel Rd. DN12—3B 60
Hazel Rd. S31—6H 125
Hazel Rd. S66—4D 82
Hazelshaw. S75—3C 22
Hazelshaw Gdns. S30—6B 50
Hazelwood Clo. S18—2A 128
Hazelwood Dri. S64—5B 56
Hazlebarrow Clo. S8—3F 123
Hazlebarrow Cres. S8—3F 123
Hazlebarrow Dri. S8—2F 123
Hazlebarrow Gro. S8—2E 123
Hazlebarrow Rd. S8—3F 123
Hazledene Cres. S72—4D 10
Hazledene Rd. S72—4D 10
Headford St. S3—5B 4 & 3D 98
Headland Dri. S10—2G 97
Headland Rd. S10—2G 97
Headlands Rd. S74—5H 37

Heads La. S30—6B 140
Heath Av. S31—4B 126
Heath Bank Rd. DN2—2A 34
Heathcote Dri. S41—5E 139
Heathcote St. S4—2H 87
Heatherbank Rd. DN4—4C 48
Heather Clo. S44—2G 139
Heather Ct. S66—5H 81
Heatherdale Rd. S66—4H 83
Heather Lea Av. S17—2C 120
Heather Lea Pl. S17—2C 120
Heather Rd. S5—6A 76
Heather Wlk. S63—6D 28
Heathfield Av. S40—2F 137
Heathfield Clo. DN3—1E 21
Heathfield Clo. S18—3D 128
Heathfield Rd. S12—3F 113
Heath Ho. DN1—1C 46
 (off Grove Pl.)
Heath Rd. S6—5B 74
Heath Rd. S30—4F 141
Heaton Clo. S18—2B 128
Heatons Bank. S62—1G 69
Heaton St. S40—3E 137
Heavygate Av. S10—5H 85
Heavygate Rd. S10—5A 86
Hedge La. S75—6B 6
Heeley Bank Rd. S2—6F 99
Heeley Grn. S2—1F 111
Heelis St. S70—1H 23
Heighton View. S31—4B 104
Helena St. S64—6E 43
Helensburgh Clo. S75—5E 13
Hellaby Euroway Ind. Est. S66
 —4A 82
Hellaby Hall Rd. S66—5B 82
Hellaby La. S66—4B 82
Hellaby View. S65—2H 81
Helliwell Ct. S30—5G 141
Helliwell La. S30—5G 141
Helmsley Av. S19—2D 124
Helmsley Clo. S31—1A 116
Helmton Dri. S8—5H 109
Helmton Rd. S8—5D 110
Helston Clo. S41—5B 138
Helston Cres. S71—4B 14
Helston Rise. S7—3A 110
Hemingfield Rd. S73—2D 38
Hemper Gro. S8—2B 122
Hemper La. S8—3B 122
Hemp Pits Rd. DN5—6D 18
Hemsworth Rd. S8—5E 111
Hendon St. S13—4H 101
Hengist Rd. DN5—1H 45
Henley Av. S8—1F 123
Henley Gro. Rd. S61—2B 78
Henley La. S61—1A 78
Henley Rd. DN2—4A 34
Henley Rd. S61—2B 78
Henley Way. S61—2A 78
Hennings Clo. DN4—4H 47
Hennings La. DN4—3H 47
Hennings Rd. DN4—6A 48
Henry Clo. S72—2C 10
Henry La. DN11—3B 62
Henry Pl. S64—6G 43
Henry Rd. S63—5G 41
Henry St. S3—6D 86
Henry St. S30—6A 50
Henry St. S31—6D 124
Henry St. S41—3B 132
Henry St. S62—4F 69
Henry St. S65—2E 79
Henry St. S70—4A 24
Henry St. S73—5D 26
Henshall St. S70—1A 24
Heppenstall La. S9—5B 88

Heptinstall St. S70—4B 24
Hepworth Dri. S31—6B 104
Hepworth Rd. DN4—4H 45
Herbert Clo. DN5—4A 32
Herbert Rd. DN5—4A 32
Herbert Rd. S7—1C 110
Herbert St. S61—2G 77
Herbert St. S64—6F 43
Herdings Ct. S12—4C 112
Herdings Rd. S12—4C 112
Herdings View. S12—4C 112
Hereford Dri. S43—3F 133
Hereford Rd. DN2—2H 33
Hereford St. S1—6D 4 & 4E 99
 (in two parts)
Hereward Rd. S5—5F 75
Hereward's Rd. S8—6H 111
Hermitage St. S2—4D 98
Hermit La. S75—5A 12
Heron Hill. S31—1C 116
Heron Mt. S2—3A 100
Herons Way. S70—3D 36
Herrick Gdns. DN4—5C 46
Herrick Rd. DN3—1H 21
Herries Av. S5—1E 87
Herries Dri. S5—1E 87
Herries Pl. S5—1E 87
Herries Rd. S5 & S6
 —1B 86 to 2G 87
Herries Rd. S. S6—1B 86
Herringthorpe Av. S65—5H 79
Herringthorpe Gro. S65—5A 80
Herringthorpe La. S65—4A 80
Herringthorpe Valley Rd. S65 &
 S66—6A 70
Herschell Rd. S7—6D 98
 (in two parts)
Hesketh Dri. DN3—3E 21
Hesley Bar. S61—3A 66
Hesley Ct. DN12—2B 58
Hesley Grange. S61—5E 67
Hesley Gro. S30—3G 65
Hesley La. S61—3A 66
Hesley Rd. DN11—5D 62
Hesley Rd. S5—2H 75
Hesley Ter. S5—2H 75
Heslow Gro. S61—2A 66
Hessey St. S13—1H 113
Hessle Rd. S6—1H 85
Hethersett Way. DN11—6C 62
Hewitt St. S64—6G 43
Hexthorpe Rd. DN4—1B 46
Heyhouse Dri. S30—6E 51
Heyhouse Way. S30—6D 50
Heysham Grn. S71—1D 14
Heywood St. S43—3F 133
Hibberd Pl. S6—3G 85
Hibberd Rd. S6—3G & 3H 85
 (in two parts)
Hibbert Ter. S70—2H 23
Hickleton St. DN12—2B 58
Hickleton Ter. S63—2G 29
Hickmott Rd. S11—5B 98
Hicks La. S3—1E 5 & 1E 99
Hickson Dri. S71—3E 15
Hicks St. S3—5E 87
Hides St. S9—3D 88
Higgitt Rd. S9—3D 88
Higham Comn. Rd. S75—3A 12
Higham Rd. S75—5A 12
Higham View. S75—6B 6
High Ash Dri. S31—4F 119
Highbury Av. DN4—3C 48
Highbury Cres. DN4—3C 48
Highbury Rd. S41—6H 131
Highbury Vale. DN12—4A 60
Highcliffe Ct. S11—6G 97
Highcliffe Dri. S11—6F 97

Highcliffe Dri. S30—3C 72
Highcliffe Dri. S64—2B 56
Highcliffe Pl. S11—1F 109
Highcliffe Rd. S11—6F 97
Highcliffe Ter. S70—1A 24
 (off Gold St.)
High Ct. S1—2F 5 & 1F 99
High Croft. S74—6A 38
Higher Albert St. S41—1A 138
Highfield. S63—5F 41
Highfield Av. S31—4A 118
Highfield Av. S41—6G 131
Highfield Av. S63—4F 29
Highfield Av. S70—3H 23
Highfield Av. S71—1A 14
Highfield Ct. S64—2A 56
Highfield Gro. S63—4A 40
Highfield La. S13 & S60
 —3B 102
Highfield La. S41—5G 131
Highfield Pk. S66—3H 83
Highfield Pl. S2—5E 99
Highfield Ridge. S73—2E 27
Highfield Rise. S6—5B 84
Highfield Rd. DN1—5E 33
Highfield Rd. DN12—3F 59
Highfield Rd. S41—6H 131
Highfield Rd. S61—5C 68
Highfield Rd. S64—2H 55
Highfield Rd. S73—3E 27
Highfields Cres. S18—3E 129
Highfields Rd. S18—3E 129
Highfields Rd. S75—5A 6
Highfield Ter. S41—6H 131
Highfield View. S60—5C 90
Highfield View Rd. S41
 (in two parts) —6H 131
High Fisher Ga. DN1—5D 32
Highgate. S9—5G 77
 (in two parts)
Highgate Clo. DN11—6E 63
Highgate Dri. S18—4G 129
Highgate La. S18—4F 129
Highgate La. S63—6E 29
Highgreave. S5—2G 75
High Greave Av. S5—2F 75
High Greave Pl. S65—2A 80
High Greave Rd. S65—1A 80
High Hazel Cres. S60—5C 90
High Hazels Clo. S9—1F 101
High Hazels Mead. S9—1F 101
High Hazels Pk. S9—1F 101
High Hooton Rd. S31 & S66
 —3G 95
High Ho. Rd. S6—4B 86
High Ho. Ter. S6—4B 86
High La. S12—6E 113
High La. S66—3F 105
Highlightley La. S18—6A 128
Highlow Clo. S40—6E 131
Highlow View. S60—2C 90
High Matlock Av. S6—5D 84
High Matlock Rd. S6—4D 84
Highmill Av. S64—2G 55
Highmoor Av. S31—5G 117
Highnam Cres. Rd. S10—2A 98
High Nook Rd. S31—5G 107
High Pavement Row. S2—3H 5
High Ridge. S70—4H 23
High Rd. DN4—4A 46
 (Balby)
High Rd. DN4—5E 45
 (Warmsworth)
High Rd. DN12—4B 60
High Royd Av. S72—1H 15
Highroyds. S70—3H 23
Highstone Av. S70—2G 23
 (Barnsley)

Highstone Av. S70—3H 23
(Worsbrough)
Highstone Cres. S70—2G 23
Highstone La. S70—3H 23
Highstone Rd. S70—2H 23
Highstone Vale. S70—2G 23
High Storrs Clo. S11—1G 109
High Storrs Cres. S11—6G 97
High Storrs Dri. S11—1F 109
High Storrs Rise. S11—6G 97
High Storrs Rd. S11—1F 109
High St. Anston, S31—3F 119
High St. Arksey, DN5—4D 18
High St. Barnby Dun, DN3
—2G 21
High St. Barnsley, S70—5G 13
High St. Beighton, S19—3G 115
High St. Bentley, DN5—2A 32
High St. Billingley, S72—2B 28
High St. Bolton-u-Dearne S63
—1A 42
High St. Brimington, S43
—3F 133
High St. Chesterfield, S40
—2A 138
High St. Conisbrough, DN12
—3E 59
High St. Darton, S75—3E 7
High St. Dodworth, S75—2B 22
High St. Doncaster, DN1—6C 32
High St. Dore, S17—2D 100
High St. Dronfield, S18—2E 129
High St. Dunsville, DN7—4G 21
High St. Ecclesfield, S30—1F 75
High St. Eckington, S31—6C 124
High St. Goldthorpe, S63—4G 29
High St. Grimethorpe, S72
—6F 11
High St. Hoyland, S74—5A 38
High St. Killamarsh, S31
—3B 126
High St. Kimberworth, S61
—2G 77
High St. La. S2—3H 5 & 2G 99
High St. Maltby, S66—4G 83
High St. Mexborough, S64
—1E 57
High St. Monk Bretton, S71
—3C 14
High St. Mosborough, S19
—2C 124
High St. Old Whittington, S41
—1A 132
High St. Rawmarsh, S62—3F 69
High St. Rotherham, S60—3D 78
High St. Royston, S71—2C 8
High St. Shafton, S72—2C 10
High St. Sheffield, S1
—3E 5 & 2F 99
High St. Staveley, S43—1C 134
High St. Swallownest. S31
—6A 104
High St. Thurnscoe, S63—1E 29
High St. Wadworth, DN11
—6H 61
High St. Wath upon Dearne S63
—5F 41
High St. Whiston, S60—2H 91
High St. Wombwell, S73—6B 26
High St. Worsbrough, S70
—4B 24
High St. La. S2—3H 5 & 2G 99
Highthorn Rd. S62—4B 56
Highton St. S6—5A 86
High Trees. S17—2D 120
High Trees. S60—6H 79
High View. S71—2D 8
High View Clo. S41—3D 138

High View Clo. S73—3F 27
Highwood Clo. S75—5A 6
Highwood Pl. S31—6C 124
Highwoods Cres. S64—6C 42
Highwoods Rd. S64—6C 42
High Wray Clo. S11—3H 109
Hilary Way. S31—6B 104
Hilda Ter. S72—6F 12
Hillary Ho. DN2—3G 33
Hillberry Rise. S40—6H 137
Hill Clo. S6—5C 84
Hill Clo. S65—5C 80
Hillcote Clo. S10—4D 96
Hillcote Dri. S10—4D 96
Hillcrest. S63—2E 29
Hill Crest. S74—6G 37
Hillcrest Dri. S30—3C 72
Hillcrest Rise. S30—4H 141
Hillcrest Rd. DN2—3G 33
Hill Crest Rd. S30—2D 64
(Chapeltown)
Hillcrest Rd. S30—4H 141
(Deepcar)
Hillcrest Rd. S41—6D 138
Hill Crest Rd. S65—2H 79
Hill End Rd. S75—6G 7
Hillfoot Rd. S3—5C 86
Hillfoot Rd. S17—4C 120
Hillman Dri. S43—5A 134
Hillsborough Arc. S6—3A 86
Hillsborough Pl. S6—3A 86
Hillsborough Rd. DN4—3C 48
Hillsborough Rd. S6—3A 86
Hills Clo. DN5—1G 45
Hillside. S19—2C 124
Hillside. S31—1F 119
Hill Side. S60—2H 91
Hillside. S71—1G 25
Hillside Av. S5—3F 75
Hillside Av. S18—3E 129
Hillside Cres. S72—3G 11
Hillside Dri. S40—3F 137
Hillside Dri. S74—6B 38
Hillside Gro. S72—3G 11
Hillside Mt. S72—3G 11
Hillside Rd. DN2—2A 34
Hills Rd. S30—3F 141
Hill St. S2—4D 98
Hill St. S71—1E 25
Hill St. S73—4E 27
Hill St. S74—6C 38
Hilltop. S72—2F 11
Hill Top Clo. S60—2B 90
Hill Top Clo. S61—3F 77
Hill Top Clo. S66—3D 82
Hill Top Cres. DN2—2A 34
Hill Top Cres. DN12—5B 60
Hill Top Cres. S19—6D 114
Hilltop Dri. S30—1B 74
Hill Top La. S30—1E 141
Hill Top La. S61—3F 77
Hill Top La. S66—2D 80
Hill Top La. S75—4D 12
Hill Top Rise. S30—1B 74
Hilltop Rd. S18—3E 129
Hill Top Rd. S30—1B 74
Hilltop Rd. S41—1A 132
Hill Top Rd. S70—3D 36
Hill Turrets Clo. S11—3F 109
Hill View Rd. S43—3E 133
Hill View Rd. S61—1F 77
Hilton Dri. S30—1F 75
Hilton St. S75—5F 13
Hindburn Clo. DN4—4A 48
Hinde Ho. Cres. S4—1A 88
Hinde Ho. Croft. S4—1A 88

Hinde Ho. La. S4—2H 87
Hinde St. S4—2A 88
Hindewood Clo. S4—1A 88
Hindle St. S70—6F 13
Hind Rd. S60—1A 92
Hipley Clo. S40—5D 130
Hipper St. S40—3A 138
Hipper St. S. S40—3A 138
Hipper St. W. S40—3G 137
Hirs Ga. S64—1G 57
Hirst Comn. La. S6—3H 73
Hirst Dri. S65—2B 80
Hobart St. S11—5D 98
Hobner La. S43—3A 134
Hobson Av. S6—4C 86
Hobson Pl. S6—4C 86
Hodder Ct. S30—1D 64
Hodgson St. S3—6C 4 & 3D 98
Hodroyd Clo. S72—4D 10
Hodroyd Cotts. S72—3F 11
Hogarth Rise. S18—3D 128
Holbeck Clo. S41—1B 138
Holbeck Grn. S9—4C 88
Holbein Clo. S18—3D 128
Holberry Clo. S10
—5A 4 & 3C 98
Holberry Gdns. S10—3C 98
Holborn Av. S18—1E 129
Holbourne Gro. S30—4B 50
Holbrook Av. S19—1F 125
Holbrook Clo. S40—5E 137
Holbrook Dri. S13—1D 112
Holbrook Grn. S19—1G 125
Holbrook Rise. S19—6F 115
Holbrook Rd. S13—6D 100
Holbrook Trading Est. S19
—1G 125
Holderness Dri. S31—5B 104
Holdings Rd. S2—4H 99
Holdroyds Yd. S75—3B 22
Holdworth La. S6—6A 72
Hole Ho. La. S30—3D 140
Holgate. S73—4H 25
Holgate Av. S5—3D 74
Holgate Clo. S5—3D 74
Holgate Cres. S5—3E 75
Holgate Dri. S5—3E 75
Holgate Mt. S70—3H 23
Holgate Rd. S5—3E 75
Holgate View. S72—2H 11
Holiwell Clo. S66—3H 83
Holkham Rise. S11—5F 109
Holland Clo. S62—6F 55
Holland Pl. S2—5E 99
Holland Rd. S2—5E 99
Holland Rd. S30—6B 50
Holland Rd. S41—1H 131
Holland St. S1—3C 4 & 2D 98
Hollens Way. S40—5B 130
Hollies Clo. S18—3G 129
Hollinberry La. S30—4A 50
Hollin Busk La. S30—5E 141
Hollin Busk Rd. S30—4E 141
Hollin Clo. DN11—3F 63
Hollin Clo. S41—3E 131
Hollindale Dri. S12—2E 113
Hollin Edge La. S30—6H 141
Holling Croft. S30—3G 141
Holling Moor La. S66—6E 81
Holling's La. S65
—5D 70 to 1H 81
Hollingwood Cres. S43—1G 133
Hollingworth Clo. S64—5H 43
Hollin Hill La. S66—5D 80
Hollin Ho. La. S6—1A 84
Hollin Rd. S30—3C 72
Hollins Clo. S6—6F 85
Hollins Ct. S6—5F 85

Hollins Dri. S6—6G 85
Hollinsend Av. S12—2E 113
Hollinsend Pl. S12—2E 113
Hollinsend Rd. S12—3C 112
Hollins La. S6—5F 85
Hollins Spring Av. S18—3E 129
Hollins Spring Rd. S18—3E 129
Hollins, The. S75—3C 22
Hollis Clo. S62—5D 54
Hollis Croft. S1—2C 4 & 1D 98
Hollis Croft. S13—1A 114
Hollis La. S41—3B 138
(in two parts)
Hollowdene. S75—4D 12
Hollowgate. DN5—1F 43
Hollow Ga. S30—2B 64
(Chapeltown)
Hollowgate. S60—4E 79
(Rotherham)
Hollow Ga. S60—2H 91
(Whiston)
Hollowgate Av. S63—3C 40
Hollow La. S19—3D 124
Hollows, The. DN4—5C 48
Holly Av. DN5—2A 32
Hollybank Av. S12—1E 113
Hollybank Clo. S12—1F 113
Hollybank Cres. S12—1E 113
Hollybank Dri. S12—1F 113
Hollybank Rd. S12—1E 113
Hollybank Way. S12—1F 113
Holly Bush La. DN3—4C 20
Hollybush St. S62—4F 69
Holly Clo. S30—3D 64
Holly Clo. S31—4A 126
Holly Cres. S66—3G 81
Hollycroft Av. S71—2D 8
Holly Dene. DN3—1F 35
Holly Dri. DN5—5B 18
Holly Gdns. S12—1E 113
Holly Ga. S70—4C 24
Holly Gro. DN11—3E 63
Holly Gro. S63—1F 55
Holly Gro. S72—2G 11
Holly Hall La. S30—1H 141
Holly Ho. La. S30—1H 73
Holly La. S1—3D 4
Holly Mt. S66—5G 81
Holly St. DN1—2C 46
Holly St. S1—3D 4 & 2E 99
(in two parts)
Holly Ter. DN4—4H 45
Holly Ter. S31—5A 104
Hollythorpe Clo. S41—5D 138
Hollythorpe Cres. S8—3E 111
Hollythorpe Rise. S8—3F 111
Hollythorpe Rd. S8—3F 111
Hollytree Av. S30—3D 82
Holmbrook Wlk. S40—6E 131
Holm Clo. S18—1B 128
Holmebank Clo. S40—1G 137
Holmebank E. S40—1G 137
Holmebank View. S40—1G 137
Holmebank W. S40—1G 137
Holme Clo. S6—3A 86
Holme Hall Cres. S40—5B 130
Holme La. S6—4H 85
Holme La. S30—2B 74
Holme Rd. S41—5A 132
Holmes Carr Cres. DN11—4B 62
Holmes Carr Rd. DN4—5B 48
Holmes Carr Rd. DN11—4B 62
Holmes Cres. S60—1E 103
Holmesdale Clo. S18—6G 123
Holmesdale Rd. S18—6F 123
Holmesfield. S61—3A 78
(off Rosebery St.)
Holmesfield Rd. S18—2A 128

Holmesfield Rd. S30—3D 72
Holmes La. S61—3A 78
Holmes La. S65—6G 57
Holmes Rd. S66—5H 81
Holmes, The. DN1—5E 33
Holme View Rd. S75—5A 6
Holme Wood Gdns. DN4—4C 48
Holme Wood La. DN3—3H 35
Holmfield Clo. DN3—4G 35
Holm Flatt St. S62—4E 69
Holmhirst Clo. S8—5C 110
Holmhirst Dri. S8—4C 110
Holmhirst Rd. S8—4C 110
Holmhirst Way. S8—4C 110
Holmoor Rd. S42—5A 136
Holyoake Av. S13—5G 101
Holyrood Rise. S66—3H 81
Holyrood Rd. DN2—6G 33
Holywell Clo. S62—6H 55
Holywell La. DN12—4E 59
Holywell La. S66—1G 83
Holywell Pl. S65—2E 79
  (off Nottingham St.)
Holywell Rd. S4 & S9—2B 88
Holywell Rd. S62—4B 56
Holywell St. S41—2A 138
Homecroft Rd. S63—4F 29
Homefield Cres. DN5—1G 31
Homestead Clo. S5—4H 75
Homestead Dri. S60—2B 90
Homestead Dri. S62—6F 55
Homestead Rd. S5—4G 75
Homestead, The. DN5—6B 18
Honeysuckle Rd. S5—6A 76
Honeywell Clo. S71—4H 13
Honeywell Gro. S71—3H 13
Honeywell La. S75—4G 13
Honeywell Pl. S71—4G 13
Honeywell St. S71—4H 13
Honister Clo. S63—4A 40
Hoober Av. S11—2G 109
Hoober Field Rd. S62—4A 54
Hoober Hall La. S62 & S63
  —2G 53
Hoober La. S62—4A 54
Hoober Rd. S11—2G 109
Hoober St. S63—4B 40
Hoober View. S62—5D 54
Hoober View. S73—2H 39
Hood Grn. Rd. S75—6A 2
Hoole La. S10—3A 98
Hoole Rd. S10—2A 98
Hoole St. S6—5A 86
Hoole St. S41—5D 138
Hooley Rd. S13—1D 114
Hooton Clo. S31—6G 95
Hooton La. S31—6G 95
Hooton La. S65—4G 71
Hooton La. S66—5E 83
Hooton Rd. S62—6C 56
Hooton St. S4—4G 87
Hope Av. S63—4F 29
Hopedale Rd. S12—3F 113
Hopefield Av. S12—3F 113
Hope Rd. S30—3E 73
Hope St. S3—2A 4 & 1C 98
Hope St. S30—3E 141
Hope St. S40—2G 137
Hope St. S60—2C 78

Hope St. S64—1E 57
Hope St. S71—1F 15
Hope St. S73—5D 26
  (Low Valley, Wombwell)
Hope St. S73—1G 39
  (Wombwell)
Hope St. S75—5F 13
  (Barnsley)
Hope St. S75—5G 7
  (Mapplewell)
Hopewell St S70—1D 24
Hopwood La. S6—1B 96
Hopwood St. S70—5G 13
Horace St. S60—4E 79
Horam Rd. S6—1B 98
Horbiry End. S31—2A 118
Horbury La. S30—3C 64
Horbury Rd. S72—5B 10
Hornbeam Clo. S30—3D 64
Hornbeam Rd. S66—3F 81
Hornby Ct. S11—6G 97
Hornby St. S70—2A 24
Horndean Rd. S5—2H 87
Horner Clo. S30—3D 140
Horner Rd. S7—6E 99
Hornes La. S75—4G 7
Horninglow Clo. DN4—4E 49
Horninglow Clo. S5—6G 75
Horninglow Mt. S5—6G 75
Horninglow Rd. S5—6G 75
Hornsby Rd. DN3—4G 35
Hornthorpe Rd. S31—6G 125
Horse Carr View. S71—1G 25
Horse Croft La. S30—1B 72
Horsemoor Rd. S63—1D 28
Horseshoe Clo. S31—4G 117
Horsewood Clo. S70—1D 22
Horsewood Rd. S13—5D 102
Horsewood Rd. S42—5D 136
Horsley Clo. S40—6C 130
Horton Clo. S19—2C 124
Horton Dri. S19—2C 124
Hough La. S73—1E 39
Houghton Rd. S31—5B 106
Houghton Rd. S63—1C 28
Houldsworth Dri. S41—3D 138
Hound Hill La. S64—4B 42
Hound Hill La. S70—5F 23
Houndkirk Rd. S11—4A 108
Hounsfield Cres. S65—2B 80
Hounsfield La. S3—4A 4
Hounsfield Rd. S3
  —3A 4 & 2C 98
Hounsfield Rd. S65—2B 80
Housley La. S30—2D 64
Housley Pk. S30—1D 64
Houstead Rd. S9—2F 101
Hoveringham Ct. S31—1A 116
Howard Dri. S41—1A 132
Howard La. S1—5F 5 & 3F 99
  (in two parts)
Howard Rd. S6—6A 86
Howard Rd. S66—4H 81
  (Bramley)
Howard Rd. S66—4H 83
  (Maltby)
Howard St. S1—4F 5 & 3F 99
Howard St. S31—4G 107
Howard St. S65—2D 78
Howard St. S70—2H 23
Howard St. S73—4G 27
Howarth Rd. S60—3D 90
Howbeck Dri. DN12—4A 60
Howbrook Clo. S30—5A 50
Howden Clo. DN4—5A 48
Howden Clo. S43—1D 134
Howden Clo. S75—4D 6
Howden Rd. S9—4C 88

Howdike La. S65—6F 57
Howe La S31—3G 95
Howlett Clo S60—2B 92
Howlett Dri S60—4C 90
Howse St. S74—5D 38
Howson Rd. S30—3F 141
Hoylake Av. S40—6E 137
Hoylake Dri. S64—4B 56
Hoyland Rd. S3—4C 86
Hoyland Rd. S74—6F 37
Hoyland St. S66—5H 83
Hoyland St. S73—1F 39
Hoy La. S64—4C 42
Hoyle Croft La. S66—1E 83
Hoyle Mill Rd. S70—1D 24
Hoyle St. S3—1C 4 & 1D 98
Hucklow Av. S40—5H 137
Hucklow Av. S43—4A 134
Hucklow Dri. S5—6H 75
Hucklow Rd. S5—1H 87
Hucknall Av. S40—1E 137
Huddersfield Rd. S75 & S70
  (Barnsley)   —3E 13
Huddersfield Rd. S75—4A 6
  (Darton)
Hudson Haven. S73—6H 25
Hudson La. S13—5E 103
Hudson Rd. S61—5G 67
Hudson's M DN1—6C 32
Humphrey Rd. S8—1C 122
Humphries Av S62—6D 54
Hungerhill Clo S61—1F 77
Hungerhill La. DN3—5B 20
Hunger Hill La. S60—2A 92
Hunger Hill Rd S60—1H 91
Hungerhill Rd S61—6F 67
Hunloke Av. S40—4F 137
Hunloke Cres. S40—4G 137
Hunningley Clo S70—2E 25
Hunningley La. S70—4D 24
Hunsdon Rd. S31—6C 124
Hunshelf Pk. S30—2E 141
Hunshelf Rd. S30—2D 64
  (Chapeltown)
Hunshelf Rd. S30—1C to 2D 140
  (in two parts, Stocksbridge)
Hunsley St. S4—3A 88
Hunster Clo. DN4—4D 48
Hunster Flat La. DN11—6D 62
Hunster Gro. DN11—5D 62
Hunstone Av. S8—2E 123
Hunter Ct. S11—6H 97
Hunter Hill Rd. S11—5A 98
Hunter Ho. Rd. S11—5A 98
Hunter Rd. S6—3H 85
Hunter's Av. S70—1C 22
Hunters Bar. S11—5A 98
Hunters Chase. S31—2F 107
Hunters Clo. S31—2F 107
Hunters Ct. S31—2F 107
Hunters Dri. S31—2F 107
Hunters Gdns. S6—2D 84
Hunters Gdns. S31—2F 107
Hunters La. S13—1E 113
Hunters Pk. S31—2F 107
Hunters Rise. S75—6D 12
Hunters Way. S31—2F 107
Huntingdon Cres S11—5C 98
Huntingdon Rd. DN2—4A 34
Huntingdon St. DN5—5A 18
Huntingtower Rd. S11—6H 97
Hunt La. DN5—4B 32
Huntley Clo. S43—3H 133
Huntley Gro. S11—1F 109
Huntley Rd. S11—1G 109
Huntsman Rd. S9—1F 101
Huntsman Rd. S43—1C 134
Hunt St. S74—6F 37

Hurl Dri. S12—2B 112
Hurley Croft. S63—4A 40
Hurlfield Av. S12—2B 112
Hurlfield Ct. S12—1C 112
Hurlfield Dri. S12—1B 112
Hurlfield Dri. S65—2H 81
Hurlfield Rd. S12—2A to 1C 112
Hurlfield View. S12—1B 112
Hurlingham Clo. S11—2A 110
Hursley Clo. S19—6G 115
Hursley Dri. S19—6G 115
Hurst Grn S30—6B 50
Hurst La. DN9—4H 63
Hutchinson La. S7—4B 110
Hutchinson La. S7—4B 110
Hutchinson Rd. S7—4B 110
Hutchinson Rd. S62—1G 69
Hutcliffe Dri. S8—5B 110
Hutcliffe Wood Rd. S8—5B 110
Hut La. S31—5C 126
Hutton Croft. S12—4B 114
Hutton Rd. S61—6H 67
Hyacinth Clo S5—6B 76
Hyacinth Rd. S5—6B 76
Hyde Pk. Ter. S2—2G 99
Hyde Pk Wlk. S2—2G 99
Hyman Clo DN4—4F 45
Hyperion Way DN11—5C 62

Ians Way S40—1E 137
Ibberson Av. S75—5F 7
Ibbotson Rd S6—5A 86
Ibsen Cres DN3—1H 21
Icknield Way. S60—3C 90
Ida's Rd. S31—5D 124
Idsworth Rd. S5—1H 87
Ilam Clo. S43—5A 134
Ilkley Cres S31—1A 116
Ilkley Rd. S5—5H 75
Illsley Rd S73—3E 27
Immingham Gro. S43—2B 134
Imperial Cres DN2—5F 33
Imperial St. S70—2H 23
Industry Rd. S9—6D 88
Industry Rd S71—6E 9
Industry St S6—5A 86
  (in two parts)
Infield La S9—1F 101
Infirmary Rd S6—5C 86
Infirmary Rd. S41—1B 138
Infirmary Rd S62—4G 69
Ingelow Av S5—4F 75
Ingfield Av. S9—1G 89
Ingleborough Croft S30—1D 64
Ingleborough Dri. DN5—1G 45
Ingleby Clo S18—2A 128
Ingle Gro DN5—1G 45
Ingleton Rd S41—6B 138
Ingleton Wlk S70—5F 13
Inglewood Av S19—6G 115
Inglewood Ct. S19—6G 115
Ingram Ct. S2—3H 99
Ingram Rd. S2—3H 99
Ingsfield La S63—1G 41
Ingshead Av S62—2F 69
Ingshead Ho S62—2F 69
Ings La. DN5—5E 19
  (Arksey)
Ings La. DN5—5F 19
  (Arksey Common)
Ings La S72—2F 27
Ings Rd DN5—3C 32
Ings Rd S73—5D 26
Ings Way DN5—5D 18
Inkerman Rd S73 4E 27
Inkersall Dri S19 - 1E 125
Inkersall Grn Rd S43 3H 133

Inkersall Rd. S43—5B 134
Insley Gdns. DN4—4C 48
Intake Cres. S75—3B 22
Intake La. S72—5C 10
Intake La. S75—4D 12
Ireland St. S43—1D 134
Irongate. S40—2A 138
(off High St.)
Ironside Clo. S14—5H 111
Ironside Pl. S14—4A 112
Ironside Rd. S14—5H 111
Ironside Wlk. S14—5H 111
Irving St. S9—1E 101
Irwell Gdns. DN4—1B 48
Islay St. S10—2H 97
Issott St. S71—4H 13
Ivanbrook Clo. S18—2A 128
Ivanhoe Av. S31—4A 118
Ivanhoe Clo. DN5—5H 31
Ivanhoe M. S31—5A 104
Ivanhoe Rd. DN3—6D 20
Ivanhoe Rd. DN4—5G 45
Ivanhoe Rd. DN12—3D 58
(Conisbrough)
Ivanhoe Rd. DN12—4B 60
(Edlington)
Ivanhoe Rd. S6—5G 85
Ivanhoe Rd. S66—5A 94
Ivanhoe Way. DN5—5H 31
Ivor Gro. DN4—3A 46
Ivy Clo. DN11—3E 63
Ivy Clo. S41—1A 132
Ivy Cottage La. S11—1C 108
Ivy Cotts. S71—1F 9
Ivy Farm Clo. S71—4F 9
Ivy Farm Croft. S65—6B 70
Ivy Gro. S10—1B 98
Ivy Hall Rd. S5—3A 76
Ivy La. S19—3G 115
Ivy Pk. Ct. S10—4E 97
Ivy Pk. Rd. S10—3E 97
Ivy Ter. S70—1A 24

Jack Close Orchard. S71—1E 9
Jackey La. S30—2B 72
Jackson Cres. S62—6E 55
Jackson Sq. S75—2B 22
Jackson St. S63—4G 29
Jackson St. S72—1G 15
Jacobs Clo. S5—5A 76
Jacobs Dri. S5—5A 76
Jamaica St. S4—4H 87
James Andrew Clo. S8—2D 122
James Andrew Cres. S8
—2C 122
James Andrew Croft. S8
—2D 122
James St. S9—2E 101
James St. S41—5A 132
James St. S60—2C 78
(in two parts)
James St. S64—6H 43
James St. S70—4A 24
(Worsbrough)
James St. S70—4C 24
(Worsbrough Dale)
James St. S71—5H 13
Janet's Wlk. S73—5G 25
Janson St. S9—3C 88
Jaques Pl. S71—5D 14
Jardine Clo. S9—5C 76
Jardine St. S9—5D 76
Jardine St. S73—1F 39
Jarratt St. DN1—1D 46
Jarrow Rd. S11—5B 98
Jasmine Av. S19—4F 115
Jaunty Av. S12—4D 112

Jaunty Clo. S12—4D 112
Jaunty Cres. S12—3D 112
Jaunty Dri. S12—4D 112
Jaunty La. S12—2D 112
Jaunty Mt. S12—4E 113
Jaunty Pl. S12—4D 112
Jaunty Rd. S12—4E 113
Jaunty View. S12—4E 113
Jaunty Way. S12—3D 112
Jaw Bones Hill. S40—5A 138
Jay La. S31—1C 116
Jedburgh Dri. S9—5C 76
Jedburgh St. S9—5C 76
Jeffcock Pl. S30—6C 50
Jeffcock Rd. S9—1E 101
Jeffcock Rd. S30—6C 50
Jefferson Av. DN2—6B 20
Jeffery Cres. S30—4F 141
Jeffrey Grn. S10—6A 96
Jeffrey St. S2—1F 111
Jenkin Av. S9—1C 88
Jenkin Clo. S9—6C 76
Jenkin Dri. S9—1C 88
Jenkin Rd. S9—6C 76
Jenny La. S72—1H 15
Jepson Rd. S5—5B 76
Jericho St. S3—1B 4 & 1C 98
Jermyn Av. S12—3G 113
Jermyn Clo. S12—4H 113
Jermyn Cres. S12—4H 113
Jermyn Croft. S75—2B 22
Jermyn Dri. S12—4H 113
Jermyn Sq. S12—4H 113
Jermyn Way. S12—4G 113
Jersey Rd. S2—6E 99
Jervis Pl. S43—5H 133
Jesmond Av. S71—2D 8
Jessamine Rd. S5—5A 76
Jessell St. S9—6B 88
Jessop St. S1—6D 4 & 3E 99
Jewitt Rd. S61—5G 67
Jew La. S1—3G 5 & 2F 99
Joan La. S66—5E 83
Joan's Wlk. S74—4B 38
Jobson Pl. S3—6D 86
Jobson Rd. S3—6D 86
Jockel Dri. S62—2F 69
John Calvert Rd. S13—1D 114
John Eaton's Almshouses. S8
—5F 111
John La. DN11—4C 62
Johnson La. S3—1F 5 & 1F 99
Johnson La. S30—6F 65
Johnson St. S3—6F 87
Johnson St. S30—3D 140
Johnson St. S65—4F 79
Johnson St. S75—5F 13
Johnstone Clo. S40—4H 137
John St. DN6—1E 17
John St. S2—4D 98
John St. S31—6D 124
John St. S40—2G 137
John St. S43—3E 133
John St. S60—3C 78
John St. S63—1F 29
John St. S64—1E 57
John St. S66—4A 94
John St. S70—1H 23
(Barnsley)
John St. S70—5A 24
(Worsbrough)
John St. S72—1B 28
(Great Houghton)
John St. S72—2A 28
(Little Houghton)
John St. S73—6A 26
John Trickett Ho. S30—2D 64
(off Lansbury Av.)

John Ward St. S13—6D 102
John West St. S30—4D 140
Joiner St. S3—1F 5
Jones Av. S73—6H 25
Jordan Cres. S61—4G 77
Jordanthorpe Centre. S8
—3F 123
Jordanthorpe Parkway. S8
—1F to 4E 123
Josephine Rd. S61—3A 78
Joseph St. S31—6D 124
Joseph St. S60—2C 78
Joseph St. S70—1H 23
Joseph St. S72—6G 11
Joshua Rd. S7—1C 110
Josselin Ct. S30—2D 64
Jossey La. DN5—1F 31 to 1A 32
Jowitt Rd. S11—1A 110
Jowitt Clo. S66—6E 83
Jubb Clo. S65—5B 80
Jubilee Cotts. S44—4G 139
Jubilee Cotts. S60—2B 90
Jubilee Ct. DN2—3A 34
Jubilee Cres. S31—2C 126
Jubilee Rd. DN1—4E 33
Jubilee Rd. S9—5D 88
Jubilee St. S60—5D 78
Jubilee Ter. S70—1B 24
Judith Rd. S31—1B 116
Judy Row. S71—3C 14
Julian Rd. S9—6D 76
Julian Way S9—6D 76
Jumble La. S30—6H 65
Jumble Rd. S11—6A 108
Junction 34 Ind. Est. S9—2G 89
Junction Clo. S73—2A 40
Junction Dri. DN11—5C 62
Junction Rd. S11—5A 98
Junction Rd. S13—6D 102
Junction St. S70—1B 24
Junction St. S73—2H 39
Junction Ter. S70—1B 24
June Rd. S13—6D 102
Juniper Rise. S31—4A 126

Katherine Rd. S66—4A 94
Katherine St. S66—5B 94
Kathleen Gro. S63—3H 29
Kathleen St. S63—3H 29
Kay Cres. S62—5C 54
Kaye Pl. S10—1B 98
Kay's Ter. S70—2E 25
Kay St. S74—6F 37
Kearsley La. DN12—5D 58
Kearsley Rd. S2—5E 99
Keats Dri. S31—5H 107
Keats Rd. DN4—5B 46
Keats Rd. S6—3B 74
Keats Rd. S41—3H 131
Keeble Martin Way. S63—5D 40
Keeper La. WF4—1H 7
Keeton Hall Rd. S31—4B 118
Keeton's Hill. S2—5D 98
Keighley Wlk. DN12—4B 58
Keilder Ct. S40—4F 137
Keir Pl. S62—1H 69
Keir St. S70—5F 13
Keir Ter. S70—5F 13
Kelburn Av. S40—4E 137
Kelham Island. S3—6E 87
Kelham St. DN1—2C 46
Kelly St. S63—4G 29
Kelsey Gdns. DN4—6C 48
Kelsey Ter. S70—2H 23
Kelso Dri. DN4—4F 45
Kelvin Gro. S73—1G 39
Kelvin St. S64—6E 43

Kelvin St. S65—6B 70
Kelvin Wlk. S6—6C 86
Kempton Gdns. S64—5G 43
Kempton Pk. Rd. DN5—3F 31
Kempton St. DN4—1B 48
Kempwell Dri. S62—5F 55
Kenbourne Gro. S7—6C 98
Kenbourne Rd. S7—6C 98
Kendal Av. S31—1H 119
Kendal Clo. DN5—2C 44
Kendal Cres. S70—5A 24
Kendal Dri. S18—2C 128
Kendal Dri. S63—2A 42
Kendal Grn. S70—5G 23
Kendal Grn. Rd. S70—5G 23
Kendal Gro. S71—1G 25
Kendall Cres. DN12—3F 59
Kendal Pl. S6—3H 85
Kendal Rd. DN5—2A 32
Kendal Rd. S6—3H 85
Kendal Rd. S41—3G 131
Kendray St. S70—6H 13
Kenilworth Clo. DN5—3F 31
Kenilworth Ct. S17—3F 109
Kenilworth Pl. S11—5A 98
Kenilworth Rd. DN4—4G 45
Kenmare Cres. DN2—4G 33
Kennedy Ct. S10—2H 97
Kennedy Dri. S63—6F 29
Kennedy Rd. S8—5C 110
Kenneth St. S65—2E 79
Kennet Vale. S40—6F 131
Kenninghall Clo. S2—6H 99
Kenninghall Dri. S2—6H 99
Kenninghall Mt. S2—6H 99
Kenninghall Pl. S2—6H 99
Kenninghall Rd. S2—6H 99
Kennington Av. DN6—2B 16
Kenrock Clo. DN5—6E 19
Kensington Rd. S5—5F 13
Kent Av. S62—6E 55
Kent Clo. S41—6H 131
Kentmere Clo. S18—2C 128
Kent Rd. DN4—4B 46
Kent Rd. S8—2F 111
Kent Rd. S61—6G 67
Kent St. S41—5C 138
Kenwell Dri. S17—4H 121
Kenwood Av. S7—6C 98
Kenwood Bank. S7—5C 98
Kenwood Clo. S70—1D 24
Kenwood Pk. Rd. S7—6C 98
Kenwood Rise. S66—3G 81
Kenwood Rd. S7—6B 98
Kenworthy Rd. S30—4D 140
Kenworthy Rd. S70—2H 23
Kenyon All. S3—2B 4
Kenyon Rd. S41—4E 139
Kenyon St. S1—2C 4 & 1D 98
Keppel. S61—6H 67
Keppel Dri. S61—5D 66
Keppel Heights. S61—5D 66
Keppel Pl. S5—3B 76
Keppel Rd. S5—3B 76
Keppel Rd. S61—5D 66
Keppel View Rd. S61—1F 77
Kepple Clo. DN11—6D 62
Keresforth Clo. S70—2E 23
Keresforth Hall Dri. S70—2E 23
Keresforth Hall Rd. S70—2F 23
Keresforth Hill Rd. S70—3D 22
Keresforth Rd. S75—3B 22
Kerwin Clo. S17—1C 120
Kerwin Dri. S17—1C 120
Kerwin Rd. S17—1C 120
Kestrel Av. S61—2C 66
Kestrel Dri. DN11—4E 63
Kestrel Dri. S31—6B 124

Kestrel Grn. S2—3A 100
Kestrel Rise. S70—3D 36
Keswick Clo. DN5—1A 32
Keswick Clo. S6—3E 85
Keswick Cres. S60—4B 90
Keswick Dri. S41—4E 131
Keswick Pl. S18—2B 128
Keswick Rd. S75—2E 7
Keswick Wlk. S71—1H 25
Keswick Way. S31—1H 119
Ket Hill La. S72—2F 11
Kettlebridge Rd. S9—2C 100
Ketton Av. S8—4F 111
Ketton Wlk. S75—4E 13
Kevin Gro. S66—5B 82
Kew Cres. S12—5B 112
Kexbrough Dri. S75—5B 6
Key Av. S74—5B 38
Keyworth Pl. S13—1A 114
Keyworth Rd. S6—2A 86
Khartoum Rd. S11—4B 98
Kibroyd Dri. S75—6A 6
Kidsley Clo. S40—6A 130
Kier Hardie Av. DN11—5E 63
Kilburn Rd. S18—2A 128
Kildale Gdns. S19—2D 124
Killamarsh La. S31—4E 127
Kilner Way. S6—6B 74
Kilnhurst Rd. S62—6G 55
Kilnhurst Rd. S65—6D 56
Kiln Rd. S61—1H 77
Kilnsea Wlk. S70—6G 13
 (off Fitzwilliam St.)
Kilton Hill. S3—5F 87
Kilton Pl. S3—5F 87
Kilvington Av. S13—6D 100
Kilvington Cres. S13—6D 100
Kilvington Rd. S13—1D 112
Kimberley St. S9—5B 88
Kimberworth Pk. Rd. S61
 (in two parts)—5F 67 & 2H 77
Kimberworth Rd. S61—2H 77
Kinder Rd. S43—5H 133
King Av. DN11—4C 62
King Av. S66—5H 83
King Ecgbert Rd. S17—4E 121
King Edward Rd. DN4—3B 46
King Edwards Gdns. S70
 —1G 23
King Edward St. S71—1D 14
Kingfield Ct. S11—6B 98
Kingfield Rd. S11—6B 98
Kingfisher Ct. DN11—4E 63
Kingfisher Rise. S61—1B 66
King George Sq. DN3—2D 20
King George's Rd. DN11—3B 62
King George Ter. S70—1B 24
King James St. S6—5B 86
Kingsclere Wlk. S40—6H 137
King's Cres. DN12—2B 60
Kingsforth La. S66—3A 94
Kingsforth Rd. S66—4A 94
Kingsgate. DN1—6D 32
Kingslake St. S9—4C 88
Kingsland Ct. S71—1F 9
Kingsley Av. DN5—5H 31
Kingsley Av. S40—5H 137
Kingsley Clo. S71—1A 14
Kingsley Cres. DN3—3G 35
Kingsley Pk. Av. S7—3H 109
Kingsley Pk. Gro. S11—3H 109
Kingsley Dri. DN6—2C 16
Kingsmead Dri. DN3—3H 49
Kingsmede Av. S40—4F 137
King's Rd. DN1—5E 33
Kings Rd. S31—6E 125
King's Rd. S64—6F 43
King's Rd. S72—4C 10

Kings Rd. S73—1G 39
King's Stocks. S72—3A 28
King's St. S72—6G 11
Kingstone Pl. S70—2F 23
Kingston Rd. DN2—5H 33
Kingston St. S4—4H 87
King St. DN1—6D 32
King St. DN3—2D 34
King St. S3—2F 5 & 1F 99
King St. S30—1E 65
King St. S31—5A 104
King St. S43—2F 133
King St. S63—4G 29
 (Goldthorpe)
King St. S63—2G 29
 (Thurnscoe)
King St. S64—2B 56
King St. S70—1H 23
King St. S74—5A 38
King St. N. S41—4A 132
King St. S. S40—6A 138
Kings Way. S60—1G 91
Kingsway. S63—1E 29
Kingsway. S73—1F 39
Kingsway. S75—4E 7
Kingsway Clo. DN11—6E 63
Kingsway Cres. S63—1E 29
Kingswood Av. S19—5A 114
Kingswood Av. S31—1E 107
Kingswood Clo. S19—5A 114
Kingswood Clo. S41—3F 131
Kingswood Cres. S74—4A 38
Kingswood Croft. S19—5A 114
Kingswood Gro. S19—5A 114
Kingwell Cres. S70—3H 23
Kingwell Croft. S70—4A 24
Kingwell Rd. S70—4H 23
Kinharvie Rd S5—6D 74
Kinnaird Av. S5—4G 75
Kinnaird Pl. S5—4G 75
Kinnaird Rd. S5—4G 75
Kinsey Rd. S30—6A 50.
Kipling Av. DN4—5H 45
Kipling Clo. S18—4G 129
Kipling Rd. DN3—1H 21
Kipling Rd S6—3A 86
Kipling Rd S41—3H 131
Kirby Clo S9—1E 101
Kirby La. S30—5H 51
Kirby St. S64—6E 43
Kirk Balk. S74—5H 37
Kirkbridge Rd. S9—4C 88
Kirkby Av DN5—3B 32
Kirkby Av. S12—3C 112
Kirkby Av. S71—5C 8
Kirkby Dri. S12—3C 112
Kirkby Rd. S12—3C 112
Kirkby View. S12—3C 112
Kirkby Way. S12—4C 112
Kirkcroft Av. S31—2B 126
Kirkcroft Av. S61—2C 66
Kirkcroft Clo. S61—2B 66
Kirkcroft Dri. S31—3B 126
Kirkcroft La. S31—3B 126
Kirk Croft Rd. S31—1E 107
Kirk Cross Cres. S71—3E 9
Kirkdale Cres. S13—4B 102
Kirkdale Dri. S13—4B 102
Kirk Edge Av. S30—5D 72
Kirk Edge Dri S30—5C 72
Kirk Edge Rd. S30—4A 72
Kirkfield Way S71—3E 9
Kirkham Clo. S71—4C 14
Kirkham Pl. S71—6F 9
Kirkhill Clo. DN3—4G 35
Kirklands Dri. S62—1E 69
Kirk Sandall Ind. Est. DN3
 —3B to 4B 20

Kirkstall Clo. DN5—4F 31
Kirkstall Clo. S31—4F 119
Kirkstall Clo. S60—2A 90
Kirkstall Rd. S11—5A 98
Kirkstall Rd. S71—6A 8
Kirkstead Rd. S61—2C 76
Kirkstone Clo. DN5—2A 32
Kirkstone Rd. S6—4A 86
Kirkstone Rd. S41—3E 131
Kirk St. DN4—1B 46
Kirk View. S74—5H 37
Kirk Way. S71—4D 14
Kirton Rd. S4—4G 87
Kitchen Rd. S73—6H 25
Kitson Dri. S71—4D 14
Kiveton La. S31—2B 118
Knab Clo. S7—2A 110
Knab Croft. S7—2A 110
Knab Rise. S7—2A 110
Knab Rd. S7—2A 110
Knapton Av. S62—1E 69
Knaresborough Clo. S31
 —6A 104
Knaresborough Rd. DN12
 —4B 58
Knaresborough Rd. S7—4A 110
Knavesmire Gdns. DN4—1B 48
Knifesmithgate. S40—2A 138
Knightwood Pl. S65—1H 79
Knollbeck Av. S73—3A 40
Knollbeck Cres. S73—3A 40
Knollbeck La. S73—2A 40
Knoll Clo. S30—3E 141
Knoll, The. S18—6H 123
Knoll, The. S40—3B 136
Knowle Clo. S6—5C 84
Knowle Ct. S11—2H 109
Knowle Croft. S11—2G 109
Knowle La. S11—2F 109
Knowle Rd. S5—3F 75
Knowle Rd. S70—3B 24
Knowle Av. S30—4F 141
Knowle Top. S19—2E 125
Knowsley St. S70—6F 13
Knutton Cres. S5—3C 74
Knutton Rise. S5—2C 74
Knutton Rd. S5—3C 74
Kyle Clo. S5—5C 74
Kyle Cres. S5—5C 74
Kynance Cres S60—4B 90

Laburnham Gro. S31—4A 126
Laburnham Gro. S70—5C 24
Laburnum Av. S66—3F 81
Laburnum Clo. S30—3E 65
Laburnum Clo. S31—3F 119
Laburnum Ct. S44—2G 139
Laburnum Dri. DN3—2G 35
Laburnum Gro. DN12—4C 58
Laburnum Gro. S30—4D 140
Laburnum Pde. S66—4D 82
Laburnum Pl. DN5—5B 18
Laburnum Rd. DN4—5H 45
Laburnum Rd. S64—5D 42
Laburnum Rd. S66—4D 82
Laburnum St. S43—2H 133
Laceby Clo. S66—2H 81
Laceby Ct. S70—2E 23
Lack Hill Rd. S65—5B 80
Ladies Spring Dri. S17—2G 121
Ladies Spring Gro. S17—2G 121
Ladock Clo. S71—4B 14
Ladybank Rd. S19—3D 124
Ladybank View. S31—5D 124
Ladybourne Ct. S17—4G 121
Ladybower La. S43—3B 134

Ladycroft. S63—1A 42
 (Bolton-upon-Dearne)
Lady Croft. S63—5E 41
 (Wath upon Dearne)
Ladycroft Rd. DN3—5F 35
Lady Field Rd. S31—6D 118
Lady Ida's Dri S31—5A 124
Lady Oak Rd. S65—1A 80
Lady's Bri. S3—1F 5 & 1F 99
Ladysmith Av. S7—1B 110
Ladywood Rd. S72—6H 11
Laird Av. S6—2G 85
Laird Dri. S6—2G 85
Laird Rd. S6—2G 85
Laithes Clo. S71—6D 8
Laithes Cres. S71—6B 8
Laithes La. S71—6B 8
Lakeland Dri. S31—1G 119
Laken Rd. DN2—5G 33
Lake View Av. S40—4E 137
Lambcote Way. S66—3H 83
Lambcroft La. S13—1C 114
Lamb Dri. S5—6B 74
Lambert Rd. S70—2C 24
Lamberts La. S65—4D 70
Lambert St. S3—1D 4 & 1E 99
Lambert Wlk S70—1C 24
Lambeth Rd. DN4—4B 46
Lamb Hill Clo. S13—6F 101
Lamb La. S71—2C 14
Lambra Rd. S70—6H 13
Lambrell Av. S31—5G 117
Lambrell Grn. S31—5G 117
Lamb Rd. S5—6B 74
Lanark Dri. S64—4G 43
Lanark Gdns. DN2—4A 34
Lancaster Av. DN2—5A 34
Lancaster Av. DN3—3D 20
Lancaster Ga. S70—5G 13
 (off St Mary's Pl.)
Lancaster Rd. S30—3D 140
Lancaster Rd. S41—3G 131
Lancaster St. S3—6D 86
Lancaster St. S63—1G 29
Lancaster St. S70—6F 13
Lancelot Clo. S40—5F 137
Lancing Rd. S2—5E 99
Landon Clo. S42—6D 136
Landsbury Av. DN11—4E 63
Landseer Clo. S14—5H 111
Landseer Clo. S18—2C 128
Landseer Ct. S66—3F 81
Landseer Dri. S14—5A 112
Landseer Pl. S14—5A 112
Landseer Wlk. S14—5A 112
Lane Cotts. S71—2E 9
Lane End. S30—6D 50
Lane End Rd. S60—6G 79
Laneham Clo. DN4—5B 48
Lane Head. S30—1H 73
Lane Head Clo. S75—3E 7
Lane Head Rise. S75—3E 7
Lane Head Rd. S17—5C 120
Laneside Clo. DN4—2A 46
Lanes, The. S66—2H 79
Lang Av. S71—5E 15
Langcliff Clo. S75—3E 7
Lang Cres. S71—5E 15
Langdale Clo. S40—6C 130
Langdale Dri. DN5—1H 31
Langdale Dri. S18—6G 123
Langdale Dri. S8—2C 110
Langdale Rd. S71—6A 14
Langdale Rd. S8—4D 112
Langdale Sq. S43—3D 132
Langdale Way. S31—6F 107
Langdon Rd. S61—1G 77

172

Louth Rd. S11—6H 97
Love La. S3—1E 5 & 1E 99
Lovell St. S4—6H 87
Love St. S3—1E 5 & 1E 99
Lovetot Av. S31—5B 104
Lovetot Rd. S61—5G 67
Lovetot St. S9—6A & 6A 88
(in two parts)
Lowburn Rd. S13—6E 101
Low Cronkhill La. S71—3G 9
Low Cudworth Grn. S72—2H 15
Lowedges Cres. S8—3D 122
Lowedges Dri. S8—3D 122
Lowedges Pl. S8—3E 123
Lowedges Rd. S8—4B 122
Lowe La. S75—6A 22
Lowell Av. DN4—5B 46
Lwr. Dolcliffe Rd. S64—6D 42
Lwr. Grove Rd. S40—2H 137
Lwr. Malton Rd. DN5—2G 31
Lwr. Thomas St. S70—1G 23
Lwr. York St. S73—6B 26
Lowfield Av. S12—6G 113
Lowfield Av. S61—4C 68
Lowfield Rd. DN2—2A 34
Lowfield Rd. S63—1B 42
Lowfields S43—1E 135
Lowfield Wlk. DN12—1B 58
(off Lime Tree Wlk.)
Low Fisher Ga. DN1—5D 32
Lowgate. DN5—2G 31
Lowgates. S43—1D 134
Low Grange Rd S63—1E 29
Low Grange Sq. S63—1E 29
Lowgreave. S65—1A 80
Lowhouse Rd. S5—2A 76
Lowlands Clo. S71—2D 14
Low La. DN4—5A 48
Low La. S61—1A 78
Low La. S66—1E 95
Low Matlock La. S6—4D 84
Low Pavement. S40—2A 138
Low Rd. DN4—4A 46
Low Rd. DN12—2E 59
Low Rd. S6—5G 85
Low Rd. S30—2D 72
Low Rd. E. DN4—5F 45
(in two parts)
Low Rd. W. DN4—6E 45
Low Row. S75—2C 6
Lowry Dri. S18—2D 128
Low St DN11—6H 61
Low St. S75—3D 22
Lowther Rd. DN1—4E 33
Lowther Rd. S6—2B 86
Low Valley Ind. Est. S73—5D 26
Low View. S75—2B 22
Loxley Av. S73—1E 39
Loxley Clo. S40—2D 136
Loxley Ct. S6—4H 85
Loxley Ct. S60—1F 91
Loxley New Rd. S6—4H 85
Loxley Rd. S6—1A 84 to 4H 85
Loxley St. S71—4F 15
Loxley View Rd. S10—6H 85
Loy Clo. S61—4A 68
Lucas Rd. S41—5G 131
Lucas St. S4—4G 87
Ludgate Clo. DN11—6E 63
Ludham Clo. S41—4H 131
Ludwell Hill. DN5—1H 43
Lugano Gro. S73—3C 26
Luke La. S6—2F 85
Lulworth Clo. S70—1B 24
Lumb La. S30—1A 72
Lumley Clo. S66—4H 83
Lumley Cres. S66—5H 83
Lumley Dri. S31—3C 106

Lumley Dri. S66—5H 83
Lumley St. S4—1H 99
Lumley St. S9—1B 100
Lump La. S30—6A 64
Lumsdale Rd. S43—3A 134
Luna Croft. S12—5B 112
Lunbreck Rd. DN4—6E 45
Lund Av. S71—4F 15
Lund Clo. S71—4F 15
Lund Cres. S71—4F 15
Lundhill Clo. S73—2G 39
Lundhill Gro S73—2G 39
Lund Hill La S71—1H 9
Lundhill Rd. S73—3G 39
Lund La. S71—4E 15
Lund Rd. S30—4D 72
Lundwood Clo S19—5C 114
Lundwood Dri S19—5C 114
Lundwood Gro S19—5C 114
Lundwood Ho DN1—1C 46
(off Bond Clo)
Lundy Rd. S18—3F 129
Lunn Rd. S72—1H 15
Lupin Way. S44—2G 139
Lupton Cres S8—3D 122
Lupton Dri S8—3D 122
Lupton Rd S8—3D 122
Lupton Wlk S8—3E 123
Luterel Dri. S31—5B 104
Luton St. S9—2D 88
Lutterworth Dri DN6 -1C 16
Lych Gate Clo DN4– 4E 49
Lydden Clo S43—3E 133
Lydford Av. S41—2B 132
Lydgate Hall Cres S10—2G 97
Lydgate La. S10—2G 97
Lyme St S60—3C 78
Lyminster Rd S6—4A 74
Lymister Av S60—1H 89
Lyncroft Clo. S60—3D 90
Lyndale Av. DN3—6C 20
Lyndhurst Clo. S11—1A 110
Lyndhurst Cres. DN3—4C 20
Lyndhurst Rd. S11—1A 110
Lyndon Av. DN6—2C 16
Lynmouth Rd. S7—2C 110
Lynn Pl. S9—3D 88
Lynton Av. S60—6G 79
Lynton Pl. S75—5B 6
Lynton Rd. S11—5B 98
Lynwood Clo. S18—2B 128
Lynwood Dri. S71—4E 9
Lyons Clo. S4—4G 87
Lyons Rd. S4—4G 87
Lyons St. S4—4G 87
Lytham Av. S31—6F 107
Lytham Av. S71—1D 14
Lytton Av. S5—4C 74
Lytton Clo. DN4—5B 46
Lytton Cres. S5—4C 74
Lytton Dri. S5—4C 74
Lytton Rd. S5—4C 74

Mabel St. S60—4F 79
Macaulay Cres. DN3—3G 35
Machin Dri. S62—5D 54
Machin La. S30—3A 140
Machon Bank. S7—1C 110
Machon Bank Rd. S7—1B 110
Mackenzie Cres. S10—3C 98
Mackenzie Cres. S30—3C 64
Mackenzie St. S11—5C 98
Mackey Cres. S72—2E 11
Mackey La. S72—2E 11
Macnaughton Rd. S75—6D 36
'acro Rd. S73—1G 39
.lam La. DN3—1G 21

Madehurst Gdns. S2—6F 99
Madehurst Rise. S2—6F 99
Madehurst Rd. S2—6F 99
Madehurst View. S2—6F 99
Madin Dri. S43—5H 133
Madingley Clo. DN4—6A 46
Madin St. S41—1A 138
Mafeking Pl. S30—1E 65
Magellan Rd. S66—3E 83
Magna Clo S66—3F 81
Magna Cres S66—3E 81
Magna La S65—6B 70
Magnolia Clo DN3—4D 20
Magnolia Clo S31—4F 119
Magnolia Clo S72—3D 10
Magnolia Ct. S10—5E 97
Magpie Gro. S2—3A 100
Mahon Av. S62—1F 69
Maidstone Rd. S6—5B 74
Main Av. DN12—2B 60
Main Av. S17—5E 121
Main Rd. S9—6E 89 to 1F 101
Main Rd S12—6G 113
Main Rd. S31—6A 124
(Marsh Lane)
Main Rd S42—4A 130
Main St DN3—2F 49
Main St DN5—3D 44
Main St DN11—6H 61
Main St S12—3B 114
Main St. S30—6A 64
(Grenoside)
Main St. S31—2F 119
(Anston)
Main St. S31—4A 104
(Aughton)
Main St. S31—6A 104
(Swallownest)
Main St. S31—1C 104
(Ulley)
Main St. S60—6D 90
(Catcliffe)
Main St. S60—3C 78
(Rotherham)
Main St. S61—3C 68
Main St. S62—1G 69
(Rawmarsh)
Main St. S62—4D 52
(Wentworth)
Main St. S63—4G 29
Main St. S64—6D 42
Main St. S65—4H 71
Main St. S66—4H 81
Main St. S73—6A 26
Majuba St. S6—5B 86
Makin St. S64—1G 57
Malcolm Clo. S70—1D 24
Malham Clo. S40—6F 131
Malham Clo. S72—2C 10
Malham Ct. S70—5F 13
(off Summer St.)
Malham Pl. S30—1D 64
Malinda St. S3—6D 86
Malin Rd. S6—4G 85
Malin Rd. S65—1B 80
Malkin St. S41—2B 138
Mallard Av. DN3—1E 21
Mallard Clo. S61—1C 66
Mallin Dri. DN12—5B 60
Mallory Av. S62—1E 69
Mallory Clo. S64—5H 43
Mallory Rd. S65—1A 80
Mallory Way S72—6C 10
Malson Way. S41—5H 131
Maltas Ct. S70—4C 24
Maltby Ho. DN1—1C 46
(off Burden Clo.)
Maltby St. S9—4C 88

Malthouse Cotts. S31—6D 118
Malting La. S4—1H 5 & 1G 99
Maltings, The. S60—4D 78
Maltkiln St. S60—4D 78
Malton Dri S31—6C 104
Malton Pl. S71—6A 8
Malton Rd DN2—4H 33
Malton Rd DN5—2F 31
Malton St. S4—4G 87
Malton Wlk S40—6H 137
Maltravers Clo. S2—3A 100
Maltravers Cres. S2—2A 100
Maltravers Pl. S2—2A 100
Maltravers Rd S2—1H 99
Maltravers St S4
—1H 5 & 1G 99
Maltravers Ter. S2—3A 100
(in two parts)
Maltravers Way. S2—2A 100
Malvern Clo S75—5D 12
Malvern Rd DN2—5A 34
Malvern Rd S9—6D 88
Malvern Rd S40—1G 137
Malwood Way S66—3H 83
Manchester Rd S10 & S6
—2A 96
Manchester Rd S30—1B 140
(Deepcar & Stocksbridge)
Mandale St DN3—1H 21
Mandeville St. S9—6E 89
Manell Ter S3—6D 86
Mangham Rd S61 & S62
—6D 68
Mangham Way. S61—6D 68
Manifold Av. S43—3B 134
Manknell Rd S41—3A 132
Mannering Rd DN4—5G 45
Manners St S3—5D 86
Manor App S61—2H 77
Manor Av. S43—4F 133
Manor Av. S63—4G 29
Manor Clo. S31—2B 118
Manor Clo. S62—5C 54
Manor Clo. S66—4F 83
Manor Ct. DN12—2B 58
Manor Ct. S71—2C 8
Manor Cres. S18—2D 128
Manor Cres. S40—2F 137
Manor Cres. S60—3B 90
Manor Cres. S72—5G 11
Manor Dri. DN2—6F 33
Manor Dri. S31—2B 118
Manor Dri. S40—2F 137
Manor Dri. S43—4F 133
Manor Dri. S60—2A 92
Manor Dri. S71—2D 8
Manor End. S70—4H 23
Manor Est. DN5—3H 17
Manor Farm Clo. DN6—1D 16
Manor Farm Clo. S31—3B 104
Manor Farm Dri. S64—3A 56
Manor Fields. S61—1G 77
Manor Gdns. S71—1H 25
Manor Gro. S71—2D 8
Manor Gro. S72—5F 11
Manor Ho. S6—5C 84
Manor Ho. Clo. S74—5A 38
Manor Ho. Rd. S61—1G 77
Manor Laith Rd. S2—3H 99
Manor La. S2—2B to 4A 100
Manor La. S31—2G 107
Manor Oak S64—3E 43
Manor Oaks Clo. S2—2A 100
Manor Oaks Pl. S2—3A 100
Manor Oaks Rd. S2
—2G 99 to 3B 100
Manor Occupation Rd. S71
—1D 8

Manor Pk. Av. S2—4B 100
Manor Pk. Centre. S2—3B 100
Manor Pk. Clo. S2—4B 100
Manor Pk. Ct. S2—4B 100
Manor Pk. Cres. S2—4B 100
Manor Pk. Dri. S2—4B 100
Manor Pk. Pl. S2—3B 100
Manor Pk. Rise. S2—3B 100
Manor Pk. Rd. S2—3B 100
Manor Pk. Way. S2—4B 100
Manor Pl. S62—2G 69
Manor Rd. DN3—1G 21
Manor Rd. DN5—2G 43
(Harlington)
Manor Rd. DN5—3A 18
(Toll Bar)
Manor Rd. S31—2F 107
(Dinnington)
Manor Rd. S31—4B 126
(Killamarsh)
Manor Rd. S31—6C 118
(Kiveton Park Station)
Manor Rd. S31—5F 117
(Wales)
Manor Rd. S40—2F & 2E 137
(in two parts)
Manor Rd. S43
—4F 133 to 1F 139
Manor Rd. S60—3B 90
Manor Rd. S61—3G 77
Manor Rd. S63—4A 40
(Brampton Bierlow)
Manor Rd. S63—1E 29
(Thurnscoe)
Manor Rd. S64—3B 56
Manor Rd. S66—4G 83
Manor Rd. S72—1G 15
Manor Sq. S63—1E 29
Manor St. S71—5F 9
Manor View. S19—2E 125
Manor View. S72—3C 10
Manor Wlk. DN11—6H 61
Manor Way. S2—1A 100
Manor Way. S31—2B 118
Manor Way. S74—5A 38
Manse Clo. DN4—3E 49
Mansel Av. S5—3C 74
Mansel Ct. S5—3C 74
Mansel Cres. S5—3C 74
Mansel Rd. S5—3C 74
Mansfeldt Cres. S41—5G 131
Mansfeldt Rd. S41—5G 131
Mansfield Cres. DN3—2D 34
Mansfield Dri. S12—1D 112
Mansfield Rd. DN4—2B 46
Mansfield Rd. S12—1C 112
Mansfield Rd. S31—2D 126
(Killamarsh)
Mansfield Rd. S31—6D 116
(Kiveton Park)
Mansfield Rd. S31
—6A 104 to 2C 116
(Swallownest & Aston)
Mansfield Rd. S41—6D 138
Mansfield Rd. S60—3E 79
Mansfield Rd. S71—5B 8
Manton Ho. DN1—1C 46
(off St James St.)
Manton St. S2—4F 99
Manvers Clo. S31—6E 107
(Anston)
Manvers Clo. S31—6B 104
(Swallownest)
Manvers Rd. S6—4A 86
Manvers Rd. S19—3F 115
Manvers Rd. S31—6A 104
Manvers Rd. S44—1G 139
Manvers Rd. S64—6C 42

Maori Av. S63—1G 41
Maple Av. DN4—3D 48
Maple Av. S66—4D 82
Maplebeck Dri. S9—1H 89
Maplebeck Rd. S9—1H 89
Maple Clo. S70—2B 24
Maple Croft Cres. S9—6B 76
Maple Croft Rd. S9—6B 76
Maple Dri. S31—4A 126
Maple Dri. S66—3F 81
Maple Gro. DN3—2F 35
Maple Gro. DN12—5B 58
Maple Gro. S9—2G 101
Maple Gro. S30—4D 140
Maple Gro. S31—5D 104
Maple Leaf Ct. S64—6D 42
Maple Pl. S30—3E 65
Maple Rd. S31—4G 117
Maple Rd. S64—6D 42
Maple Rd. S75—4E 7
(Mapplewell)
Maple Rd. S75—2B 50
(Tankersley)
Maple St. S43—3H 133
Mapperley Rd. S18—2A 128
Mappin's Rd. S60—6C 90
Mappin St. S1—3B 4 & 2D 98
Mapplebeck Rd. S30—6C 50
Maran Av. S73—4G 27
Marcham Dri. S19—3G 115
March Bank. S65—4E 71
March Flatts Rd. S65—5E 71
March Ga. DN12—4E 59
March St. DN12—3E 59
March St. S9—4D 88
March Vale Rise. DN12—4E 59
Marchwood Av. S6—5E 85
Marchwood Clo. S6—1G 137
Marchwood Dri. S6—4E 85
Marchwood Rd. S6—5E 85
Marcliff Clo. S6—5D 80
Marcliff Cres. S66—5D 80
Marcliff La. S66—5D 80
Marcus Dri. S3—6F 87
Mardale Clo. S41—2G 131
Marden Rd. S7—1C 110
Margaret Clo. S31—1B 116
Margaret Rd. S73—4D 26
Margaret Rd. S73—4D 26
(Darfield)
Margaret Rd. S73—1G 39
(Wombwell)
Margaret St. S1—4E 99
Margaret St. S66—6H 83
Margate Dri. S4—3H 87
Margate St. S4—3A 88
Margate St. S72—6G 11
Margerison St. S8—6E 99
Margetson Cres. S5—3D 74
Margetson Dri. S5—3D 74
Margetson Rd. S5—3D 74
Marian Rd. DN3—4C 20
Marina Rise. S73—4C 26
Marion St. S6—1H 85
Markbrook Dri. S30—5A 50
Market Hill. S70—6G 13
Market Pde. S70—6H 13
Market Pl. DN1—6D 32
Market Pl. S1—2F 5 & 1F 99
Market Pl. S30—2F 65
(Chapeltown)
Market Pl. S40—2A 138
Market Pl. S60—3D 78
Market Pl. S72—6B 10
Market Pl. S73—1G 39
Market Rd. DN1—5D 32
Market Sq. S13—1C 114
Market Sq. S63—4G 29

Market St. DN6—5D 16
Market St. S13—1C 114
Market St. S30—2F 65
(Chapeltown)
Market St. S31—6D 124
Market St. S43—1C 134
Market St. S60—3D 78
Market St. S63—4G 29
(Goldthorpe)
Market St. S63—1E 29
(Thurnscoe)
Market St. S64—1E & 1F 57
(in two parts, Mexborough)
Market St. S64—2C 56
(Swinton)
Market St. S70—6G 13
Market St. S72—6B 10
Market St. S74—4A 38
Markfield Dri. S66—3F 81
Markham Av. DN3—2E 35
Markham Av. DN12—3C 58
Markham Cres. S43—1D 134
Markham Ho. DN1—1C 46
(off Burden Clo.)
Markham La. S43 & S44
—4F 135
(in two parts)
Markham Rd. DN12—3B 60
Markham Rd. S40—3H 137
Markham Sq. S44—6E 135
Markham Ter. S8—1D 110
Mark La. S10—1A 108
Mark St. S70—6G 13
Marlborough Av. DN5—5H 31
Marlborough Clo. S31—6D 106
Marlborough Rise. S31
—1C 116
Marlborough Rd. DN2—5F 33
Marlborough Rd. S10—2A 98
Marlborough Ter. S70—1G 23
Marlcliffe Rd. S6—1G 85
Marlow Clo. DN2—4A 34
Marlowe Dri. S65—4H 79
Marlowe Rd. DN3—1H 21
Marlowe Rd. S65—4H 79
Marlow Rd. DN2—4A 34
Marmion Rd. S11—6H 97
Marples Clo. S8—6D 98
Marples Dri. S8—6D 98
Marquis Gdns. DN3—2H 21
Marr Grange La. DN5—2A 30
Marrick Ct. S30—2D 64
Marrion Rd. S62—1G 69
Marriott La. S7—4B 110
Marriott Pl. S62—6D 54
Marriott Rd. S7—4B 110
Marriott Rd. S64—1C 56
Marrison Dri. S31—3A 126
Marr Ter. S10—4F 97
Marsala Wlk. S73—3D 26
Marsden Ind. Est. S13—3H 101
Marsden La. S3—2B 4 & 1D 98
Marsden Pl. S40—1A 138
(Newbold Rd.)
Marsden Pl. S40—3F 137
(Old Rd.)
Marsden Rd. S30—3E 141
Marsden St. S40—2A 138
Marshall Av. DN4—4A 46
Marshall Clo. S62—4F 69
Marshall Gro. S63—6F 41
Marshall Hall. S10—4B 98
Marshall Rd. S8—5C 110
Marsh Av. S18—6F 123
Marsh Clo. S19—3C 124
Marshfield. S70—2D 36
Marshfield Gro. S43—1E 135
Marsh Ga. DN5—5B 32

Marsh Hill. S66—1C 83
Marsh Ho. Rd. S11—2F 109
Marsh La. DN3—1A 20
Marsh La. DN5—4D & 3C 18
(in two parts)
Marsh La. S10—2F 97
Marsh Rd. DN5—4B 32
Marsh St. S30—3F 141
Marsh St. S60—4C 78
Marsh St. S73—6B 26
Marsh View. S31—6G 125
Marson Av. DN6—2B 16
Marston Clo. S18—3B 128
Marston Cres. S71—5B 8
Marstone Cres. S17—4E 121
Marston Rd. S10—1H 97
Martin Ct. S31—6C 124
Martin Cres. S5—3F 75
Martindale Ter. S30—2E 65
(off Greenland Gdns.)
Martin La. S74—2H 37
Martin Rise. S31—6C 124
Martin Rise. S61—1C 66
Martin's Rd. S71—4E 15
Martin Well's Rd. DN12—4C 60
Marton Rd. DN5—2H 17
Marvell Rd. DN5—3F 31
Mary Ann Clo. S71—5D 14
Mary La. S73—4F 27
Mary's Pl. S75—5D 12
Mary's Rd. S73—4F 27
Mary St. S1—4E 99
Mary St. S31—6D 124
Mary St. S60—2C 78
Mary St. S72—2A 28
Mary St. S75—3A 12
Masbrough St. S60—3B 78
(in two parts)
Masefield Clo. S31—5G 107
Masefield Rd. DN2—2A 34
Masefield Rd. S13—6E 101
Masefield Rd. S63—4C 40
Masham Rd. DN4—4C 48
Mason Av. S31—4B 104
Mason Cres. S13—6F 101
Mason Dri. S31—4B 104
Mason Gro. S13—6F 101
Mason Lathe Rd. S5—4A 76
Mason St. S63—4G 29
Masons Way. S70—2C 24
Mason Way. S74—4H 37
Massey Rd. S13—2D 114
Masson Clo. S40—6F 131
Mastall La. DN5—5F 19
Masters Cres. S5—4F 75
Masters Rd. S5—4F 75
Mather Av. S9—2D 100
Mather Cres. S9—2D 100
Mather Dri. S9—2D 100
Mather Rd. S9—2D 100
Mather Wlk. S9—2D 100
Matilda La. S1—6F 5 & 3F 99
Matilda St. S1—5D 4 & 3E 99
(in two parts)
Matilda Way. S1—5E 5 & 3E 99
Matlock Dri. S43—6A 134
Matlock Rd. S6—6A 86
Matlock Rd. S42 & S40—6D 136
Matlock Rd. S71—1B 14
Mattersey Clo. DN4—6C 40
Matthews Dri. S66—6F 81
Matthews La. S8—6G 111
Matthew St. S3—6D 86
Maugerhay. S8—6G 111
Mauncer Cres. S13—6B 102
Mauncer Dri. S13—6B 102
Mauncer La. S13—1B 114
Maun Way. S5—6G 75

Maurice St. S62—4F 69
Mawfa Av. S14—5H 111
Mawfa Cres. S14—5H 111
Mawfa Dri. S14—5H 111
Mawfa La. S14—4H & 5H 111
(in two parts)
Mawfa Rd. S14—6H 111
Mawfa Wlk. S14—5H 111
Mawfield Rd. S75—3B 12
Maxey Pl. S8—1E 111
Maxfield Av. S10—2A 98
Maxwell St. S4—5G 87
Maxwell Way. S4—5G 87
May Av. DN4—5H 45
May Av. S41—1C 132
Maycock Av. S61—5F 67
May Day Grn. S70—6H 13
May Day Grn. Arc. S70—6H 13
Mayfield. S71—3B 14
Mayfield Cres. DN11—5D 62
Mayfield Cres. S70—3G 23
Mayfield Rd. DN5—4A 32
Mayfield Rd. S10
      —6A 96 to 1B 108
Mayfield Rd. S40—3E 137
Mayflower Cres. DN4—6E 45
Mayflower Dri. DN4—6E 45
Maynard Rd. S40—4H 137
Maynard Rd. S60—1A 92
May Rd. S6—3H 85
May Ter. S70—6E 13
Maythorn Clo. S75—5G 7
May Tree Clo. S19—6E 115
May Tree Croft. S19—6E 115
May Tree La. S19—6E 115
McConnel Cres. DN11—4B 62
McIntyre Rd. S30—3D 140
McLaren Cres. S66—5G 83
McMahon Av. S43—5H 133
McManus Av. S62—5F 55
Meaburn Clo. DN4—4D 48
Meadowland Rise. S72—3H 15
Meadow Av. S62—6D 54
Meadow Bank Av. S7—6B 98
Meadow Bank Rd. S11—6B 98
Meadow Bank Rd. S63—4F 77
Meadow Clo. S18—5G 123
Meadow Clo. S43—1D 132
Meadow Clo. S65—6C 70
Meadow Cres. S19—2B 124
Meadow Cres. S71—1F 9
Meadow Cres. S72—6F 11
Meadow Croft. DN3—5E 21
Meadow Croft. S72—2C 10
Meadowcroft Gdns. S19
      —1E 125
Meadowcroft Glade. S19
      —1E 125
Meadowcroft Rise. S19
      —1E 125
Meadow Dri. S30—2C 64
Meadow Dri. S64—3A 56
Meadow Dri. S71—3D 14
Meadow Dri. S73—4F 27
Meadow Field Rd. DN3—1E 21
Meadow Gate La. S19—6H 115
Meadow Gro. S17—5E 121
Meadow Gro. Rd. S17—5D 120
Meadow Hall Rd. S9—1D 88
Meadowhall Rd. S61—4F 77
Meadowhead. S8—6D 110
Meadow Head Av. S8—2C 122
Meadow Head Clo. S8—2C 122
Meadow Head Dri. S8—2C 122
Meadowhill Rd. S41—5D 138
Meadow La. DN12—2E 57
Meadow La. S62—5D 54
Meadow La. S66—5G 83

Meadow La. S75—6C 6
Meadow Rise. DN3—1E 21
Meadow Rise. DN11—6H 61
Meadow Rd. S71—2F 9
Meadow Spur. S65—6D 70
Meadows, The. S31—2A 118
Meadow St. S3—1B 4 & 6D 86
Meadow St. S31—3C to 3C 106
(in two parts)
Meadow St. S61—3A 78
Meadow St. S71—5H 13
Meadow Ter. S11—5A 98
Meadow View. S40—5C 136
Meadow View. S70—4A 24
Meadow View Clo. S74—6H 37
Meadow View Rd. S8—1D 122
Meadow View Rd. S62—5B 56
Meadstead Dri. S71—2D 8
Meads, The. S8—1F 123
Mead, The. S41—5C 138
Meadway Dri. S17—2C 120
Meadway, The. S17—2D 120
Meakin St. S41—5D 138
Mede, The. DN6—2B 16
Medley View. DN12—4F 59
Medlock Clo. S13—4A 102
Medlock Clo. S42—6D 136
Medlock Cres. S13—3A 102
Medlock Croft. S13—3A 102
Medlock Dri. S13—4A 102
Medlock Rd. S13—4A 102
Medlock Rd. S40—5E 137
Medlock Way. S13—3A 102
Medway Pl. S73—2H 39
Meersbrook Av. S8—2D 110
Meersbrook Pk. Rd. S8—1E 111
Meersbrook Rd. S8—2F 111
Meetinghouse La. S1
      —2F 5 & 1F 99
Meetinghouse La. S13—1C 114
Mekyll Clo. S66—3F 81
Melbeck Ct. S30—2C 64
Melbourne Av. S10—3A 98
Melbourne Av. S18—2A 128
Melbourne Av. S31—5C 104
Melbourne Av. S63—1H 41
Melbourne Rd. DN4—5G 45
Melbourne Rd. S30—3C 140
Melbourn Rd. S10—1A 98
Melciss Rd. S66—5E 81
Meld Clo. DN11—6D 62
Melford Clo. S75—4F 7
Melford Dri. DN4—1G 61
Melfort Glen. S10—2F 97
Mell Av. S74—5A 38
Melling Av. DN5—6H 31
Melling Clo. S40—5H 137
Mellington Clo. S8—5G 111
Mellor La. S18—2A 130
Mellor Rd. S73—1F 39
Mellor Way. S40—6A 138
Mellow Fields Rd. S31—1D 106
Mellwood Gro. S73—3E 39
Melrose Clo. S40—2E 137
Melrose Clo. S66—5H 93
Melrose Gro. S60—1G 91
Melrose Rd. S3—4F 87
Melrose Way. S71—5D 14
Melton Av. S63—4G 29
Melton Av. S73—3B 40
Melton Ct. DN12—1B 58
Meltonfield Clo. DN3—4G 35
Melton Gdns. DN5—2D 44
Melton Grn. S63—5C 40
Melton Gro. S19—5A 114
Melton High St. S63—5C 40
Melton Rd. DN5—2A 44 to 6H 31

Melton St. S64—1G 57
Melton St. S73—3B 40
Melton Ter. S70—4C 24
Melton Wood Gro. DN5—2C 44
Melville Av. DN4—4A 46
Melville Cres. S43—1F 139
Melville Rd. S9—3D 88
Melville St. S73—6B 26
Melvina Cres. S75—3F 13
Melwood Ct. DN3—5G 35
Memesia Clo. S31—3E 119
Memoir Gro. DN11—6C 62
Mendip Clo. S75—5D 12
Mendip Cres. S40—1D 136
Mendip Rise. S60—4D 90
Merbeck Gro. S30—5C 50
Mercaston Clo. S40—6C 130
Mercel Av. DN3—1G 35
Mercia Dri. S17—3E 121
Meredith Cres. DN4—5B 46
Meredith Rd. S6—3H 85
Mere Gro. DN3—2E 35
Mere La. DN3—6E 21 to 2E 35
Merlin Clo. S70—3D 36
Merlin Way. S5—6G 73
Merlin Way. S61—1C 66
Merrick Clo. S40—6F 131
Merrill Rd. S63—1E 29
Merton La. S9—5D 76
Merton Rise. S9—5D 76
Merton Rd. S9—5C 76
Metcalfe Av. S31—3A 126
Methley Clo. S12—1B 112
Methley Ho. DN1—1C 46
(off Grove Pl.)
Methley St. S72—1H 15
Mews Ct. S19—5A 114
Mews Ct. S63—2A 42
Mexborough Rd. S63—2B 42
Meynell Clo. S40—3E 137
Meynell Cres. S5—5B 74
Meynell Rd. S5—5B 74
Meynell Way. S31—3A 126
Meyrick Dri. S75—6B 6
Michael Croft. S63—5D 40
Michael Rd. S71—5E 15
Michael's Est. S72—6G 11
Micklebring Gro. DN12—5C 58
Micklebring Way. S66—2B 82
Mickleden Way. S75—6C 12
Mickley La. S17 & S18—5E 121
Middcliff Ct. S19—6E 115
Middle Av. S62—2F 69
Middleburn Clo. S70—2A 24
Middlecliff Clo. S19—6E 115
Middlecliff Cotts. S72—2A 28
Middlecliff Ct. S19—6E 115
Middlecliff La. S72
      —1G 27 to 2A 28
Middlecliff Rise. S19—6E 115
Middlecroft Rd. S43—4A 134
Middle Dri. S60—2F 91
Middlefield Clo. S17—2C 120
Middlefield Croft. S17—2C 120
Middlefield Rd. DN4—4B 48
Middlefield Rd. S60—1G 91
Middlefields Dri. S60—2A 92
Middlegate. DN5—6G to 6G 17
(in two parts)
Middleham Clo. DN4—4C 48
Middle Hay Clo. S14—2A 112
Middle Hay Pl. S14—3A 112
Middle Hay Rise. S14—3A 112
Middle Hay View. S14—3A 112
Middle La. S6—5G 85
Middle La. S30—1H 73
Middle La. S65—2F 79
Middle La. S S65—3G 79

Middle Pavement. S40—2A 138
(off Low Pavement)
Middle Pl. S65—2H 79
Middlesex St. S70—1H 23
Middleton Av. S31—5E 107
Middleton Dri. S43—6H 133
Middleton La. S30—1B 74
Middleton Rd. S65—3F 79
Middlewood Rd. S6
      —5G 73 to 3A 86
Middlewood Rd. N. S30—4F 73
Midfield Rd. S10—1G 97
Midhill Rd. S2—6F 99
Midhope Way. S75—6C 12
Midhurst Rd. S6—3H 73
Midland Rd. S61—3A 78
Midland Rd. S64—2C 56
Midland Rd. S71—1E 9
Midland St. S1—4E 99
Midland St. S70—6H 13
Midland Ter. S41—6B 138
Milano Rise. S73—4D 26
Milbanke St. DN1—5D 32
Milburn Ct. S19—6G 115
Milburn Gro. S19—6G 115
Milden Pl. S70—2A 24
Milden Rd. S6—1G 85
Milefield View. S72—6F 11
Mile Oak Rd. S60—6G 79
Miles Clo. S5—2E 87
Miles Rd. S5—2D 86
Miles Rd. S30—6C 50
Mile Thorn La. DN1—4D 32
Milford Rd. S43—6A 134
Milford St. S9—3D 88
Milgate St. S71—1F 9
Milgrove Cres. S30—5B 50
Milking La. S73—4A 40
Millais Rise. S66—2F 81
Millard La. S66—4G 83
Millbank Clo. S30—1B 64
Mill Clo. S31—5F 95
(Brookhouse, Laughton)
Mill Clo. S31—3B 118
(Todwick)
Millcross La. S18—1A 130
Milldale Clo. S40—6E 131
Milldale Rd. S17—4F 121
Mill Dri. S41—4C 130
Milldyke Clo. S60—2B 92
Miller Croft. S13—1A 114
Miller Dale Dri. S60—4D 90
Miller Rd. S7—6D 98
Miller St. S30—3H 141
Millfield Ct. DN3—1E 21
Millfield Rd. DN5—1C 32
Mill Fields. S31—3A 118
Mill Ga. DN5—1B 32
Mill Grn. S43—1C 134
Mill Hill. S60—2A 92
Mill Hill. S73—5H 25
Millhill Clo. DN3—5G 35
Mill Hills. S31—2B 118
Millhouses La. S11 & S7
      —2H 109
Millhouses St. S74—6A 38
Millicent Sq. S66—5C 83
Millindale. S66—4G 83
Mill La. DN3—3G 49
Mill La. DN4—3D 44
Mill La. DN5—2G 43
Mill La. DN6—1D 16
Mill La. S3—1F 5 & 1B 98
Mill La. S17—4F 121
Mill La. S18—2F 129
(Dronfield)
Mill La. S30—3H 141
(Deepcar)

175

Mill La. S31—2F 119
  (Anston)
Mill La. S40—3F 137
Mill La. S60—1D 102
Mill La. S62—4B 52
Mill La. S63—6C 40
Mill La. S75—4C 6
Millmoor La. S60—3C 78
Millmoor Rd. DN4—3C 48
Millmoor Rd. S73—5D 26
Millmount Rd. S8—2D 110
Millmount Rd. S74—6B 38
Mill Rd. S30—6F 65
Mill Rd. S31—5D 124
Mill Rd. S60—1D 102
Millsands. S3—1F 5 & 1F 99
Millside. S72—2C 10
Millside Wlk. S72—2C 10
Millstone Clo. S18—1B 128
Millstone Dri. S31—5D 104
Mill Stream Clo. S40—4E 137
Mill St. DN3—3F 35
Mill St. S41—2B 138
Mill St. S60—4D 78
Mill St. S61—3B 68
Mill St. S71—6B 14
Millthorpe Rd. S5—5H 75
Mill View. S63—2H 41
Mill Wlk. S3—1F 5 & 1F 99
Millwood Rd. DN4—6H 45
Millwood View. S6—4C 84
Milner Clo. S66—3H 81
Milner Ga. DN12—2G 59
Milner Ga. La. DN12—3F 59
Milner Rd. DN4—4H 45
Milnes St. S70—1A 24
Milne St. S75—3A 12
Milnrow Cres. S5—3D 74
Milnrow Dri. S5—3D 74
Milnrow Rd. S5—3D 74
Milnrow View. S5—3D 74
Milton Av. DN5—5H 31
Milton Clo. S63—3C 40
Milton Ct. DN1—1C 46
Milton Ct. S64—2A 56
Milton Cres. S40—5A 138
Milton Cres. S74—6A 38
Milton Gdns. DN3—3F 35
Milton Gro. DN3—5D 20
Milton Gro. S73—1G 39
Milton La. S3—6C 4 & 3D 98
Milton Pl. S43—1D 134
Milton Rd. S7—6D 98
Milton Rd. S30—2B 64
Milton Rd. S31—5G 107
Milton Rd. S63—3H 29
Milton Rd. S64—6E 43
Milton Rd. S65—1F 79
Milton Rd. S74—6A 38 to 1A 52
Milton St. S1 & S3
  —6B 4 & 3D 98
Milton St. S60—1D 78
Milton St. S64—2A 56
Milton St. S66—5F 83
Milton Wlk. DN1—1C 46
Minimum Ter. S40—3G 137
Minna Rd. S3—4F 87
Minneymoor Hill. DN12—2F 59
Minneymoor La. DN12—3F 59
Minster Clo. DN4—4E 49
Minster Clo. S30—1G 75
Minster Rd. S30—1F 75
Minster Way. S71—4D 14
Minto Rd. S6—3H 85
Miriam Av. S40—5C 136
Mission Field. S73—3A 40
Mitchell Clo. S70—4D 24
Mitchell Rd. S8—5D 110

Mitchell Rd. S73—4A 26
Mitchell St. S3—2A 4 & 1C 98
Mitchell St. S70—4E 25
Mitchelson Av. S75—2A 22
Moat La. S66—2G 93
Modena Ct. S73—3C 26
Moffat Gdns. DN7—6B 20
Moffatt Rd. S2—6F 99
Molineaux Clo. S5—4H 75
Molineaux Rd. S5—3G 75
Molineux Av. S43—2B 134
Molloy Pl. S8—1E 111
Molloy St. S8—1E 111
Mona Av. S10—1A 98
Mona Rd. DN4—3B 46
Mona Rd. S10—6A 86
Mona St. S75—5F 13
Monckton Rd. S5—6B 76
Moncrieffe Rd. S7—1C 110
Monk's Bri. Rd. S31—3C 106
Monks Clo. S61—5E 67
Monkspring. S70—4C 24
Monks Way. S71—4D 14
Monk Ter. S71—2E 15
Monkwood Rd. S41—3F 131
Monkwood Rd. S62—6D 54
Monmouth Dri. DN2—3G 33
Monmouth St. S3—5A 4 & 3C 98
Monsal Cres. S43—5H 133
Monsal Cres. S71—6C 8
Monsal St. S63—1E 29
Mons St. S9—2E 89
Montague Av. DN12—3C 58
Montague St. DN1—5D 32
Montague St. S11—4C 98
Montague St. S72—5C 10
Montagu Rd. DN5—1G 45
Montagu St. S64—1G 57
Monteney Cres. S5—1E 75
Monteney Rd. S5—2E 75
Montfort Dri. S3—5F 87
Montgomery Av. S7—6C 98
Montgomery Ct. S11—2G 109
Montgomery Dri. S7—6C 98
Montgomery Gdns. DN2—3A 34
Montgomery Rd. S7—6C 98
Montgomery Rd. S63—5E 41
Montgomery Sq. S63—5F 41
Montgomery Ter. Rd. S6
  —6D 86
Montrose Av. DN2—4H 33
Montrose Av. S75—4D 6
Montrose Ct. S11—3F 109
Montrose Pl. S18—1B 128
Montrose Rd. S7—2A 110
Moonpenny Way. S18—2E 129
Moonshine La. S5—6D 74
Moorbank Clo. S10—3D 96
Moorbank Clo. S73—5H 25
Moorbank Clo. S75—3E 13
Moorbank Dri. S10—2D 96
Moorbank Rd. S10—2D 96
Moorbank Rd. S73—4H 25
Moorbank View. S73—4H 25
Moorbridge Cres. S73—2B 40
Moor Cres. S19—2C 124
Moorcrest Rise. S75—3F 7
Moorcroft Av. S10—6B 96
Moorcroft Clo. S10—6B 96
Moorcroft Dri. S10—6B 96
Moorcroft Rd. S10—6B 96
Moordale View. S62—6A 56
Moor End Rd. S10—1A 98
Moore St. S3—1C 4 & 4D 98
Moorfield Av. S65—2H 81
Moorfield Clo. S65—2H 81
Moorfield Dri. DN3—4F 35
Moorfield Gro. S65—2H 81

Moorfields. S3—1D 4 & 1E 99
Moorfoot. S1—6D 4
Moor Gap. DN3—3H 49
Moorgate Av. S10—1B 98
Moorgate Av. S60—5E 79
Moorgate Chase. S60—4E 79
Moorgate Ct. S60—4E 79
Moorgate Cres. S18—3F 129
Moorgate Gro. S60—5E 79
Moorgate La. S60—5E 79
Moorgate Rd. S60—4E 79
Moorgate St. S60—3D 78
Moor Grn. Clo. S75—6C 12
Moorhead. S1—5D 4
Moorhouse Clo. S60—2B 92
Moorhouse La. S60—2A 92
Moorhouse La. S75—1B 84
Moorland Av. S70—6D 12
Moorland Av. S75—3F 7
Moorland Ct. DN1—6E 33
Moorland Cres. S75—3F 7
Moorland Dri. S30—3C 140
Moorland Gro. DN4—2A 48
Moorland Pl. S6—5C 84
Moorlands. S66—5D 80
Moorlands Cres. S60—2A 92
Moorland View. S12—5C 112
Moorland View. S31—6C 104
Moorland View Rd. S40
  —5E 137
Moor La. DN3—2B 20
Moor La. S44—6A 139
Moor La. S63—4D 40
Moor La. S66—1B 83
Moor La. S70—6D 36
Moor La. N. S65—5H 71
Moor La. S. S65—1H 81
Moorlawn Av. S42—6A 136
Moor Ley. S70—2C 36
Moor Oaks Rd. S10—2A 98
Moor Rd. S63—4F 41
Moor Rd. S65—3H 79
Moorside Clo. S19—1C 124
Moorside Clo. S75—5F 7
Moorsyde Av. S10—6H 85
Moorsyde Cres. S10—6H 85
Moor, The. S1—6D 4 & 3E 99
Moorthorpe Gdns. S19—5H 113
Moorthorpe Grn. S19—5H 113
Moorthorpe Way. S19—5H 113
  (in two parts) & 5C 114
Moor Valley. S19—5H 113
Moor View. DN3—3H 49
Moorview Clo. S43—4D 132
Moorview Ct. S17—4H 121
Moor View Dri. S8—4C 110
Moor View Rd. S8—5C 110
Moor View Rd. S43—1E 135
Moor View Ter. S11—2E 109
Moorwoods Av. S30—2E 65
Moorwoods La. S30—2E 65
Moray Pl. S18—1B 128
Mordaunt Rd. S2—1B 112
Morgan Av. S5—1D 86
Morgan Clo. S5—6D 74
Morgan Rd. DN2—5A 34
Morgan Rd. S5—1D 86
Morland Clo. S14—4B 112
Morland Dri. S14—4B 112
Morland Pl. S14—4B 112
Morland Rd. S14—4A 112
Morley Av. S40—1E 137
Morley Clo. S18—2A 128
Morley Pl. DN12—4D 58
Morley Rd. DN1—4E 33
Morley Rd. S61—6G 67
Morley St. S6—4H 85
Morley St. S62—3F 69

Morpeth Gdns. S3—1B 4
Morpeth St. S3—1B 4 & 1D 98
Morpeth St. S65—3E 79
Morrall Rd. S5—2E 75
Morrel St. S66—5G 83
Morris Av. S41—6G 131
Morris Av. S62—5F 55
Morris Cres. DN4—5G 45
Morris Dri. S41—6G 131
Morrison Av. S66—3G 83
Morrison Dri. DN11—5E 63
Morrison Pl. S73—3E 27
Morrison Rd. S73—3D 26
Morris Rd. DN4—5G 45
Mortain Rd. S60—1F 91
Mortains. S31—1B 118
Morthen Hall La. S66—4F 93
Morthen La. S60—5C 92
Morthen La. S66—3E 93
Morthen Rd. S66
  —5F 81 to 4A 94
Mortimer Rd. S66—5H 83
Mortimer St. S1—6F 5 & 3F 99
Mortlake Rd. S5—1H 87
Mortomley Clo. S30—6C 50
Mortomley Hall Gdns. S30
  —6C 50
Mortomley La. S30—6C 50
Morton Clo. S71—2D 14
Morton Pl. S30—1A 74
Morton Rd. S64—6F 43
Mosborough Hall Dri. S19
  —4E 125
Mosborough Moor. S19
  —6A 114
Mosborough Parkway. S12
  —2H 113
Mosborough Rd. S13—6D 100
Moscar Cotts. S7—3B 110
Moss Clo. S66—5F 81
Mossdale Av. S19—2D 124
Mossdale Clo. DN5—2G 13
Moss Dri. S31—4B 126
Moss Gro. S12—4D 114
Moss Rd. S17—5A 120
Moss View. S19—3B 124
Moss Way. S19
  —2D 124 to 3D 114
Moston Wlk. S40—6G 137
Motehall Dri. S2—4C 100
Motehall Pl. S2—4D 100
Motehall Rd. S2—4C 100
Motehall Way. S2—4C 100
Motte, The. S61—1H 77
Mottram St. S71—5H 13
Mound Rd. S40—4A 138
Mount Av. S72—5G 11
Mountbatten Dri. S30—2B 64
Mountcastle St. S41—3H 131
Mountcastle Wlk. S41—3H 131
Mount Clo. S70—2H 23
Mount Cres. S74—4H 37
Mountenoy Rd. S60—4D 78
Mountford Croft. S17—4E 121
Mount Pleasant. DN4—4A 46
Mt. Pleasant. S30—1E 65
Mt. Pleasant. S70—5B 24
Mt. Pleasant. S72—5G 11
Mt. Pleasant Clo. S30—1E 65
Mt. Pleasant Rd. S61—2B 78
Mt. Pleasant Rd. S63—1F 55
Mount Rd. S3—4D 86
Mount Rd. S30—2C 64
Mount Rd. S72—5G 11
Mount St. S11—4D 98
Mount St. S61—2B 78
Mount St. S70—1G 23
Mount St. S71—1F 25

Mount Ter. S73—6A 26
Mount, The. DN3—6E 21
Mt. Vernon Av. S70—2H 23
Mt. Vernon Cres. S70—3A 24
Mt. Vernon St. S70
—4H 23 to 2A 24
Mount View. DN12—4B 60
Mt. View Av. S8—4E 111
Mt. View Gdns. S8—4E 111
Mt. View Rd. S8—5E 111
Mount Wlk. S73—5G 25
Mousehole La. S65—6C 70
Mouse Pk. Ga. S30—1F 73
Mowbray Gdns. S65—1A 80
Mowbray Pl. S65—1A 80
Mowbray St. S3—6E 87
Mowbray St. S65—1A 80
Mowson Cres. S30—4D 72
Mowson Dri. S30—4D 72
Mowson La. S30—4D 72
Moxon Clo. S30—4G 141
Mucky La. S30—1C 140
(Smithy Moor)
Mucky La. S30—5B 140
(Whitwell Moor)
Mucky La. S71—6G 15
Muglet La. S66—6H 83
Muirfield Av. S64—3C 56
Muirfield Clo. S41—5B 132
Muirfield Clo. S72—4C 10
Mulberry Clo. DN5—4F 31
Mulberry Rd. S31—1G 119
(Anston)
Mulberry Rd. S31—6G 125
(Eckington)
Mulberry St. S1—3F 5 & 2F 99
Mulberry Way. S31—4H 125
Mulehouse Rd. S10—1G 97
Mundella Pl. S8—4E 111
Mungy La. S65—5B 70
Munsbrough La. S61—5B 68
Munsbrough Rise. S61—4B 68
Munsdale. S61—4B 68
Murdoch Pl. S71—6A 8
Murdock Rd. S5—5D 74
Murrayfield Dri. S19—3E 125
Murray Rd. S11—6H 97
Murray Rd. S31—2C 126
Murray Rd. S62—1G 69
Musard Pl. S43—2B 134
Musard Way. S31—3A 126
Musgrave Cres. S5—2E 87
Musgrave Dri. S5—2E 87
Musgrave Pl. S5—2E 87
Musgrave Rd. S5—2D 86
Musgrove Av. S65—5E 71
Muskoka Av. S11—2E 109
Muskoka Dri. S11—1E 109
Mutual St. DN4—1B 46
Myers Av. S30—1D 72
Myers Gro. La. S6—5E 85
Myers La. S6—6A 72
Mylnhurst Rd. S11—2H 109
Mylor Ct. S71—4C 14
Mylor Rd. S11—1G 109
Myndon Wlk. DN12—2C 58
Myrtle Cres. S66—4G 81
Myrtle Gro. S31—5G 117
Myrtle Gro. S43—2G 133
Myrtle Rd. S2—6E 99
Myrtle Rd. S73—6A 26
Myrtle Springs. S12—2B 112
Myrtle St. S75—5E 13
Myton Rd. S9—1C 100

Nairn Dri. S18—2B 128
Nairn St. S10—2H 97

Nancy Rd. S72—6H 11
Nanny Hill. S30—3E 141
Nanny Marr Rd. S73—4E 27
Napier Mt. S70—4H 23
Napier St. S11—4C 98
Narrow La. S31—2G 119
Narrow Twitchell. S60—3E 79
(off Hollowgate)
Narrow Wlk. S10—2A 98
Naseby Av. DN5—3F 31
Naseby St. S9—1C 88
Nathan Ct. S19—6F 115
Nathan Dri. S19—5F 115
Nathan Gro. S19—5E 115
Navan Rd. S2—6C 100
Naylor Gro. S30—3C 72
Naylor Gro. S75—2B 22
Naylor Rd. S30—2C 72
Naylor St. S62—4F 69
Neale Bank. S43—4D 132
Neale Rd. DN2—1H 33
Nearcroft Rd. DN4—4B 48
Needham Way. S7—2A 110
Needlewood. S75—3B 22
Neepsend La. S3—5D 86
Neild Rd. S74—5B 38
Neill Rd. S11—5A 98
Nelson Av. S71—3B 14
Nelson Clo. S60—3D 90
Nelson Mandela Wlk. S2
(off Saxonlea Av.) —4D 100
Nelson Pl. S30—2B 64
Nelson Rd. DN11—4B 62
Nelson Rd. DN12—3B 60
Nelson Rd. S6—5F 85
Nelson Rd. S66—4H 83
(in three parts)
Nelson St. S41—5A 132
Nelson St. S65—2E 79
Nelson St. S70—6G 13
Nemesia Clo. S31—3E 119
Nesfield Clo. S41—3F 131
Nesfield Way. S5—5H 75
Nether Av. S30—6B 64
Nether Av. S31—3A 126
Nether Cantley La. DN3—1F 49
Nether Cres. S30—6B 64
Netherdene Rd. S18—2E 129
(in two parts)
Nether Edge Rd. S7—1C 110
Netherfield. S65—1H 79
Netherfield Clo. S30—3H 141
Netherfield Ct. S65—1F 79
Netherfield La. S62—1F 69
Netherfield Rd. S10—1H 97
Netherfield Rd. S40—5C 136
Nethergate. S6—6C 84
Nethergreen Av. S31—2B 126
Nethergreen Gdns. S31
—2B 126
Nethergreen Rd. S11—5F 97
Nether Hall Rd. DN1—5D 32
Nether La. S30—5F 65
Netherleigh Rd. S40—2D 136
Nether Ley Av. S30—2E 65
Nether Ley Ct. S30—2E 65
Nether Ley Croft. S30—2E 65
Nether Ley Gdns. S30—2E 65
Nethermoor Av. S31—2B 126
Nethermoor Clo. S31—2B 126
Nethermoor Dri. S31—2B 126
Nethermoor Dri. S66—1G 93
Nethermoor La. S31—2B 126
Nether Rd. S30—6F 65
Nether Shire La. S5—2G 75
Netherthorpe. S43—1E 135

Netherthorpe Clo. S43—2D 134
Netherthorpe La. S31—3A 126
Netherthorpe Pl. S3
—1B 4 & 6D 86
Netherthorpe Rd. S3
—3A 4 & 1C 98
Netherthorpe Rd. S43—1D 134
Netherthorpe St. S3
—1B 4 & 1D 98
Netherthorpe Wlk. S3
—1B 4 & 1D 98
Netherthorpe Way. S31
—6E 107
Nether Wheel Row. S13
—2G 113
Netherwood Rd. S73—4B 26
Nettleham Rd. S8—4D 110
Neville Av. S70—2D 24
Neville Clo. S3—5F 87
Neville Clo. S70—2D 24
Neville Clo. S73—5H 25
Neville Ct. S73—5H 25
Neville Cres. S70—2D 24
Neville Dri. S3—5F 87
Neville Rd. S61—6H 67
Neville St. S60—2D 78
Nevis Clo. S40—1F 137
Newark Clo. S75—3F 7
Newark Rd. S64—6C 42
Newark St. DN11—3C 62
Newark St. S9—4C 88
New Beetwell St. S40—2A 138
Newbold Av. S41—5G 131
Newbold Back La. S40
(in two parts) —5F to 6F 131
Newbold Dri. S41—5G 131
Newbold Rd. S41
—3C 130 to 1A 138
Newbold Ter. DN5—4H 31
Newbolt Rd. DN4—5B 46
Newbould Cres. S19—4G 115
Newbould La. S10—3A 98
Newbridge Dri. S43—3D 132
Newbridge La. S41 & S43
—1A 132
Newbridge St. S41—2A 132
Newburn Dri. S9—1G 89
Newburn Rd. S9—1F 89
(off Town St.)
Newbury Rd. S10—1H 97
Newbury Way. DN5—3F 31
Newby Cres. DN4—6A 46
Newby Rd. S41—3E 131
Newcastle St. S31—6E 107
Newcastle St. S1—3C 4 & 2D 98
Newcomen Rd. DN5—4A 32
New Cross Dri. S13—1A 104
New Cross Wlk. S13—6A 102
New Cross Way. S13—1A 114
Newdale Av. S72—2G 15
Newent La. S10—1H 97
Newfield Ct. S10—5D 96
Newfield Cres. S17—2C 120
Newfield Cres. S63—6D 40
Newfield Croft. S17—1C 120
Newfield Farm Clo. S14
—2A 112
Newfield Grn. Rd. S2—1H 111
Newfield La. S17—2C 120
Newfields Av. S71—3D 14
Newgate Clo. S30—6C 50
New Hall Av. S66—1G 93
New Hall Cres. S30—2B 140
New Hall La. S30—3A 140
Newhall La. S66—6A 82
New Hall La. S71—2H 25
Newhall Rd. DN3—3E 21

Newhall Rd. S9—4B 88
New Hall Rd. S40—3F 137
New Haven Clo. S40—4D 136
New Hill. DN12—3E 59
Newhill Rd. S63—6D 40
Newhill Rd. S71—2A 14
New Ings. DN3—3E 35
Newington Av. S72—5B 10
Newington Clo. DN4—4D 48
Newington Dri. S31—6C 104
Newington Rd. S11—5A 98
Newland Av. S66—3F 83
Newland Av. S72—2G 15
Newland Dale. S41—1A 138
Newland Gdns. S41—6G 131
Newland Rd. S71—6A 8
Newlands Av. S12—1C 112
Newlands Av. S40—2E 137
Newlands Clo. DN4—4D 48
Newlands Dri. DN5—4H 31
Newlands Dri. S12—1C 112
Newlands Gro. S12—1D 112
Newlands Rd. S12—1C 112
New La. DN5—2C 44
New La. DN11—4E 63
New La. S63—5H 27
New Lodge Cres. S71—6A 8
Newlyn Dri. S71—6A 8
Newlyn Pl. S8—4D 110
Newlyn Rd. S8—4D 110
Newman Av. S71—4E 9
Newman Clo. S9—5D 76
Newman Ct. S9—5D 76
Newman Ct. S60—1G 91
Newman Dri. S9—5C 76
Newman Rd. S9—6C 76
Newman Rd. S60—1G 91
Newmarch St. S9—6G 77
Newmarket Rd. DN4—1B 48
New Mill Bank. S30—6E 141
New Orchard La. S66—4A 94
New Orchard Rd. S66—4A 94
New Queen St. S41—1A 138
New Rd. S30—3F 141
(Deepcar)
New Rd. S31—1E 119
(Anston)
New Rd. S31—5F 107
(Dinnington)
New Rd. S31—3D 116
(Wales)
New Rd. S42—5A 136
New Rd. S61—4D 76
New Rd. S63—5F 41
New Rd. S73—4F 39
New Rd. S75—3E 7
(Mapplewell)
New Rd. S75—6B 36
(Tankersley)
Newsam Rd. S62—4B 56
Newsham Rd. S8—3D 110
Newsome Av. S73—6H 25
New Sq. S40—2A 138
New Station Rd. S64—2C 56
Newstead Av. S12—5G 113
Newstead Av. S30—1D 72
Newstead Clo. S12—4G 113
Newstead Clo. S18—2A 128
Newstead Clo. S65—1H 79
Newstead Dri. S12—5G 113
Newstead Gro. S12—4G 113
Newstead Rise. S12—5H 113
Newstead Rd. DN5—1H 31
Newstead Rd. S12—4G 113
Newstead St. S71—5A 8
Newstead Way. S12—5G 113
(in two parts)
New St. DN1—2C 46

New St. DN5—1A 32
New St. S1—2E 5 & 1E 99
New St. S19—2G 125
New St. S30—3G 141
(Deepcar)
New St. S30—5B 50
(High Green)
New St. S31—4F 107
(Dinnington)
New St. S31—1E 107
(Laughton)
New St. S40—3A 138
New St. S60—5D 90
New St. S61—3B 68
(Greasbrough)
New St. S61—3B 66
(Thorpe Hesley)
New St. S62—2F 69
New St. S63—2B 42
New St. S64—6H 43
New St. S70—1G 23 to 6H 13
(in two parts, Barnsley)
New St. S70—5A 24
(Worsbrough Bridge)
New St. S70—5C 24
(Worsbrough Dale)
New St. S71—2E 9
(Royston)
New St. S71—1E 25
(Stairfoot)
New St. S72—1A 28
(Great Houghton)
New St. S72—6G 11
(Grimethorpe)
New St. S73—4E 27
(Darfield)
New St. S73—4D 38
(Hemingfield)
New St. S73—6C 26
(Wombwell)
New St. S74—6F 37
New St. S75—3B 22
(Dodworth)
New St. S75—4F 7
(Mapplewell)
New St. La. S2—2H 5 & 1G 99
Newton Av. S30—2B 140
Newton Dri. DN5—6H 31
Newton Dri. S65—3G 79
Newton La. DN5—6H 31
Newton La. S1—6E 5 & 3E 99
Newton La. S30—2B 140
Newton Pl. S61—4B 66
Newton Rd. S30—6C 50
Newton St. S65—3G 79
Newton St. S70—5F 13
Newtown Av. S71—1D 8
Newtown Av. S72—2H 15
Newtown Grn. S72—2H 15
New Tree Dri. DN11—6H 61
New Winterwell. S63—4D 40
New World Centre. S61—1G 77
Niagara Rd. S6—6A 74
Nicholas La. S63—4E 29
Nicholas St. S41—6D 138
Nicholas St. S70—6F 13
Nicholson Av. S63—6D 40
Nicholson Av. S75—3A 12
Nicholson Pl. S8—1F 111
Nicholson Rd. DN4—2A 46
Nicholson Rd. S8—1E 111
Nichols Rd. S6—6G 85
Nickerwood Dri. S31—1B 116
Nidderdale Pl. S66—3G 81
Nidderdale Rd. S61—4H 67
Nidd Rd. S9—6C 88
Nidd Rd. E. S9—6D 88
Nightingale Clo. S60—4D 78

Nightingale Croft. S61—1C 66
Nightingale Rd. S30—1B 74
Nightingale St. S9—6D 88
Nile St. S10—3A 98
Ninian Gro. DN4—3C 48
Noble St. S74—6B 38
Noblethorpe Rd. S62—6D 56
Nodder Rd. S13—5E 101
Noehill Pl. S2—4D 100
Noehill Rd. S2—4D 100
Nook End. S6—5D 84
Nookery Clo. S66—3H 83
Nooking Clo. DN3—2G 35
Nook La. S6—5C 84
Nook, The. S10—1B 98
Nora St. S63—3H 29
Norbeck Cres. DN4—6E 45
Norbeck Rd. DN4—6E 45
Norborough Rd. DN2—4F 33
Norborough Rd. S9—1G 89
Norbriggs Rd. S43—1F 135
Norbrook Way. S60—2B 92
Norburn Dri. S31—3B 126
Norbury Clo. S18—2B 128
Norbury Clo. S40—5D 130
Norcroft. S70—3H 23
Norfolk Clo. S42—5D 136
Norfolk Clo. S71—3B 14
Norfolk Ct. S65—2E 79
Norfolk Dri. S31—1G 119
Norfolk Hill. S30—6A 64
Norfolk La. S1—5E 5
Norfolk Pk. Av. S2—4H 99
Norfolk Pk. Dri. S2—4G 99
Norfolk Pk. Rd. S2—4G 99
Norfolk Pl. S66—4G 83
Norfolk Rd. DN4—5B 46
Norfolk Rd. S2—5H 5 & 3G 99
Norfolk Rd. S72—1A 28
Norfolk Row. S1—3E 5 & 2E 99
Norfolk St. S1—4E 5 & 2E 99
(in two parts)
Norfolk St. S65—2E 79
Norfolk Way. S60—1G 91
Norgreave Way. S19—2E 125
Norman Clo. S70—4A 24
Norman Clo. S71—3C 14
Norman Cres. DN5—2G 31
Norman Cres. DN11—4C 62
Normancroft Av. S2—4E 101
Normancroft Cres. S2—4E 101
Normancroft Dri. S2—4D 100
Normancroft Way. S2—4E 101
Normandale Av. S6—3E 85
Normandale Rd. S6—4B 86
Norman St. S9—4C 88
Norman St. S63—1G 29
Normanton Gdns. S4—4G 87
Normanton Gro. S13—1H 113
Normanton Hill. S13—1E 113
Normanton Spring Ct. S13
—1H 113
Normanton Spring Rd. S13
—2G 113
Normanville Av. S60—2B 90
Norrel's Croft. S60—5F 79
Norris Rd. S6—3H 85
Norroy St. S4—5H 87
Norstead Cres. S66—4H 81
Northampton Rd. DN2—4A 34
N. Anston Trading Est. S31
—5B 106
N. Bridge Rd. DN5—5B 32
N. Carr La. S73—1E 27
N. Church St. S1—1E 5 & 1E 99
N. Cliffe Rd. DN12—2D 58
North Clo. S71—2E 9
Northcote Av. S2—1F 111

Northcote Ho. S8—4D 110
(off Chantrey Rd.)
Northcote Rd. S2—1F 111
Northcote Ter. S75—5E 13
North Cres. S31—1C 126
North Cres. S44—5E 135
North Cres. S65—2G 79
North Dri. S60—1D 78
Northern Av. S2—6A 100
Northern Comn. S18—6H 121
Northfield Av. S10—6H 85
Northfield Av. S62—6F 55
Northfield La. DN3—1G 21
Northfield La. S66—4E 81
Northfield Rd. DN4—4A 32
Northfield Rd. S10—1H 97
Northfield Rd. S60—2D 78
North Ga. S31—6D 124
North Ga. S64—1G 57
Northgate. S75—3E 13
North Gro. S44—5E 135
N. Hill Rd. S5—5D 74
Northlands. DN6—1C 16
Northlands. S71—1E 9
Northlands Rd. S5—5D 74
North Mall. DN1—6C 32
(off French Ga.)
North Pl. S65—2G 79
North Pl. S75—4D 12
N. Quadrant. S5—5H 75
North Rd. S44—2F 139
North Rd. S65—1H 79
North Rd. S71—1F 9
Northside Rd. S63—5F 41
North Sq. DN12—3C 60
North St. DN4—2E 47
North St. DN12—3C 60
North St. S6—6D 86
North St. S60—2C 78
North St. S62—6G 55
North St. S64—2C 56
North St. S73—3E 27
North Ter. S41—6B 138
Norththorpe. S75—3D 22
Northumberland Av. DN2
—4H 33
Northumberland Av. S74
—4A 38
Northumberland La. DN12
—2A 58
Northumberland Rd. S10
—2B 98
Northumberland Way. S71
—1G 25
North View. S31—6B 104
North View. S72—6F 11
Norton Av. S8, S14 & S12
—6H 111
Norton Av. S40—5C 136
Norton Church Rd. S8—6F 111
Norton Grn. Clo. S8—6G 111
Norton Hammer La. S8—3C 110
Norton La. S8
—2E 123 to 5H 111
Norton Lees Clo. S8—4E 111
Norton Lees Cres. S8—3E 111
Norton Lees La. S8—3D 110
Norton Lees Rd. S8—2D 110
Norton Lees Sq. S8—3E 111
Norton Pk. Av. S8—1F 123
Norton Pk. Cres. S8—1E 123
Norton Pk. Dri. S8—1E 123
Norton Pk. Rd. S8—2E 123
Norton Pk. View. S8—1E 123
Norton Rd. DN2—4H 33
Norton Rd. S63—4D 40
Norville Cres. S73—3F 27
Norwich Rd. DN2—2G 33

Norwich Row. S2—5H 5 & 2G 99
Norwith Rd. DN4—5B 48
Norwood Av. S5—1F 87
Norwood Av. S41—6D 138
Norwood Av. S66—3F 83
Norwood Clo. S5—2F 87
Norwood Clo. S41—6E 139
Norwood Clo. S66—3F 83
Norwood Cres. S31—2D 126
(Killamarsh)
Norwood Cres. S31—5G 117
(Kiveton Park)
Norwood Dri. DN5—4B 18
Norwood Dri. S5—2F 87
Norwood Dri. S72—2G 11
Norwood Dri. S75—2A 12
Norwood Grange Dri. S5—1F 87
Norwood Pl. S31—2D 126
Norwood Rd. DN12—3D 58
Norwood Rd. S5—2F 87
Norwood St. S65—6B 70
Nostel Ho. DN1—1C 46
(off Grove Pl.)
Nostell Fold. S75—3B 22
Nostell Pl. DN4—5B 48
Nottingham Cliff. S3—5F 87
Nottingham Clo. DN5—3F 31
Nottingham Clo. S31—3F 119
Nottingham Clo. S71—2G 25
Nottingham St. S3—5F 87
Nottingham St. S65—2E 79
Novello St. S66—5H 83
Nowill Ct. S8—1E 111
Nowill Pl. S8—1E 111
Nunnery Cres. S60—5C 90
Nunnery Dri. S2—1B 100
Nunnery Ter. S2—2B 100
Nursery Cres. S31—1F 119
Nursery Dri. S30—1F 75
Nursery Dri. S60—5C 90
Nursery Gdns. S70—2E 25
Nursery Gro. S30—1G 75
Nursery La. DN5—4C 44
Nursery La. S3—1F 5 & 6F 87
Nursery Rd. S31—1G 119
Nursery Rd. S31—5A 104
(Swallownest)
Nursery St. S3—1F 5 & 6F 87
Nursery St. S70—1G 23
Nuttall Pl. S2—2H 99
Nutwell Clo. DN4—5C 48
Nutwell La. DN3—2F 49 to 3G 35

Oakamoor Clo. S40—6D 130
Oak Apple Clo. S6—4C 84
Oak Av. S63—6G 41
Oak Bank Av. S41—1B 132
Oakbank Clo. S64—5B 56
Oakbank Ct. S17—4E 121
Oakbrook Ct. S10—5F 97
Oakbrook Rd. S11—5F 97
Oakbrook View. S10—4G 97
Oak Clo. S31—4A 126
Oak Clo. S64—6C 42
Oak Clo. S66—3F 81
Oak Clo. S74—6H 37
Oakdale. S70—4B 24
Oakdale Clo. DN3—6D 20
Oakdale Clo. S70—5B 24
Oakdale Pl. S61—4H 77
Oak Dale Rd. DN4—1C 60
Oak Dale Rd. S7—1B 110
Oakdale Rd. S31—2H 119
Oakdale Rd. S61—4H 77
Oakdell. S18—6H 123
Oakdene. DN11—5D 62

178

Oaken Wood Clo. S61—2C 66
Oaken Wood Rd. S61—2B 66
Oakes Grn. S9—5A 88
Oakes Pk. View. S14—6H 111
Oakes St. S9—5D 76
Oakfern Gro. S30—5B 50
Oakfield Av. S40—4D 136
Oakfield Ct. S75—4E 7
Oakfield Wlk. S75—5C 12
Oak Gro. DN3—1E 35
Oak Gro. DN12—4C 58
Oakham Dri. S3—5D 86
Oakham Pl. S75—4E 13
Oak Hill. S65—1G 79
Oakhill Rd. DN2—3H 33
Oak Hill Rd. S7—1B 110
Oakhill Rd. S18—1G 129
Oakholme Rd. S10—3A 98
Oakland Rd. S6—3H 85
Oaklands Av. S71—3D 14
Oaklands Dri. DN4—3B 48
Oaklands Gdns. DN4—4B 48
Oaklands Pl. S63—6E 41
Oak Lea. S61—4B 68
Oak Lea. S70—5C 24
Oak Lea Av. S63—4C 40
Oakley Av. S40—1G 137
Oakley Rd. S13—3G 101
Oak Lodge Rd. S30—6A 50
Oak Pk. S10—3H 97
Oak Pk. Rise. S70—2A 24
Oak Pl. S10—3H 97
Oak Rd. DN3—1E 35
Oak Rd. S12—5C 112
Oak Rd. S39—1F 115
Oak Rd. S63—1F 29
(Thurnscoe)
Oak Rd. S63—6G 41
(Wath upon Dearne)
Oak Rd. S64—6C 42
Oak Rd. S66—4D 82
Oak Rd. S72—3D 10
Oaks Av. S30—3C 140
Oaks Cres. S70—1C 24
Oaks Farm Dri. S75—4D 6
Oaks Farm La. S44—3G 139
Oaks Fold. S5—3A 76
Oaks Fold Av. S5—4A 76
Oaks Fold Rd. S5—4A 76
Oaks La. S5—4A 76
Oaks La. S30—2A 140
Oaks La. S61—6E 67
Oaks La. S71 & S70—6C 14
(in two parts)
Oak St. S8—6E 99
Oak St. S19—1C 124
Oak St. S43—2G 133
Oak St. S70—6F 13
Oak Ter. DN1—2C 46
Oak Ter. Av. S72—6B 10
Oak Tree Clo. S75—5B 6
Oak Tree Cotts. S44—4G 139
Oak Tree Rd. DN3—2H 49
Oakwell Clo. S66—3G 83
Oakwell La. S71—6A 14
Oakwell Ter. S71—6A 14
Oakwood Av. S5—2D 74
Oakwood Av. S71—1E 9
Oakwood Cres. S30—4D 72
Oakwood Cres. S60—5G 79
Oakwood Cres. S62—6E 55
Oakwood Cres. S71—1D 8
Oakwood Dri. DN3—4E 35
(Armthorpe)
Oakwood Dri. DN3—3H 49
(Branton)
Oakwood Dri. S60—5G 79

Oakwoou Hall Dri. S60—1F 91
Oakwood Rd. DN4—4H 45
Oakwood Rd. S71—1D 8
Oakwood Rd. E. S60—6G 79
Oakwood Rd. W. S60—6F 79
Oakwood Sq. S75—5A 6
Oakworth Clo. S19—3E 125
Oakworth Dri. S19—3D 124
Oakworth Gro. S19—3D 124
Oakworth View. S19—3D 124
Oates Av. S62—2F 69
Oates Clo. S61—2A 78
Oates St. S61—2A 78
Oberon Cres. S73—3D 26
Occupation La. S6—2D 84
Occupation La. S12—4G 113
Occupation Rd. S41—3H 131
Occupation Rd. S62—4H 51
(Harley)
Occupation Rd. S62—3E 69
(Parkgate)
Ochre Dike Clo. S19—5E 115
Ochre Dike La. S19—5D 114
Ochre Dike Wlk. S61
          —3H 67 to 3A 68
Octavia Clo. S60—1C 90
Odom Ct. S2—1F 111
Ogden Pl. S8—1E 123
Ogden Rd. DN2—1B 34
Oil Mill Rd. S60—3D 78
Oldale Clo. S13—2C 114
Oldale Ct. S13—1C 114
Oldale Gro. S13—1C 114
Oldcotes Rd. S31—2F 107
Old Cotts. S41—2C 138
Old Cross La. S63—5F 41
Old Farm Ct. S64—5C 42
Oldfield Av. DN12—3B 58
Oldfield Av. S6—5D 84
Oldfield Clo. S6—5D 84
Oldfield Gro. S6—5D 84
Oldfield Rd. S6—6C 84
Oldfield Rd. S65—2B 80
Old Field Shutt La. S65—1D 80
Oldfield Ter. S6—6D 84
Old Fulwood Rd. S10—6D 96
Old Garden Dri. S65—2G 79
Old Gate La. S65—6C 70
Old Hall Clo. DN5—2E 45
Old Hall Clo. S31—1D 106
Old Hall Cres. DN5—1B 32
Old Hall Dri. S66—4H 81
Old Hall Pl. DN5—1B 32
Old Hall Rd. DN5—1B 32
Old Hall Rd. S9—4C 88
Old Hall Rd. S70—1B 36
Old Hay Clo. S17—3D 120
Old Hay Gdns. S17—3C 120
Old Hay La. S17—4C 120
Old Hexthorpe. DN4—2H 45
Old Hill. DN12—3E 59
Old Hill La. S65—2D 80
Old La. S19—2G 125
Old La. S30—3A 72
Old Mill La. S70 & S71—4G 13
Old Mill Rd. DN12—4F 59
Old Pk. Av. S8—2B 122
Old Pk. Rd. S8—2B 122
Old Peverel Rd. S44—6E 135
Old Quarry Av. S31—4F 117
Old Retford Rd. S13—5C 102
Oldridge Clo. S40—5D 130
Old Rd. DN12—5B 58 to 3E 59
Old Rd. S40—2C 136 to 3F 137
Old Rd. S71—2A 14

Old Row. S74—6D 38
Oldroyd Row. S75—3B 22
(off Stainborough Rd.)
Old School La. S60—5D 90
Old Sheffield Rd. S60—4D 78
Old St. S2—2G 99
Old Warren Vale. S62—6G 55
Oldwell Clo. S17—5D 120
Old Wortley Rd. S61—1G 77
Old Yew Ga. S30—1E 73
Olive Clo. S31—6B 104
Olive Cres. S12—5C 112
Olive Gro. Rd. S2—6F 99
Olive Rd. S19—2D 124
Olive Rd. S30—3D 140
Oliver Rd. DN4—4A 46
Oliver Rd. S7—3A 110
Olivers Dri. S9—1F 101
Olivers Mt. S9—1F 101
Oliver St. S64—6D 42
Olive Ter. S6—4D 84
Olivet Rd. S8—4D 110
Ollerton Rd. S71—4A 8
Onchan Rd. S6—6E 85
Onesmoor Bottom. S30—3A 72
Onslow Rd. S11—6H 97
Orange St. S1—3C 4 & 2D 98
Orchard Av. S31—6E 107
Orchard Clo. S5—2F 75
Orchard Clo. S31—6G 95
(Laughton)
Orchard Clo. S60—5D 90
Orchard Clo. S71—2C 14
Orchard Clo. S75—4F 7
Orchard Cres. S5—2F 75
Orchard Flatts Cres. S61
          —5A 68
Orchard Gdns. S31—3F 119
Orchard La. S1—3E 5 & 2E 99
Orchard La. S19—4F 115
Orchard La. S31—5F 117
Orchard Lea Dri. S31—6B 104
Orchard Pl. S1—3E 5 & 2E 99
Orchard Pl. S31—3B 126
Orchard Pl. S60—3C 78
Orchard Pl. S63—5D 40
Orchard Rd. S5—5A 86
Orchard Sq. S18—1B 128
Orchard St. DN4—2B 46
Orchard St. S1—3E 5 & 2E 99
Orchard St. S30—4H 141
(Deepcar)
Orchard St. S30—2D 72
(Oughtibridge)
Orchard St. S63—5G 29
(Goldthorpe)
Orchard St. S63—1E 29
(Thurnscoe)
Orchard St. S73—6B 26
Orchards Way. S40—4F 137
Orchard, The. S31—1G 119
Orchard View Rd. S40—1E 137
Orchard Wlk. S71—4H 13
Orchid Clo. S44—2G 139
Orchid Way. S31—3E 119
Ordnance Pl. S9—4B 88
Ordnance Ter. S61—3H 77
(off Up. Clara St.)
Orgreave Clo. S13—4C 102
Orgreave Cres. S13—4C 102
Orgreave Dri. S13—4C 102
Orgreave Ho. DN1—1C 46
(off Burden Clo.)
Orgreave La. S13—3B 102
Orgreave Pl. S13—3B 102
Orgreave Rise. S13—5D 102
Orgreave Rd. S13—4B 102
Orgreave Rd. S60—1C 102

Orgreave Way. S13—5C 102
Oriel Mt. S10—6C 96
Oriel Rd. S10—6D 96
Oriel Way. S71—4D 14
Ormesby Clo. DN4—1G 61
Ormesby Clo. S18—2A 128
Ormesby Cres. DN5—4G 31
Ormesby Way. S66—4H 81
Ormond Clo. S8—3F 123
Ormond Clo. S42—6D 136
Ormond Dri. S8—3F 123
Ormonde Way. DN11—5C 62
Ormond Rd. S8—3F 123
Ormond Way. S8—2F 123
Ormsby Rd. S41—4H 131
Orpen Dri. S14—5A 112
Orpen Way. S14—5A 112
Orphanage Rd. S3—3F 87
Orwell Clo. S73—2H 39
Orwins Clo. S41—4F 131
Osbert Dri. S66—4A 94
Osborne Av. S66—2B 16
Osborne Av. S31—5C 104
Osborne Clo. S11—6A 98
Osborne Ct. S11—6A 98
Osborne Ct. S71—3D 14
Osborne Dri. S31—2B 118
Osborne Rd. DN2—5F 33
Osborne Rd. S11—6A 98
Osborne Rd. S31—5B 118
(Kiveton Park)
Osborne Rd. S31—2B 118
(Todwick)
Osborne St. S70—1A 24
Osgarthorpe Cres. S4—3G 87
Osgathorpe Dri. S4—3G 87
Osgathorpe Rd. S4—3G 87
Osmaston Rd. S8—5D 110
Osmond Dri. S70—4A 24
Osmond Pl. S70—4A 24
Osmund Rd. S31—6B 124
Osprey Av. S70—3D 36
Osprey Gdns. S2—3A 100
Osprey Rd. S31—1C 116
Oswestry Rd. S5—5G 75
Oswin Av. DN4—4A 46
Otley Clo. DN12—2E 59
Otley Wlk. S6—5B 86
Otter St. S9—5B 88
Oughtibridge Bri. S30—2D 72
Oughtibridge La. S30—2E 73
Oulton Av. S66—3H 81
Oulton Dri. S72—6C 10
Oulton Rise. S64—5H 43
Ouseburn Croft. S9—6C 88
Ouseburn Rd. S9—6C 88
Ouseburn St. S9—6C 88
Ouse Rd. S9—6C 88
Ouse Ter. DN12—2E 59
Outgang La. DN12—2E 59
Outgang La. S66—6H 83
Outram Rd. S2—3A 100
Outram Rd. S41—5H 131
Oval Rd. S65—2H 79
Oval, The. DN4—2A 48
Oval, The. DN6—1B 16
Oval, The. DN12—2E 59
Oval, The. S5—6H 75
Oval, The. S31—1G 119
Overcroft Rise. S17—5D 120
Overdale Av. S70—3B 24
Overdale Gdns. S17—3C 120
Overdale Rise. S17—3C 120

Overdale Rd. S73—2G 39
Overend Clo. S14—3H 111
Overend Dri. S14—3H 111
Overend Rd. S14—3H 111
Overend Way. S14—3H 111
Oversley Rd. DN2—3F 33
Oversley St. S9—6G 77
Overton Clo. S43—1D 134
Overton Rd. S6—1H 85
Owen Clo. S6—3B 74
Owen Clo. S65—1E 79
Owen Pl. S6—3B 74
Owen Wlk. S6—3B 74
Owler Ga. S30—1A 72
Owler La. S4—2H 87 to 2A 88
 (in three parts)
Owlerton Grn. S6—3B 86
Owlet La. S4—2A 88
Owlings Pl. S6—3G 85
Owlings Rd. S6—2G 85
Owlthorpe Greenway. S19
  —6D 114 to 6H 115
Owlthorpe La. S19—1B 124
Owlthorpe Rise. S19—1B 124
Owram St. S73—4E 27
Ox Carr. DN3—3E 35
Ox Close Av. S17—4G 121
Ox Close Av. S61—6G 67
Oxclose Dri. S18—2A 128
Oxclose La. S18—2A 128
Oxford Clo. S43—3F 133
Oxford Clo. S61—4C 68
Oxford Pl. DN1—1C 46
Oxford Pl. S71—1E 25
Oxford Rd. S43—3F 133
Oxford St. DN11—4C 62
Oxford St. S6—1B 98
Oxford St. S64—6C 42
Oxford St. S65—2G 79
Oxford St. S70—2A 24
Oxford St. S71—1E 25
Oxley Clo. S30—3C 140
Oxley Gro. S60—5F 79
Oxspring Bank. S5—1B 86
Oxted Rd. S9—1C 88
Oxton Dri. DN4—5F 45
Oxton Rd. S71—5C 8

Packer's Row. S40—2A 138
Packhorse La. S30—5C 50
Packington Rd. DN4—4F 49
Packman La. S31—6D 118
Packman Rd. S62—4C 54
Packman Rd. S63—4B 40
 (Wath upon Dearne)
Packmans Clo. S30—6A 64
Packmans Way. S30—6A 64
Packwood Clo. S66—3H 83
Paddock Clo. S75—4G 7
Paddock Cres. S2—2A 112
Paddock Rd. S75—4G 7
Paddocks, The. S31—6C 104
Paddocks, The. S43—1G 135
Paddocks, The. S65—5E 71
Paddock, The. S61—3D 66
Paddock, The. S73—3E 27
Paddock Way. S18—1F 129
 (in two parts)
Padley Clo. S75—2A 22
Padley Way. S5—5H 75
Padua Rise. S73—4D 26
Page Hall Rd. S4—2H 87
Pagenall Dri. S31—5B 104
Paget St. S9—4B 88
Pagoda St. S9—4B 88
Paisley Clo. S43—3A 134
Palermo Fold. S73—3D 26

Palgrave Cres. S5—5C 74
Palgrave Rd. S5—5B 74
Palington Gro. DN4—2C 48
Pall Mall. S70—6H 13
Palm Av. DN3—2G 35
Palmer Cres. S18—3F 129
Palmer Rd. S9—5E 89
Palmerston Av. S66—3E 83
Palmerston Rd. S10—2B 98
Palmer St. DN4—2E 47
Palmer St. S9—6B 88
Palmers Way. S66—5H 93
Palm Gro. DN12—4C 58
Palm Hollow Clo. S66—5D 80
Palm La. S6—5A 86
Palm St. S6—5A 86
Palm St. S75—4F 13
Pamela Dri. DN4—5E 45
Pangbourne Rd. S63—1E 29
Pantry Grn. S70—5C 24
Pantry Well. S70—5C 24
Paper Mill Rd. S5—2A 76
Parade, The. S12—1C 112
Parade, The. S62—6E 55
Parade, The. S74—6H 37
Paradise La. S1—2E 5
Paradise Sq. S1—2E 5 & 1E 99
Paradise St. S1—2E 5 & 1E 99
Parish Way. S71—4D 14
Park Av. DN3—2D 34
Park Av. DN5—2E 45
Park Av. DN12—4E 59
Park Av. S10—5H 97
Park Av. S18—1F 129
 (Dronfield)
Park Av. S30—3E 65
 (Chapeltown)
Park Av. S31—6E 107
Park Av. S60—1A 92
Park Av. S64—6E 43
Park Av. S70—6G 13
Park Av. S71—6B 8
 (Athersley)
Park Av. S71—2F 9
 (Royston)
Park Av. S72—2H 11
 (Brierley)
Park Av. S72—5B 10
 (Cudworth)
Park Av. S72—5G 11
 (Grimethorpe)
Park Clo. DN3—3F 35
Park Clo. DN5—2E 45
Park Clo. S40—6A 138
Park Clo. S64—2A 56
Park Clo. S65—5D 70
Park Clo. S75—5G 7
Park Cotts. S70—6A 24
Park Ct. S30—1A 74
Park Cres. DN4—6E 45
Park Cres. S10—3B 98
Park Cres. S30—1F 75
Park Cres. S71—2F 9
Park Dri. DN5—2D 44
Park Dri. S30—3D 140
Park Dri. S31—6H 103
Park Dri. S41—4B 138
Park Dri. S75—5D 22
Park Dri. Way. S30—2D 140
Park End Rd. S63—5F 29
Parker Av. S44—1F 139
Parker's La. S10—2A 98
Parkers La. S17—1D 120
Parker's Rd. S10—2A 98
Parker's Ter. S70—4C 36
Parker St. S70—6F 13
Parkers Yd. S41—2B 138
Parkfield Pl. S2—5E 99

Parkfield Rd. S65—3F 79
Parkgate Av. DN12—3C 58
Park Grange Clo. S2—5H 99
Park Grange Croft. S2—4G 99
Park Grange Dri. S2—5G 99
Park Grange Mt. S2—5G 99
Park Grange Mt. S2
  —4G 99 to 5A 100
Park Grange View. S2—5H 99
Park Gro. S30—2D 140
Park Gro. S62—6F 55
Park Gro. S66—4H 81
Park Gro. S70—1G 23
Park Hall Av. S42—5D 136
Parkhead Clo. S71—1C 8
Parkhead Ct. S11—3F 109
Parkhead Cres. S11—3F 109
Parkhead Rd. S11—4E 109
Park Hill. S31—6E 125
 (Eckington)
Park Hill. S31—6H 103
 (Swallownest)
Park Hill. S73—3F 27
Parkhill Cres. DN3—2H 21
Parkhill Rd. DN3—2H 21
Park Hill Rd. S73—6C 26
Park Hollow. S73—1H 39
Park Ho. La. S9—2H 89
Parkinson St. DN4—1D 32
Parklands. DN3—6D 20
Park La. DN4—1A 48
Park La. DN12—6C 58
Park La. S10—3B 98
Park La. S30—2E 141
 (Deepcar)
Park La. S30—4E 51
 (High Green)
Park La. S41—4H 131
Park La. S65—1A 83
 (Braithwell Common)
Park La. S65—4D 70
 (Thrybergh)
Park La. Ct. S65—4D 70
Parkman Rd. S62 & S63
  —4C 54 to 6C 40
Park Nook. S65—5C 70
Park Pl. S65—2H 79
Park Rd. DN1—6D 32
Park Rd. DN5—6A 18
Park Rd. DN12—4D 58
Park Rd. S6—5F 85
Park Rd. S40—4H 137
Park Rd. S63—1E 29
 (Thurnscoe)
Park Rd. S63—6E 41
 (Wath upon Dearne)
Park Rd. S64—6E 43
 (Mexborough)
Park Rd. S64—3H 55
 (Swinton)
Park Rd. S65—2H 79
Park Rd. S70—2E 23
 (Barnsley)
Park Rd. S70—6A 24
 (Worsbrough)
Park Rd. S72—2H 11
 (Brierley)
Park Rd. S72—6G 11
 (Grimethorpe)
Parkside La. S6—6D 84
Parkside Rd. S6—2A 86
Parkside Rd. S74—1F 51
Parkside Shopping Centre. S31
  —2B 126
Parkson Rd. S60—1H 91
Park Spring Clo. S2—5G 99
Park Spring Dri. S2—5G 99
Park Spring Gro. S2—5G 99

Park Spring Pl. S2—5G 99
Park Spring Way. S2—5G 99
Park Sq. S2—3H 5 & 2F 99
Parkstone Cres. S66—5B 82
Parkstone Delph. S12—5C 112
Parkstone Way. DN2—2A 34
Park St. S31—6A 104
Park St. S40—6A 138
Park St. S61—2B 78
Park St. S62—1F 69
Park St. S70—1G 23
Park St. S73—1G 39
Park Ter. DN1—6D 32
Park Ter. S30—3F 65
Park Ter. S31—5B 118
Park Ter. S65—5C 70
Park Vale Dri. S65—5D 70
Park View. DN6—2E 17
Park View. S41—6D 138
Park View. S44—6C 42
Park View. S66—3H 83
 (in two parts)
Park View. S70—2F 23
 (Barnsley)
Park View. S70—4B 24
 (Worsbrough)
Park View. S71—1F 9
Park View. S72—2H 11
 (Brierley)
Park View. S72—3C 10
 (Shafton)
Park View Av. S19—2E 125
Parkview Ct. S8—5E 111
Park View Rd. S6—2A 86
Park View Rd. S30—3E 65
Park View Rd. S61—4E 77
Park View Rd. S75—4H 7
Park View Ter. S9—6E 89
Parkway. DN3—4F 35
Park Way. DN6—1D 16
Parkway Av. S9—1B 100
Parkway Clo. S9—1B 100
Parkway Dri. S9—2C 100
Parkway Mkt. S9—1D 100
Parkway N. DN2—3F 33
Parkway S. DN2—3F 33
Parkwood Ind. Est. S3—5E 87
Parkwood Rise. DN3—2E 21
Parkwood Rd. S3—2D to 5D 86
Parkwood Rd. N. S5—2D 86
Parma Rise. S73—4C 26
Parsley Hay Clo. S13—4H 101
Parsley Hay Dri. S13—4H 101
Parsley Hay Rd. S13—4H 101
Parsonage Clo. S19—3D 124
Parsonage Cres. S6—5A 86
Parsonage St. S6—5A 86
Parson Cross Rd. S6—5A 74
Parson La. S73—3A 22
Partridge Clo. S31—6B 124
Partridge Flatt Rd. DN4—5D 48
Partridge Pl. S31—1C 116
Partridge Rise. DN3—2H 21
Partridge Rd. DN3—2H 21
Partridge View. S2—3A 100
Parwich Clo. S40—6C 130
Passfield Rd. DN11—5E 63
Passhouses Rd. S4—3F 87
Pasture Gro. S31—6C 124
Pasture La. S63—5H 27
Pastures Rd. S64—6H 43
Pastures, The. S31—2A 118
Paternoster Row. S1
  —5F 5 & 3F 99
Paterson Clo. S30—2D 104
Paterson Rd. S31—4G 107
Patmore Rd. S5—5H 75
Paton Gro. S43—3D 132

Patterdale Clo. S18—2C 128
Patterdale Way. S31—1H 119
Pavement, The. S2—3H 5
Pavilion La. S60—1B 90
Paxton Ct. S14—3B 112
Paxton La. S10—3B 98
Paxton Rd. S41—6C 132
Payler Clo. S2—5C 100
Paynes Cres. S62—6E 55
Peacehaven. DN3—2H 21
Peacock Clo. S61—1B 66
Peakdale Cres. S12—2G 113
Peake Av. DN12—3C 58
Peak La. S66—6E 83
Peak Pl. S43—4B 134
Peak St. S71—6C 8
Peak View Rd. S40—1F 137
Pearce Rd. S9—2E 101
Pearce Wlk. S9—1E 101
Pea Royd La. S30—2E 141
Pearson Cres. S73—4H 25
Pearson Pl. S8—2D 110
Pearson's Clo. S65—5A 80
Pearson's Field. S73—6B 26
Pearson St. S30—2D 140
Pear St. S11—4C 98
Peartree Av. S63—1E 29
Pear Tree Av. S66—4G 81
Pear Tree Clo. S31—4A 126
Pear Tree Clo. S43—3G 133
Pear Tree Clo. S60—3D 90
Pear Tree Rd. S5—3H 75
Pearwood Cres. DN4—6H 45
Peashill St. S62—2F 69
Peatfield Rd. S31—2D 126
Peckham Rd. S30—1D 64
Pedley Av. S19—1E 125
Pedley Clo. S19—6E 115
Pedley Dri. S19—1E 125
Pedley Gro. S19—6E 115
Peel Clo. S66—3E 83
Peel Pde. S70—6G 13
Peel Pl. S71—4A 14
Peel Sq. S70—6G 13
Peel St. S10—3A 98
Peel St. S70—6G 13
(Barnsley)
Peel St. S70—2H 23
(Worsborough Common)
Peel St. Arc. S70—6G 13
Peel Ter. S10—2C 98
Peet Wlk. S74—4B 38
Peg Folly. S30—3A 140
Peggy La. S30—6A 66
Pelham St. S9—3B 88
Pell's Clo. DN1—6C 32
Pembrey Ct. S19—5G 115
Pembridge Ct. S71—1E 9
Pembroke Av. DN4—5A 46
Pembroke Cres. S30—1C 64
Pembroke Rise. DN5—3F 31
Pembroke Rise. S31—3F 119
Pembroke Rd. S18—3E 129
Pembroke St. S11—4C 98
Pembroke St. S61—3H 77
Pendeen Rd. S11—5F 97
Penistone Rd. S6—2A to 6D 86
Penistone Rd. S30—1A 64
(Chapeltown)
Penistone Rd. S30
(Grenoside) —1B 74 to 5B 64
Penistone Rd. N. S6
—1A 86 & 6A 74
Penistone St. DN1—5D 32
Penley St. S11—5D 98
Penmore Clo. S41—4C 138

Penmore La. S41—5C 138
Penmore St. S41—5C 138
Pennine Centre, The. S1—2D 4
Pennine View. S30—5D 140
Pennine View. S75—3E 7
Pennine Way. S40—6E 131
Pennine Way. S75—5D 12
Pen Nook Clo. S30—5G 141
Pen Nook Dri. S30—5G 141
Pen Nook Gdns. S30—5G 141
Penns Rd. S2—1G 111
Penny Hill La. S31 & S66
—1D 104
Pennyholme Clo. S31—5B 118
Penny La. S17—5C 120
Penny Piece La. S31—1F 119
Penny Piece Pl. S31—1F 119
Penrhyn Rd. S11—6A 98
Penrhyn Wlk. S71—1G 25
Penrith Clo. S5—1C 86
Penrith Cres. S5—1C 86
Penrith Gro. S71—1G 25
Penrith Rd. DN2—5A 34
Penrith Rd. S5—1C 86
Penrose Pl. S13—1A 114
Penshurst Clo. S65—1H 79
Penthorpe Clo. S12—1D 112
Pentland Clo. S40—6E 131
Pentland Gdns. S19—5D 114
Pentland Rd. S18—2B 128
Penton St. S1—3D 4
Penyghent Clo. S30—1D 64
Pepper Clo. S61—5F 67
Pepper St. S74—3A 38
Percy St. S3—6D 86
Percy St. S65—3E 79
Peregrine Dri. S70—3D 36
Peregrine Way. S31—4H 127
(in two parts)
Perigree Rd. S8—4C 110
Periwood La. S8—4C 110
Perkyn Rd. S5—2H 75
Perkyn Ter. S5—2H 75
Perseverance St. S70—6F 13
Persimman Clo. DN11—6D 62
Perth Clo. S64—5G 43
Petal Clo. S66—3H 83
Peter Av. S30—4H 141
Peterborough Clo. S10—5A 96
Peterborough Dri. S10—4A 96
Peterborough Rd. S10—4A 96
Peterdale Clo. S43—3E 133
Peterdale Rd. S43—3E 133
Petersgate. DN5
—1G 31 to 6H 17
Peter's Rd. DN12—4B 60
Peter St. S61—2G 77
Peter St. S66—4A 94
Petre Dri. S4—3A 88
Petre St. S4—4H 87
Pettyclose La. S41—6D 132
Petunia Rd. DN3—4D 20
Petworth Croft. S71—1D 8
Petworth Dri. S11—5F 109
Pevensey Av. S41—5G 131
Pevensey Ct. S41—4G 131
Peveril Clo. S31—4A 118
Peveril Cres. S71—6C 8
Peveril Rd. DN4—5G 45
Peveril Rd. S11—6H 97
Peveril Rd. S31—5E 125
Peveril Rd. S41—4H 131
Pexton Rd. S4—3G 87
Pheasant Bank. DN11—4E 63
Philip La. S30—5A 50
Philip Rd. S70—2D 24
Phillimore Rd. S9—5D 88
Phillips Rd. S6—2D 84

Phoenix Gro. S60—1B 90
Phoenix Rd. S12—6E 113
Phoenix Rd. S60—5G 77
Piccadilly. DN5—1A 32
Piccadilly Rd. S41—3B 138
Piccadilly Rd. S64—4A 56
Pickering Cres. S31—6A 104
Pickering Rd. DN5—4A 18
Pickering St. S3—4D 86
Pickering St. S9—3D 88
Pickhill's Av. S30—4H 29
Picking La. S30—1F 75
Pickmere Rd. S10—1H 97
Pickton Clo. S40—3F 137
Pickup Cres. S73—1F 39
Piece End. S30—5B 50
(in two parts)
Piece End Clo. S30—5B 50
Pieces N., The. S60—3H 91
Pieces S., The. S60—3H 91
Pighills La. S18—5F 123
Pike Clo. S40—6D 130
Pike Low Gro. S75—5H 7
Pike Rd. S60—2C 90
Pilgrim St. S3—4F 87
Pilley Grn. S75—6B 36
Pilley La. S75—5A 36
Pinchmill Hollow. S66—1F 93
Pirich Mill La. S60—2C 92
Pindale Av. S43—4A 134
Pindar Oaks Cotts. S70—1B 24
Pindar Oaks St. S70—1A 24
Pindar St. S70—1B 24
Pine Av. S31—4F 119
Pine Clo. S31—4A 126
Pine Clo. S66—3G 81
Pine Clo. S70—3C 24
Pine Croft. S30—3E 65
Pinecroft Way. S30—3E 65
Pinefield Av. DN3—1E 21
Pine Gro. DN12—5C 58
Pinehall Dri. S71—3D 14
Pine Hall Rd. DN3—1E 21
Pinehurst Rise. S64—3B 56
Pine Rd. DN4—3D 48
Pine St. S43—3G 133
Pine View. S40—2D 136
Pine Wlk. S64—5B 56
Pinewood Av. DN3—1F 35
Pinewood Av. DN4—6G 45
Pinfold. S63—5E 41
Pinfold Clo. S42—5A 136
Pinfold Clo. S64—3A 56
Pinfold Clo. S71—1E 25
Pinfold Cotts. S72—1H 15
Pinfold Hill. S70—3A 24
Pinfold La. S3—4F 87
Pinfold La. S60—3E 79
Pinfold La. S71—2E 9
Pinfold La. S73—4F 27
Pinfolds Lands. S64—1F 57
Pinfold St. S1—3D 4 & 2E 99
Pinfold St. S31—6D 124
Pingle Av. S7—4A 110
Pingle Rd. S7—4H 109
Pingle Rd. S31—2C 126
Pingles Cres. S65—5C 70
Pinner Rd. S11—5A 98
Pinstone St. S1—5E 5 & 3E 99
Pipe Ho. La. S62—6F 55
(in two parts)
Piper Clo. S5—6E 75
Piper Cres. S5—5E 75
Pipering La. DN5—2G to 2H 31
(in two parts)
Piper La. S31—6D 104
Piper La. S42—2A 136
Piper Rd. S5—6F 75

Pipeyard La. S31—6C 124
Pipworth La. S31—5F 125
Pisagh Ho. Rd. S10—2A 98
Pitchard Clo. S12—4B 114
Pitchford La. S10—4D 96
Pit La. S12—1C 112
Pit La. S60—1F 103
Pit La. S61—3B 66
Pit La. S73—1C 38
Pit Row. S73—5E 39
Pitsmoor Rd. S3—5E 87
Pittam Clo. DN3—3F 35
Pitt Clo. S1—4B 4
Pitt La. S1—4B 4
Pitt St. S31—6H 125
Pitt St. S1—3H 77
Pitt St. S64—1G 57
Pitt St. S70—6G 13
Pitt St. S73—4C 26
Pitt St. N. S61—3H 77
Pitt St. W. S70—6F 13
Plane Clo. DN4—3D 48
Plane Dri. S66—4G 81
Planet Rd. DN6—1E 17
Plank Ga. S30—1E 73
Plantation Av. DN4—1F 63
Plantation Av. S31—1G 119
(Anston)
Plantation Av. S31—4F 107
(Dinnington)
Plantation Av. S71—2F 9
Plantation Clo. S66—3F 83
Plantation Rd. S8—1E 111
Plantin Rise. S19—2E 125
Plantin, The. S19—2E 125
Plaster Pits La. DN5—5D 30
Platt St S3—5E 87
Platts Comn. Ind. Est. S74
—4H 37
Platts Dri. S19—3G 115
Platts La. S30—2E 73
Playford Yd. S74—3H 37
Pleasant Clo. S12—1D 112
Pleasant Pl. S40—2F 137
Pleasant Rd. S12—1D 112
Pleasant View. S71—3G 13
Pleasley Rd. S60 & S31—2H 91
Plover Ct. DN11—4E 63
Plover Ct. S22—3A 100
Plover Croft. S61—1C 66
Plover Dri. S70—3D 36
Plover Way. S44—2F 139
Plowmans Way. S61—4H 67
Plowright Clo. S14—2H 111
Plowright Dri. S14—2H 111
Plowright Mt. S14—2H 111
Plowright Way. S14—2H 111
Plumber St. S70—6F 13
Plumbley Hall Rd. S19—2C 124
Plumbley La. S19—3B 124
Plumbleywood La. S19
—3A 124
Plum La. S3—1E 5 & 1E 99
Plumpers Rd. S9—1F 89
Plumpton Av. S64—5G 43
Plumpton Pk. Rd. DN4—6E 49
Plum St. S3—1E 5 & 1E 99
Plunket Rd. DN2—5F 33
Plymouth Rd. S7—2C 110
Pocknedge La. S42—4A 136
Pogmoor La. S75—5C 12
Pogmoor Rd. S75—5D 12
Pog Well La. S75—4A 64
Polka Ct. S3—4E 87
Pollard Av. S5—6C 74
Pollard Cres. S5—6C 74
Pollard Rd. S5—6C 74

Pollard St. S61—3G 77
Pollitt St. S75—4G 13
Pollyfox Way. S75—2B 22
Pomona St. S11—4C 98
Pond Clo. S6—5D 84
Pond Hill. S1—3G 5 & 2F 99
Pond Rd. S6—5D 84
Pond St. S1—3F 5 & 2F 99
Pond St. S40—3A 138
Pond St. S70—1G 23
(in two parts)
Pontefract Rd. S71
　　　—6H 13 to 1G 15
Pontefract Rd. S72—5B 10
Pontefract Rd. S73—3B to 1B 40
Poole Pl. S9—1E 101
Poole Rd. S9—1D 100
Poolsbrook Av. S43—3E 135
Poolsbrook Cres. S43—3E 135
Poolsbrook Rd. S44—5E 135
Poolsbrook Sq. S43—3E 135
Poolsbrook View. S43—3E 135
Pools La. S71—2G 9
Pool Sq. S1—4E 5 & 2E 99
Pope Av. DN12—3B 58
Pop La. DN12—3E 59
Poplar Av. S19—2F 115
Poplar Av. S30—4D 140
Poplar Av. S40—3D 136
Poplar Av. S63—4G 29
Poplar Av. S65—5C 70
Poplar Av. S72—3C 10
Poplar Clo. S18—4G 129
Poplar Clo. S30—2C 72
Poplar Clo. S31—4A 126
Poplar Clo. S64—5D 42
Poplar Dri. DN2—3A 34
Poplar Dri. S60—3B 90
Poplar Dri. S63—1F 55
Poplar Glade. S66—5F 81
Poplar Gro. DN4—1C 60
Poplar Gro. DN12—5D 58
Poplar Gro. S64—2B 56
Poplar Gro. S65—1H 81
Poplar Nook. S31—4G 117
Poplar Pl. DN3—3F 35
Poplar Rise. S66—3D 82
Poplar Rd. S30—2C 72
Poplar Rd. S31—6H 125
Poplar Rd. S73—1G 39
Poplars Rd. S70—2B 24
Poplar Ter. DN5—1B 32
Poplar Ter. S71—1F 9
Poplar Way. S60—6C 90
Popple St. S4—2H 87
Porter Av. S75—5E 13
Porter Brook View. S11—5B 98
Porter St. S43—1C 134
Porter Ter. S11—5A 98
Porter Ter. S75—5D 12
Portland Av. S31—6C 104
Portland Bldgs. S6—6C 86
(off Portland St.)
Portland Clo. S31—5E 107
Portland La. S1—4B 4 & 2D 98
Portland Pl. S66—4G 83
Portland Rd. DN11—6D 62
Portland Rd S19—5G 115
Portland St. S6—6C & 6C 86
(in two parts)
Portland St. S64—2B 56
Portland St. S70—1B 24
Portland Wlk. S6—5C 86
Portobello. S1—3B 4 & 2D 98
Portobello La. S1—3B 4 & 2D 98
Portobello St. S1—3C 4 & 2D 98
Portsea Rd. S6—3H 85
Pot Ho. La. S30—3D 140

Potterdyke Av. S62—5F 55
Potter Hill. S61—4C 68
Potter Hill La. S30—6A 50
Potters Ga. S30—6A 50
(in two parts)
Pottery Clo. S62—2F 69
Pottery La. E. S41—4B 132
Pottery La. W. S41—4A 132
Poucher St. S61—3F 77
Poulton St. S71—1D 14
Powder Mill La. S70—6C 24
Powell St. S3—2A 4 & 1C 98
Powell St. S70—5B 24
Powley Rd. S6—4B 74
Poynton Av. S31—2C 104
Poynton Way. S31—2C 104
Poynton Wood Cres. S17
　　　—3G 121
Poynton Wood Glade. S17
　　　—3G 121
Prescott Rd. S6—1G 85
Preston Av. S74—4C 38
Preston St. S8—6E 99
Preston Way. S71—1D 14
Prestwich St. S9—5D 76
Prestwood Gdns. S30—2C 64
Priest Croft La. S73—1D 26
Priestley Av. S62—6H 55
Priestley Av. S75—5A 6
Priestley Clo. DN4—6H 45
Priestley St. S2—4F 99
Primrose Av. S5—5A 76
Primrose Av. S73—4D 26
Primrose Circ. DN11—5E 63
Primrose Clo. S63—6D 28
Primrose Ct. S41—1H 137
Primrose Cres. S19—4F 115
Primrose Dri. S30—1F 75
Primrose Hill. S6—5B & 5C 86
(in two parts)
Primrose Hill. S60—1C 78
Primrose Hill. S74—6A 38
Primrose La. S31—1C 126
Primrose Way. S74—1A 52
Primulas Clo. S31—3E 119
Prince Arthur St. S75—5F 13
Princegate. DN1—6D 32
Prince of Wales Rd. S2 & S9
　　　—6C 100
Prince's Cres. DN12—2B 60
Prince's Rd. DN4—2H 47
Princess Clo. S63—1H 41
Princess Ct. S2—5D 100
Princess Dri. S30—4E 141
Princess Gdns. S73—1F 39
Princess Gro. S75—6A 36
Prince's Sq. DN3—3D 20
Princess Rd. S18—1E 129
Princess Rd. S63—4G 29
Princess Rd. S64—6F 43
Princess St. DN6—3D 16
Princess St. S4—6H 87
Princess St. S31—3C 106
Princess St. S41—1H 137
Princess St. S43—2F 133
Princess St. S63—4D 40
Princess St. S70—6G 13
Princess St. S72—4C 10
Princess St. S73—6A 26
Princess St. S74—6F 37
Princess St. S75—4E 7
Prince's St. DN1—6D 32
Princes St. S60—3B 78
Prince St. S64—1B 56
Pringle Rd. S60—2B 90
Printing Office St. DN1—6C 32
Prior Rd. DN12—4D 58

Priory Av. S7—5D 98
Priory Clo DN12—2E 59
Priory Clo. S30—6E 65
Priory Cres. S71—4E 15
Priory Pl. DN1—6C 32
Priory Pl. S7—5D 98
Priory Pl. S71—3E 15
Priory Rd. S7—6C 98
Priory Rd. S30—6E 65
Priory Rd. S63—1A 42
Priory Rd. S71—3E 15
Priory Ter. S7—5D 98
Priory Way. S31—6C 104
Private Dri. S43—3G 133
Probert Av. S63—4F 29
Proctor Pl. S6—3A 86
Progress Dri. S66—5H 81
Prospect Clo. S66—5H 81
Prospect Cotts. S70—2H 23
Prospect Dri. S17—4H 121
Prospect Dri. S17—4F 121
Prospect Pl. DN1—1C 46
Prospect Pl. S17—3G 121
Prospect Rd. DN5—3A 18
Prospect Rd. S2—6E 99
Prospect Rd. S17—4G 121
Prospect Rd. S18—6G 123
Prospect Rd. S41—1H 131
Prospect Rd. S63—6E 29
Prospect St. S70—6F 13
Prospect St. S72—6B 10
Prospect Ter. S40—1G 137
Providence St. S70—1H 23
Providence Rd. S6—5H 85
Providence St. S60—3C 78
Providence St. S61—4C 68
Providence St. S73—5D 26
Psalter Ct. S11—6A 98
Psalter La. S11—6H 97 to 5C 98
Psalters La. S61—3H 77 & 3A 78
Pullman Clo. S43—1D 134
Pump Riding. DN12—4D 60
Purbeck Av. S40—1F 137
Purbeck Ct. S19—5D 114
Purbeck Gro S19—5D 114
Purbeck Rd. S19—5D 114
Purcell Clo. S66—5H 83
Pye Av. S75—5E 7
Pye Bank Clo. S3—5E 87
Pye Bank Dri. S3—5E 87
Pye Bank Rd. S3—5E 87
Pym Rd. S64—6E 43
Pynot Rd. S41—1B 132

Quadrant, The. S17—4E 121
Quail Rise. S2—3A 100
Quaker Clo. S63—6D 40
Quaker La. DN4—5F 45
Quaker La. S71—1G 25
Quantock Way. S40—6D 130
Quarry Bank Rd. S41—3C 138
Quarry Clo. S60—3A 90
Quarry Clo. S75—5B 6
Quarryfield La. S66—3F 83
(Maltby)
Quarry Field La. S66—6F 81
(Wickersley)
Quarry Hill. S19—1A 124
Quarry Hill. S60—3D 78
Quarry Hill Rd. S63—1E 55
Quarry La. DN6—3C 16
Quarry La. S11—1A 110
Quarry La. S31—1F 119
Quarry La. S40—3E 137
Quarry La. S61—1C 78
Quarry La. S64—4D 42
Quarry La. S73—4G 27

Quarry Rd. S13—3H 101
Quarry Rd. S17—4E 121
Quarry Rd. S31—2A 126
Quarry Rd. S74—2H 37
Quarry St. S62—1F 69
Quarry St. S64—1F 57
Quarry St. S70—1H 23
Quarry St. S71—2A 14
Quarry St. S72—6B 10
Quarry Vale Gro. S12—3E 113
Quarry Vale Rd. S12—3E 113
Queen Av. DN11—4C 62
Queen Av. S66—5G 83
Queen Mary Clo. S2—6C 100
Queen Mary Cres. DN3—3D 20
Queen Mary Cres. S2—5C 100
Queen Mary Rd. S2—5B 100
Queen Mary Rd. S40—4D 136
Queen Mary's Rd. DN11—4C 62
Queen Mary St. S66—6H 83
Queen's Av. S31—5G 117
Queen's Av. S64—1B 56
Queen's Av. S72—2H 27
Queen's Av. S75—5F 13
Queensberry Rd. DN2—5A 34
Queen's Cres. DN12—2B 60
Queens Cres. S74—6E 37
Queen's Dri. DN5—3A 32
Queen's Dri. S72—4C 10
(Cudworth)
Queen's Dri. S72—2B 10
(Shafton)
Queen's Dri. S75—4E 13
(Barnsley)
Queen's Dri. S75—2B 22
(Dodsworth)
Queens Gdns. S73—1F 39
Queens Gdns. S75—4E 13
Queensgate. DN1—1D 46
Queensgate. S30—1B 74
Queen's Rd. DN1—5E 33
Queens Rd. S2—6E 99
Queens Rd. S19—3F 115
Queen's Rd. S31—6A 104
Queen's Rd. S71—6H 13
Queen's Rd. S72—4C 10
Queens Row S3—1C 4 & 1D 98
Queen's Ter. S64—6E 43
Queen St DN4—3B 46
(in two parts)
Queen St S1—2E 5 & 1E 99
Queen St S19—2C 124
Queen St S30—2E 65
(Chapeltown)
Queen St. S31—3F 107
(Dinnington)
Queen St. S31—6E 125
(Eckington)
Queen St S40—1H 137
Queen St S43—2F 133
(Brimington)
Queen St S43—3B 134
(Staveley)
Queen St S62—6G 55
Queen St S63—4G 29
(Goldthorpe)
Queen St S63—2G 29
(Thurnscoe)
Queen St S64—2B 56
Queen St S65—2G 79
Queen St S70—6H 13
Queen St S72—6G 11
Queen St S73—3F 27
Queen St S74—6E 37
Queen St N. S41—3A 132
Queen St S. S70—6H 13
Queensway. S60—1F 91

182

Queensway. S70—4B 24
Queensway. S71—1E 9
Queensway. S74—5B 38
Queensway. S75—4E 13
Queen Victoria Rd. S17—5F 121
Quern Way. S73—3E 27
Quest Av. S73—3E 39
Quiet La. S10—1B 108
Quilter Rd. S66—5H 83
Quoit Grn. S18—2F 129
Quorn Dri. S40—6C 130

Raby Rd. DN2—4F 33
Raby St. S9—6G 77
Racecommon La. S70—2F 23
Racecommon Rd. S70—2F 23
Racecourse Mt. S41—3H 131
Racecourse Rd. S41—3H 131
Racecourse Rd. S64—2G 55
Race St. S70—6G 13
Racker Way. S6—4H 85
Rackford La. S31—3H 119
Rackford Rd. S31—2G 119
Radbourne Comn. S18—2B 128
Radbourn Rd. DN11—5C 62
Radcliffe Mt. DN5—5A 18
Radcliffe Rd. DN5—5A 18
Radcliffe Rd. S71—5B 8
Radford St. S3—2B 4 & 1D 98
Radiance Rd. DN1—4E 33
Radley Av. S66—4F 81
Radnor Clo. S19—5G 115
Radnor Way. DN2—3A 34
Raeburn Clo. S14—5A 112
Raeburn Pl. S14—4A 112
Raeburn Rd. S14—5A 112
Raeburn Way. S14—5A 112
Ragusa Dri. DN11—6D 62
Raikes St. S64—1D 56
Rails Rd. S6—1A 96
Railway Av. S60—6C 90
Railway Cotts. S60—5C 90
Railway Cotts. S75—2A 22
Railway Ter. S31—5A 118
Railway Ter. S41—6B 138
Railway Ter. S60—3C 78
Railway Ter. S63—4F 29
Railway View. S63—4G 29
Rainborough Rd. S63—5B 40
Rainbow Av. S12—3B 114
Rainbow Clo. S12—3C 114
Rainbow Cres. S12—3C 114
Rainbow Dri. S12—3C 114
Rainbow Gro. S12—3C 114
Rainbow Pl. S12—5C 114
Rainbow Rd. S12—3C 114
Rainbow Wlk. S12—3B 114
 (off Carter Lodge Dri.)
Rainbow Way. S12—3B 114
Rainford Dri. S71—1D 14
Rainford Sq. DN3—2D 20
Rainton Rd. DN1—1E 47
Raisen Hall Pl. S5—1E 87
Raisen Hall Rd. S5—6D 74
Rakes La. DN12—6D 60
Raleigh Dri. S30—2B 64
Raleigh Rd. S2—1F 111
Raleigh Ter. DN4—5G 45
Raley St. S70—2F 23
Ralph Ellis Dri. S30—4D 140
Ralph Rd. S43—1E 135
Ralston Ct. S19—3D 124
Ralston Croft. S19—3E 125
Ralston Gro. S19—3D 124
Ralston Pl. S19—3D 124
Ramper La. DN3—2G 21
Ramper Rd. S66—2D 94

Rampton Rd. S7—6D 98
Ramsay Cres. DN5—3H 31
Ramsden Rd. DN4—1A 46
Ramsden Rd. S60—4F 79
Ramsey Av. S40—4F 137
Ramsker Dri. DN3—4F 35
Ranby Rd. S11—6H 97
Randall Pl. S2—5D 98
Randall St. S2—4E 99
Randall St. S31—6G 125
Rands La. DN3—2G 35
Raneld Mt. S40—5E 137
Rangeley Rd. S6—6G 85
Range Rd. S4—2B 88
Ranmoor Chase. S10—4H 97
Ranmoor Cliffe Rd. S10—4E 97
Ranmoor Clo. S41—4C 138
Ranmoor Ct. S10—5G 97
Ranmoor Cres. S10—4F 97
Ranmoor Ho. S10—3C 98
Ranmoor Pk. Rd. S10—4F 97
Ranmoor Rd. S10—4F 97
Ranskill Ct. S9—4E 89
Ranworth Clo. DN5—4G 31
Ranworth Rd. S66—4H 81
Raseby Av. S19—5E 115
Raseby Clo. S19—5E 115
Raseby Pl. S19—5E 115
Rasen Clo. S64—5G 43
Ratcliffe Rd. S11—5B 98
Ratten Row. DN11—6H 61
Ratten Row. S75—3A 22
Ravencar Rd. S31—6B 124
Ravencarr Pl. S2—4C 100
Ravencarr Rd. S2—4C 100
Raven Dri. S61—1C 66
Ravenfield Clo. S19—5A 114
Ravenfield Dri. S71—2A 14
Ravenfield La. S65—1G 71
Ravenfield Rd. DN3—4G 35
Ravenholt. S70—5A 24
Raven Rd. S7—1B 110
Ravenscar Dri. DN12—2A 58
Ravens Clo. S75—5F 7
Ravens Ct. S70—5B 24
Ravenscroft Av. S13—5G 101
Ravenscroft Clo. S13—5G 101
Ravenscroft Ct. S13—5G 101
Ravenscroft Cres. S13—5G 101
Ravenscroft Dri. S13—5G 101
Ravenscroft Oval. S13—5G 101
Ravenscroft Pl. S13—5G 101
Ravenscroft Rd. S13—6G 101
Ravenscroft Way. S13—5G 101
Ravensdale Clo. S43—5A 134
Ravensdale Rd. S18—2A 128
Ravensfield. DN12—1B 58
Ravensmead Ct. S63—2A 42
Ravenswood Rd. S40—6C 130
Ravensworth Rd. DN1—1E 47
Ravensworth Rd. S9—3D 88
Ravine, The. S5—2A 76
Rawlins Ct. S18—5G 123
Rawmarsh Hill. S62—3F 69
Rawmarsh Rd. S60—2D 78
Rawmarsh Shopping Cen. S62
 —2F 69
Rawson Clo. DN4—2D 48
Rawson Rd. S65—2E 79
Rawsons Bank. S30—1F 75
Rawson Spring Av. S6—1B 86
Rawson Spring Rd. S6—1B 86
Rawson Spring Way. S6
 —1B 86
Rawson St. S6—4C 86
Raybould Rd. S61—6H 67

Rayleigh Av. S43—3D 132
Rayls Rise. S31—2B 118
Rayls Rd. S31—2B 118
Raymond Rd. DN5—3H 31
Raymond Rd. S70—1D 24
Raynald Rd. S2—4C 100
Raynard Rd. DN4—4H 45
Raynor Sike La. S30—1A 72
Reader Cres. S64—1B 56
Reaper Cres. S30—1C 64
Reasbeck Ter. S71—2H 13
Reasby Av. S65—1H 81
Rebecca Row. S70—1H 23
Recreation Av. S66—5B 94
Recreation La. DN11—4C 62
Recreation Rd. DN6—3D 16
Recreation Rd. S43—6F 133
Recreation Rd. S63—4F 41
Rectory Clo. S30—3E 141
Rectory Clo. S31—5E 125
Rectory Clo. S63—1D 28
Rectory Clo. S73—1F 39
Rectory Gdns. DN1—5E 33
Rectory Gdns. DN12—6A 60
Rectory La. S63—1D 28
Rectory M. DN5—3D 44
Rectory Rd. S31—4B 126
Rectory Rd. S43—1C 134
Rectory Rd. S44—6E 135
Rectory St. S62—3F 69
Rectory Way. S71—4D 14
Redbourne Rd. DN5—6B 18
Redbrook Av. S41—5B 138
Redbrook Croft. S19—4A 114
Redbrook Gro. S19—4A 114
Redbrook Rd. S75—3C 12
Redcar Clo. DN12—3A 58
Redcar Rd. S10—2A 98
Redcliffe Clo. S75—3D 12
Redfearn St. S71—5H 13
Redfern Av. S19—6D 114
Redfern Ct. S19—6D 114
Redfern Dri. S19—6D 114
Redfern Gro. S19—6D 114
Red Fern Gro. S30—4D 140
Redgrave Pl. S66—3F 81
Redgrove Way. S40—5E 137
Redhall Clo. DN3—3E 21
Red Hill. S31—2B 4 & 1D 98
Red Hill. S31—5B 118
Redhill Av. S70—2C 24
Redhill Ct. DN11—6H 61
Red Ho. La. DN6—1A & 1C 16
 (in two parts)
Red House Wlk. S40—6F 131
Redland La. S7—4B 110
Redland Way. S66—3E 83
Red La. S10—4A 98
Red La. S41—2C 132
Redmarsh Av. S62—6E 55
Redmires Rd. S10—4A 96
Red Oak La. S6—4C 84
Redrock Rd. S60—1G 91
Redscope Cres. S61—5F 67
Redscope Rd. S61—6F 67
Redthorne Way. S72—2B 10
Redthorn Rd. S13—5H 101
Redthorpe Crest. S75—3C 12
Redvers Buller Rd. S40—4A 138
Redwood Av. S31—4A 126
Redwood Av. S71—2E 9
Redwood Clo. S74—6H 37
Redwood Dri. S66—4C 82
Redwood Glen. S30—3D 64
Reedham St. S66—4H 81
Reform St. S62—5F 69
Regency Ter. S30—2E 65
 (off Greenhead Gdns.)

Regent Av. DN3—4G 35
Regent Ct. DN1—6E 33
Regent Ct. S6—3B 86
Regent Cres. S71—6B 8
Regent Gdns. S70—4G 13
Regent Gro. DN11—5E 63
Regent Ho. S70—6H 13
Regent Sq. DN1—6E 33
Regent St. DN4—4A 46
Regent St. S1—3B 4 & 2D 98
Regent St. S61—3H 77
Regent St. S70—5H 13
Regent St. S74—6E 37
Regent St. S. S70—5H 13
Regents Way. S31—6C 104
Regent Ter. DN1—6E 33
Regent Ter. S3—4B 4 & 2D 98
Regina Cres. S72—3E 11
Reginald Rd. S70—2D 24
Regina Rd. S73—1H 39
Rembrandt Dri. S18—2C 128
Remington Av. S5—2D 74
Remington Dri. S5—2D 74
Remington Rd. S5—2D 74
Remount Rd. S61—5F 67
Remount Way. S61—5F 67
Renathorpe Rd. S5—3H 75
Rencliffe Av. S60—6F 79
Reneville Clo. S5—1E 75
Reneville Clo. S60—5E 79
Reneville Ct. S60—5D 78
Reneville Cres. S5—1E 75
Reneville Dri. S5—1E 75
Reneville Rd. S60—5D 78
Reney Av. S8—3B 122
Reney Cres. S8—3B 122
Reney Dri. S8—3B 122
Reney Rd. S8—2C 122
Reney Wlk. S8—3B 122
Renishaw Av. S60—1H 91
Renshaw Clo. S30—5A 50
Renshaw Rd. S11—1G 109
Renton St. S11—4D 98
Renville Clo. S62—6E 55
Renway Rd. S60—6G 79
Repton Clo. S40—6C 130
Repton Pl. S18—2A 128
Reresby Cres. S60—1A 92
Reresby Dri. S60—1A 92
Reresby Rd. S60—1H 91
Reresby Rd. S65—5E 71
Reresby Wlk. DN12—1B 58
Reservoir Rd. S10—2A 98
Reservoir Rd. S31—1A 104
Reservoir Ter. S40—1G 137
Retford Rd. S13—4B 102
Retford Wlk. DN11—4F 63
Revell Clo. S65—2B 80
Revill Clo. S66—3F 83
Revill La. S13—1C 114
Rex Av. S7—3H 109
Reynard La. S6—6B 84
Reynolds Clo. S18—3C 128
Reynolds Clo. S66—3F 81
Rhodes Av. S41—6G 131
Rhodes Av. S61—5F 67
Rhodes Dri. S60—1A 92
Rhodesia Ct. DN4—3B 48
Rhodesia Rd. S40—3E 137
Rhodes St. S2—4H 5 & 2G 99
Rhodes Ter. S70—1A 24
Ribble Croft. S30—1E 65
Ribblesdale Dri. S12—6H 113
Ribble Way. S5—6G 75
Riber Av. S71—6C 8
Riber Clo. S6—5D 84
Riber Clo S43—6A 134

Riber Ter. S40—3G 137
Ribston Ct. S9—6C 88
Ribston Rd. S9—1C 100
Richard Av. S71—1A 14
Richard La. DN11—4C 62
Richard Rd. S60—4E 79
Richard Rd. S71—1A 14
Richard Rd. S75—5B 6
Richards Ct. S2—1F 111
Richardson Wlk. S73—5H 25
Richards Rd. S2—6E to 6F 99
(in two parts)
Richard St. S70—6F 13
Richards Way. S62—1G 69
Richmond Av. S13—5G 101
Richmond Av. S75—6B 6
Richmond Clo. S40—5G 137
Richmond Gro. S13—5G 101
Richmond Hall Av. S13—5F 101
Richmond Hall Cres. S13
—6F 101
Richmond Hall Dri. S13—5F 101
Richmond Hall Rd. S13—5F 101
Richmond Hall Way. S13
—6F 101
Richmond Hill Rd. DN5—1G 45
Richmond Hill Rd. S13—6G 101
Richmond Pk. Av. S13—3G 101
Richmond Pk. Av. S61—3F 77
Richmond Pk. Clo. S13—4G 101
Richmond Pk. Cres. S13
—3G 101
Richmond Pk. Croft. S13
—3G 101
Richmond Pk. Dri. S13—4G 101
Richmond Pk. Gro. S13—4G 101
Richmond Pk. Rise. S13
—3F 101
Richmond Pk. Rd. S13—4G 101
Richmond Pk. View. S13
—4G 101
Richmond Pk. Way. S13
—4G 101
Richmond Pl. S13—6F 101
Richmond Rd. DN5—2F 31
Richmond Rd. S13
—1E 113 to 4H 101
Richmond Rd. S61—3G 77
Richmond Rd. S63—1E 29
Richmond St. S3—5F 87
Richmond St. S70—6F 13
Richworth Rd. S13—5H 101
Ricknald Clo. S31—4B 104
Ridal Av. S30—2C 140
Ridal Clo. S30—2C 140
Ridal Croft. S30—2C 140
Riddings Clo. S2—6C 100
Riddings Clo. S66—5B 94
Rider Rd. S6—3A 86
Ridge Balk La. DN6—2B 16
Ridgehill Av. S12—2C 112
Ridgehill Gro. S12—2D 112
Ridge Rd. DN6—5D 16
Ridge Rd. S65—2E 79
Ridge, The. S10—4C 96
Ridge View Clo. S9—6C 76
Ridge View Dri. S9—6C 76
Ridgewalk Way. S70—3H 21
Ridgeway S65—2A 80
Ridgeway Clo. S65—2B 80
Ridgeway Clo. S66—5A 82
Ridgeway Cres. S12—2C 112
Ridgeway Cres. S71—4E 9
Ridgeway Dri. S12—1C 112
Ridgeway Rd. S12—1C 112
Ridgeway Rd. S60—3C 90
Ridgeway, The. S18—6H 123
Ridgewood Av. DN3—6D 20

Ridgway Av. S73—3E 27
Riding Clo. S66—4E 81
Ridings Av. S71—2B 14
Ridings, The. S71—2C 14
Rig Clo. S61—6H 67
Rig Dri. S64—2G 55
Riggotts La. S40—6F 137
Riggotts Way. S42—3A 130
Riggs High Rd. S6—6A 84
Riggs Low Rd. S6—6A 84
Riley Av. DN4—5H 45
Riley Rd. S63—6F 41
Rimington Rd. S73—6B 26
Rimini Rise. S73—4C 26
Ringinglow Rd. S11
—3A 108 to 1H 109
Ringstead Av. S10—3E 97
Ringstead Cres. S10—3E 97
Ringstone Gro. S72—2H 11
Ringway. S63—6D 28
Ringwood Av. S41—4G 131
Ringwood Av. S43—3A 134
Ringwood Cres. S19—5G 115
Ringwood Dri. S19—5G 115
Ringwood Gro. S19—5G 115
Ringwood Rd. S19—5G 115
Ringwood Rd. S43—3F 133
Ripley Gro. S75—3D 12
Ripley St. S6—4A 86
Ripon Av. DN2—2F 33
Ripon St. S9—6B & 6B 88
(in two parts)
Ripon Way. S31—6A 104
Rippon Ct. S62—6F 55
Rippon Cres. S6—3H 85
Rippon Rd. S6—3H 85
Risedale Rd. S63—5H 29
Rise, The. S31—2G 119
Rise, The. S64—3H 55
Rising St. S3—5F 87
Rivelin Bank. S6—4H 85
Rivelin Glen Cotts. S6—1E 97
Rivelin Pk. Ct. S6—5G 85
Rivelin Pk. Cres. S6—5G 85
Rivelin Pk. Dri. S6—6G 85
Rivelin Pk. Rd. S6—6G 85
Rivelin Rd. S6—5G 85
Rivelin St. S6—5H 85
Rivelin Ter. S6—5G 85
Rivelin Valley Rd. S6
—2A 96 to 4H 85
Riverdale Av. S10—5G 97
Riverdale Pk. Caravan Pk. S43
—1E 135
Riverdale Rd. DN5—1G 31
Riverdale Rd. S10—4G 97
Riverhead. DN5—2D 44
River La. S1—4G 5 & 2F 99
Riverside Clo. S6—3F 85
Riverside Clo. S73—4G 27
Riverside Cres. S42—6A 136
Riverside Dri. DN5—2E 45
River Ter. S6—3A 86
River View Rd. S30—2D 72
Riviera Mt. DN5—4B 32
Riviera Pde. DN5—4B 32
Rix Rd. S62—5B 56
Roache Dri. S63—5E 29
Roach Rd. S11—6A 98
Robert Av. S71—5D 14
Robert Rd. S8—2D 122
Robert's Av. DN12—4F 59
Robertshaw Cres. S30—3F 141
Robertson Dri. S6—5H 85
Robertson Rd. S6—5G 85
Roberts Rd. DN4—2B 46
Roberts Rd. DN12—4C 60
Roberts St. S72—6B 10

Roberts St. S73—1E 39
Robert St. S60—3B 78
Robert St. S70—5A 24
Robey St. S4—2H 87
Robinbrook La. S12—6E 113
Robincroft. S40—6H 137
Robinets Rd. S61—4A 68
Robin Hood Av. S71—1F 9
Robin Hood Chase. S6—4C 84
Robin Hood Cres. DN3—6E 21
Robin Hood Rd. DN3—6E 21
Robin Hood Rd. S9—5C 76
Robin La. S19—2F 115
Robin Pl. S31—1C 116
Robins Clo. S31—6C 104
Robinson Rd. S2—3G 99
Robinson's Sq. S70—4C 36
Robinson St. S60—5D 78
Robinson Way. S31—3A 126
Rob Royd. S70—4E 23
Rob Royd. S75—3B 22
Roche. S19—1E 125
(off Shortbrook Dri.)
Roche Clo. S71—4B 14
Roche End. S31—2A 118
Rocher Av. S30—2C 74
Rocher Clo. S30—2C 74
Rocher Gro. S30—2C 74
Rochester Clo. S10—4A 96
Rochester Dri. S10—4A 96
Rochester Rd. S10—4A 96
Rochester Rd. S31—4F 119
Rochester Rd. S71—3B 14
Rochester Row. DN5—4F 31
Rockcliffe Dri. DN11—6H 61
Rockcliffe Rd. S62—3F 69
Rockingham. S19—1E 125
(off Shortbrook Dri.)
Rockingham Clo. S1—5D 4
Rockingham Clo. S18—2A 128
Rockingham Clo. S40—2E 137
Rockingham Ga. S1
—5D 4 & 3E 99
Rockingham Ho. DN1—1C 46
(off Elsworth Clo.)
Rockingham Ho. S62—1G 69
Rockingham La. S1
—4D 4 & 2E 99
Rockingham Rd. DN2—4E 33
Rockingham Rd. S62—1G 69
Rockingham Rd. S64—3G 55
Rockingham Rd. S75—3C 22
Rockingham Row. S70—5D 36
Rockingham St. S1
—3C 4 & 2D 98
Rockingham St. S70—5D 36
Rockingham St. S71—3G 13
Rockingham St. S74—5F 37
Rockingham Way. S1
—5D 4 & 3E 99
Rockingham Way. S61—4H 67
Rockland Vs. S65—5C 70
Rocklea Clo. S64—3A 56
Rockley Av. S70—3C 36
Rockley Clo. S40—6H 137
Rockley Cres. S70—4C 36
Rockley La. S75 & S70—6E 23
Rockley Nook. DN2—2H 33
Rockley Rd. S6—1H 85
Rockleys. S75—3C 22
Rockley View. S75—5B 36
Rockmount Rd. S9—5D 76
Rock Pl. S30—3F 141
Rock St. S3—6E 87
Rock St. S70—5F 13
Rockwood Clo. S30—2C 64
Rockwood Clo. S75—4D 6

Roden Way. S62—5C 54
Rodge Croft. S41—P 0
Rodger Rd. S13—6D 102
Rodger St. S61—2B 78
Rodley La. S2—5F 5
Rodman Dri. S13—5D 102
Rodman St. S13—5D 102
Rod Moor Rd. S18—5H 121
Rodney Hill. S6—3D 84
Rodsley Clo. S40—6D 130
Roebuck Hill. S74—3B 38
Roebuck Rd. S6—1B 98
Roebuck St. S73—2F 39
Roeburn Clo. S75—3E 7
Roecar Clo. S41—1B 132
Roe Croft Clo. DN5—1D 44
Roehampton Rise. DN5—4F 31
Roehampton Rise. S60—2A 90
Roehampton Rise. S71—1F 25
Roe La. S3—3F 87
Roewood Ct. S3—3F 87
(off Orphanage Rd.)
Roger Rd. S71—5E 15
Rojean Rd. S30—1B 74
Rokeby Dri. S5—3E 75
Rokeby Rd. S5—3E 75
Roland Row. S2—2G 99
Rolleston Av. S66—5E 83
Rolleston Rd. S5—5G 75
Rollet Clo. S2—5C 100
Rollin Dri. S6—2H 85
Rolling Dales Clo. S66—3E 83
Rolls Cres. S62—5C 54
Roman Cres. S60—1C 90
Roman Cres. S62—1E 69
Romandale Gdns. S2—4E 101
Roman Ridge Rd. S9—6D 76
Roman Rd. DN4—1E 47
Roman Rd. S75—6B 6
Roman St. S63—1G 29
Romney Clo. S66—3F 81
Romney Dri. S18—2C 128
Romney Gdns. S2—1F 111
Romsdal Rd. S10—1A 98
Romwood Av. S64—2G 55
Ronald Rd. DN4—3A 46
Ronald Rd. S9—1E 101
Ronksley Cres. S5—3H 75
Ronksley Rd. S5—3H 75
Rookdale Clo. S75—3D 12
Rookery Clo. S31—4G 117
Rookery Rd. S64—3H 55
Rookhill. S70—4C 24
Ropery Row. S2—1G 99
Rosamond Av. S17—3G 121
Rosamond Clo. S17—3G 121
Rosamond Ct. S17—3G 121
Rosamond Dri. S17—4G 121
Rosamond Glade. S17—3G 121
Rosamond Pl. S17—3G 121
Rosa Rd. S10—1A 98
Roscoe Bank. S6—1D 96
Roscoe Ct. S6—5F 85
Roscoe Dri. S6—5F 85
Roscoe Mt. S6—6F 85
Roscoe Rd. S3—6D 86
Rose Av. DN4—3B 46
Rose Av. S19—4F 115
Rose Av. S44—2G 139
Rose Av. S73—2D 26
Rosebery St. S61—3A 78
Rosebery St. S70—1D 24
Rosebery Ter. S70—1A 24
Rose Clo. S60—4D 90
Rose Cottage. DN3—1H 21
Rose Ct. S66—5E 81
Rose Cres. DN5—2G 31
Rose Cres. S62—1H 69

Rosedale Av. S62—1G 69
Rosedale Clo. S31—5C 104
Rosedale Gdns. S11—5B 98
Rosedale Gdns. S70—6E 13
Rosedale Rd. DN5—5A 18
(Bentley)
Rosedale Rd. DN5—2F 31
(Doncaster)
Rosedale Rd. S11—5B 98
Rosedale Rd. S31—5B 104
Rosedale Way. S66—3G 81
Rose Dri. S66—4G 81
Rose Garth Av. S31—5B 104
Rosegarth Clo. DN5—2H 31
Rose Gro. DN3—3E 35
Rose Gro. S73—5H 25
Rose Hill. DN4—2A 48
Rose Hill. S40—2H 137
Rosehill Av. S62—6G 55
Rosehill Ct. S70—5G 13
Rose Hill E. S40—2A 138
Rose Hill Rise. DN4—2A 48
Rosehill Rd. S62—1F 69
Rose Hill W. S40—2H 137
Rose Ho. DN3—3E 35
Rose La. S31—5D 94
Roselle St. S6—3A 86
Rosemary Av. S66—4E 81
Rosemary Ct. S10—6A 86
(off Heavygate Rd.)
Rosemary Rd. S19—3F 115
Rosene Cotts. S42—4A 130
Rose Pl. S73—5A 26
Rose Tree Av. S72—6B 10
Rose Tree Ct. S72—6B 10
Roseville. S73—3E 27
Rose Wood Clo. S41—3F 131
Rosewood Dri. DN3—2G 21
Roslin Rd. S10—2A 98
Rossendale Clo. S40—5G 137
Rosser Av. S12—5B 112
Rossetti Mt. S66—3F 81
Rossington Ho. DN1—2C 46
(off Elsworth Clo.)
Rossington Ri. S11—5A 98
Rossington St. DN12—1B 58
Rossiter Rd. S61—3C 68
Rosslyn Av. S31—5C 104
Rosslyn Cres. DN5—5B 18
Ross St. S9—1F 101
Rosston Rd. S66—4H 83
Rostholme Sq. DN5—5B 18
Roston Clo. S18—2B 128
Rothay Clo. S18—3C 128
Rothay Rd. S4—2B 88
Rothbury Clo. S19—5G 115
Rothbury Ct. S19—5G 115
Rothbury Way. S60—2D 90
Rother Av. S43—3D 132
Rother Ct. S60—1F 91
Rother Cres. S60—1E 103
Rotherham Clo. S31—1D 126
Rotherham La. S31—6E 95
Rotherham Rd. S13—3B 102
Rotherham Rd. S19—3G 115
(Beighton)
Rotherham Rd. S19—2F 125
(Halfway)
Rotherham Rd. S31—4F 125
(Eckington)
Rotherham Rd. S31—2D 126
(Killamarsh)
Rotherham Rd. S31—3C 106
(Laughton Common)
Rotherham Rd. S31—6A 104
(Swallownest)
Rotherham Rd. S31 & S43
(Woodall)   —5E 127

Rotherham Rd. S60—5D 90
(Catcliffe)
Rotherham Rd. S60 & S62
(Parkgate)   —6E 69
Rotherham Rd. S63—5B 40
Rotherham Rd. S66—4C 82
Rotherham Rd. S71
               —1H 13 to 5D 14
Rotherham Rd. S72
               —3H 27 to 1A 28
Rotherham Rd. Nth. S19
               —2F 125
Rotherham St. S9—4C 88
Rotherhill Clo. S65—2G 79
Rothermoor Av. S31—5G 117
Rother Rd. S60—6D 78
Rotherside Rd. S31—5F 125
Rotherstoke Clo. S60—5E 79
Rother St. S73—3A 40
Rother Ter. S60—6D 78
Rothervale Clo. S19—3G 115
Rothervale Rd. S40—5A &
(in two parts)   6A 138
Rother Valley Way. S19
               —2H 125
Rother View Rd. S60—6D 78
Rotherway. S60—3E 91
Rother Way. S66—3A 82
Rotherwood Av. S13—5D 102
Rotherwood Clo. DN5—3F 31
Rotherwood Cres. S66—5A 94
Rotherwood Rd. S31—2C 126
Rothey Gro. S40—6B 130
Rough La. S30—1H 73
Roughwood Grn. S61—4A 68
Roughwood Rd. S61—5G 67
Roughwood Way. S61—5G 67
Roundel St. S9—6B 88
Round Grn. La. S75—5D 22
Roundwood Ct. S70—5A 24
Roundwood Gro. S62—2G 69
Roundwood Way. S73—3D 26
Rowan Clo. S30—3E 65
Rowan Ct. DN2—3A 34
Rowan Dri. S66—4G 81
Rowan Dri. S75—4D 12
Rowan Garth. DN5—3A 32
Rowan Mt. DN2—3H 33
Rowan Rise. S66—4D 82
Rowan Rd. S31—6H 125
Rowan Tree Dell. S17—6E 121
Rowan Tree Rd. S31—4H 125
Rowborn Dri. S30—5F 73
Rowdale Cres. S12—2F 113
Rowell La. S6—3B 84
Rowena Av. DN3—6D 20
Rowena Dri. DN5—3E 31
Rowena Dri. S66—4A 94
Rowena Rd. DN12—3D 58
Rowland Pl. DN1—1C 46
Rowland Rd. S2—5E 99
Rowland Rd. S75—4E 13
Rowland St. S3—6E 87
Rowland St. S71—1F 9
Rowms La. S62—2C 56
Rowsley Cres. S43—3A 134
Rowsley St. S2—4F 99
Row, The. DN3—2F 49
Roxby Clo. DN4—5B 48
Roxton Av. S8—1D 122
Roxton Rd. S8—6C 110
Royal Av. DN1—5E 33
Royale Clo. S31—6E 125
Royal St. S70—6G 13
Royalty La. DN5—1H 19
Royd Av. S72—1H 15
Royd Av. S75—4F 7
Royd Clo. S70—5H 23

Roydfield Clo. S19—5D 114
Roydfield Dri. S19—5D 114
Roydfield Gro. S19—5D 114
Royd La. S30—5F 141
Royd La. S75—4A 12
Royds Av. S60—1A 92
Royds Clo. Cres. S65—5C 70
Royds La. S4—5A 88
Royds La. S74—6E 39
Royds Moor Hill. S60—2D 92
Royd, The. S30—5F 141
Royd View. S72—2G 11
Roy Kilner Rd. S73—5H 25
               • to 5A 26
Royston Av. DN5—2A 32
Royston Av. S19—5A 114
Royston Clo. S19—5A 114
Royston Clo. S42—6D 136
Royston Cotts. S74—5H 37
Royston Croft. S19—5A 114
Royston Gro. S19—5A 114
(off Royston Clo.)
Royston Hill. S74—5H 37
Royston La. S71—3E 9
Royston Rd. S72—4A 10
Rubens Clo. S18—2D 128
Rubens Row. S2—3H 5
Rudyard Rd. S6—3A 86
Rufford Av. S71—5C 8
Rufford Clo. S40—4G 137
Rufford Ct. S19—5G 115
Rufford Pl. S65—1H 79
Rufford Rise. S19—5E 115
Rufford Rise. S63—5E 29
Rufford Rd. DN4—2F 47
Rufus La. DN11—4B 62
Rugby St. S3—5F 87
Rundle Dri. S7—6C 98
Rundle Rd. S7—6C 98
Rundle Rd. S30—3D 140
Runnymede Rd. DN2—5H 33
Rupert Rd. S7—2C 110
Rural Cres. DN3—3H 49
Rural La. S6—1F 85
Rushby St. S4—2H 87
Rushdale Av. S8—2E 111
Rushdale Mt. S8—2E 111
Rushdale Rd. S8—2E 111
Rushdale Ter. S8—2E 111
Rushey Clo. S62—5E 55
Rushleigh Ct. S17—2D 120
Rushley Av. S17—1D 120
Rushley Clo. S17—1D 120
Rushley Dri. S17—1D 120
Rushley Rd. S17—1D 120
Rushworth Clo. S75—5A 6
Ruskin Av. S64—5F 43
Ruskin Clo. S63—4C 40
Ruskin Dri. DN3—3G 35
Ruskin Rd. DN4—5A 46
Ruskin Sq. S8—1E 111
Russell Clo. S71—2B 14
Russell Ct. S11—5G 109
Russell Pl. S66—3G 83
Russell Rd. S62—6C 56
Russell St. S3—1E 5 & 6E 87
Russell St. S65—1E 79
Rustlings Clo. S10—5F 97
Rustlings Rd. S11—5G 97
Rustlings View. S11—5H 97
Ruston Clo. S40—5D 130
Ruthin St. S4—3A 88
Ruth Sq. S10—3C 98
Ruthven Dri. DN4—4F 45
Rutland Av. S30—6D 106
Rutland La. DN11—4B 62
Rutland Pk. S10—3A 98
Rutland Pl. S73—1D 38

Rutland Rd. S3—5D 86
Rutland Rd. S40—2H 137
Rutland St. DN1—5E 33
Rutland St. S3—5E 87
Rutland St. S41—1A 132
Rutland Way. S3—5D 86
Rutland Way. S74—4E 13
Ryan Pl. S62—3F 69
Rydal Clo. S18—2B 128
Rydal Clo. S31—6F 107
Rydal Cres. S41—3G 131
Rydalhurst Av. S6—1G 85
Rydall Pl. DN5—1H 31
Rydal Rd. S8—2C 110
Rydal Rd. S31—6F 107
Rydal Ter. S71—6A 14
Rydal Way. S64—5G 43
Ryder Clo. S40—5G 137
Rye Bank. S60—2B 92
Rye Croft. S71—1A 14
Ryecroft Glen Rd. S17—1G 121
Ryecroft Rd. S62—1A 70
Ryecroft View. S17—1D 120
Ryedale Wlk. DN5—2E 31
Ryefield Gdns. S11—2G 109
Ryegate Cres. S10—2H 97
Ryegate Rd. S10—3G 97
Ryehill Av. S40—3C 136
Ryeview Gdns. S61—5B 68
Ryhill Dri. S19—5A 114
Ryle Rd. S7—6C 98
Rylstone Ct. S12—4B 114
Rylstone Gro. S12—5B 114
Rylstone Wlk. S70—3D 24
Ryton Av. S73—2H 39
Ryton Clo. S66—4G 83
Ryton Rd. S31—3F 119

Sackerville Ter. S31—3H 125
Sackup La. S75—4D 6
Sackville Clo. S42—5D 136
Sackville Rd. S10—1H 97
Sackville St. S70—5F 13
Saddler Av. S19—6D 114
Saddler Clo. S19—6D 114
Saddler Grn. S19—6D 114
Saddler Gro. S19—6D 114
Sadler Ga. S70—5G 13
Sadler's Ga. S73—5A 26
St Agnes Rd. DN4—1G 47
St Aidan's Av. S2—5H 99
St Aidan's Clo. S2—4A 100
St Aidan's Dri. S2—4A 100
St Aidan's Mt. S2—5A 100
St Aidan's Pl. S2—5A 100
St Aidan's Rd. S2—5A 100
St Aidan's Way. S2—5A 100
St Albans Clo. S10—4C 96
St Albans Dri. S10—4B 96
St Albans Rd. S10—4B 96
St Alban's Way. S66—5E 81
St Andrew Rd. S30—4G 141
St Andrew Rd. S74—5A 38
St Andrew's Clo. S11—6B 98
St Andrew's Clo. S64—4B 56
St Andrews Cres. S74—5A 38
St Andrews Rise. S40—5E 137
St Andrew's Rd. DN12—4D 58
St Andrew's Rd. S11—6B 98
St Andrews Rd. S74—5A 38
St Andrew's Sq. S63—1A 42
St Andrew's Ter. DN4—2E 47
St Andrew's Wlk. S60—2A 90
St Andrew's Way. DN3—1E 21
St Andrews Way. S71—2G 25
St Anne's Dri. S71—6F 9
St Anne's Rd DN4—1G 47
St Ann's Rd. S30—3F 141

St Ann's Rd. S65—1E 79
St Anthony Rd. S10—1G 97
St Augustines Av. S40—5A 138
St Augustines Cres. S40
—5A 138
St Augustines Dri. S40—4A 138
St Augustines Mt. S40—5A 138
St Augustines Rise. S40
—5A 138
St Augustine's Rd. DN4—2A 48
St Augustines Rd. S40—5H.137
St Austell Dri. S75—3A 12
St Barbara's Clo. S66—5E 83
St Barbara's Rd. S73—4D 26
St Barnabas La. S2—5E 99
St Barnabas Rd. S2—5E 99
St Bartholomew's Clo. S66
—5E 83
St Bart's Ter. S70—1H 23
St Bede's Rd. S60—3E 79
St Catherine's Av. DN4—3C 46
St Catherine's Way. S75—5D 12
St Cecilia's Rd. DN4—2G 47
St Chad's Sq. DN12—1B 58
St Chads Way. DN5—2E 45
St Charles St. S9—5A 88
St Christophers Clo. S71
—2G 25
St Christopher's Cres. DN5
—3G 31
St Clement's Clo. DN5—3F 31
St Clements Clo. S71—2G 25
St David Rd. S30—4G 141
St David's Dri. DN5—3F 31
St David's Dri. S31—4F 119
St David's Dri. S60—2A 90
St David's Dri. S71—1F 25
St David's Rise. S40—5F 137
St David's Rd. DN12—3D 58
St Dominic's Clo. DN5—3D 44
St Edmund's Av. S66—5A 94
St Edward's Av. S70—1F 23
St Elizabeth Clo. S2—5F 99
St Eric's Rd. DN4—3B 48
St Francis Boulevd. S71—6F 9
St George Ga. DN1—6C 32
St George Rd. S30—4G 141
St George's Av. S64—2A 56
St George's Clo. S3
—2A 4 & 2C 98
St George's Ct. S3—3B 4
St George's Dri. S60—3A 90
St George's Rd. DN4—2A 48
St George's Rd. S70—6G 13
St George's Ter. S3
—3B 4 & 2D 98
St Giles Ga. DN5—4F 31
St Giles Sq. S30—2D 64
St Helen Rd. S30—5G 141
St Helen's Av. S71—2B 14
St Helen's Boulevd. S71—1B 14
St Helen's Clo. S41—1A 108
St Helen's Clo. S60—2F 103
St Helen's La. DN5—1H 43
St Helen's Rd. DN4—1G 47
St Helen's Rd. DN3—3D 20
St Helen's St. S41—1A 108
St Helen's St. S74—5C 38
St Helen's View. S71—2C 14
St Helen's Way. S71—2D 14
St Helier Dri. S75—5D 12
St Hilda Av. S70—6E 13
St Hilda Clo. S30—5G 141
St Hilda's Rd. DN4—1G 47
St James Av. S31—3F 119
St James Clo. DN3—3D 20
St James Clo. S41—4C 138
St James Clo. S63—5G 41

St James' Clo. S70—5A 24
St James Ct. DN1—1D 46
St James' Dri. S65—4H 71
St James' Gdns. DN4—2B 46
St James' Row. S1
—3E 5 & 2E 99
St James's Bri. DN4—1C 46
St James St. DN1—1C 46
St James Sq. S74—5A 38
(off High St. Hoyland)
St James' St. S1—3E 5 & 2E 99
St James' View. S65—4H 71
St James Wlk. S13—5D 102
St Joan Av. S30—5G 141
St John's Av. S60—3B 78
St John's Av. S75—3A 12
St John's Clo. S2—1G 99
St John's Clo. S65—1G 79
St Johns Ct. S60—2B 78
St John's Gdns. S2—2G 99
St Johns Grn. S61—6G 67
St John's Mt. S41—3H 131
St Johns Pl. S43—2B 134
St John's Rd. DN4—3A 46
St John's Rd. DN12—3B 60
St John's Rd. S2—2G 99
St John's Rd. S30—4H 141
St John's Rd. S31—1E 107
St John's Rd. S41—4G to 3H 131
(in two parts)
St John's Rd. S43—2A 134
St John's Rd. S64—2A 56
St John's Rd. S65—1G 79
St John's Rd. S70—1G 23
St John's Rd. S72—1H 15
St John's Wlk. S64—3D 42
St John's Wlk. S71—2F 9
St Joseph's Ct. S31—4F 107
St Joseph's Rd. S13—3H 101
St Lawrence Rd. S9—6G 77
St Leger Av. S31—3C 106
St Leonard's Av. S65—5D 70
St Leonard's Clo. S31—5F 107
St Leonards Dri. S41—4C 138
St Leonard's La. S65—2F 79
St Leonard's Lea. DN5—3G 31
St Leonard's Rd. S65—2E 79
St Leonards Way. S71—2G 25
St Lukes Way. S71—4C 14
St Margaret Av. S30—4G 141
St Margaret's Av. DN5—1G 43
St Margaret's Dri. S40—2H 137
St Margaret's Rd. S64—2H 55
St Margaret's Rd. S2—2G 47
St Margarets Rd. S30—2F 75
St Mark Rd. S30—4G 141
St Mark's Cres. S10—3B 98
St Mark's Rd. S40—2G 137
St Martin Clo. S30—4G 141
St Martins Av. DN5—3G 31
St Martin's Clo. S75—6D 12
St Mary Cres. S30—5G 141
St Mary's Clo. S30—6E 65
St Mary's Cres. DN1—5E 33
St Mary's Cres. S64—1A 56
St Mary's Dri. DN3—3G 35
St Mary's Dri. S60—5C 90
St Mary's Ga. S2—4D 98
St Mary's Ga. S41—2B 138
St Mary's Ga. S63—5G 13
St Marys La. S30—6E 65
St Mary's Pl. S41—2B 138
St Mary's Pl. S70—5G 13
St Mary's Rd. DN1—4E 33
St Mary's Rd. DN12—4C 60
St Mary's Rd. S2—6F 5 & 4E 99
St Mary's Rd. S62—2G 69
St Mary's Rd. S63—3H 29

St Mary's Rd. S73—1E 39
St Mary's Ter. S30—6E 141
(off Walders La.)
St Mary's View. S61—4B 68
St Matthews Way. S71—4C 14
St Matthias Rd. S30—5G 141
St Michaels Av. DN11—3E 63
St Michael's Av. S71—1D 14
St Michael's Av. S64—1B 56
St Michaels Clo. S30—1F 75
St Michaels Cres. S30—2F 75
St Michael's Rd. DN4—2H 47
St Michaels Rd. S30—1F 75
St Nicholas Rd. S62—1G 69
St Oswald's Dri. DN3—5D 20
St Owens Dri. S75—5D 12
St Patrick Rd. S30—4G 141
St Patrick's Rd. DN2—4G 33
St Patrick's Way. DN5—3F 31
St Paul Clo. S30—4G 141
St Paul Clo. S31—2A 118
St Pauls Av. S41—6D 138
St Paul's Pde. DN5—4F 31
St Paul's Pde. S1—4E 5
St Paul's Pde. S71—1F 25
St Peter Av. S30—4H 141
St Peter's Clo. S1—2E 5 & 1E 99
St Peter's Clo. S60—3A 90
St Peter's Dri. DN12—4D 58
St Peter's Rd. DN4—4G 45
St Peter's Rd. DN12—4D 58
St Peter's Ter. S70—1A 24
St Philip's Clo. S66—5E 83
St Philip's Dri. S41—5B 138
St Philip's La. S3—6D 86
St Philip's Rd. S3—2A 4 &
(in three parts)1C 98 to 6D 86
St Quentin Clo. S17—4H 121
St Quentin Dri. S17—4H 121
St Quentin Mt. S17—4H 121
St Quentin Rise. S17—4H 121
St Quentin View. S17—4H 121
St Ronan's Rd. S7—6D 98
St Sepulchre Ga. DN1—6C 32
St Sepulchre Ga. W. DN4 & DN1
—1C 46
St Stephens Dri. S31—5B 104
St Stephen's Rd. S65—2E 79
St Stephen's Wlk. S3—1C 98
St Thomas Rd. S10—2H 97
St Thomas's Clo. DN4—5G 45
St Thomas's Rd. S75—3C 12
St Thomas St. S1—3C 4 & 2D 98
St Thomas St. S40—3E 137
St Ursula's Rd. DN4—1G 47
St Veronica Rd. S30—4H 141
St Vincent Av. DN1—5E 33
St Vincent Av. DN6—1B 16
St Vincent Rd. S1—5E 33
St Vincent's Av. DN3—4G 49
St Wandrilles Clo. S30—6F 65
St Wilfreds Rd. DN4—2A 48
St Wilfrid's Rd. S2—5E 99
Salcey Sq. S40—4F 137
Sale Hill. S10—3H 97
Salerno Way. S73—3C 26
Sale St. S74—6F 37
Salisbury Av. S18—3E 129
Salisbury Av. S41—4G 131
Salisbury Cres. S41—4H 131
Salisbury Rd. DN4—2A 46
Salisbury Rd. S10—1H 97
Salisbury Rd. S18—4F 129
Salisbury Rd. S66—3F 83
Salisbury St. S75—4F 13
Salmon Rd. S11—5D 98
Salt Box La. S30—2A 74

Saltergate. S40—2H 137
Saltersbrook. S63—4F 29
Saltersbrook Rd. S73—2D 26
Samson St. S2—3G 99
Samuel Clo. S2—6H 99
Samuel Dri. S2—6H 99
Samuel Pl. S2—5H 99
Samuel Rd. S2—6H 99
Samuel Rd. S75—4D 12
Samuel Sq. S75—4D 12
Samuel St. DN4—5H 45
Sandall Beat La. DN2—3B 34
Sandall Beat Rd. DN4—6H 33
Sandall Carr Rd. DN3—4C 20
Sandall La. DN3—2B 20
Sandall Pk. Dri. DN2—2A 34
Sandall Rise. DN2—3H 33
Sandall Stones Rd. DN3
(in two parts) —5B to 4C 20
Sandal Rd. DN12—4C 58
Sandalwood Clo. DN2—1A 34
Sandalwood Rise. S64—5B 56
Sandbeck Clo. S71—4G 13
Sandbeck Ct. DN12—1B 58
Sandbeck Ho. DN1—1C 46
(off Grove Pl.)
Sandbeck Pl. S11—5B 98
Sandbeck Rd. DN4—1F 47
Sandbeck Way. S66—4A 82
Sandbed Rd. S3—2A 88
Sandbergh Rd. S61—5G 67
Sandby Ct. S14—5A 112
Sandby Croft. S14—5A 112
Sandby Dri. S14—5A 112
Sandcliffe Rd. DN2—3H 33
Sanderby Dri. S65—2H 81
Sanderson Rd. S9—1D 88
Sanderson St. S9—4B 88
Sandford Gro. Rd. S7—2C 110
Sandford Rd. DN4—5A 46
Sandhill Clo. S62—6H 55
Sandhill Ct. S72—1B 28
Sandhill Rd. S62—6H 55
Sandhurst Pl. S10—1A 98
Sandiway. S40—5E 137
Sandown Clo. S31—6B 124
Sandown Gdns. DN4—5E 43
Sandown Rd. S64—5F 43
Sandpiper Rd. S61—1B 66
Sandringham Av. S60—2H 91
Sandringham Clo. S44—1G 139
Sandringham Pl. S65—1H 81
Sandringham Rd. DN2—6G 33
Sandringham Rd. S9—5C 76
Sandringham Rd. S44—1G 139
Sandrock Dri. DN4—4C 48
Sands Clo. S14—3A 112
Sandstone Av. S9—1B 88
Sandstone Clo. S9—6C 76
Sandstone Dri. S9—1B 88
Sandstone Rd. S9—1B 88
Sandwith Rd. S31—2A 118
Sandy Acres Clo. S19—6F 115
Sandy Acres Dri. S19—6F 115
Sandybridge La. S72—1B 10
Sandy Flatt La. S66—2E 93
Sandygate. S63—5F 41
Sandygate Ct. S10—3D 96
Sandygate Cres. S33—1F 55
Sandygate Gro. S10—3D 96
Sandygate La. S10—3E 97
Sandygate Pk. S10—3D 96
Sandygate Pk. Cres. S10
—3D 96
Sandygate Pk. Rd. S10—3D 96
Sandygate Rd. S10—3D 96
Sandy La. DN4—2G 47

Sandy La. S66—6H 81 & 6A 82 (Bramley)
Sandy La. S66—4B 94 (Thurcroft)
Sandy La. S73—1A 38
Sandymount Rd. S63—5G 41
Sanforth St. S41—5A 132
Sankey Sq. S63—4F 29
Sarah St. S61—3B 78
Sarah St. S64—1E 57
Sark Rd. S2—6E 99
Saundby Clo. DN4—4A 48
Saunders Pl. S2—2A 100
Saunders Rd. S2—2A 100
Saunder's Row. S73—1E 39
Savage La. S17—2D 120
Savile St. S4—6G 87
Savile St. E. S4—5H 87
Savile Way. S72—2H 11
Saville Hall La. S75—3B 22
Saville Rd. S60—2H 91
Saville Rd. S63—5E 41
Saville Rd. S75—3B 22
Saville St. S65—6A 70
Saville Ter. S70—1G 23
Sawdon Rd. S11—4C 98
Sawn Moor Av. S66—5B 94
Sawn Moor Rd. S66—6B 94
Sawston Clo. DN4—1G 61
Saxon Cres. S70—4A 24
Saxonlea Av. S2—4D 100
Saxonlea Ct. S2—4E 101
Saxonlea Cres. S2—4E 101
Saxonlea Dri. S2—4D 100
Saxon Rd. S8—1E 111
Saxon Rd. S31—5B 118
Saxon St. S63—1G 29
Saxon St. S72—1H 15
Saxton Av. DN4—3A 48
Saxton Clo. S74—5D 38
Saxton Dri. S60—2F 91
Sayers Clo. DN5—1G 43
Scafell Pl. S31—1H 119
Scaftworth Clo. DN4—4A 48
Scammadine Clo. S60—3D 90
Scamming La. S31—6H 95
Scampton Lodge. S5—1F 87
Scarborough Clo. S31—6E 107
Scarborough Cres. S66—5G 83
Scarborough Farm Ct. S66 —4F 83
Scarborough La. DN11—4B 62
Scarborough Rd. S9—6E 89
Scarborough Rd. S66—4F 81
Scaresdale Rd. S41—3A 132
Scarfield Clo. S71—1F 25
Scargill Croft. S1—2F 5 & 1F 99
Scar La. S71—1F 25
Scarlet Oak Meadow S6—5C 84
Scarll Rd. DN4—2A 46
Scarsdale Clo. S18—3F 129
Scarsdale Cres. S43—4D 132
Scarsdale Cross. S18—2F 129 (off Scarsdale Rd.)
Scarsdale Rd. S8—4D 110
Scarsdale Rd. S18—2E 129
Scarsdale Rd. S41—3A 132
Scarsdale St. S31—4G 107
Scarth Av. DN4—3B 46
Scawsby La. DN5—1D 30
Scawthorpe Av. DN5—1F 31
Sceptone Gro. S72—2C 10
Sceptre Gro. DN11—6C 62
Schofield Dri. S73—3E 27
Schofield Pl. S73—3E 27
Schofield Rd. S30—3F 141
Schofield Rd. S73—3E 27

Schofield St. S64—6D 42
Scholes Grn. S61—3E 67
Scholes La. S61—4C to 1D 66
Scholes View. S30—6F 65
Scholes View. S74—6A 38 (Hoyland)
Scholes View. S74—4B 38 (Jump)
Scholey Rd. S66—4F 81
Scholey St. S3—6F 87
Scholfield Cres. S66—5H 83
School Av. S19—2E 125
School Board La. S40—2G 137
School Clo. S19—2F 125
School Clo. S31—5F 117
Schoolfield Dri. S62—6F 55
School Grn. La. S10—6B 96
School Gro. S31—6C 104
School Hill. S60—2A 92
School Hill. S72—6B 10
School La. DN3—3F 49
School La. S2—3H 5 & (in two parts) 2G 99
School La. S6—6C 84
School La. S8—2D 122 (Greenhill)
School La. S8—6G 111 (Norton)
School La. S18—2E 129
School La. S30—6A 64 (Grenoside)
School La. S65—4D 70
School La. Clo. S8—6G 111
School Rd S19—4G 115
School Rd. S10—2H 97
School Rd. S30—6C 50
School Rd. S31—1D 106 (Laughton)
School Rd. S31—5D 116 (Wales)
School Rd. S41—4A 132
School Rd. S66—5B 94
School St. S2—3H 5 & 2G 99
School St. S19—2D 124
School St. S31—4F 107 (Dinnington)
School St. S31—6D 124 (Eckington)
School St. S31—6A 104 (Swallownest)
School St. S63—1A 42 (Bolton-upon-Dearne)
School St. S63—1F 29 (Thurnscoe)
School St. S65—5C 70
School St. S70—1D 24
School St. S72—5B 10
School St. S73—3F 27 (Darfield)
School St. S73—3E 39 (Hemingfield)
School St. S73—6B 26 (Wombwell)
School St. S75—4F 13 (Barnsley)
School St. S75—4C 6 (Darton)
School St. S75—4G 7 (Mapplewell)
School St. Flats. S2—3H 5
School Ter. DN12—3D 58
School Wlk. DN12—1B 58 (Conisbrough)
School Wlk. DN12—6A 60 (Old Edlington)
School Wlk. S66—4F 83
Scofton Pl. S9—4D 88
Scorah's La. S64—2G 55

Scotia Clo. S2—5B 100
Scotia Dri. S2—5B 100
Scotland St. S3—1C 4 & 1D 98
Scot La. DN1—6D 32
Scott Av. DN5—1G 43
Scott Av. DN12—3C 58
Scott Clo. S66—5A 94
Scott Cres. DN3—4C 20
Scott Hill. DN5—3D 44
Scott Rd. S4—3G 87
Scott St. S4—3A 88
Scott Wlk. S66—3D 82
Scott Way. S30—3D 64
Scovell Av. S62—6D 54
Scowerdons Clo. S12—2H 113
Scowerdons Dri. S12—2H 113
Scraith Wood Dri. S5—1C 86
Scrooby La. S62—4D 68
Scrooby Pl. S61—4C 68
Scrooby St. S61—4C 68
Sea Breeze Ter. S13—5G 101
Seabrook Rd. S2—3H 99
Seagrave Av. S12—3D 112
Seagrave Cres. S12—4C 112
Seagrave Dri. S12—3D 112
Seagrave Rd. S12—3D 112
Searby Rd. S66—2H 81
Seaton Clo. S2—3B 100
Seaton Cres. S2—3B 100
Seaton Gdns. DN11—6D 62
Seaton Pl. S2—3B 100
Seaton Way. S2—3B 100
Sebastian View. S60—1C 90
Second Av. DN6—3E 17
Second La. S31—4G 119
Second La. S66—1G 93
Sedan St. S4—4G 87
Sedbergh Cres. S41—4F 131
Sedge Clo. S66—5H 81
Sedgefield Way. S64—5F 43
Sedgemoor Clo. S40—1D 136
Sedgley Rd. S6—3B 86
Sefton Ct. S10—6E 97
Sefton Rd. S10—6E 97
Selborne Rd. S10—3G 97
Selborne St. S9—6B 88
Selborne St. S65—1E 79
Selby Clo. S31—6A 104
Selby Clo. S40—5E 137
Selby Rd. DN2—4G 33
Selby Rd. S4—2H 87
Selby Rd. S71—6B 8
Selhurst Cres. DN4—4C 48
Selhurst Rd. S41—6H 131
Selkirk Av. DN4—5F 45
Selkirk Rd. DN2—3A 34
Sellars Rd. S61—6G 67
Sellars Row. S30—5B 50
Sellers St. S8—1D 110 to 6D 98 (in two parts)
Selly Oak Gro. S8—3G 123
Selly Oak Rd. S8—3G 123
Selmer Ct. S43—3D 132
Selwyn St. S65—1E 79
Senior Rd. DN4—1A 46
Senior Rd. S9—1F 101
Seniors Pl. S30—1E 65
Sennen Croft. S71—4B 14
Serlby Ho. DN1—1C 46 (off Grove Pl.)
Serpentine Wlk. S8—1E 123
Setcup La. S31—6H 125
Seth Ter. S70—1A 24
Setts Mkt. S1—2G 5
Sevenfields Ct. S6—2G 85
Sevenfields La. S6—2G 85
Severn Ct. S10—2B 98

Severn Rd. S10—2B 98
Severnside Dri. S13—6A 102
Severnside Gdns. S13—6A 102
Severnside Pl. S13—6A 102
Severnside Wlk. S13—6A 102
Sewell Rd. S19—3F 125
Sexton Dri. S66—5H 81
Seymore Rd. S31—1B 116
Seymour Rd. S43—2G 135
Seymour Rd. S66—4H 83
Shackleton Rd. DN2—6B 20
Shady Side. DN4—2H 45 (in two parts)
Shaftesbury Av. DN2—6H 33
Shaftesbury Av. DN6—1B 16
Shaftesbury Av. S40—2F 137
Shaftesbury Dri. S74—6H 37
Shaftesbury Ho. DN2—4A 34
Shaftesbury St. S70—1E 25
Shaftholme La. DN5—1B 18
Shaftholme Rd. DN5—2D 18
Shafton Rd. S60—1H 91
Shakespeare Av. DN5—5H 31
Shakespeare Cres. S18 —3G 129
Shakespeare Dri. S31—5G 107
Shakespeare Rd. DN5—6B 18
Shakespeare Rd. S63—4D 40
Shakespeare Rd. S65—1F 79
Shaldon Gro. S31—6B 104
Shalesmoor. S3—6D 86
Shambles St. S70—6G 13
Shambles, The. S40—2A 138
Shap Clo. S42—6E 131
Shardlow Gdns. DN4—5D 48
Sharlston Gdns. DN11—4F 63
Sharpe Av. S8—1C 122
Sharpfield Av. S62—5E 55
Sharrard Clo. S12—2D 112
Sharrard Dri. S12—2D 112
Sharrard Gro. S12—1D 112
Sharrard Rd. S12—2D 112
Sharrow La. S11—5C 98
Sharrow Mt. S11—6B 98
Sharrow St. S11—5D 98
Sharrow Vale Rd. S11—5A 98
Sharrow View. S7—5C 98
Shaw Ct. DN3—4G 35
Shawfield Clo. DN3—1E 21
Shawfield Rd. S71—6F 9
Shaw La. DN2—1B 34
Shaw La. S70—6F 13
Shaw La. S71—4F 9
Shaw La. S75—3G 7
Shaw La. Ind. Est. DN2—1C 34
Shaw Rd. DN12—2C 60
Shaw Rd. S65—1G 79
Shawsfield Rd. S60—6F 79
Shaws Row. S40—3F 137
Shaw St. S9—1D 88
Shaw St. S18—5G 123
Shaw St. S41—3A 132
Shaw St. S70—6F 13
Shay Ho. La. S30—4D 140
Shay Rd. S30—3D 140
Shay, The. DN4—4C 48
Sheaf Bank. S2—6E 99
Sheaf Clo. DN12—4F 59
Sheaf Ct. S70—2D 24
Sheaf Cres. S63—2B 42
Sheaf Gdns. Ter. S2—4F 99
Sheaf Mkt. S1—2G 5
Sheaf Sq. S1—5F 5 & 3F 99
Sheaf St. S1—4G 5 & 2F 99
Sheardown St. DN4—1B 46
Sheards Dri. S18—2C 128
Shearman Av. S61—5G 67
Shearwood Rd. S10—2B 98

Sheep Bri. La. DN11—3E 63
Sheepbridge La. S41—1G 131
Sheepcote Rd. S31—3A 126
Sheep Cote Rd. S60—6B 80
Sheep Dike La. S66—4G 93
Sheephill Rd. S11—4A 108
Sheep La. DN5—6A 30
Sheffield La. S60—6C 90
Sheffield Parkway. S2, S9 &
   S60—2H 5 & 1G 99
Sheffield Rd. DN4—1B 60
Sheffield Rd. DN12—5B 58
Sheffield Rd. S9—2E 89 to 6H 77
Sheffield Rd. S12—5H 113
Sheffield Rd. S13—1A 114
 (Woodhouse)
Sheffield Rd. S13 & S31
 (Woodhouse Mill) —5E 103
Sheffield Rd. S18—6D 122
 (Dronfield)
Sheffield Rd. S31—2F 119
 (Anston)
Sheffield Rd. S31—1B 118
 (Aston)
Sheffield Rd. S31—3D 124
 (Eckington)
Sheffield Rd. S31—2H 125
 (Killamarsh)
Sheffield Rd. S41
  —5A 132 to 1H 131
Sheffield Rd. S60—6H 77
Sheffield Rd. S70—1H 23
 (Barnsley)
Sheffield Rd. S70—2C 36
 (Birdwell)
Sheffield Rd. S74—6E 37
Sheldon Av. DN12—4F 59
Sheldon La. S6—5C 84
Sheldon Rd. S7—1C 110
Sheldon Rd. S30—3E 141
Sheldon Rd. S60—6D 130
Sheldon Row. S3—1G 5 & 1F 99
Sheldon St. S2—4E 99
Sheldrake Clo. S61—2B 66
Shelf St. S2—4F 99
Shelley Av. DN4—5B 46
Shelley Dri. DN3—3G 35
Shelley Dri. S18—4G 129
Shelley Dri. S31—5H 107
Shelley Dri. S71—4A 14
Shelley Gro. DN5—6H 31
Shelley Rise. DN6—1C 16
Shelley Rd. S65—3H 79
Shelley Way. S63—4C 40
Shenstone Dri. S65—5H 79
Shenstone Rd. S6—1A 86
Shenstone Rd. S65—5H 79
Shepcote La. S9—4E 89
Shepcote Way. S9—4E 89
Shephards Clo. DN12—2B 58
Shepherd Dri. S30—1C 64
Shepherd La. S63—2F 29
Shepherd St. S3—1C 4 & 1D 98
Shepherd St. S70—1H 23
Shepley Croft. S30—1C 64
Shepley St. S40—3F 137
Shepley's Yd. S40—2A 138
Sheppard Rd. DN4—4A 46
Shepperson Rd. S6—2H 85
Sherbourne Av. S41—3G 131
Sherburn Ga. S30—1D 64
Sherburn Rd. S71—6A 8
Sherde Rd. S6—6C 86
Sheridan Av. DN4—5C 46
Sheridan Ct. S71—4B 14
Sheridan Dri. S65—3A 80
Sheridan Rd. DN3—1H 21

Sheringham Clo. S30—6B 50
Sheringham Gdns. S30—6B 50
 (off Sheringham Clo.)
Sherwood Av. DN3—5D 20
Sherwood Av. DN5—3F 31
Sherwood Av. DN12—4C 58
Sherwood Chase. S17—4E 121
Sherwood Cres. S60—3E 79
Sherwood Dri. DN4—6G 45
Sherwood Glen. S7—6H 109
Sherwood Pl. S18—2B 128
Sherwood Rd. DN11—5E 63
Sherwood Rd. S18—2B 128
Sherwood Rd. S31—2C 126
Sherwood St. S40—4B 138
Sherwood Way. S72—4A 10
Shetland Gdns. DN2—4A 34
Shetland Rd. S18—3F 129
Shield Av. S70—4A 24
Shinwell Av. S43—4H 133
Shipcroft Clo. S73—1G 39
Ship Hill. S60—3D 78
Shipman Ct. S19—2D 124
Shipton St. S6—6C 86
Shirburn Gdns. DN4—2D 48
Shirebrook Rd. S8—1E 111
Shirecliffe Clo. S3—3F 87
Shirecliffe La. S3—4E 87
Shirecliffe Rd. S5—1E 87
Shiregreen La. S5—5A to 6B 76
Shiregreen Ter. S5—4H 75
Shirehall Cres. S5—2H 75
Shirehall Rd. S5
  —3H 75 to 2A 76
Shireoaks Rd. S18—1G 129
Shires Clo. DN5—2D 44
Shirland Av. S71—1A 14
Shirland La. S9—5C 88
Shirland St. S41—1A 138
Shirley Clo. S40—6D 130
Shirley Rd. DN4—2A 46
Shirley Rd. S3—4F 87
Shore Ct. S10—3H 97
Shoreham Av. S60—2G 91
Shoreham Dri. S60—2F 91
Shoreham Rd. S60—2F 91
Shoreham St. S2 & S1
  —6F 5 & 5E 99
Shore La. S10—3G 97
Shortbrook Bank. S19—1E 125
Shortbrook Clo. S19—1F 125
Shortbrook Croft. S19—1F 125
Shortbrook Dri. S19—1E 125
Shortbrook Rd. S19—1E 125
Shortbrook Wlk. S19—1F 125
 (off Eastcroft Way.)
Shortbrook Way. S19—1E 125
Short Ga. DN11—6F 61
Short La. DN4—4H 47
Shortridge St. S9—5B 88
Short Rd. DN2—5A 34
Short Row. S71—2H 13
Shorts La. S17—3B 120
Short St. S9—2D 88
Short St. S74—6F 37
Short Wood Clo. S70—2D 36
Shortwood Vs. S74—3F 37
Shotton Wlk. DN1—1C 46
Shrewsbury Almshouses. S2
  —5H 5 & 3G 99
Shrewsbury Rd. S2
  —6G 5 & 3F 99
Shrewsbury Ter. S17—5B 120
 (off Butts Hill)
Shrewsbury Ter. S61—3H 77
Shrogs Wood Rd. S60—6B 80
Shubert Clo. S13—5B 102

Shude Hill. S1—2G 5
Shude La. S1—3G 5 & 2F 99
Sibbering Row. S30—4H 141
Sicey Av. S5—5H to 1H 75
Sicey La. S5—3H 75
Sidcop Rd. S72—5B 10
Siddall St. S1—3B 4 & 2D 98
Sidlaw Clo. S42—6E 131
Sidney Rd. DN2—5H 33
Sidney St. S1—6E 5 & 3E 99
Sidney St. S64—2B 56
Sidons Clo. S61—5G 67
Siemens Clo. S9—1G 89
Siena Clo. S73—4C 26
Sikes Rd. S31—2F 119
Silkstone Clo. S12—3G 113
Silkstone Cres. S12—3G 113
Silkstone Dri. S12—3F 113
Silkstone Pl. S12—3G 113
Silkstone Rd. S12—3F 113
Silkstone View. S74—3A 38
Silver Birch Av. S10—6C 96
Silverdale Clo. DN3—3H 49
Silverdale Clo. S11—3G 109
Silverdale Clo. S41—2G 131
Silverdale Ct. S11—3H 109
 (off Silverdale Gdns.)
Silverdale Cres. S11—2G 109
Silverdale Croft. S11—3G 109
Silverdale Dri. S71—2D 14
Silverdale Gdns. S11—3H 109
Silverdale Glade. S11—3H 109
Silverdale Rd. S11—2G 109
Silverdales. S31—4G 107
Silver Hill Rd. S11—2H 109
Silver Jubilee Clo. DN2—3A 34
Silver Mill Rd. S2—5E 99
Silvermoor Dri. S65—1H 81
Silverstone Av. S72—6C 10
Silver St. DN1—6D 32
Silver St. S1—2E 5 & 1E 99
Silver St. S65—5C 70
Silver St. S70—1G 23 to 6H 13
 (in two parts)
Silver St. S75—3B 22
Silver St. Head. S1
  —2D 4 & 1E 99
Silverwood Ho. DN1—2C 46
 (off Elsworth Clo.)
Silverwood View. DN12—3D 58
Silverwood Wlk. S66—3F 81
Simcrest Av. S31—4B 126
Simmonite Rd. S66—1H 67
Simons Way. S73—4H 25
Simpson Pl. S64—6D 42
Sims St. S1—2D 4 & 1E 99
Sincil Way. DN4—4C 48
Singleton Cres. S6—4A 86
Singleton Gro. S6—4A 86
Singleton Rd. S6—4A 86
Sitka Clo. S71—2D 8
Sitwell. S19—1E 125
 (off Shortbrook Way.)
Sitwell Av. S30—3C 140
Sitwell Av. S40—4H 137
Sitwell Dri. S60—6G 79
Sitwell Gro. S60—1G 91
Sitwell Gro. S64—3B 56
Sitwell La. S66—6F 81
Sitwell Park Rd. S60—6B 80
Sitwell Pl. S7—5D 98
Sitwell Rd. S7—5D 98
 (in two parts)
Sitwell St. S31—6C 124
Sitwell Ter. S66—6F 81
 (off Sitwell La.)
Sitwell Vale. S60—6F 79
Sivilla Rd. S62—5B 56

Skelton Av. S75—4F 7
Skelton Clo. S13—2B 114
Skelton Dri. S13—1C 114
Skelton Gro. S13—1B 114
Skelton La. S13—1B 114
Skelton La. S19—4F 115
Skelton Rise. S30—3D 72
Skelton Rd. S8—2E 111
Skelton Wlk. S13—1C 114
Skelton Way. S13—1B 114
Skelwith Clo. S4—2B 88
Skelwith Clo. S41—3F 131
Skelwith Dri. S4—1B 88
Skelwith Rd. S4—2B 88
Skew Hill La. S30—1H 73
Skiddaw Clo. S40—5F 131
Skiers View Rd. S74—6G 37
Skiers Way. S74—6G 37
Skinnerthorpe Rd. S4—2H 87
Skipton Clo. DN12—2A 58
Skipton Rd. S4—3G 87
Skipton Rd. S31—6A 104
Skipwith Sq. DN11—5C 62
Skye Edge Av. S2—3H 99
Skye Edge Rd. S2—3H 99
Slack Fields La. S30—1B 72
Slack La. S40—2D 136
Slacks La. S66—6H 81
Slade Rd. S64—3A 56
Slaidburn Av. S30—1D 64
Slate St. S2—6F 99
Slayleigh Av. S10—5C 96
Slayleigh Dri. S10—5D 96
Slayleigh La. S10—5C 96
Slayleigh La. S10—5C 96
Sleaford St. S9—5B 88
Sledgate Dri. S66—6D 80
Sledgate La. S66—6D 80
Sledmere Rd. DN5—3G 31
Slinn St. S10—6A 86
Slitting Mill La. S9—5B 88
Smallage La. S13—4F 103
Smalldale Rd. S12—3F 113
Smeaton Clo. S65—1H 81
Smeaton St. S11—5D 98
Smelter Wood Av. S13—6G 101
Smelter Wood Clo. S13—6G 101
Smelter Wood Ct. S13—6G 101
Smelter Wood Cres. S13
  —6H 101
Smelter Wood Dri. S13—6G 101
Smelter Wood La. S13—6G 101
Smelter Wood Pl. S13—6H 101
Smelter Wood Rise. S13
  —6H 101
Smelter Wood Rd. S13—6G 101
Smelter Wood Way. S13
  —6G 101
Smeltinghouse La. S18
  —1A 130
Smillie Rd. DN11—5E 63
Smith Av. S43—4H 133
Smith Cres. S41—4D 138
Smithey Clo. S30—1B 64
Smithfield. S3—1D 4 & 1E 99
Smithfield Av. S41—6C 138
Smithfield Rd. S12—5C 112
Smithies La. S75 & S71—3G 13
Smithies Rd. S64—1B 56
Smithies St. S71—3G 13
Smithley La. S73—6F 25
Smith Rd. S30—3D 140
Smith Sq. DN4—4H 45
Smith St. DN4—4H 45
Smith St. S9—6E 89
Smith St. S30—2E 65
Smith St. S73—6C 26

Smithy Bri. La. S73
    —4F to 5H 39
Smithy Carr Av. S30—2D 64
Smithy Carr Clo. S30—2D 64
Smithy Clo. S61—6H 67
Smithy Croft. S18—1A 128
Smithy Grn. Rd. S71—2H 13
Smithy Moor Av. S30—1A 140
Smithy Moor La. S30—1A 140
Smithy Wood Cres. S8—3C 110
  (in two parts)
Smithy Wood La. S75—3B 22
Smithy Wood Rd. S8—3C 110
Smithy Wood Rd. S30—3H 65
Snail Hill. S60—3D 78
Snailsden Way. S75—5H 7
Snaithing La. S10—4E 97
Snaithing Pk. Clo. S10—4E 97
Snaithing Pk. Rd. S10—4E 97
Snake La. DN12—4F 59
Snape Hill. S18—1E 129
Snapehill Clo. S18—6E 123
Snapehill Cres. S18—6E 123
Snapehill Dri. S18—6E 123
Snape Hill La. S18—1E 129
Snape Hill Rd. S73—4D 26
Snelston Clo. S18—2A 128
Snetterton Clo. S72—6C 10
Snig Hill. S3—2F 5 & 1F 99
Snowberry Clo. S64—5A 56
Snowden Ter. S73—6B 26
Snowdon Way. S60—4D 90
Snow Hill. S75—3B 22
Snow Hill Row. S2—2H 5
Snow La. S3—1D 4 & 1E 99
Snydale Rd. S72—6B 10
Soaper La. S18—1E 129
Soap Ho. La. S13—1F 115
Society St. DN1—6D 32
Sokell Av. S73—1E 39
Solario Way. DN11—6C 62
Solferino St. S11—4D 98
Solly St. S1—3B 4 & 1D 98
Solway Rise. S18—1B 128
Somercotes Rd. S12—2F 113
Somersall La. S40—5C 136
Somersall Pk. Rd. S40—4C 136
Somersby Av. DN5—5H 31
Somersby Av. S42—6D 136
Somerset Ct. S72—1H 15
Somerset Dri. S43—2F 133
Somerset Rd. DN1—1D 46
Somerset Rd. S3—5F 87
Somerset Rd. S3—5F 87
Somerset St. S66—5H 83
Somerset St. S70—5F 13
Somerset St. S72—1H 15
Somerton Dri. DN4—4C 48
Somerville Ter. S6—5B 86
Sopewell Rd. S61—3F 77
Sorby Hall. S10—4H 97
Sorby Rd. S31—6H 103
Sorby St. S4—6G 87
Sorby Way. S66—6E 81
Soresby St. S40—2A 138
Sorrel Rd. S66—3G 81
Sorrelsykes Clo. S60—3H 91
Sorrento Way. S73—2D 26
Sothall Clo. S19—4F 115
Sothall Ct. S19—4F 115
Sothall Grn. S19—4F 115
Sough Hall Av. S61—2B 66
Sough Hall Cres. S61—2B 66
Sough Hall Rd. S61—3B 66
Sousa St. S66—5H 83
Southall St. S8—1E 111
South Av. S64—3H 55
Southbourne Ct. S17—3D 120

Southbourne Hall. S10—3B 98
Southbourne Rd. S10—3A 98
South Clo. S71—3E 9
Southcote Dri. S18—2B 128
South Ct. S17—2E 121
South Cres. S31—2C 126
South Cres. S44—6E 135
South Cres. S65—2H 79
South Cres. S75—2B 22
Southcroft Gdns. S7—1D 110
Southcroft Wlk. S7—1D 110
(off Southcroft Gdns.)
Southdown Av. S40—1E 137
South Dri. S63—2H 41
South Dri. S71—3E 9
Southend Pl. S2—3A 100
Southend Rd. S2—3A 100
Southern St. S9—2E 89
Southey Av. S5—6E 75
Southey Clo. S5—6D 74
Southey Cres. S5—6D 74
Southey Cres. S66—4G 83
Southey Dri. S5—6E 75
Southey Grn. Clo. S5—6D 74
Southey Grn. Rd. S5
    —5B 74 to 5E 75
Southey Hall Clo. S61—2B 66
Southey Hall Dri. S5—6E 75
Southey Hall Rd. S5—6D 74
Southey Hill. S5—5C 74
Southey Pl. S5—6D 74
Southey Rise. S5—6D 74
Southey Rd. S66—4G 83
Southey Wlk. S5—6D 74
Southfield Av. S41—6D 138
Southfield Cotts. S71—4E 9
Southfield Cres. S63—2D 28
Southfield La. S63—3D 28
Southfield Rd. DN3—2E 35
Southgate. S31—6E 125
Southgate. S74—5A 38
Southgate. S75—4E 13
Southgrove Rd. S10—4B 98
Southlands Way. S31—6C 104
South La. S1—6C 4 & 4D 98
Southlea Av. S74—6B 38
Southlea Clo. S74—6B 38
Southlea Dri. S74—6A 38
Southlea Rd. S74—6B 38
South Lodge Ct. S40—2D 136
South Mall. DN1—6C 32
(off French Ga.)
Southmoor Av. DN3—3E 35
Southmoor Clo. S43—1F 139
South Pde. DN1—6E 33
South Pde. S3—6E 87
South Pl. S40—3F 137
  (Barker La.)
South Pl. S40—3A 138
  (South St.)
South Pl. S73—6H 25
South Pl. S75—4D 12
South Rd. S6—5A 86
South Rd. S30—6B 50
South Rd. S61—2G 77
South Rd. S75—2B 22
Southsea Rd. S13—1A 114
South St. DN4—2D 46
South St. DN6—5D 16
South St. S2—3H 5 & 2G 99
South St. S19—3D 124
South St. S31—4F 107
South St. S40—3A 138
South St. S61—4C 68
  (Greasbrough)
South St. S61—4G 77
  (Kimberworth & Rotherham)
South St. S62—1G 69

South St. S66—4B 94
South St. S70—6F 13
South St. S73—4E 27
South St. S75—3B 22
South St. N. S43—1D 132
South Ter. S31—4D 116
S. Vale Dri. S65—5D 70
South View. S19—2G 125
South View. S31—5H 117
South View. S72—6F 11
South View. S73—4E 27
S. View Clo. S6—2E 85
S. View Cres. S7—6D 98
S. View Rise. S6—2E 85
S. View Rd. S7—5D 98
S. View Rd. S74—6H 37
S. View Ter. S60—6C 90
Southway. S19—1E 125
Southwell Rise. S64—5F 43
Southwell Rd. DN2—3F 33
Southwell Rd. S4—2B 88
Southwell Rd. S62—1H 69
Southwell St. S75—5F 13
Spa Brook Clo. S12—3H 113
Spa Brook Dri. S12—2H 113
  (in two parts)
Spa La. S13—2C 114
Spa La. S41—2B to 3B 138
  (in two parts)
Spa La. Croft. S13—1C 114
Spalton Rd. S62—3F 69
Spansyke St. DN4—1B 46
Sparkfields. S75—5F 7
Spark La. S75—6E 7
Spa View Av. S12—4H 113
Spa View Dri. S12—4H 113
Spa View Pl. S12—4H 113
Spa View Rd. S12—4H 113
Spa View Ter. S12—4H 113
Spa View Way. S12—4H 113
Spa Well Cres. S60—6E 91
Speedwell Ind. Est. S43
    —2C 134
Speeton Rd. S6—4A 86
Spencer Av. DN1—5E 33
Spencer Av. S43—1F 135
Spencer Dri. S65—2H 81
Spencer Rd. S2—6E 99
Spencer St. S40—1A 138
Spencer St. S64—6C 42
Spencer St. S70—6G 13
Spencer St. S65—4H 79
Spilsby Clo. DN4—5E 49
Spinkhill Av. S13—5E 101
Spinkhill Dri. S13—5F 101
Spinkhill Rd. S13—6E 101
Spinkhill Rd. S31—6B 106
Spinners Wlk. S60—4E 79
(off Warwick St.)
Spinney Clo. S60—6G 79
Spinneyfield. S60—1G 91
Spinney Hill. DN5—3D 44
Spinney, The. DN3—1E 21
Spinney, The. DN4—6H 45
Spinney, The. S43—3D 132
Spitalfields. S3—6F 87
Spital Gdns. S41—4C 138
Spital Hill. S4—6G 87
Spital La. S4—6G 87
Spital La. S41
    —3B 138 to 4E 139
Spital St. S3—6F 87
Spital St. S4—6G 87
Spofforth Rd. S9—6C 88
Spooner Rd. S10—3A 98
Spoon Glade. S6—5C 84
Spoonhill Rd. S6—5F 85

Spoon La. S6—5A 84
Spoon M. S6—5C 84
Spoon Way. S6—5C 84
Spotswood Clo. S14—3A 112
Spotswood Dri. S14—2A 112
Spotswood Mt. S14—3H 111
Spotswood Pl. S14—3H 111
Spotswood Rd. S14—3H 111
Spout Copse. S6—5B 84
Spout La. S6—5B 84
Spout Spinney. S6—5B 84
Springbank. S73—4F 27
Springbank Clo. S71—5E 9
Spring Bank Rd. DN12—5D 58
Spring Bank Rd. S40—2H 137
Spring Clo. S60—2A 92
Spring Clo. Dell. S14—3B 112
Spring Clo. Mt. S14—3B 112
Spring Clo. View. S14—3A 112
Spring Cres. DN5—2D 44
Spring Croft. S61—6H 67
Springcroft Dri. DN5—1G 31
Springdale Rd. DN2—4G 33
Spring Dri. S73—3A 40
Springfield. S63—1G 41
Springfield Av. S7—2A 110
Springfield Av. S40—2F 137
Springfield Clo. DN3—4G 35
Springfield Clo. S7—3A 110
Springfield Clo. S31—6C 124
Springfield Clo. S73—4F 27
Springfield Cres. S73—4F 27
Springfield Cres. S74—6G 37
Springfield Dri. S65—5E 71
Springfield Glen. S7—3H 109
Springfield Path. S64—1E 57
Springfield Pl. S70—6F 13
Springfield Rd. DN12—3C 60
Springfield Rd. S7—3A 110
Springfield Rd. S62—6C 56
Springfield Rd. S66—4E 81
Springfield Rd. S72—6F 11
Springfield Rd. S74—6F 37
Springfield St. S70—6F 13
Springfield Ter. S31—6C 106
Springfield Ter. S70—6F 13
Spring Gdns. DN1—6C 32
Spring Gdns. S71—3C 14
Spring Gdns. S74—5A 38
Spring Hill. S10—1A 98
Springhill Av. S73—3A 40
Spring Hill Rd. S10—1A 98
Spring Ho. Rd. S10—1A 98
Spring La. DN5—5D 30
Spring La. S2—5A 100
Spring La. S71—5E 9
Spring La. WF4—1G 7
Springmill Ter. S30—2D 140
Spring Pl. S40—2A 138
Spring St. S3—1E 5 & 1E 99
Spring St. S65—2E 79
Spring St. S70—1G 23
Spring Vale Av. S70—5H 23
Springvale Clo. S66—3F 83
Springvale Rd. S6 & S10—6B 86
Spring Vale Rd. S43—3D 132
Springvale Wlk. S6—6B 86
Spring View Rd. S10—1A 98
Spring Wlk. S65—2E 79
Spring Wlk. S73—5H 25
Spring Water Av. S12—4A 114
Spring Water Clo. S12—4H 113
Spring Water Dri. S12—4A 114
Springwell Clo. S66—3H 83
Springwell La. DN4 & DN11
    —5H 45
Springwood. S5—1C 86
Springwood Av. S31—4A 104

189

Spring Wood Clo. S41—3E 131
Springwood Ho. DN1—1C 46
 (off Elsworth Clo.)
Springwood La. S30—6A 50
Springwood Dri. DN5—1G 31
Springwood Rd. S8—1E 111
Springwood Rd S74—6G 37
Sprink Hall La. S30—4D 140
Sprotbrough Rd. DN5—6H 31
Spruce Av S66—4G 81
Spruce Av. S71—2D 8
Spruce Rise. S31—4A 126
Spurley Hey Gro. S30—4E 141
Spurr St. S2—5F 99
Square E., The. S66—2G 81
Square, The. S31—5F 117
Square, The. S42—4B 130
Square, The. S62—4H 51
Square, The. S70—1F 23
Square, The. S71—6E 15
Square W., The. S66—2F 81
Squirrel Croft. S61—3H 67
Stacey Cres. S72—6F 11
Stacey Dri. S65—4D 70
Stacye Av. S13—1D 114
Stacye Rise. S13—1D 114
Stadium St. S62—5E 69
Stafford Clo. S18—1A 128
Stafford Cres. S60—2F 91
Stafford Dri. S60—2F 91
Stafford La. S2—3H 99
Stafford M. S2—3H 99
 (off Stafford La.)
Stafford Pl. DN12—2B 58
Stafford Rd. DN6—3E 17
Stafford Rd. S2—3H 99
Stafford St. S2—3G 99
Stafford Way. S30—2D 64
Stag Clo. S60—6A 80
Stag Cres. S60—6A 80
Stag La. S60—6H 79
Stainborough Clo. S75—3B 22
Stainborough La. S75—6A 22
Stainborough Rd. S75—3B 22
Stainborough View. S70
 —4H 23
Stainborough View. S75
 —5B 36
Staincross Comn. S75—3F 7
Staindrop View. S30—1E 65
Stainforth Rd. DN3—2H 21
Stainmore Av. S19—5G 115
Stainton Clo. S71—1G 13
Stainton La. S66—2H 83
Stainton Rd. S11—5H 97
Stainton St. DN12—2B 58
Stairfoot Ind. Est. S70—2E 25
Stair Rd. S4—3G 87
Staithes Wlk. DN12—1C 58
Stalker Lees Rd. S11—5B 98
Stalker Wlk. S11—4C 98
Stamford St. S9—4B 88
Stamford Way. S75—3F 7
Stanage Rise. S12—2F 113
Stanage Way. S40—6C 130
Standhill Cres. S71—6A 8
Standish Av. S5—3E 87
Standish Clo. S5—2E 87
Standish Dri. S5—2E 87
Standish Rd. S5—2E 87
Standon Cres. S9—4C 76
Standon Dri. S9—4C 76
Standon Rd. S9—4C 76
Stand Rd. S41—3H 131
Staneford Ct. S19—6D 114
Stanford Rd. S18—2A 128
Stanford Rd. S66—5H 83
Stanford Way. S42—5D 136

Stanground Rd. S2—4D 100
Stanhope Gdns. S75—4E 13
Stanhope Rd. DN1—4E 33
Stanhope Rd. S12—2E 113
Stanhope St. S70—6F 13
Staniforth Av. S31—6B 124
Staniforth Cres. S31—2A 118
Staniforth Rd. S9—6B 88
Stanley Av. S43—5H 133
Stanley Gdns. DN4—2B 46
Stanley Gro. S31—5D 104
 (in two parts)
Stanley La. S3—6F 87
Stanley Pl. S9—2E 89
Stanley Rd. DN5—2F 31
Stanley Rd. S8—2F 111
Stanley Rd. S30—1B 64
 (Chapeltown)
Stanley Rd. S30—3E 141
 (Stocksbridge)
Stanley Rd. S70—2E 25
Stanley Sq. DN3—3D 20
Stanley St. S3—1G 5 & 6F 87
Stanley St. S31—2B 126
Stanley St. S41—3C 138
Stanley St. S60—3D 78
Stanley St. S70—6F 13
Stanley Ter. S66—4D 82
Stannington Rd. S6
 —5B 84 to 4H 85
Stannington View Rd. S10
 —1G 97
Stanton Cres. S12—3F 113
Stanwell Av. S9—5C 76
Stanwell Clo. S9—5C 76
Stanwell St. S9—5C 76
Stanwell Wlk. S9—5C 76
Stanwood Av. S6—5F 85
Stanwood Cres. S6—5F 85
Stanwood Dri. S6—5F 85
Stanwood Rd. S6—5F 85
Staple Grn. S65—5E 71
Stapleton Rd. DN4—6F 45
Star La. DN12—3E 59
Starling Mead. S2—3A 100
Starnhill Clo. S30—6G 65
Station App. DN1—6C 32
 (off Factory La.)
Station Bk. La. S41—2B 138
Station Cotts. S75—4A 6
Station La. S9—1C 88
Station La. S30—2D 72
Station La. S41 & S43—1B 132
Station Rd. DN3—1D 20
Station Rd. DN5—6D 18
Station Rd. DN11—4E 63
Station Rd. DN12—2E 59
Station Rd. S9—1E 101
Station Rd. S13—1C 114
Station Rd. S19
 —2D 124 to 2H 125
Station Rd. S30—2F 65
 (Chapeltown)
Station Rd. S30—3H 141
 (Deepcar)
Station Rd. S30—6G 65
 (Ecclesfield)
Station Rd. S31—6E 125
 (Eckington)
Station Rd. S31—3H 125
 (Killamarsh)
Station Rd. S31—5H 117
 (Kiveton Park)
Station Rd. S31—2C 106
 (Laughton Comn, Dinnington)
Station Rd. S31—6B 126
 (Spinkhill)

Station Rd. S41—2B 138
 (Chesterfield)
Station Rd. S41—2A 132
 (Whittington Moor)
Station Rd. S43—3C 132
 (Brimington)
Station Rd. S43—2F 133
 (Hollingwood)
Station Rd. S60—5C 90
 (Catcliffe)
Station Rd. S60—3B 78
 (Rotherham)
Station Rd. S60—1E 103
 (Treeton)
Station Rd. S63—1A 42
 (Bolton-upon-Dearne)
Station Rd. S63—1F 29
 (Thurnscoe)
Station Rd. S63—4F 41
 (Wath upon Dearne)
Station Rd. S64—1E & 1E 57
 (in two parts)
Station Rd. S70—5F 13
 (Barnsley)
Station Rd. S70—5C 24
 (Worsbrough)
Station Rd. S71—2F 15
 (Lundwood)
Station Rd. S71—1D 8
 (Royston)
Station Rd. S73—6C & 6C 26
 (in two parts)
Station Rd. S75—4C 6
 (Darton)
Station Rd. S75—2A 22
 (Dodworth)
Station Rd. Ind. Est. S73—5C 26
Station St. S64—2B 56
Station Ter. S41—3C 132
Station Ter. S71—1G 9
Station Way. S31—2C 106
Staton Av. S19—3G 115
Stauton Rd. DN4—4E 49
Staveley La. S31—6E 125
Staveley Rd. S8—6E 99
Staveley Rd. S43—1E 133
 (New Whittington)
Staveley Rd. S43—3D 134
 (Poolsbrook)
Staveley Rd. S44—6C 134
Staveley St. DN12—2B 60
Steade Rd. S7—6D 98
Steadfast St. S9—4C 88
Steadfield Rd. S74—6G 37
Steadfolds La. S66—5C 94
Steadlands, The. S62—6D 54
Stead La. S74—6F 37
Stead St. S31—6D 124
Steel City Trading Est. S9
 —6D 76
Steele Av. S43—5H 133
Steele St. S74—6E 37
Steelhouse La. S3
 —1E 5 & 1E 99
Steel Rd. S11—5A 98
Steel St. S61—4A 78
Steeping Clo. S43—3E 133
Stemp St. S11—5D 98
Stenson Ct. DN4—3A 46
Stenton St. S8—2D 122
Stentons Ter. S64—1F 57
Stephen Dri. S10—2F 97
Stephen Dri. S30—1H 73
Stephen Hill. S10—2F 97
Stephen Hill Rd. S10—2G 97
Stephen La. S30—1H 73
Stephenson Hall. S10—3A 98
Stephenson Pl. S40—2A 138

Stephenson Pl. S64—1B 56
Stephenson Rd. S43—2C 134
Stepney Row. S2—2H 5
Stepney St. S2—2H 5 & 1G 99
Stepping La. S30—1H 73
Sterland St. S40—2G 137
Sterndale Rd. S7—4A 110
Steven Cres. S30—2D 64
Stevenson Dri. S65—4H 79
Stevenson Dri. S75—3A 12
Stevenson Rd. DN4—5B 46
Stevenson Rd. S9—5A 88
Stevenson Way. S9—5B 88
Stevens Rd. DN4—2B 46
Steventon Rd. S65—5E 71
Stewart Rd. S11—5B 98
Stewarts Rd. S62—1H 69
Stewart St. DN1—1C 46
Sticking La. S64—4B 42
Stirling St. DN1—1C 46
Stockarth Clo. S30—5F 73
Stockarth La. S30—4E 73
Stockbridge Av. DN5—2A 32
Stockbridge La. DN5—6C 18
Stockil Rd. DN4—1E 47
Stock Av. S2—4A 100
Stocks Grn. Ct. S17—5D 120
Stocks Grn. Dri. S17—5D 120
Stocks Hill. S30—6E 65
Stocks Hill Clo. S71—4E 9
Stock's La. S62—2F 69
Stock's La. S75—5E 13
Stockton Clo. S3—6F 87
Stockton Pl. S3—6F 87
Stockwell Av. S31—6G 117
Stockwell La. S31—6F 117
Stockwith La. S74—4F 37
Stoke St. S9—6A 88
Stoket La. S31—6D 92
Stokewell Rd. S63—4C 40
Stonecliffe Clo. S2—4C 100
Stonecliffe Dri. S30—5D 140
Stonecliffe Pl. S2—4C 100
Stonecliffe Rd. S2—4C 100
Stonecliffe Wlk. DN12—1C 58
Stone Clo. S18—6G 123
Stone Clo. S65—2H 81
Stone Clo. Av. DN4—1B 46
Stone Cotts. DN5—2H 17
Stone Cres. S66—4F 81
Stonecroft Rd. S17—4E 121
Stone Cross Dri. DN5—1D 44
Stonecross Gdns. DN4—3E 49
Stone Delf. S10—4C 96
Stone Font Gro. DN4—4D 48
Stonegarth Clo. S72—1H 15
Stonegravels Croft. S19
 —3E 125
Stonegravels Way. S19
 —3F 125
Stone Gro. S10—2B 98
Stone Hill Dri. S31—6B 104
Stonehill Rise. DN5—1G 31
Stonehill Rise. S72—1H 15
Stone La. S13—2A 114
Stoneley Clo. S12—6D 112
Stoneley Cres. S12—6D 112
Stonelow Ct. S18—1F 129
 (off Paddock Way)
Stonelow Cres. S18—1G 129
Stonelow Grn. S18—1F 129
Stonelow Rd. S18—1F 129
Stone Moor Rd. S30—4C 140
Stone Riding. DN12—4A 60
 (Edlington)
Stone Riding. DN12—6D 60
 (Edlington Wood)
Stone Rd. S18—5G 123

Stone Row. S40—3G 137
Stonerow Way. S60—6E 69
Stonesdale Clo. S19—2D 124
Stones Inge. S30—6B 50
Stone St. S19—2D 124
Stone St. S71—3G 13
Stonewood Ct. S10—3D 96
Stonewood Gro. S10—3D 96
Stoney Ga. S30—5B 50
Stonyford Rd. S73—5D 26
Stony La. S30—2B 72
Stony Wlk. S6—4A 86
Stoops La. DN4—4H 47
Stoops Rd. DN4—4B 48
Stopes Rd. S6—5A 84
Stoppard Row. S40—3E 137
Store St. S2—4F 99
Storey's Ga. S73—6H 25
Storey St. S64—2A 56
Storforth La. S40 & S41
　　—6A 138
Storforth La. Ter. S41—5C 138
Storforth La. Trading Est S40
　　—5B 138
Storm St. S8—6E 99
Storrs Bri. S6—2A 84
Storrs Bri. La. S6—2A 84
Storrs Carr. S6—3A 84
Storrs Grn. S6—4A 84
Storrs Hall Rd. S6—5H 85
Storrs La. S6—4A 84
Storrs La. S30—3A 50
Storrs Rd. S40—3D 136
Storth Av. S10—5E 97
Storth La. S10—5E 97
Storth La. S31
　　—4F 117 to 2A 118
Storth Pk. S10—6D 96
Storthwood Ct. S10—4E 97
Stothard Rd. S10—1H 97
Stour Clo. S43—3E 133
Stour La. S6—1F 85
Stovin Dri. S9—5D 88
Stovin Gdns. S9—5D 88
Stovin Way. S9—4E 89
Stow Bri. La. S60—5C 92
Stowe Av. S7—3A 110
Stradbroke Av. S13—6F 101
Stradbroke Clo. S13—6G 101
Stradbroke Cres. S13—6G 101
Stradbroke Dri. S13—6G 101
Stradbroke Pl. S13—6G 101
Stradbroke Rise. S40—5E 137
Stradbroke Rd. S13
　　—6F 101 to 1B 114
Stradbroke Wlk. S13—6F 101
Stradbroke Way. S13—6G 101
Strafford Av. S70—3H 23
Strafford Av. S74—5D 38
Strafford Gro. S70—5D 36
Strafford Pl. S61—2A 66
Strafford Rd. DN2—4E 33
Strafford Rd. S61—5G 67
Strafford St. S75—5A 6
Strafford Wlk. S75—3B 22
Straight La. S63—4G 29
Straight Riding. DN12—5C 60
Strait La. S63—5E 41
Stratford Rd. S10—4D 96
Strathmore Gro. S63—5F 41
Strathmore Rd. DN2—6G 33
Strathtay Rd. S11—6H 97
Strauss Cres. S66—5H 83
Strawberry Av. S5—3F 75
Strawberry Gdns. S71—1E 9
Strawberry Lee La. S17
　　—4B 120
Straw La. S6—6C 86

Streatfield Cres. DN11—4C 62
Streetfield Cres. S19—3D 124
Streetfield La. S19—3E 125
Streetfields. S19—3E 125
Street La. S62—3F 53
Strelley Av. S8—6C 110
Strelley Rd. S8—6C 110
Strelley Rd. S71—5A 8
Stretton Clo. DN4—3E 49
Stretton Rd. S11—6A 98
Stretton Rd. S71—2A 14
Stride, The. S40—6H 137
Stringers Croft. S60—2B 92
Stringvale Clo. S66—1G 93
Stripe Rd. DN11—4E 63
Struan Rd. S7—2A 110
Strutt Rd. S3—4E 87
Stuart Clo. S41—5C 132
Stuart Rd. S30—3F 65
Stuart St. S63—1G 29
Stubbin Clo. S62—6D 54
Stubbing Ho. La. S6—2G 73
Stubbing La. S30—6C 72
Stubbing Rd. S40—6H 137
Stubbin La. S5—5G 75
Stubbin La. S62—5C 54
Stubbin Rd. S62—6B 54
Stubbins Hill. DN12—3B 60
Stubbins Riding. DN12—4C 60
Stubbs Cres. S61—6H 67
Stubbs Rd. S73—1E 39
Stubbs Wlk. S61—6H 67
Stubley Clo. S18—1C 128
Stubley Hollow. S18—6C 122
Stubley La. S18—1B 128
Stubley Pl. S18—1C 128
Studfield Cres. S6—3F 85
Studfield Dri. S6—2F 85
Studfield Gro. S6—3F 85
Studfield Hill. S6—3F 85
Studfield Rise. S6—2F 85
Studfield Rd. S6—3F 85
Studley Ct. S9—1E 101
Studmoor Rd. S61—5F 67
Studmoor Wlk. S61—5F 67
Stump Cross Gdns. S63—1H 41
Stump Cross Rd. S63—6E 41
Stumperlowe Av. S10—5E 97
Stumperlowe Clo. S10—5E 97
Stumperlowe Cres. Rd. S10
　　—5D 96
Stumperlowe Croft. S10—4D 96
Stumperlowe Hall Chase. S10
　　—4D 96
Stumperlowe Hall Rd. S10
　　—5D 96
Stumperlowe La. S10—5D 96
Stumperlowe Mans. S10
　　—5D 96
Stumperlowe Pk. Rd. S10
　　—5D 96
Stumperlowe View. S10—4D 96
Stupton Rd. S9—1C 88
Sturge Croft. S2—1F 111
Sturton Clo. DN4—5A 48
Sturton Dri. S65—6C 70
Sturton Rd. S4—3G 87
Sub-Station La. S41—3A 132
(off Queen St. N.)
Sudbury Clo. S40—6D 130
Sudbury Dri. S31—6C 104
Sudbury St. S3—6D 86
Sudhall Clo. S41—3F 131
Sudhall Ct. S41—3F 131
Suffolk Clo. S31—1G 119
Suffolk La. S2—6G 5
Suffolk Rd. DN4—5B 46
Suffolk Rd. S2—6F 5 & 3F 99

Suffolk View. DN12—3B 58
Sulby Gro. S70—3D 24
Summerdale Rd. S72—1G 15
Summerfield. S10—3A 98
Summerfield. S65—3E 79
Summerfield Cres. S43
　　—3D 132
Summerfield Rd. S18—6F 123
Summerfield Rd. S40—4H 131
Summerfield St. S11—4C 98
Summer La. S17—5D 120
Summer La. S71—1D 8
Summer La. S73—6H 25
Summerley Wlk. S40—6F 131
Summer Rd. S71—1D 8
Summerskill Grn. S43—4A 134
Summer St. S3—1C 98
Summer St. S70—5F 13
(in two parts)
Summerwood La. S18—6D 122
Summerwood Pl. S18—1D 128
Sumner Rd. S65—1F 79
Sunderland St. S11—4C 98
Sunderland Ter. S70—1A 24
Sundew Croft. S30—5B 50
Sundew Gdns. S30—5B 50
Sundown Pl. S13—5H 101
Sundown Rd. S13—5H 101
Sunningdale Clo. S40—5G 137
Sunningdale Clo. S64—4B 56
Sunningdale Dri. S72—5C 10
Sunningdale Mt. S11—2A 110
Sunningdale Rise. S40—5E 137
Sunningdale Rd. S31—5F 107
Sunny Bank. S10—4C 98
Sunny Bank. S30—6B 50
(High Green)
Sunny Bank. S74—5C 38
Sunnybank Cres. S60—3C 90
Sunnybank Dri. S72—2H 15
Sunny Bank La. S30—6E 141
Sunny Bar. DN1—6D 32
Sunnyside. DN3—4C 20
Sunnyside Clo. S31—1G 119
Sunny Springs. S41—1A 138
Sunnyvale Av. S17—5D 120
Sunnyvale Rd. S17—5D 120
Sunrise Mnr. S74—3A 38
Surbiton St. S9—3D 88
Surrey Clo. S70—2H 23
Surrey La. S1—4F 5 & 3F 99
(in two parts)
Surrey Pl. S1—4F 5 & 2E 99
Surrey St. DN4—4B 46
Surrey St. S1—4E 5 & 2E 99
Surtees Clo. S66—2E 83
Sussex Gdns. DN12—2B 58
Sussex Rd. S4—6G 87
Sussex Rd. S30—2E 65
Sussex St. DN4—4B 46
Sussex St. S4—1H 5 & 6G 87
Suthard Cross Rd. S10—1H 97
Sutherland Ho. DN2—3G 33
Sutherland Rd. S4—5G 87
Sutherland St. S4—5H 87
Sutton Av. S71—5B 8
Sutton Cres. S43—4A 134
Sutton Rd. DN3—2E 21
Sutton St. DN4—2A 46
Sutton St. S3—3A 4 & 1C 98
Swaddale Av. S41—5B 132
Swaith Av. DN5—2H 31
Swaithedale. S70—4C 24
Swaithe View. S70—4D 24
Swale Clo. S63—1B 42
Swale Ct. S60—1F 91
Swaledale Rd. S7—2B 110
Swale Dri. S30—2C 64

Swale Gdns. S9—1E 101
Swale Rd. S61—4A 68
Swallow Clo. S70—3D 36
Swallow Ct. DN11—4E 63
Swallow Hill Rd. S75—6E 7
Swallow La. S31—1C 116
Swallow's La. S19—1C 124
Swallow St. S9—4B 88
Swallow Wood Ct. S13—1A 114
Swamp Wlk. S6—4B 86
Swanbourne Clo. S41—5C 138
Swanbourne Pl. S5—5G 75
Swanbourne Rd. S5—4G 75
Swanee Rd. S70—2B 24
Swannington Clo. DN4—4F 49
Swan Rd. S31—1C 116
Swan St. DN5—5B 18
Swan St. S9—4C 88
Swan St. S60—4D 78
Swanwick St. S41—1A 132
Swarcliffe Rd. S9—6C 88
Sweyn Croft. S70—4A 24
Swifte Rd. S60—6G 79
Swift Rise. S61—1C 66
Swift Rd. S30—1B 74
Swift St. S75—5F 13
Swift Way. S2—4A 100
Swinburne Av. DN4—5B 46
Swinburne Av. DN6—2C 16
Swinburne Clo. DN3—1H 21
Swinburne Pl. S65—4H 79
Swinburne Rd. S65—4H 79
Swinscoe Way. S40—6C 130
Swinston Hill Rd. S31—5F 107
Swinton Rd. S64—1D 56
(in two parts)
Swinton St. S3—6E 87
Sycamore Av. DN3—2G 35
Sycamore Av. S18—6E 123
Sycamore Av. S31—5F 117
Sycamore Av. S40—4G 137
Sycamore Av. S66—4G 81
Sycamore Av. S72—6B 10
Sycamore Cres. S63—6G 41
Sycamore Dri. S31—4A 126
Sycamore Dri. S71—2C 8
Sycamore Farm Clo. S66
　　—6F 81
Sycamore Gro. DN4—3D 48
Sycamore Gro. DN12—4C 58
Sycamore Ho. Rd. S5—3B 76
Sycamore La. S43—2G 133
Sycamore Rd. DN3—2H 21
Sycamore Rd. S30—1F 75
(Ecclesfield)
Sycamore Rd. S30—4C 140
(Stocksbridge)
Sycamore Rd. S43—2F 133
Sycamore Rd. S64—6C 42
Sycamore Rd. S65—4H 69
Sycamores, The. DN5—1F 31
Sycamore St. S19—3F 115
(Beighton)
Sycamore St. S19—1C 124
(Mosborough)
Sycamore St. S75—5E 13
Sycamore Wlk. S63—1F 29
Sydney Rd. S6—1B 98
Sydney St. S40—2G 137
Sydney Ter. S70—1H 23
Sykes Av. S75—5F 13
Sykes Ct. S64—4B 56
Sykes St. S70—2F 23
Sylvan Clo. S41—4B 138
Sylvan Clo. S66—3H 83
Sylvester Av. DN4—2C 46
Sylvester Gdns. S1
　　—6E 5 & 3E 99

Sylvester St. S1—6E 5 & 3E 99
Sylvestria Ct. DN11—4E 63
Sylvia Clo. S13—6D 102
Sylvia Rd. S18—5H 129
Symes Gdns. DN4—2D 48
Symonds Av. S62—5C 54
Symons Cres. S5—5D 74

Tadcaster Clo. DN12—3A 58
Tadcaster Cres. S8—3D 110
Tadcaster Rd. S8—3D 110
Tadcaster Way. S8—3D 110
Taddington Rd. S40—6D 130
Tait Av. DN12—5B 60
Talbot Av. DN3—2H 21
Talbot Circle. DN3—2H 21
Talbot Cres. S2—5H 5 & 3G 99
Talbot Cres. S42—6D 138
Talbot Gdns. S2—5H 5 & 3G 99
Talbot Pl. S2—3G 99
Talbot Rd. S2—3G 99
Talbot Rd. S64—2D 56
Talbot St. S2—5H 5 & 3G 99
Talbot St. S41—6D 138
Talmont Rd. S11—1H 109
Tamar Clo. S75—4A 12
Tanfield Clo. S71—1C 8
Tanfield Rd. S6—2B 86
Tanfield Way. S66—5F 81
Tankersley La. S74—1D 50
Tannery Clo. S13—1B 114
Tannery St. S13—1B 114
Tan Pit La. S63—6F 29
Tansley Dri. S9—5D 76
Tansley St. S9—5D 76
Tansley Way. S43—5A 134
Tanyard. S75—3A 22
Tap La. S40—2G 137
Taplin Rd. S6—3H 85
Tapton. S10—2A 98
Tapton Bank. S10—3G 97
Tapton By Pass. S41—5B 132
Tapton Ct. S10—3H 97
Tapton Cres. Rd. S10—3H 97
Tapton Grange. S43—6E 133
Tapton Gro. S43—6E 133
Tapton Hill Rd. S10—2G 97
Tapton Ho. Rd. S10—3H 97
Tapton La. S41—2B 138
Tapton Pk. S41—6C 132
Tapton Pk. Rd. S10—4F 97
Tapton Ter. S41—1B 138
Tapton Vale. S41—6C 132
Taptonville Cres. S10—3A 98
Taptonville Rd. S10—2A 98
Tapton Wlk. S10—3H 97
Tapton Way. S44—2F 139
Tarleton Clo. DN3—3E 21
Tasker Rd. S10—1H 97
Tasman Gro. S66—3E 83
Tatenhill Gdns. DN4—4E 49
Taunton Av. S9—5D 76
Taunton Gdns. S64—5G 43
Taunton Gro. S9—5D 76
Taverner Clo. S30—4B 50
Taverner Croft. S30—5C 50
 (off Taverner Way.)
Taverner Way. S30—5B 50
Tavistock Rd. S7—1D 110
Tay Clo. S18—1B 128
Taylor Cres. S41—4D 138
Taylor Row. S70—1H 23
Taylor's Clo. S62—5E 69
Taylor's La. S62—5E 69
Taylor St. DN12—3F 59
Taylor St. S63—1F 29

Taylor Wlk. S64—4A 56
Tay St. S6—1B 98
Teesdale Rd. S12—6H 113
Teesdale Rd. S61—4H 67
Teeside Clo. DN5—4F 31
Telford Cres. S43—1D 134
Telford Rd. S9—4A 32
Telson Clo. S64—2G 55
Temperance St. S64—2B 56
Tempest Av. S73—2E 27
Templar Clo. S66—5H 93
Temple Cres. S66—5H 81
Temple Gdns. DN4—4E 49
Temple Rd. S60—6H 77
Temple Way. S71—4D 14
Ten Acre Rd. S61—1H 77
Tenby Gdns. DN4—4A 46
Tennyson Av. DN3—3F 35
Tennyson Av. DN5—5H 31
Tennyson Av. S40—2H 137
Tennyson Av. S64—5F 43
Tennyson Clo. S31—5G 107
Tennyson Rise. S63—6D 44
Tennyson Rd. DN5—6B 18
Tennyson Rd. S6—5B 86
Tennyson Rd. S65—4G 79
Tennyson Rd. S66—5G 83
Tennyson Rd. S71—3B 14
Tenter Balk La. DN6—2C 16
Tenterden Rd. S5—5H 73
Tenter La. DN4—5E 45
Tenter Rd. DN4—5E 45
Tenters Grn. S70—5H 23
Tenter St. S1—2D 4 & 1E 99
Tenter St. S60—2C 78
Terminus Rd. S7—4A 110
Terrace Rd. S62—3F 69
Terrace, The. S5—6A 76
Terrace Wlk. S11—5A 98
Terrey Rd. S17—4E 121
Terry St. S9—3D 88
Tetney Rd. S10—3F 97
Teynham Dri. S5—1D 86
Teynham Rd. S5—1C 86
Thackeray Av. S62—6H 55
Thames St. S60—2C 78
Thatch Pl. S61—4A 68
Thealby Gdns. DN4—4A 48
Theatre La. S41—2B 138
Thellusson Av. DN5—3E 31
Theobald Av. DN4—2F 47
Theobald Clo. DN4—2E 47
Thicket Dri. S66—3H 83
Third Av. DN6—3E 17
Thirlmere Clo. S63—2A 42
Thirlmere Ct. S64—5H 43
Thirlmere Dri. S18—1E 129
Thirlmere Dri. S31—1H 119
Thirlmere Gdns. DN3—4D 20
Thirlmere Rd. S8—2C 110
Thirlmere Rd. S41—4E 131
Thirlmere Rd. S71—6A 14
Thirlwall Av. DN12—3C 58
Thirlwell Rd. S8—1E 111
Thirsk Clo. DN12—3A 58
Thirza St. S6—5C 86
Thomas St. DN12—4B 60
Thomas St. S1—5C 4 &
 (in two parts)   3D & 3D 98
Thomas St. S31—5H 117
Thomas St. S62—6D 56
Thomas St. S64—1B 56
Thomas St. S70—1H 23
 (Barnsley)
Thomas St. S70—4A 24
 (Worsbrough)
Thomas St. S73—4F 27
Thompson Clo. S41—3A 132

Thompson Clo. S62—5C 54
Thompson Clo. S63—5F 41
Thompson Clo. S66—2E 83
Thompson Dri. S64—4A 56
Thompson Gdns. S30—5A 50
Thompson Hill. S30—6A 50
Thompson Rd. S11—4B 98
Thompson Rd. S73—1F 39
Thompson St. S41—4A 132
Thomson Av. DN4—4H 45
Thomson Av. DN12—3A 60
Thondale Rise. S60—3D 90
Thoresby Av. DN4—2F 47
Thoresby Av. S71—4C 14
Thoresby Clo. S31—6D 104
Thoresby Pl. S43—5A 134
Thoresby Pl. S65—1H 79
Thoresby Rd. S6—4A 86
Thornborough Clo. S2—6G 99
Thornborough Pl. S2—6G 99
Thornborough Rd. S2—6F 99
Thornbridge Av. S12—4F 113
Thornbridge Clo. S12—4F 113
Thornbridge Cres. S12—4G 113
Thornbridge Cres. S40—6H 137
Thornbridge Dri. S12—4F 113
Thornbridge Gro. S12—4F 113
Thornbridge Pl. S12—4F 113
Thornbridge Rise. S12—4G 113
Thornbridge Rd. S12—5F 113
Thornbridge Way. S12—4G 113
Thorncliff Cres. S40—6A 138
Thorncliffe La. S30—6D 50
Thorncliffe Vs. S30—6D 50
Thorndene Clo. S41—5A 132
Thorndon Rd. S4—5H 87
Thorndon Way. S40—5E 137
Thorne Clo. S71—6A 8
Thorne End Rd. S75—3F 7
Thornely Av. S75—1B 22
Thorne Rd. DN1, DN2 & DN3
        —6D 32
Thorne Rd. S7—2C 110
Thornfield Av. S40—4D 136
Thornfield Ct. S41—6A 132
Thorn Garth. DN5—3A 32
Thornham Clo. DN3—4F 35
Thornhill Av. DN2—3H 33
Thornhill Av. S60—4B 90
Thornhill Edge. S60—2C 78
Thorn La. DN2—5B 20
Thornlea Ct. DN12—4A 60
Thornley Cotts. S75—2B 22
Thornley Cres. S63—1E 29
Thornley Sq. S63—1D 28
Thornley Vs. S70—4C 36
Thorn Rd. S62—4B 56
Thornsett Ct. S11—5C 98
Thornsett Gdns. S17—2F 121
Thornsett Rd. S7—5C 98
Thorntondale Rd. DN5—2F 31
Thornton Pl. S18—2A 128
Thornton Rd. S70—2C 24
Thornton St. S61—4G 77
Thornton Ter. S61—4G 77
Thornton Ter. S70—2C 24
Thorntree Clo. S61—3B 66
Thorntree Ct. S40—6H 137
Thorntree La. S75—4F 13
Thorntree Rd. S61—4B 66
Thornville Rd. S9—6D 88
Thorogate. S62—6E 55
Thorold Pl. DN3—2D 20
Thorp Clo. S2—5E 99
Thorpe Av. S18—5G 123
Thorpe Bridle Rd. S31—6F 119
Thorpe Dri. S19—6E 115
Thorpefield Clo. S61—2B 66

Thorpefield Dri. S61—2B 66
Thorpe Grn. S19—6D 114
Thorpe Ho. Av. S8—3E 111
Thorpe Ho. Rise. S8—3E 111
Thorpe Ho. Rd. S8—3E 111
Thorpe La. DN5—2D 44
Thorpe St. S61—2B 66
Threatre Yd. S40—2A 138
 (off Low Pavement)
Three Nooks La. S72—4B 10
Threshfield Way. S12—4B 114
Thrumpton Rd. S71—4B 8
Thrush Av. S60—3D 90
Thrush St. S6—5H 85
Thruxton Clo. S72—5C 10
Thrybergh Ct. DN12—2D 58
Thrybergh Hall Rd. S62—1H 69
Thrybergh La. S65—4E 71
Thundercliffe Rd. S61—2D 76
Thurcroft Ho. DN1—1C 46
 (off St James St.)
Thurley Pl. S9—4D 88
Thurnscoe Bri. La. S63—3F 29
Thurnscoe La. S72—1B 28
Thurnscoe Rd. S63—1A 42
Thurstan Av. S8—1C 122
Tiber View. S60—2C 90
Tickhill Rd. DN4 & DN11—4A 46
Tickhill Rd. S66—4H 83
Tickhill Sq. DN12—2B 58
Tickhill St. DN12—1B 58
Tideswell Clo. S43—3A 134
Tideswell Rd. S5—6G to 5H 75
Tilford Rd. S13—1C 114
Tillotson Clo. S8—1E 111
Tillotson Rise. S8—1E 111
Tillotson Rd. S8—1E 111
Tiltshills La. DN5—1B 18
Tilts La. DN5—1D 18
Timothy Wood Av. S70—3D 36
Tingle Bri. Av. S73—4E 39
Tingle Bri. Cres. S73—4E 39
Tingle Bri. La. S73—4E 39
Tingle Clo. S73—4E 39
Tinker La. S6 & S10—6H 85
Tinker La. S74—5E 37
Tinker Rd. S62—1G 69
Tinsley Ind. Est. S9—5E 89
Tinsley Pk. Clo. S9—4E 89
Tinsley Pk. Rd. S9—4D 88
Tinsley Rd. S74—4H 37
Tipsey Hill. S75—4H 7
Tipton St. S9—1C 88
Tissington Clo. S40—6D 130
Tithe Barn Av. S13—6C 102
Tithe Barn Clo. S13—6C 102
Tithe Barn La. S13—6C 102
Tithe Barn Way. S13—6B 102
Tithe Laithe. S74—5A 38
Titterton Clo. S9—5C 88
Titterton St. S9—5C 88
Tiverton Clo. S64—3B 56
Tivydale Dri. S75—6C 6
Toad La. S66—6H 93
Tockwith Rd. S9—6D 88
Todmorden Clo. DN12—2A 58
Todwick Ho. Gdns. S31
        —1A 118
Todwick Rd. S8—4C 110
Todwick Rd. S31—5A 106
Toecroft La. DN5—2B 44
Tofield Rd. DN11—5G 61
Tofts La. S6—1C 96
Toftstead. DN3—4F 35
Toftwood Av. S10—1G 97
Toftwood Rd. S10—1H 97
Togo Bldgs. S63—2E 29
Togo St. S63—2E 29

193

Valentine Cres. S5—4G 75
(in two parts)
Valentine Rd. S5—4G 75
Vale Rd. S3—4D 86
Vale Rd. S65—5D 70
Valiant Gdns. DN5—6G 31
Valley Cres. S41—3C 138
Valley Dri. DN3—3H 49
Valley Dri. S31—2B 126
Valley Dri. S63—5E 41
Valley Rd. S8—1E 111
Valley Rd. S12—4C 114
Valley Rd. S30—1C 64
Valley Rd. S31—2B 126
Valley Rd. S41—3C 138
Valley Rd. S64—3H 55
Valley Rd. S73—5C 26
Valley Rd. S75—4E 7
Valley View Clo. S31—6H 125
Valley Way. S74—5A 38
Vancouver Dri. S63—1H 41
Vanguard Trading Est. S40
—6B 138
Varley Gdns. S66—3F 81
Varney Rd. S63—6E 41
Vaughan Av. DN1—5D 32
Vaughon Rd. S75—4D 12
Vaughton Hill. S30—3H 141
Vauxhall Clo. S9—5D 76
Vauxhall Rd. S9—5D 76
Venetian Cres. S73—4D 26
Ventnor Pl. S7—5D 98
Venus Ct. S60—1C 90
Verdant Way. S5—4H 75
Verdon St. S3—5F 87
Verelst Av. S31—4B 104
Vere Rd. S6—1A 86
Vernon Av. S70—2H 23
Vernon Clo. S70—2H 23
Vernon Cres. S70—4H 23
Vernon Delph. S10—2F 97
Vernon Dri. S30—2E 65
Vernon Rd. S17—3E 121
Vernon Rd. S40—2F 137
Vernon Rd. S60—6H 79
Vernon Rd. S70—4H 23
Vernon St. S70—5D 36
Vernon St. S71—5H 13
Vernon St. S74—6H 37
Vernon St. N. S71—5H 13
Vernon Ter. S10—3G 97
Vernon Ter. S70—1A 24
(off Gold St.)
Vernon Way. S66—3E 83
Vernon Way. S75—4D 12
Verona Rise. S73—4E 27
Vesey St. S62—3F 69
Vicarage Clo. DN4—4E 49
Vicarage Clo. S64—1G 57
Vicarage Clo. S65—1B 80
Vicarage Cres. S30—1A 74
Vicarage La. S17—2D 120
Vicarage La. S65—3D 78
Vicarage La. S71—2E 9
Vicarage Rd. S9—4B 88
Vicarage Rd. S30—1A 74
Vicarage Way. DN5—5E 19
Vicar Cres. S13—3F 27
Vicar La. S1—3E 5 & 2E 99
Vicar La. S13—6B 102
Vicar La. S40—2A 138
Vicar Rd. S63—4E 41
Vicar Rd. S73—4E 27
Vickers Dri. S5—6H 75
Vickers Rd. S5—1H 87
Vickers Rd. S30—6B 50
Victoria Av. S43—1D 134
Victoria Av. S65—3F 79

Victoria Av. S70—5G 13
Victoria Clo. S30—3D 140
Victoria Cres. S70—4C 36
(off Chapel St.)
Victoria Cres. S75—5F 13
Victoria Cres. W. S75—5F 13
Victoria Gro. S43—6F 133
Victoria La. DN11—4C 62
Victoria Rd. S63—4D 40
Victoria Rd. S64—6E 43
Victoria Rd. S70—5G 13
Victoria Rd. S71—1F 9
Victoria Rd. S73—2B 26
Victoria Sta. Rd. S4
—1G 5 & 1F 99
Victoria St. S3—4B 4 & 2D 98
Victoria St. S18—1D 128
Victoria St. S30—3D 140
(Stocksbridge)
Victoria St. S31—4G 107
Victoria St. S41—1A 138
Victoria St. S43—2F 133
Victoria St. S60—5D 90
(Catcliffe)
Victoria St. S60—3B 78
(Rotherham, in two parts)
Victoria St. S62—6C 56
Victoria St. S63—4G 29
Victoria St. S64—6C 42
Victoria St. S66—6G 83
Victoria St. S70—5G 13
(Barnsley)
Victoria St. S70—1D 24
(Stairfoot)
Victoria St. S72—6B 10
Victoria St. S73—3F 27
Victoria St. S74—5B 38
Victoria St. N. S41—1H 131
Victoria St. W. S40—3E 137
Victoria Ter. S10—2A 98
(off Parker's La.)
Victoria Ter. S31—5A 118
Victoria Ter. S70—1A 24
Victoria Vs. S6—6C 86
(off Blake Gro. Rd.)
Victor Rd. S17—2F 121
Victor St. S6—4B 88
Victor Ter. S70—1A 24
View Rd. S2—6E 99
View Rd. S65—1G 79
Viking Way. S31—4B 118
Villa Gdns. DN5—2A 18
Village St. DN6—1D 16
Villa Pk. Rd. DN4—3C 48
Villa Rd. DN6—2D 16
Villiers Clo. S2—1A 112
Villiers Dri. S2—1A 112
Vincent Cres. S40—3D 136
Vincent Rd. S7—5D 98
Vincent Rd. S65—2H 81
Vincent Rd. S71—4F 15
Vincent Ter. S63—2H 29
Vine Clo. S60—3C 78
Vine Clo. S71—3C 14
Vine St. S9—6E 89
Viola Bank. S30—3D 140
Violet Av. DN12—4B 60

Violet Av. S19—4E 115
Violet Bank Rd. S7—1C 110
Vivian Rd. S5—1H 87
Vizard Rd. S74—5C 38
Volunteer Yd. DN1—5C 32
Vulcan Ho. S65—2G 79
Vulcan Rd. S9—1E 89

Wadbrough Rd. S11—4B 98
Waddington Rd. S75—5D 12
Waddington Ter. S64—1F 57
Wade Clo. S60—5F 79
Wade Meadow. S6—2G 85
Wade St. S4—2A 88
Wade St. S75—5D 12
Wadsley La. S6—1G 85
Wadsley Pk. Cres. S6—2G 85
Wadsworth Av. S12—2E 113
Wadsworth Clo. S12—1F 113
Wadsworth Dri. S12—2E 113
Wadsworth Rd. S62—5C 54
Wadsworth Rd. S12—2E 113
Wadsworth Rd. S66—5H 81
Wadworth Av. DN11—4F 63
Wadworth Hill. DN11—6H 61
Wadworth Rise. S65—6C 70
Wadworth St. DN12—2C 58
Wager La. S72—2G 11
Wagon Rd. S61—5B 68
Waingate. S3—2F 5 & 1F 99
Wainscott Clo. S71—2D 14
Wainwright Av. S13—5F 101
Wainwright Av. S73—6H 25
Wainwright Cres. S13—5F 101
Wainwright Pl. S73—6H 25
Wainwright Rd. DN4—1E 47
Wainwright Rd. S61—6H 67
Wakefield Rd. WF4, S75 & S71
—1G 7
Wake Rd. S7—6C 98
Walbank Rd. DN3—3G 35
Walbert Av. S63—2E 29
Walbrook. S70—5B 24
Walden Av. DN5—6G 17
Walden St. S2—6F 99
Walders Av. S6—1G 85
Walders La. S30—6E 141
Walesmoor Av. S31—3F 127
Wales Pl. S6—5B 86
Wales Rd. S31—5F 117
Waleswood Rd. S31—2H 115
Waleswood View. S31—1B 116
Waleswood Vs. S31—4D 116
Walford Rd. S31—3A 126
Walgrove Av. S40—4F 137
Walgrove Rd. S40—4F 137
Walker Clo. S30—1A 74
Walker La. S65—2E 79
Walker Pl. S65—2E 79
Walker Rd. S61—6H 67
Walker Rd. S75—6D 36
Walker's La. S31—3B 126
Walkers Ter. S71—2C 14
Walker St. S3—6F 87
Walker St. S62—1H 69
Walker St. S64—2C 56
Walker View. S62—1H 69
Walkley Bank Clo. S6—4A 86
Walkley Bank Rd. S6
—5G 85 to 5A 86
Walkley Cres. Rd. S6—5H 85
Walkley La. S6—3A 86
Walkley Rd. S6—5A 86
Walkley St. S6—5A 86
Walkley Ter. S6—5G 85
Walk, The. S65—2H 79
Walk, The. S70—5C 36

Wallace Rd. DN4—5G 45
Wallace Rd. S3—4D 86
Waller Rd. S6—5G 85
Walling Clo. S9—1D 88
Walling Rd. S9—1D 88
Wall St. S70—1G 23
Walney Fold. S71—1D 14
Walnut Dri. S31—5F 107
(Dinnington)
Walnut Dri. S31—4A 126
(Killamarsh)
Walnut Gro. S64—5D 42
Walnut Pl. S30—3D 64
(in two parts)
Walnut Tree Hill. DN11—6H 61
Walpole Clo. DN4—6H 45
Walpole Gro. S31—4B 104
Walseker La. S31—1G 127
Walsham Dri. DN5—4G 31
Walshaw Rd. S30—4D 72
Walters Rd. S66—4H 83
Walter St. S6—4B 86
Walter St. S60—2C 78
Waltham Gdns. S19—5G 115
Waltham St. S70—1A 24
Waltheof Rd. S2—5C 100
Walton Back La. S42—6A 136
Walton Clo. S18—1A 128
Walton Clo. S40—4G 137
Walton Ct. S8—1C 122
Walton Cres. S40—4G 137
Walton Dri. S40—4G 137
Waltonfields Rd. S40—3F 137
Walton Ho. DN1—1C 46
(off Grove Pl.)
Walton Rd. S11—4B 98
Walton Rd. S40—3F 137
Walton St. S75—4E 13
Walton St. N. S75—4E 13
Walton Wlk. S40—3G 137
Wannop St. S62—4F 69
Wansfell Rd. S4—2B 88
Wansfell Ter. S71—6A 14
Wapping, The. S65—6H 57
Warburton Clo. S2—6G 99
Warburton Gdns. S2—6G 99
Warburton Rd. S2—6G 99
Warde Aldam Cres. S66—4E 81
Warde Av. DN4—5H 45
Warden Clo. DN4—3E 49
Warden St. S9—2D 88
Warden St. S60—6D 78
Wardgate Way. S40—6C 130
Wardlow Clo. S40—5H 137
Wardlow Rd. S12—2F 113
Ward Pl. S7—5D 98
Wardsend Rd. S6—1B 86
Wardsend Rd. N. S6—6A 74
Ward St. S3—6E 87
Wareham Ct. S19—5G 115
Warehouse La. S63—5E 41
Warley Rd. S2—4A 100
Warminster Clo. S8—3E 111
Warminster Cres. S8—3F 111
Warminster Dri. S8—4F 111
Warminster Gdns. S8—4E 111
Warminster Pl. S8—5F 111
Warminster Rd. S8—3E 111
Warmsworth Halt Ind. Est. DN4
—1C 60
Warmsworth Rd. DN4—5G 45
Warner Av. S75—5D 12
Warner Pl. S75—5E 13
Warner Rd. S6—2H 85
Warner Rd. S75—5D 12
Warner St. S41—4B 138
Warnington Dri. DN4—6E 49

194

Warning Tongue La. DN3 & DN4
—3F 49
Warren Av. S62—6E 55
Warren Clo. DN2—5G 33
Warren Cres. S70—2H 23
Warren Dri. S61—1H 77
Warreners Dri. S65—5D 70
Warren Gdns. S30—5F 51
Warren Hill. S30—5E 51
Warren House Clo. S66—4H 81
Warren La. DN4—6D 48
Warren La. S30—4D 50 to 5F 51
(in two parts)
Warren La. S75—2F 7
Warren Mt. S61—1H 77
Warren Pl. S70—2H 23
Warren Quarry La. S70—2H 23
Warren Rise. S18—6G 123
Warren Rd. DN12—4D 58
Warren Rd. S66—4F 81
Warren St. S4—6H 87 & 6A 88
(in two parts)
Warren, The. S31—6D 104
Warren Vale. S62 & S64—6G 55
Warren Vale Rd. S64—2G 55
Warren View. S70—1H 23
Warren Wlk. S71—1F 9
Warrington Rd. S10—1B 98
Warris Clo. S61—6G 67
Warris Pl. S2—2H 99
Warsop Rd. S71—4A 8
Warwick Rd. DN2—6H 33
Warwick Rd. S71—3B 14
Warwick St. S10—1A 98
Warwick St. S40—6B 138
Warwick St. S60—4E 79
Warwick St. S. S60—4E 79
Warwick Ter. S10—1A 98
Warwick Way. S31—6E 107
Wasdale Av. S19—3E 125
Wasdale Clo. S19—3E 125
Washfield Cres. S60—1E 103
Washfield La. S60—1E 103
Washford Rd. S9—5A 88
Wash Ho. La. S40—3E 137
Washington Av. DN5—2A 32
Washington Av. DN12—3B 58
Washington Av. S73—1D 38
Washington Rd. DN6—2D 16
Washington Rd. S11—5D 98
Washington Rd. S30—6F 65
Washington Rd. S63—5F 29
Washington St. S64—6F 43
Wasteneys Rd. S31—2B 118
Watch Ho. La. DN5—3H 31
Watch St. S13—5E 103
Waterdale. DN1—1D 46
Waterdale Rd. S70—5H 23
Waterdale Shopping Centre
(off Waterdale) DN1—6D 32
Waterfall Rd. S9—6E 89
Waterfield Pl. S70—1E 25
Wateringbury Gro. S43
—1D 134
Watering La. S71—1A 26
Water La. S17—2F 121
Water La. S60—4D 78
Water La. S62—2C 52
Water La. S65—1G 71
Waterloo Rd. S3—4C 86
Waterloo Rd. S70—6F 13
Waterloo Wlk. S6—6D 86
Watermead. S63—2B 42
Water Slacks Clo. S13—1B 114
Water Slacks Dri. S13—1B 114
Water Slacks La. S13—1A 114
Water Slacks Rd. S13—1B 114
Water Slacks Wlk. S13—1B 114

Water Slacks Way. S13
—1B 114
Watersmeet Rd. S6—4H 85
Water St. S3—1E 5 & 1E 99
Waterthorpe Clo. S19—1F 125
Waterthorpe Cres. S19—1F 125
Waterthorpe Gdns. S19
—1F 125
Waterthorpe Glade. S19
—1F 125
Waterthorpe Glen. S19—1F 125
Waterthorpe Greenway. S19
—4D 114
Waterthorpe Rise. S19—6F 115
Watery St. S3—6D 86
Wath Rd. S7—1C 110
Wath Rd. S63—1A 42
(Bolton-upon-Dearne)
Wath Rd. S63—5B 8
(Wath upon Dearne)
Wath Rd. S64—5B 42
(Brampton)
Wath Rd. S73—1H 39
(Brampton)
Wath Rd. S73—4E 39
(Hemingfield)
Wath Rd. S74—1D 52
Wath Wood Bottom. S63
—2E 55
Wath Wood Dri. S64—2F 55
Wath Wood Rd. S63—1F 55
Watkinson Gdns. S19—6E 115
Watnall Rd. S71—5B 8
Watson Clo. S61—1H 77
Watson Glen. S61—1E 77
Watson Rd. S10—3A 98
Watson Rd. S61—1H 77
Watson St. S74—2F 37
Watsons Wlk. S1—2F 5
Watt La. S10—3F 97
Waveney Dri. S75—4A 12
Waverley Av. DN4—4G 45
Waverley Av. DN12—3E 59
Waverley Av. S31—4A 118
Waverley Av. S66—5B 94
Waverley Cotts. S13—2H 101
Waverley La. S13—2H 101
Waverley Rd. S9—1E 101
Waverley View. S66—6C 90
Waycliffe. S71—4C 14
Wayford Av. S41—4B 138
Wayford Av. S66—3H 81
Wayland Av. S70—4H 23
Wayland Rd. S11—5B 98
Wayside. S43—3D 132
Weakland Clo. S12—5H 113
Weakland Cres. S12—4H 113
Weakland Dri. S12—4H 113
Weakland Way. S12—4H 113
Weaver Clo. S75—4A 12
Weavers Clo. S30—6A 64
Webb Av. S30—4G 141
Webbs Av. S6—5E 85
Webley Clo. DN2—4A 34
Webster Clo. S61—1E 77
Webster Cres. S61—1F 77
Webster Croft. S41—1B 132
Webster St. S9—2D 88
Wedgewood Clo. S62—2F 69
Weedon St. S9—2D 88
Weet Shaw La. S72—4A 10
Weetwood Dri. S11—2G 109
Weetwood Rd. S60—1G 91
Weigh La. S2—2G 99
Weir Head. S9—2D 88
Welbeck Clo. S18—1A 128
Welbeck Clo. S43—5B 134
Welbeck Dri. S31—6D 104
Welbeck Pl. S65—1H 79

Welbeck Rd. DN4—1F 47
Welbeck Rd. S6—5H 85
Welbeck St. S75—5F 13
Welbury Gdns. S19—3E 125
Welby Pl. S8—2D 110
Welfare Av. DN12—3C 58
Welfare Av. S40—2F 137
Welfare Rd. DN6—4D 16
Welfare Rd. S63—1F 29
Welfare View. S63—5F 29
Welfare View. S75—1B 22
Welham Dri. S60—5E 79
Welland Clo. S3—5D 86
Welland Ct. S75—4A 12
Welland Cres. S74—5C 38
Wellbourne Clo. S30—3G 65
Wellcarr Rd. S8—5E 111
Well Ct. S12—4B 114
Well Croft. S30—6B 50
Wellcroft Clo. DN2—3A 34
Well Grn. S65—5E 71
Wellesley Rd. S10—2B 98
Wellfield Clo. S12—6G 113
Wellfield Rd. S6—6B 86
Wellfield Rd. S61—5G 67
Wellfield Rd. S75—4F 13
Wellgate. DN12—3E 59
Wellgate. S60—3E 79
Wellgate. S75—4F 7
Wellgate Mt. S60—3E 79
Wellgate Ter. S60—3E 79
Well Grn. Rd. S6—6B 84
Wellhead Rd. S8—1E 111
Well Hill Gro. S71—1E 9
Well Hill Rd. S30—1H 141
Wellington Av. S31—6D 106
Wellington Clo. S71—3B 14
Wellington Cres. S70—3C 24
Wellington Gro. DN2—3A 32
Wellington Pl. S70—6F 13
Wellington Rd. DN12—3B 60
Wellington Rd. S6—5E 85
Wellington St. S1—5C 4 & 3D 98
Wellington St. S63—4G 29
Wellington St. S64—6E 43
Wellington St. S70—6G 13
Welling Way. S61—2G 77
Well La. DN11—6H 61
Well La. S6—1F 85
Well La. S12—3B 114
Well La. S30—6A 64
Well La. S31—3A 104
Well La. S60—1E 103
(Treeton)
Well La. S60—4B 92
(Upper Whiston)
Well La. S60—2H 91
(Whiston)
Well La. S63—5E 41
Well La. S71—2C 14
Well Meadow Dri. S3—2B 4
Well Meadow St. S3
—1B 4 & 1D 98
Well Rd. S8—1E 111
Wells Rd. DN2—3F 33
Wells St. S72—1H 15
Well's St. S75—5C 6
Wells, The. S31—2F 119
Well St. S70—6F 13
Well View Rd. S61—1F 77
Wellway, The. S66—2F 81
Welney Pl. S6—5A 74
Welshpool Pl. S40—2F 137
Welshpool Yd. S40—3F 137
Welton Clo. DN4—5A 48
Welwyn Clo. S12—3D 112
Welwyn Clo. S40—2F 137
Welwyn Rd. S12—3D 112

Wembley Av. DN12—3C 58
Wenlock Clo. S40—1F 137
Wenlock Cres. S40—1E 137
Wenlock St. S13—4H 101
Wensley Clo. S4—2A 88
Wensley Ct. S4—1A 88
Wensley Ct. S60—1E 91
Wensley Cres. DN4—4D 48
Wensley Croft. S4—1A 88
Wensleydale Dri. S60—4D 90
Wensleydale Rd. DN5—2F 31
Wensleydale Rd. S61—4H 67
Wensley Dri. S4—1A 88
Wensley Gdns. S4—1A 88
Wensley Grn. S4—1A 88
Wensley Rd. S71—6A 8
Wensley Rd. S30—6A 50
Wensley St. S4—1A 88
Wensley St. S63—1D 28
Wensley Way. S43—3A 134
Wentworth Av. S11—5F 109
Wentworth Av. S31—1D 116
Wentworth Av. S40—5G 137
Wentworth Clo. S61—2A 66
Wentworth Cres. S75—5H 7
Wentworth Ho. DN1—1C 46
(off St James St.)
Wentworth Pk. S75—1B 50
Wentworth Pk. S62—6E 53
Wentworth Pl. S61—5E 67
Wentworth Rd. DN2—4E 33
Wentworth Rd. S18—2A 128
Wentworth Rd. S61—2B 66
Wentworth Rd. S62 & S64
—4C 54
Wentworth Rd. S74—2H 37
(Blacker Hill)
Wentworth Rd. S74—1C 52
(Elsecar)
Wentworth Rd. S74—4C 38
(Jump)
Wentworth Rd. S75—5B 6
(Darton)
Wentworth Rd. S75—5G 7
(Mapplewell)
Wentworth Rd. S70—4C 36
Wentworth St. S71—4G 13
Wentworth View. S73—2F 39
Wentworth View. S74—6A 38
Wentworth Way. S31—6G 107
Wentworth Way. S75—3B 22
(Dodworth)
Wentworth Way. S75—1B 50
(Tankersley)
Wentworth Woodhouse. S62
—5E 53
Wescoe Av. S72—1A 28
Wesley Av. S31—5B 104
Wesley La. S10—2H 97
Wesley Pl. S31—3F 119
Wesley Rd. S30—6A 50
(in two parts)
Wesley Rd. S31—4H 117
Wesley St. S70—6H 13
Wessenden Clo. S75—6C 12
Wessex Gdns. S17—4D 120
West Av. DN4—4A 46
West Av. DN6—2B 16
West Av. S62—1F 69
West Av. S63—2H 41
West Av. S71—1F 9
West Av. S73—6H 25
Westbank Clo. S18—5F 123
Westbank Ct. S18—5G 123
Westbank Dri. S31—3E 119
W. Bank La. S1—3D 4 & 2E 99
W. Bank Rise. S31—3E 119
West Bar. S3—1E 5 & 1E 99
Westbar Grn. S1—2D 4 & 1E 99

West Bars. S40—2H 137
West Bawtry Rd. S60—2D 90
Westbourne Gdns. DN4—6H 45
Westbourne Gro. S40—2D 136
Westbourne Gro. S75—4F 13
Westbourne Rd. S10—4A 98
Westbourne Ter. S70—6E 13
Westbrook Bank. S11—5B 98
Westbrook Clo. S40—3B 136
Westbrook Dri. S40—3B 136
Westbrook Rd. S30—2E 65
Westbury Av. S30—3F 65
Westbury Clo. S75—3D 12
Westbury St. S9—6B 88
Westby Cres. S60—2H 91
West Clo. S61—1G 77
West Cres. S30—3C 140
West Cres. S44—6E 135
Westcroft Cres. S19—1E 125
Westcroft Dri. S19—2E 125
Westcroft Gdns. S19—1E 125
Westcroft Glen. S19—2E 125
Westcroft Gro. S19—2E 125
W. Don St. S6—5C 86
W. End Av. DN5—2A 32
W. End Av. S71—2C 8
W. End Cres. S71—2C 8
W. End La. DN11—4A 62
W. End Rd. S63—4B 40
W. End View. S31—6H 125
Westerdale Rd. DN5—2B 32
Western Av. S31—5F 107
Western Bank. S10—2B 98
Western Clo. S31—5F 107
Western Rd. S10—1A 98
Western Rd. S65—2G 79
Western St. S70—5G 13
Western Ter. S73—6A 26
Westfield. S19—1E 125
Westfield Av. S12—4C 114
Westfield Av. S31—4A 104
Westfield Av. S40—4D 136
Westfield Centre. S19—1E 125
Westfield Cres. S19—1C 124
Westfield Cres. S63—1D 28
Westfield Gro. S12—4B 114
Westfield La. DN5—1F 43
Westfield La. S75—2A 12
Westfield Northway. S19
—1E 125
Westfield Rd. DN3—3E 35
Westfield Rd. DN4—3B 46
Westfield Rd. S18—3G 129
Westfield Rd. S31—4A 126
Westfield Rd. S62—4E 69
Westfield Rd. S66—4H 81
Westfield Rd. S73 & S63—5A 40
Westfields. S70—5A 24
Westfields. S71—1C 8
Westfield Southway. S19
—1E 125
Westfield St. S70—6F 13
Westfield Ter. S1—4C 4 & 2D 98
Westgate. S60—4D 78
West Ga. S64—6G 43
Westgate. S70—6G 13
Westgate. S71—3B 14
West Gro. DN2—4G 33
West Gro. S71—1C 8
Westhaven. S72—2H 15
West Hill. S61—3E 77
Westhill La. S3—4B 4 & 2D 98
Westholme Rd. DN4—2B 46
W. Kirk La. S72—2A 28
W. Laith Ga. DN1—6C 32
Westland Clo. S19—6E 115
Westland Gdns. S19—6E 115
Westland Gro. S19—1E 125

Westland Rd. S19—1E 125
West La. S6—1A 84
West La. S31—4H 103
West La. S66—2D 94
West Mall. DN1—6C 32
(off French Ga.)
Westminster Av. S10—4B 96
Westminster Clo. S10—4B 96
Westminster Cres. DN2—4H 33
Westminster Cres. S10—4B 96
Westminster Ho. DN2—4A 34
W. Moor Cres. S75—6C 12
W. Moor La. DN3—1H 35
W. Moor La. S63 & DN5—1D 42
Westmoor Rd. S43—1F 139
Westmoreland St. S6—6C 86
Westmoreland Way. DN5
—2C 44
Westmorland La. DN12—2B 58
Westmorland St. DN4—5H 45
W. Mount Av. S63—3C 40
Westnall Ho. S30—2D 72
(off Glossop Row.)
Westnall Rd. S5—2H 75
Westnall Ter. S5—2H 75
Weston Clo. S40—5C 130
Weston Rd. DN4—5A 46
Weston St. S3—2A 4 & 1C 98
Westover Rd. S10—3E 97
W. Park Dri. S31—6H 103
W. Pinfold. S71—2E 9
Westpit Hill. S63—4A 40
West Pl. DN5—6B 18
W. Quadrant. S5—6H 75
West Rd. S64—6D 42
West Rd. S75—5D 12
West St. DN1—6C 32
West St. DN12—3E 59
West St. S1—4B 4 & 2D 98
West St. S18—1D 128
West St. S19—4F 115
West St. S31—3F 119
(Anston)
West St. S31—6H 125
(Eckington)
West St. S40—1H 137
West St. S63—4G 29
(Goldthorpe)
West St. S63—5E 41
(in two parts,
Wath upon Dearne)
West St. S64—1E 57
West St. S66—4B 94
West St. S70—5A 24
West St. S71—1F 9
West St. S73—4E 27
(Darfield)
West St. S73—6A 26
(Wombwell)
West St. S74—5G 37
West St. La. S1—3D 4 & 2E 99
Westthorpe Rd. S31—4B 126
W. Vale Gro. S65—5D 70
West View. S43—2B 134
West View. S70—2G 23
W. View Clo. S17—4F 121
W. View Cres. S63—5E 29
W. View La. S17—3F 121
W. View Rd. S41—5G 131
W. View Rd. S61—3E 77
W. View Rd. S64—1E 57
W. View Ter. S70—5B 24
Westville Rd. S75—4F 13
Westwell Pl. S19—3D 124
Westwick Cres. S8—2B 122
Westwick Gro. S8—2C 122
Westwick La. S42—2A 136
Westwick Rd. S8—3B 122

Westwood Av. S43—3A 134
Westwood Ct. S70—5G 13
Westwood La. S30—1A 50
Westwood La. S43—1F 139
Westwood New Rd. S30 & S75
—6A 50
Westwood New Rd. S70—6D 36
(off Sheffield Rd.)
Westwood Rd. S11—5F 97
Westwood Rd. S30—5B 50
Westwood Rd. S44—1G 139
Wetherby Clo. DN5—4F 31
Wetherby Ct. S9—1E 101
Wetherby Dri. S31—6A 104
Wetherby Dri. S64—5F 43
Wetlands La. S41—1D 138
Wet Moor La. S63—4E 41
Whaley Rd. S75—2B 12
Wharfe Ct. S60—1E 91
Wharfedale Dri. S30—2C 64
Wharfedale Rd. S75—5C 12
Wharf La. S9—6F 77
Wharf La. S41—1A 138
Wharf La. S43—1D 134
Wharf Rd. DN1—4D 32
Wharf Rd. S62—6C 56
Wharf St. S2—2H 5 & 1G 99
Wharf St. S64—2C 56
Wharf St. S71—4A 14
Wharncliffe. S75—3C 22
Wharncliffe Av. S31—5C 104
Wharncliffe Av. S63—5F 41
Wharncliffe Clo. S62—5D 54
Wharncliffe Clo. S74—1H 51
Wharncliffe Rd. S10
—6A 4 & 3C 98
Wharncliffe Rd. S30—6B 50
Wharncliffe St. DN4—1A 46
Wharncliffe St. S65—2E 79
Wharncliffe St. S70—6F 13
Wharncliffe St. S71—5F 9
Wharton Av. S31—6A 104
Wheatacre Rd. S30—3E 141
Wheata Dri. S5—2F 75
Wheata Pl. S5—2F 75
Wheata Rd. S5—3E 75
Wheatbridge Rd. S40—2G 137
Wheatcroft Rd. S62—1H 69
Wheathill Cres. S5—3H 75
Wheathill Clo. S43—1F 139
Wheathill La. S41—1D 138
Wheatley Clo. S71—3H 13
Wheatley Gro. S13—4G 101
Wheatley Hall Rd. DN2
—3E 33 to 1B 34
Wheatley Pk. Rd. DN5—5A 18
Wheatley Pl. DN12—2B 58
Wheatley Rise. S75—3F 7
Wheatley Rd. S61—6G 67
Wheatley Rd. S62—6C 56
Wheatley Rd. S70—2E 25
Wheatley St. DN12—2B 58
Wheats La. S1—2E 5
Wheeldon Cres. S43—3D 132
Wheeldon La. S40—2A 138
Wheeldon St. S1—3B 4 & 2D 98
Wheel Hill. S1—3G 5 & 2F 99
Wheel La. S30—1B 74
(Grenoside)
Wheel La. S30—2B 72
(Oughtibridge)
Wheel, The. S30—1D 74
Wheldrake Rd. S5—1H 87
Whernside Av. S30—1D 64
Whinacre Clo. S8—3F 123
Whinacre Pl. S8—3E 123
Whinacre Wlk. S8—3E 123

Whinfell Clo. DN6—1D 16
Whinfell Ct. S11—5E 109
Whin Hill Rd. DN4—3D 48
Whinmoor Rd. S5—6B 76
Whinmoor Rd. S30—6A 50
Whinnifred Rd. S63—5H 41
Whins, The. S62—2C 68
Whiphill Clo. DN4—4C 48
Whiphill La. DN3—4G 35
Whiphill Top La. DN3—1H 49
Whirlow Ct. Rd. S11—5F 109
Whirlowdale Clo. S11—5F 109
Whirlowdale Cres. S7—4H 109
Whirlowdale Rise. S11—5F 109
Whirlowdale Rd. S11 & S7
—5E 109
Whirlow Farm M. S11—4F 109
Whirlow Gro. S11—5F 109
Whirlow La. S11—4E 109
Whirlow Pk. Rd. S11—5F 109
Whiston Brook View. S60
—2A 92
Whiston Grange. S60—2G 91
Whiston Gro. S60—5F 79
Whiston Vale. S60—3H 91
Whitaker Clo. DN11—6D 62
Whitaker Sq. DN11—5C 62
Whitbeck Clo. DN11—6H 61
Whitburn Rd. DN1—1E 47
Whitby Rd. DN11—5C 62
Whitby St. S9—6E 89
Whitcomb Dri. DN11—6D 62
Whitebank Clo. S41—4B 138
Whitecotes La. S40—5F 137
White Croft. S1—2D 4 & 1E 99
Whitecroft Cres. S60—3C 90
White Cross La. DN11—4G 61
White Cross La. S70—4D 24
White Cross Rise. S70—4D 24
White Cross Rd. S72—2H 15
White Edge Clo. S40—6F 131
White Ga. S31—1H 119
Whitegate Wlk. S61—4G 67
Whitehall Rd. S61—3H 67
Whitehall Way. S61—4A 68
Whitehead Av. S30—3F 141
Whitehead St. S43—1D 134
Whitehill Av. S60—3C 90
White Hill Av. S70—6C 12
Whitehill Dri. S60—4C 90
White Hill Gro. S70—6D 12
Whitehill La. S60—2C 90
Whitehill Rd. S60—3C 90
White Hill Ter. S70—6C 12
Whitehouse La. S6—5B 86
Whitehouse Rd. S6—5B 86
Whitehouses. S41—4B 138
White La. S12
—4C 112 to 6G 113
White La. S30—6F 51
Whitelea Gro. S64—1D 56
Whitelea Gro. Trading Est S64
—1D 56
Whitelea Rd. S64—2C 56
White Leas. S40—1D 136
Whiteley La. S10—6C 96
Whiteleys Av. S62—6A 54
Whiteley Wood Clo. S11—6F 97
Whiteley Wood Rd. S11
—1E 109
Whitelow La. S17—1A 120
White Rd. S43—1E 135
White Rose Ho. S60—4D 78
White's La. S2—2H 99
White Thorns Clo. S8—3F 123
White Thorns Dri. S8—4F 123
White Thorns View. S8—3F 123
Whiteways Clo. S4—3H 87

Whiteways Dri. S4—3H 87
Whiteways Gro. S4—3H 87
Whiteways Rd. S4—3H 87
Whitewood Clo. S71—2D 8
Whitfield Rd. S10—6C 96
Whitfield Rd. S62—6D 54
Whitham Rd. S10—3A 98
Whiting St. S8—1E 111
Whitley La. S30—6B 64 to 5F 65
Whitley View Rd. S61—4D 76
Whitney Clo. DN4—6G 45
Whittier Rd. DN4—5A 46
Whittington Hill. S41—2A 132
Whittington St. DN1—4D 32
Whitting Valley Rd. S41
      —2A 132
Whitton Clo. DN4—5A 48
Whitton Pl. S44—6E 135
Whitwell Cres. S30—3D 140
Whitwell La. S30—4C 140
Whitwell St. S9—1F 101
Whitwell View. DN11—4F 63
Whitworth Croft. S10—3F 97
Whitworth La. S9—4C 88
Whitworth Rd. S10—4E 97
Whitworth Rd. S41—5A 132
Whitworth's Bldgs. S63—1G 29
(off Clarke St.)
Whitworth St. S63—4G 29
Whitworth Way. S63—4E 41
Whixley Rd. S9—6D 88
Whybourne Gro. S60—4E 79
Whybourne Ter. S60—3E 79
Whyn View. S63—1E 29
Wicker. S3—1G 5 & 1D 98
Wicker La. S3—1G 5 & 1F 99
Wickersley Rd. S60—5G 79
Wickett Hern Rd. DN3—3H 35
Wickfield Clo. S12—2H 113
Wickfield Dri. S12—2H 113
Wickfield Gro. S12—3G 113
Wickfield Pl. S12—2G 113
Wickfield Rd. S12—3H 113
Wicklow Rd. DN2—4G 33
Widdop Clo. S13—5F 101
Widdop Croft. S13—5F 101
Wigfield Dri. S70—4H 23
Wigfull Rd. S11—4A 98
Wigley Rd. S43—5A 134
Wignall Av. S66—5D 80
Wikeley Way. S43—3D 132
Wike Rd. S71—5E 15
Wilberforce Rd. DN2—6B 20
Wilberforce Rd. S31—2F 119
Wilbrook Rise. S75—3C 12
Wilby La. S70—1A 24
Wilcox Clo. S6—4B 74
Wilcox Grn. S61—3A 68
Wilcox Rd. S6—4A 74
Wild Av. S62—6C 54
Wildflower Clo. DN11—6C 62
Wilding Clo. S61—1G 77
Wilding Way. S61—1G 77
Wilford Rd. S71—4A 8
Wilfred St. S60—3D 78
Wilfred Ter. S70—1G 23
Wilfrid Rd. S9—6C 88
Wilkin Hill. S18—2A 130
Wilkinson Av. DN11—5E 63
Wilkinson Dri. S43—4H 133
Wilkinson La. S10
      —4A 4 & 2C 98
Wilkinson Rd. S74—6C 38
Wilkinson St. S10
      —4A 4 & 2C 98
Wilkinson St. S70—1H 23
Willan Dri. S60—6C 90
Wilbury Dri. S12—1C 112

Willey St. S3—1G 5 & 1D 98
William Clo. S19—3D 124
William Cres. S19—2D 124
William La. DN3—3B 62
Williamson Rd. S11—6B 98
Williams Rd. DN5—3H 31
William St. S10—6A 4 & 3C 98
William St. S31—6D 124
William St. S41—5A 132
William St. S60—3E 79
William St. S62—3G 69
William St. S63—3E 29
(Goldthorpe)
William St. S63—5F 41
(Wath upon Dearne)
William St. S64—2C 56
William St. S70—4A 24
William St. S73—6A 26
William St. N. S41—1H 131
Willington Rd. S5—5G 75
Willis Rd. S6—2H 85
Willman Rd. S71—4F 15
Willoughby St. S4—1A 88
Willow Av. DN4—3D 48
Willow Av. S62—2G 69
Willow Bank. S75—3G 13
Willow Bri. Rd. DN5—4B 32
Willow Clo. S31—4F 119
Willow Clo. S60—4D 90
Willow Clo. S66—3G 81
Willow Clo. S72—6B 10
Willow Clo. S74—6G 37
Willow Ct. S44—2G 139
Willow Ct. S63—6E 41
Willow Cres. S30—3E 65
Willow Dene Rd. S72—6G 11
Willow Dri. S9—2G 101
Willow Dri. S64—6D 42
Willow Dri. S66—3G 81
Willow Garth. S62—1G 69
Willowgarth Av. S60—3C 90
Willow Garth Rd. S41—3E 131
Willow Gro. S31—5D 104
Willow La. DN11—4E 63
Willow La. S63—2B 42
Willow Rd. DN3—2G 35
Willow Rd. S30—5D 140
Willow Rd. S31—4A 126
Willow Rd. S63—1F 29
(Thurnscoe)
Willow Rd. S63—1G 55
(Wath upon Dearne)
Willow Rd. S66—4D 82
Willows, The. S61—5F 67
Willow St. DN12—3F 59
Willow St. S70—1F 23
Willow Wlk. DN5—4A 18
Wilsic Ho. DN1—1C 46
(off Grove Pl.)
Wilson Av. S62—1E 69
Wilson Dri. S65—6C 70
Wilson Gro. S71—3F 15
Wilson Pl. S8—1E 111
Wilson Rd. S11—5A 98
Wilson Rd. S18—5G 123
Wilson Rd. S30—4H 141
Wilson St. S3—5E 87
Wilson St. S18—3F 129
Wilson St. S73—6H 25
Wilson Wlk. S73—3C 22
Wilstrop Rd. S9—6D 88
Wilthorpe Av. S75—3E 13
Wilthorpe Cres. S75—3E 13
Wilthorpe Farm Rd. S75—3E 13
Wilthorpe Gdns. S19—4A 114
Wilthorpe Grn. S75—3E 13
Wilthorpe La. S75—3D 12
Wilthorpe Rd. S75—3C 12

Wilton Clo. S62—2F 69
Wilton Ct. S61—2A 78
Wilton Pl. S10—3C 98
Wiltshire Av. DN12—2B 58
Wiltshire Rd. DN2—3A 34
Wimborne Cres. S41—4G 131
Winberry Av. S31—2G 119
Wincanton Clo. S64—5F 43
Winchester Av. DN2—3G 33
Winchester Av. S10—5B 96
Winchester Clo. S10—5B 96
Winchester Ct. S65—2E 79
(off Nottingham St.)
Winchester Cres. S10—5B 96
Winchester Dri. S10—5B 96
Winchester Ho. DN5—3F 31
Winchester Rd. S10—5B 96
Winchester Rd. S41—4G 131
Winchester Way. DN5—3G 31
Winchester Way. S60—2A 90
Winchester Way. S71—2G 25
Wincobank Av. S5—6A 76
Wincobank Clo. S5—6B 76
Wincobank La. S4—2B 88
Wincobank Rd. S5—6B 76
Winco Rd. S4—2B 88
Winco Wood La. S9—6B 76
Windermere Av. DN2—4A 34
Windermere Av. S18—2C 128
Windermere Av. S63—5G 29
Windermere Clo. S64—5H 43
Windermere Ct. S31—1G 119
Windermere Cres. DN3—3D 20
Windermere Grange. DN12
      —4B 60
Windermere Rd. S8—2C 110
Windermere Rd. S41—4E 131
Windermere Rd. S71—6A 14
Winders Pl. S73—1F 39
Windgate Hill. DN12—2F 59
Windham Clo. S71—4H 13
Windham Dri. DN3—1H 21
Windhill Av. S64—6G 43
Windhill Av. S75—2E 7
Windhill Cres. S64—5G 43
Windhill Cres. S75—2E 7
Windhill Dri. S75—2E 7
Windhill La. S75—2E 7
Windhill Mt. S75—2E 7
Windhill Ter. S64—5G 43
Windle Rd. DN4—2A 46
Windle Sq. DN3—3D 20
Windmill Av. DN12—4F 59
Windmill Av. S72—5G 11
Windmill Balk La. DN6—3C 16
Windmill Dri. DN11—6H 61
Windmill Greenway. S19
      —4E 125
Windmill Hill La. S30—3C 64
Windmill La. S5—5A 76
Windmill Rd. S31—1G 119
Windmill Rd. S73—1D 38
Windmill St. S9—3B 88
Windmill Ter. S71—1D 8
Windsor Av. S75—3A 6
Windsor Clo. S66—3H 81
Windsor Ct. S11—3F 109
Windsor Cres. S31—4B 1
Windsor Cres. S72—2H 27
Windsor Dri. S18—2A 128
Windsor Dri. S75—2B 22
Windsor Rise. S31—1C 116
Windsor Rd. DN2—5F 33
Windsor Rd. DN12—2D 58
Windsor Rd. S8—1D 110
Windsor Rd. S61—3B 66
Windsor Sq. S63—1G 29
Windsor St. S4—5H 87 & 6A 88
(in two parts)

Windsor St. S63—1G 29
Windsor St. S74—4H 37
Windsor Wlk. DN5—3G 31
Windsor Wlk. S31—4E 119
Windsor Wlk. S47—4C 138
Windy Ho. La. S2—6C 100
Windy Ridge. S31—4A 104
Winfield Rd. S63—6F 41
Wingerworth Av. S8—1B 122
Wingerworth Way. S40
      —6H 137
Wingfield Clo. S18—3A 128
Wingfield Clo. S61—4A 68
Wingfield Cres. S12—2E 113
Wingfield Rd. S61—4H 67
Wingfield Rd. S71—1A 14
Winholme. DN3—3F 35
Winifred Rd. S60—3C 78
Winkley Ter. S5—4A 76
Winlea Av. S65—5C 80
Winnat Pl. S43—4A 134
Winnats Clo. S40—6E 131
Winn Clo. S6—6H 73
Winn Dri. S6—6H 73
Winn Gdns. S6—6H 73
Winn Gro. S6—6H 73
Winnipeg Rd. DN5—6B 18
Winsford Rd. S6—4A 74
Winster Clo. S70—3D 36
Winster Ct. S41—1A 138
Winster Rd. S6—1A 86
Winster Rd. S43—3A 134
Winston Av. S30—2B 140
Winter Av. S75—5E 13
Winter Hill La. S61—2G 77
Winterhill Rd. S61—3F 77
Winter Rd. S75—5E 13
Winter St. S3—1C 98
Winter Ter. S75—5E 13
Winterton Clo. DN4—5B 48
Winterton Gdns. S12—4C 114
Winterwell Rd. S63—4C 40
Winton Clo. S70—2A 24
Winton Rd. DN2—5H 33
Wiseton Rd. S11—5A 98
Wisewood Av. S6—3G 85
Wisewood La. S6—3G 85
Wisewood Pl. S6—3G 85
Wisewood Rd. S6—3G 85
Witham Ct. S40—2E 137
Witham Ct. S75—4A 12
Withens Av. S6—1H 85
Withens Ct. S75—4E 7
Witney St. S8—5E 99
Wivelsfield Rd. DN4—4G 45
Woburn Clo. DN4—6G 45
Woburn Pl. S11—5F 109
Woburn Pl. S75—3B 22
Wolfe Clo. S40—4F 137
Wolfe Dri. S6—4B 74
Wolfe Rd. S6—4B 74
Wollaton Av. S17—4G 121
Wollaton Clo. S17—5A 8
Wollaton Dri. S17—4G 121
Wollaton Rd. S17—5F 121
Wolseley Rd. S8—6E 99
Wolsey Av. DN6—6G 33
Wolverley Rd. S13—1A 114
Wombwell Av. S63—6E 41
Wombwell By-Pass. S73
      —5A 26
Wombwell La. S70 & S73
      —2E 25
Wombwell La. S74—1H 37
Wombwell Rd. S74—4A 38
Woodall La. S31—3G 127
Woodall Rd. S31—4D 126
Woodall Rd. S65—4A 80

Woodall Rd. S. S65—5A 80
Woodbank Cres. S8—2D 110
Woodbank Rd. S6—1A 96
Woodbine Rd. S9—4B 88
Woodbourne Rd. S9—5B 88
Woodbourn Hill. S9—6B 88
Woodbridge Rise. S40—5D 136
Woodburn Dri. S30—3G 65
Woodbury Clo. S9—4C 76
Woodbury Rd. S9—4C 76
Wood Cliffe. S10—1B 108
Wood Clo. S30—3G 65
Wood Clo. S62—6E 55
Woodcock Clo. S61—5H 67
Woodcock Pl. S2—2H 99
Woodcock Rd. S74—6A 38
Wood Croft. S61—6H 67
Woodcross Av. DN4—4E 49
Woodend Clo. S6—4G 85
Woodend Dri. S6—4G 85
Woodfarm Av. S6—5F 85
Woodfarm Clo. S6—5E 85
Woodfarm Dri. S6—5E 85
Woodfarm Pl. S6—5F 85
Woodfield Av. S64—6F 43
Woodfield Clo. S73—3E 27
Woodfield Rd. DN3—4G 35
Woodfield Rd. DN4—4A 46
(in two parts)
Woodfield Rd. S10—6H 85
Woodfield Rd. S63—5B 40
Wood Fold. S3—4E 87
Woodfoot Rd. S60—2F 91
Woodford Rd. DN3—1H 21
Woodgrove Rd. S9—5D 76
Woodgrove Rd. S65—2A 80
Woodhall Rd. S73—3E 27
Woodhead Dri. S74—2H 37
Woodhead La. S74—1A 38
Woodhead Rd. S2—5E 99
Woodhead Rd. S30—5A 64
(Grenoside)
Woodhill Rise. S64—3B 56
Woodholm Pl. S11—2H 109
Woodholm Rd. S11—2H 109
Woodhouse Av. S19—3F 115
Woodhouse Clo. S62—5D 54
Woodhouse Ct. S19—3F 115
Woodhouse Cres. S19—3F 115
Woodhouse Gdns. S13—1C 114
Woodhouse Grn. S66—4A 94
Wood Ho. La. DN11—5G 61
Woodhouse La. S19—2E 115
Woodhouse La. S44—6H 135
Woodhouse La. WF4—1F 7
Woodhouse Rd. DN2—3E 33
Woodhouse Rd. S12—1D 112
Woodhouse Rd. S74—6A 38
Woodland Av. S31—2G 119
Woodland Clo. S60—6C 90
Woodland Clo. S66—6G 81
Woodland Dri. S12—5D 112
Woodland Dri. S31—2G 119
Woodland Dri. S70—1D 22
Woodland Gdns. S66—4H 83
Woodland Gro. S63—1F 55
Woodland Pl. S17—4F 121
Woodland Rd. S8—4F 111
Woodland Rd. S63—1F 55
Woodlands. S43—4D 132
Woodlands Av. S19—2F 115
Woodlands Clo. S31—4B 104
Woodlands Cres. S64—3G 55
Woodlands Rd. DN6—3D 16
Woodlands Rd. S74—3A 38
Woodlands, The. S10—3G 97
Woodlands View. S73—3C 38
Woodlands View S74—4A 38

Woodlands Way. DN12—2B 58
Woodland View. DN6—3C 16
Woodland View. S12—5D 112
Woodland View. S17—2G 121
Woodland View. S64—1G 57
Woodland View. S72—2H 15
Woodland View Rd. S6—5G 85
Woodland Vs. S75—6C 36
Woodland Wlk. S40—6B 130
Woodland Way. S65—5A 80
Wood La. DN11—3E 61
Wood La. DN12—6B 60
Wood La. S6—5E 85
Wood La. S60—4A 90
(Brinsworth)
Wood La. S60—6D 78
(Canklow)
Wood La. S60—1F 103
(Treeton)
Wood La. S66—6G 93
(Thurcroft)
Wood La. S66—6G 81
(Wickersley)
Wood La. S71—3A 8 to 3E 9
(in two parts)
Woodlea Gro. DN3—3F 35
Woodlea Way. DN2—2A 34
Woodleigh Clo. S40—6B 130
Woodleys Av. S62—5E 55
Woodman Dri. S64—3G 55
Woodmoor St. S71—5F 9
Woodnook La. S42—6B 130
Woodpecker Clo. S31—1C 116
Wood Rd. S6—3H 85
Wood Rd. S61—6H 67
Woodrove Av. S13—6D 100
Woodrove Clo. S13—6D 100
Woodroyd Av. S71—4E 9
Wood Royd Rd. S30—3G 141
Woodseats. S30—4B 64
Woodseats Ho. Rd. S8—5D 110
Woodseats Rd. S8—2C 110
Woodsetts Rd. S31—1G 119
Woodsett Wlk. DN12—3G 59
Woodside Av. S31—2D 126
Woodside Av. S63—5F 41
Woodside Clo. S40—1D 136
Woodside Clo. S66—4H 83
Woodside Ct. S66—5H 83
(off Tickhill Rd.)
Woodside La. S3—5E & 5E 87
(in two parts)
Woodside La. S30—6A 64
Woodside Rd. DN5—1G 31
Woodside Wlk. S61—4B 68
Woodspring Ct. S4—3A 88
Woodstock Rd. DN4—4G 45
Woodstock Rd. S6—3E 85
Woodstock Rd. S7—1C 110
Woodstock Rd. S75—3F 13
Wood St. DN1—6D 32
Wood St. S6—5C 86
Wood St. S64—6D 42
(Mexborough)
Wood St. S64—2C 56
(Swinton)
Wood St. S65—5C 70
Wood St. S70—1G 23
Wood St. S73—1E 39
Wood Ter. S60—6D 78
Woodthorpe Clo. S2—5C 100
Woodthorpe Cres. S13—5E 101
Woodthorpe Rd. S13—6E 101
Woodthorpe Rd. S43—1G 135
Woodvale Clo. S40—5C 136
Woodvale Rd. S10—4H 97
Woodview. DN5—2D 44
Wood View. S66—4H 83

Wood View. S70—5D 36
Wood View. S74—6C 38
Wood View La. S75—4D 12
Wood View Pl. S60—6D 78
Woodview Rd. S6—4A 86
Woodview Ter. S11—5E 97
Woodville Hall. S10—4C 98
Wood Wlk. S64—5D 42
Wood Wlk. S74 & S73—3A 38
Woodway, The. S66—2F 81
Woofindin Av. S11—6E 97
Woofindin Rd. S10—6D 96
Wooldale Clo. S19—5A 114
Wooldale Dri. S19—5A 114
Wooley Av. S73—1E 39
Woollen La. S6—6C 86
Woollen Wlk. S6—5C 86
Woolley Colliery Rd. S75—4C 6
Woolley Edge La. S75—1D 6
(off Elsworth Clo.)
Woolley Ho. DN1—2C 46
Woolley Rd. S30—3C 140
Woolley Wood Rd. S5—2A 76
Worcester Av. DN2—2F 33
Worcester Clo. S10—4B 96
Worcester Dri. S10—4B 96
Worcester Rd. S10—4A 96
Wordsworth Av. DN4—5A 46
Wordsworth Av. S5
—6C 74 to 1F 75
Wordsworth Av. S31—5G 107
Wordsworth Clo. S5—5C 74
Wordsworth Cres. S5—5C 74
Wordsworth Dri. DN5—5H 31
Wordsworth Dri. S5—5C 74
Wordsworth Dri. S65—3G 79
Wordsworth Pl. S18—4G 129
Wordsworth Rd. S41—3H 131
Wordsworth Rd. S63—4C 40
Wordsworth Rd. S71—3B 14
Workhouse La. S3
—1E 5 & 1E 99
Works La. S44—3H 139
Worksop Rd. S9—5C 88
Worksop Rd. S31—3F 119
(Anston)
Worksop Rd. S31—6E 105
(Aston)
Worksop Rd. S31—6B 104
(Swallownest)
Worksop Rd. S43—1E 135
Works Rd. S43—1H 133
Worral Av. S60—6E 91
Worral Clo. S70—3H 23
Worral Dri. S30—4D 72
Worrall Rd. S30—1C 64
(High Green)
Worrall Rd. S30 & S6—5D 72
(Worrall)
Worry Goose La. S60—1A 92
Worsbrough Rd. S70—3D 36
Worsbrough Rd. S74—2H 37
Worsbrough View. S75—5B 36
Worthing Cres. DN12—3F 59
Worthing Rd. S9—6A 88
Wortley Av. DN12—3C 58
Wortley Av. S64—2B 56
Wortley Av. S73—4H 25
Wortley Dri. S30—2E 73
Wortley Rd. S30—3H 141
(Deepcar)
Wortley Rd. S30—5A 50
(High Green)
Wortley Rd. S61—1G 77 & 2B 78
(in two parts)
Wortley St. S70—6G 13
Wortley View. S74—2H 37
Wostenholm Rd. S7—6D 98

Wragby Rd. S11—5G 97
Wragg La. S31—2H 115
Wragg Rd. S2—3A 100
Wreakes La. S18—6D 122
Wreakin Pl. S9—2E 89
Wrelton Clo. S71—2D 8
Wren Bank. S2—3A 100
Wren Pk. Clo. S40—6H 137
Wrens Way. S70—3D 36
Wren View. S70—2H 23
Wright Cres. S73—1F 39
Wright's Hill. S2—5D 98
Wrightson Av. DN4—6E 45
Wrightson Ter. DN5—3B 32
Wright St. S31—1G 119
Wroxham Way. DN5—4G 31
Wulfric Clo. S2—5B 100
Wulfric Pl. S2—5B 100
Wulfric Rd. S2—5C 100
Wulfric Rd. S31—6C 124
Wyatt Av. S11—1A 110
Wybourn Ho. Rd. S2—2A 100
Wybourn Ter. S2—2A 100
Wychwood Clo. DN4—1F 61
Wychwood Croft. S19—5G 115
Wychwood Glen. S19—5G 115
Wychwood Gro. S19—5G 115
Wycombe St. S71—5E 15
Wyedale Ct. S41—4G 131
Wyedale Croft. S19—3F 115
Wyndthorpe Av. DN4—4C 48
Wyn Gro S73—2A 40
Wynmoor Cres. S73—3A 40
Wynyard Rd. S6—2H 85
Wythburn Rd. S41—4E 131
Wyvern Gdns. S17—3E 121

Yarborough Ter. DN5—4B 32
Yardley Sq. S3—2A 4 & 1C 98
Yarmouth St. S9—2D 88
Yarncliff Clo. S40—6F 131
Yarwell Dri. S66—3E 83
Yates Clo. S66—6E 81
Yealand Clo. DN6—1D 16
Yeldersley Clo. S40—6D 130
Yeomans Rd. S6—6C 86
Yeomans Way. S31—3F 119
Yewdale. S70—4B 24
Yew Greave Cres. S5—2D 74
Yew La. S5—2C 74
Yews Av. S70—4B 24
Yews Clo. S30—5D 72
Yews La. S70—4B to 1B 24
Yews Pl. S70—2B 24
Yew Tree Av. S31—2H 119
Yew Tree Cres. DN11—3E 63
Yew Tree Dri. S9—2H 89
Yew Tree Dri. S31—4A 126
Yew Tree Rd. S40—5C 136
Yew Tree Rd. S66—3C 82
Yewtrees La. S30—6D 140
Yoredale Av. S30—1D 64
York Gdns. DN4—2B 48
York Gdns. S63—4D 40
York La. S66—4F 93
York Rise. S31—6A 104
York Rd. DN5—1F 31 to 4B 32
York Rd. S9—6E 89
York Rd. S30—3D 140
York Rd. S65—2E 79
York Sq. S64—1E 57
York St. DN11—3C 62
York St. S1—2E 5 & 1E 99
York St. S41—6C 138
York St. S63—1G 29
York St. S64—6D 42
York St. S70—6G 13